HENRI TAJFEL

This book offers a biographical account of Henri Tajfel, one of the most influential European social psychologists of the twentieth century, offering unique insights into his ground-breaking work in the areas of social perception, social identity, and intergroup relations.

The author, Rupert Brown, paints a vivid and personal portrait of Tajfel's life, his academic career and its significance to social psychology, and the key ideas he developed. It traces Tajfel's life from his birth in Poland just after the end of World War I, his time as a prisoner-of-war in World War II, his work with Jewish orphans and other displaced persons after that war, and thence to his short but glittering academic career as a social psychologist.

Based on a range of sources including interviews, archival material, correspondence, photographs, and scholarly output, Brown expertly weaves together Tajfel's personal narrative with his evolving intellectual interests and major scientific discoveries. Following a chronological structure with each chapter dedicated to a significant transition period in Tajfel's life, the book ends with an appraisal of two of his principal posthumous legacies: the European Association of Social Psychology, a project always close to Tajfel's heart and for which he worked tirelessly; and the 'social identity approach' to social psychology initiated by Tajfel over forty years ago and now one of the discipline's most important perspectives.

This is fascinating reading for students, established scholars, and anyone interested in social psychology and the life and lasting contribution of this celebrated scholar.

Rupert Brown is Professor of Social Psychology at the University of Sussex. He obtained his PhD under Tajfel in 1979 and has been an active researcher in the field of intergroup relations throughout his career. He was the recipient of the 2014 Tajfel medal, awarded by the European Association of Social Psychology for distinguished lifetime achievement. He is the author of two widely used student texts (*Group Processes* and *Prejudice*) and over 180 scientific articles and book chapters.

EUROPEAN MONOGRAPHS IN SOCIAL PSYCHOLOGY

Sponsored by the European Association of Social Psychology

Series Editor: *Professor Rupert Brown, Department of Psychology, University of Kent, Canterbury, Kent CT2 7NP*

The aim of this series is to publish and promote the highest quality of writing in European social psychology. The editor and the editorial board encourage publications which approach social psychology from a wide range of theoretical perspectives and whose content may be applied, theoretical or empirical. The authors of books in this series should be affiliated to institutions that are located in countries which would qualify for membership of the Association. All books will be published in English, and translations from other European languages are welcomed. Please submit ideas and proposals for books in the series to Rupert Brown at the above address.

Published

Conflict and Decision-Making in Close Relationships
Erich Kirchler, Christa Rodler, Erik Hölzl, and Katja Meier

Stereotyping as Inductive Hypothesis Testing
Klaus Fiedler and Eva Walther

Intergroup Relations in States of the Former Soviet Union
Louk Hagendoorn, Hub Linssen, and Sergei Tumanov

The Social Psychology of Ethnic Identity
Maykel Verkuyten

Consumer Culture, Identity and Well-Being
Helga Dittmar

Judging Passions: Moral emotions in persons and groups
Roger Giner-Sorolla

The Psychology of Human Values
Gregory Maio

HENRI TAJFEL

Explorer of Identity and Difference

Rupert Brown

Routledge
Taylor & Francis Group

LONDON AND NEW YORK

First published 2020
by Routledge
2 Park Square, Milton Park, Abingdon, Oxon OX14 4RN

and by Routledge
52 Vanderbilt Avenue, New York, NY 10017

Routledge is an imprint of the Taylor & Francis Group, an informa business

© 2020 Rupert Brown

British Library Cataloguing-in-Publication Data
A catalogue record for this book is available from the British Library

Library of Congress Cataloging-in-Publication Data
A catalog record has been requested for this book

ISBN: 978-1-138-58980-3 (hbk)
ISBN: 978-1-138-58981-0 (pbk)
ISBN: 978-0-429-49138-2 (ebk)

Typeset in Bembo
by Newgen Publishing UK
Printed and bound by CPI Group (UK) Ltd, Croydon, CR0 4YY

This book is dedicated with love to my large (and still growing) family: my wife Lyn, my children Jon, Kirsten, and Amy, their spouses Alice, Heddy, and Colin, and my five grandchildren Rosa, Hannah, Issa, Celia, and Lily.

CONTENTS

PREFACE

This is a book about Henri Tajfel, one of the most influential European social psychologists of the twentieth century. During his lifetime, he made significant scientific contributions to our understanding of social perception, intergroup relations, and social identity, as well as helping to create a successful professional association for European social psychologists. Since his death, that already considerable impact grew enormously and is now visible far beyond the geographical and disciplinary boundaries within which he originally worked. His ideas have inspired subsequent generations of scholars who have extended them into several new areas of enquiry.

Of his many intellectual achievements, the one for which he is most well-known is his Social Identity Theory. In this theory he sought to link his early work on social categorisation to many phenomena associated with people's group memberships: ingroup loyalty and disaffection; ingroup favouritism and intergroup discrimination; social stereotypes; and motivations to bring about or resist social change.

Two recurring ideas underlie his explanation of all these phenomena. The first is that to understand them one must recognise that there are fundamental differences between people's behaviour when they are acting as group members – when their *social identities* are engaged – and their behaviour when they are acting as individuals – when only their *personal* identities are relevant. The second is the importance of always being aware of and taking account of the *social contexts* in which people find themselves. It was never sufficient, he believed, to construct theories of intergroup relations which use conceptions of people as asocial human 'cognitive processors' or biologically driven 'organisms'.

This book is not just about Tajfel the social scientist, it is also about Tajfel the man. Indeed, I believe it is impossible to do proper justice to his many scientific and professional contributions without appreciating his own personal life story. To gain that appreciation the same two phrases, *social identity* and *social context*, serve us well. Tajfel had a large repertoire of social identities – a Polish Jew, a French then British citizen, a social scientist, a multiple émigré – all of which provided him with several and sometimes conflicting vantage points from which to observe and interpret the world. And the social contexts in which he lived – interwar Poland (where anti-Semitism was rife), the Second World War (which he experienced as a prisoner-of-war of the Germans), immediate post-war Europe (in which he had to rebuild his life in the aftermath of the Holocaust), and Europe 1950–1982 (a period dominated by the Cold War and political upheaval) – were all pivotal in shaping his intellectual passions throughout his life.

Three themes will recur in the story of his life. One is the importance of his Jewish identity. Although he was a secular rather than a practising Jew, his Jewish background was always integral to his identity and provided the backdrop for all his work, which was ultimately to understand the psychological underpinnings of the Holocaust. A second theme is his geographical and cultural rootlessness. He was a man constantly on the move: he lived in at least seven different countries and had no fewer than three official nationalities in his life; his career was punctuated with several visiting fellowships to overseas research centres. And third is his boundless curiosity. This was clearly evident in all his own scholarly work but manifested itself early on with an enthusiastic interest in cultivating the intellectual endeavours of others.

These themes, together with the brief snapshots of his life and work above, explain my chosen subtitle, *'Explorer of Identity and Difference'*. The two main pre-occupations of his academic career were people's reliable tendency to exaggerate the differences they perceive between objects or people that fall into different categories, and the extension of that phenomenon to social identity, where he argued that underlying people's social identities is a basic need to see their group as positively distinct from other groups. The subtitle, then, attempts to capture those two concerns in a literal sense. In addition, though, it is meant to convey something of his wider outlook. He was always an iconoclast, forever exploring and developing ideas that ran counter to the mainstream scientific thinking of the day.

A word is in order about methodology and ethics. Like any biographer, and especially a biographer of a subject who is no longer alive, I have been mainly reliant on the testimony of others. It is true that I got to know Tajfel quite well towards the end of his life – I was his PhD student and research assistant – and so have some first-hand observations with which to triangulate the evidence from my informants and library archives. But for the period from the end of the Second World War to the early 1970s (when I first met him), I have had to piece together the jigsaw of his life mostly from interviews I conducted with many colleagues now quite elderly or deceased. As a psychologist, I approached these interviews with a preconception of the fragile and tenuous nature of long-term memory for people and episodes. In the event, though, I was constantly astonished by the vividness and precision of these informants' recollections. Wherever possible, when I have quoted from these informants, I have sought their confirmation as to the accuracy of what they told me and their permission to report it in the pages of this book. Sadly, in a few cases, this proved impossible because the informants died since granting me the interview.

I tried to cross-check the interview testimony with that provided by others or with that in various library archives. Frustratingly, though, such archival evidence was exceedingly sparse before about 1967. This date marked one of Tajfel's professional relocations and I suspect that in the move to his new academic home in that year, the vast majority of his papers were consigned to the rubbish bin. Thankfully, after 1967 most of his correspondence has been conserved.

Of Tajfel's early life (prior to 1945), very little documentary evidence exists. No letters from this period could be found. Moreover, his 'official' documents – birth certificates, identity cards, school enrolments and the like – were almost certainly destroyed in the conflagration of the Holocaust. I have located a few fragments from this period, mostly of a genealogical variety but, for the most part, I have had to rely on historiography – ethnographic accounts of Polish life in the interwar period and of life behind barbed wire during the Second World War. These accounts necessarily provide only a general – but hopefully typical – picture of life in those eras rather than the particulars of Tajfel's own experiences.

Tajfel is no longer with us but some members of his immediate family are still alive. This means that, on occasion, I felt I had to withhold some information out of a respect for their privacy, both when they specifically requested it or when I regarded it as necessary. In making these judgements, I tried always to follow Voltaire's maxim: 'To the living we owe consideration, to the dead only the truth'. Thus, in the pages of this book I have endeavoured to present the unvarnished truth about Tajfel himself, whilst mostly maintaining a veil of discretion about members of his family. I followed that same Voltaire maxim by occasionally anonymising certain (still living) informants who reported particularly sensitive material.

The first seven chapters of the book follow a conventional chronological structure, beginning with his birth and ending with his death. These chapters cover seven episodes of his life of varying durations (between five and eighteen years). Any such temporal segmentation is somewhat arbitrary but, in this case, was not completely random. The choice of chapter boundaries was dictated by what seemed to me to be significant transition points in his life. Throughout these seven chapters, I attempt to weave the personal narrative of his life with his evolving intellectual interests and his major scientific discoveries. This is most apparent from Chapter 4 onwards, which marks the beginning of his academic career. In Chapters 4–7, from time to time I provide a detailed description and analysis of his most significant papers, and the empirical research on which they were based. Sometimes, it was necessary to set that research against the theoretical debates and controversies of the time. My intention in adopting this approach is to provide readers, whether students or established scholars, an appreciation of why those papers have acquired the legendary status they have, and a discussion of whether (or not) that reputation is merited.

The eighth and final chapter deals with two of his principal posthumous legacies: the *European Association of Social Psychology*, a project always close to Tajfel's heart and for which he worked tirelessly; and an appraisal of the 'social identity approach' that he was responsible for initiating over forty years ago. In both cases, I contrast his ambitions for these projects with their subsequent evolution since his death.

ACKNOWLEDGEMENTS

I am deeply indebted to dozens of people who have helped me with this project. They are too numerous to name in their entirety but I would like to single out some individuals whose assistance has been especially important to me over the past five years.

Anne Tajfel was enthusiastic about the book from the very beginning and furnished me with much invaluable information about her husband and many wonderful photographs, several of which appear in the pages that follow. I am very grateful to her and I hope she will feel I have done Henri justice, notwithstanding her occasional misgivings about what I have written.

I would also like to thank the former residents of the Villa Essor, Le Vésinet, and Miravelle homes for giving so generously of their time. Their recollections of the time they spent under Tajfel's care in the 1940s were a moving testament to the resilience of youth after the trauma of war. Pierre Aron, Marcel Frydman, Victor Graimont, Maurice Michower, Jacques Schlaf, and Maurice Weksler, I thank you all most warmly.

Sadly, some of Tajfel's oldest and dearest friends are no longer alive. However, I was privileged to have been able to speak with them before they left us and I would like here to acknowledge their contributions: Jerry Bruner, Harry Hurwitz, and Gustav Jahoda, I was enriched and inspired by our conversations together.

The same can be said for most of the other 50 or so interviews I conducted for this biography. In addition to them being enjoyable exercises in nostalgia, they provided me with innumerable new insights into Tajfel's character and work. I do not have the space to name them all here but they are acknowledged in the notes throughout the text. Special mention, though, must be made of Mick Billig who was so encouraging of the project from the start and who gave unstintingly of his time in conversation and correspondence. Steve Reicher and Craig McGarty should also be recognised for their continual support of my work, and Steve especially for his insightful comments on Chapter 8.

I have had the very good fortune to have had a small and dedicated cadre of readers of early drafts of the manuscript. Their sharp eyes and wise comments have meant that the book, for all of its undoubted failings, is not nearly as bad as it might have been. Thank you especially: Robin Banerjee, Kay Deaux, Ian Dey, Laura Ferraresi, Ginette Herman, and Jenny Paterson. Laura Ferraresi was also of immeasurable assistance in navigating the (to me) unfathomable waters of social media and in locating several of Tajfel's surviving relatives. Francine Tajfel also merits a special note of thanks for her help with the Tajfel family genealogy, as does Eddy van Avermaet for guiding me through the labyrinth that is the KU Leuven archive and commenting so thoughtfully on part of Chapter 8.

Like any biography, his book has benefited from my unfettered access to several library archives. Over the past five years I have spent many pleasurable hours foraging in these wonderful places and I would like here to acknowledge the assistance provided by the archivists at the Wellcome Collection (London), the Harvard University Library, the Bentley Historical Library (Michigan), the Katholieke Universiteit Leuven Bibliotheken, Linacre College (Oxford), and the Emanuel Ringelblum Jewish Historical Institute (Warsaw). Yours can be a solitary profession but historians and biographers (especially this one) are forever in your debt.

Tajfel lived in many countries during his life and, as a result, acquired fluency in several languages. Sadly, I lack his multilingual capacity and have had to rely on the assistance of others to help me with the translation of documents. So, thank you Richard Bourhis, Sarah Carter, Jean-Claude Croizet, Dariusz Doliński, Ginette Herman, Olga Kuzawińska, and Hélène Rozenberg for helping me make sense of all those French, Polish, and Russian materials I sent your way. Talking of translation, a big thank you is also due to Charlotte Rea who was faced with the unenviable task of 'translating' my terrible handwriting so speedily and accurately into a typescript that the rest of the world could read.

Last, but very much not least, I should acknowledge the generous financial support provided by the *European Association of Social Psychology* which allowed me to kick-start this project, and *The Leverhulme Trust* which was brave (or foolish) enough to award me, the most novice of biographers, a Senior Research Fellowship which freed me from my normal university duties to enable me to see it through to its conclusion. I sincerely hope that neither organisation will feel that their investment has been wasted.

ABBREVIATIONS

AIVG	L'Aide aux Israélites Victimes de la Guerre
BHL	Bentley Historical Library
BPS	British Psychological Society
EASP	European Association of Social Psychology
FF	Ford Foundation
HUA	Harvard University Archives
KUL	Katholieke Universiteit Leuven Bibliotheken
LCA	Linacre College Archive
OSE	Oeuvre de Secours aux Enfants
SIT	Social Identity Theory
WC	The Wellcome Collection, London
WoS	Web of Science

1

POLAND

1919–1936

1919: birth of a nation, birth of a social scientist

The twentieth year of the twentieth century was a momentous one for the people of Poland as a whole, and for one Polish family in particular. We will come to the particularity presently but, in that year, for the first time for over a hundred years, Poles could properly say that they had their country back. For the previous 123 years, their country had been invaded, partitioned, and subjugated by the Austrian, Prussian, and Russian empires. With the signing of the First World War Armistice in November 1918, suddenly Poles had a country they could call their own again, although it was far from clear what the boundaries of that country actually were. Indeed, the next two years would see a period of intense diplomatic and military activity to establish exactly where the lines demarcating Poland from her neighbours should be drawn.[1]

On the diplomatic front, the negotiations began in January 1919 at the Paris Peace Conference and culminated six months later on 28 June with the signing of the Versailles Treaty. However, the final definition of Poland's frontiers had less to do with this diplomatic activity than with two years of sustained warfare, waged on no fewer than six different fronts simultaneously: Ukraine, Posnania, Silesia, Lithuania, Czechoslovakia, and the Soviet Union.[2] Of these, the latter proved to be the most decisive for Poland's immediate (and subsequent) future. It began in February 1919 with an attack by the Polish army in a small town in the North West of Poland, Bereza Kartuska, and continued for nearly two more years with various ebbs and flows of the Polish and Soviet armies. The details of this war need not detain us here, except in one respect, towards its end, at the river Vistula.

The river Vistula is the largest and longest river in Poland. It rises in the Carpathian mountains in the south and snakes its way northward via Warsaw to Danzig (Gdansk) on the Baltic Sea. It seems to have been regarded as being of strategic importance by the Soviets. As early as January 1919, the Soviet Supreme Command launched a military reconnaissance called Target Vistula.[3] Twenty months later, in August 1920, the Soviet Army crossed the Vistula at a small town called Włocławek, storming the bridge there and cutting the crucial railway line between Warsaw and Danzig. In that same month, in and around Warsaw, some 160 km to the south-east of Włocławek, the Battle of Warsaw was fought, resulting in a rout of the Soviet army, a Polish victory which became known as 'The Miracle on the Vistula'.[4]

The Second Polish Republic of 1919 did not initially enjoy a very positive international reputation. The country was variously described as 'the monstrous bastard of the Peace of Versailles' (Molotov), 'a farce' (E.H. Carr), 'an economic impossibility whose only industry is Jew-baiting' (J.M Keynes), and a country 'drunk with the new wine of liberty supplied to her by the Allies', which 'fancied herself as the resistless mistress of Central Europe' (Lloyd George).[5]

If relations with her neighbours and the international community were somewhat fraught in 1919, the situation within Poland was hardly a bed of roses either. The first elections to the Polish National Assembly, The Sejm, were held in January 1919 and the new administration was immediately confronted with a social and economic situation that can only be described as chaotic. The unfortunate legacy of its recent rule from Berlin, Moscow, and Vienna was that, in 1919, there were at least six different currencies in circulation, five separate regional administrations, four languages used in the army, three legal codes, two or three incompatible railway gauges, and no fewer than eighteen political parties contesting the election.[6] Nor was Poland immune from the economic turbulence that was rocking the rest of Europe. Nowhere was this more obvious than in the instability of its currency. In 1918, an American dollar would buy you 9 Polish marks; by 1923, it would fetch you 15 million marks.[7]

The rapidly changing demographics of the fledgling country did not help either. The 1921 Census recorded a total population of just over 27 million, of which approximately one-third comprised various minority groups: 14.3% Ukrainian, 10.5% Jewish, 3.9% German, 3.9% Byelorussian. Just ten years later, the national population had grown to 32 million, an increase of over 18%.[8] Its ethnic make-up varied greatly between different geographical regions and, especially, between urban and rural populations. Włocławek, that town that had been briefly occupied in 1920 by the Soviets, had in that year a Jewish population of nearly 25% of its 39,000 inhabitants.[9]

The early years of the new Polish Republic were also a time of great political flux. Perhaps not surprisingly, waging war on so many different fronts had given rise to a strong nationalistic sentiment. This nationalism found expression not only in hostility towards Poland's erstwhile and current enemies, especially Russia, but also towards its several minority groups. Opinions vary as to the extent of anti-semitism in Poland in the immediate aftermath of World War I, and as to whether Jews experienced disproportionately more discrimination than other minority groups,[10] but there can be little doubt that life for many Jews in Poland in 1919 was distinctly

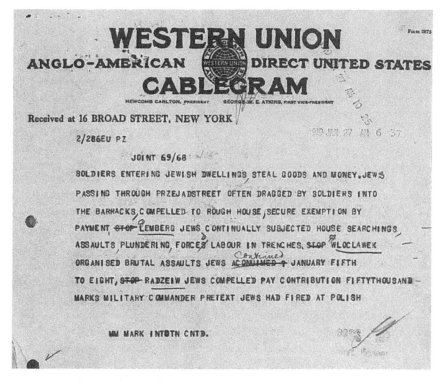

FIGURE 1.1 Telegram describing anti-semitic violence in Włocławek, January, 1919.
Source: American Jewish Joint Distribution Committee Archive (reproduced with permission).

uncomfortable. For example, according to one account, there were anti-Jewish riots in Włocławek in January 1919, with physical assaults on individual Jews and vandalism of Jewish owned businesses (Figure 1.1).[11] A year later, in that same town, at the height of the Soviet offensive towards the Vistula, it seems that there was more anti-Semitic violence and looting. According to this same source, Polish soldiers, who had been drafted to Włocławek to assist with the fortifications, forced Jewish workers to shout, 'Long live Poland, let the Jews die'.[12]

Anti-Semitism was never far from the surface in the Polish media, especially in the Catholic press, and in political discourse.[13] This was particularly evident in the ultra-right wing National Democrat and Christian Democrat parties during the 1920s, but was also visible in other parties once the Sanacja government came to power after a coup in 1926.[14] Here are the words of a particularly vile song that was circulated in Wloclawek and elsewhere at various times between 1923 and 1931. It was sung to the tune of the Polish national anthem:

> Poland is not dead yet, as long as we are still alive/ What the treason of Judah took from us, we shall take back with our work./ Jews, begone from here…/

They have taken over industry, trade, they are buying cities,/ They don't want to celebrate on Sunday, their impertinence is growing stronger./ When our brave soldiers were beating up the enemy,/ Evil Jews were shooting at them from their windows like the Apache./ Our crops are being eaten by locusts in summer and in winter,/ A self-acclaimed national minority wants to control us./ This Jewish viper is crawling in its golden skin,/ It's choking Poland and killing it with venom.[15]

By the 1930s, new measures were introduced into several sectors – the economy, professions, education – which were either openly or indirectly discriminatory against the Jewish community.[16] For example, Jews were effectively barred from many State occupations (e.g., army, civil service); several professions and universities imposed numerical quotas – so called 'numerus clausus' – to restrict the numbers of Jews and other minorities so that their proportions in the organisation did not exceed their proportions in the population at large. Apparently, there were even separate benches in some university lecture theatres for Jews and Christians – known as 'ghetto benches'. And a variety of regulations were implemented – e.g., prohibition of the ritual slaughter of animals, compulsory market days on Saturdays (the Jewish Sabbath), all of which hit Jewish businesses disproportionately.[17] Sometimes, indeed, Jewish businesses in Włocławek in the 1930s were marked with black spots.[18]

There was one other event in Włocławek in 1919 that we now need to record. On 22 June, six days before the signing of the Treaty of Versailles, Ruchla Perle Tajfel, wife of Icek Henyn Tajfel, gave birth to a baby boy, Hersz Mordcha Tajfel, although he was usually known by the Polish version of his name, Heniek Tajfel. In comparison to all the upheavals in Poland that year, this was an unremarkable event: a new arrival to a Jewish family in a small provincial town in the north-west of Poland. Yet, for future generations of social scientists, this day would prove momentous enough in its own way. For that same Heniek Tajfel would later become Henri Tajfel, one of the most influential European social psychologists of the twentieth century.

The Tajfel family

It is conventional in biographies to say something about genealogy, to trace the family roots of one's subject. I do so here, not merely out of respect for convention but to place on record the (very large) extended family from which Heniek came. To anticipate a little, the fact that, in common with most Jewish families in Poland at that time, so few members of this family survived the Holocaust was to have a profound psychological impact on Heniek and was to influence many of his later intellectual concerns.

Let me begin with Heniek's immediate family[19] (Figure 1.2). As we know, his parents were Icek and Ruchla. Icek was the eldest son of Wolf Tajfel (or 'Wolek' as he was sometimes known) who, in turn, was son of Jciek and Malka Tajfel (neé Opiesinski). Wolf was married to Miriam (neé Dyszel) and was the patriarch of the

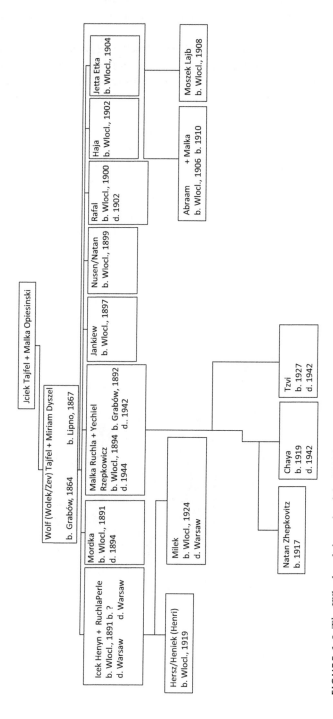

FIGURE 1.2 The Włocławek branch of the Tajfels.

family, father to no fewer than *ten* children, of whom two died in early childhood.[20] Wolf was born in Grabów in 1864. Grabów is a small town about 70 km south of Włocławek.

We know from various sources that Wolf, Heniek's grandfather, was a well-to-do landowner and business man. In the earliest records from the late nineteenth century, Wolf is described as a butcher,[21] but the Włocławek Yizkor[22] book notes that subsequently (in 1920) he set up a leather business, the First Włocławek Tannery, with three others,[23] a fact confirmed by various business and telephone directories from the 1920s and 1930s where he is listed under the leather (*skóry*) trade section. These directories show him living at various addresses, but principally on 3 Maja Street, no. 26 ('3 Maja' means 3 May, Polish National Day) which, to this day, is an elegant tree-lined avenue running through the centre of Włocławek down to the Vistula. The Włocławek Register Office records him as also being in the wool trade.[24] A contemporaneous photograph of his shop on 3 Maja is shown in Figure 1.3. The sign by the front door ('Konfekcja Męska i Damska') means 'Ready-made clothing for men and women'. Konfekcja would also include leather gloves, bags and belts.[25]

FIGURE 1.3 The Tajfel shop at 3 Maja Street (No. 26) (between 1925 and 1931).

Source: https://fotopolska.eu/3_Maja_26_Wloclawek (reproduced with permission).

Icek, Heniek's father, went into the family business. The Włocławek Register Office has him listed as an owner of 'leather and wool selling by retail and in bulk (wholesale)' and he lived for some years (certainly, 1922–1924) at the same address as his father, 3 Maja Street no. 26. Indeed, it is the contention of the Włocławek Register Office that Heniek was probably born in this house.[26] It seems that Icek was not a conspicuous success at business. There are various financial documents in the Włocławek town archive, one of which indicated that he had been late in submitting some business registration document and would be subject to a fine. Heniek's widow also told me that Heniek had described his father, while being a very good chess player, as being no good at running his business.[27] Although he and Ruchla subsequently moved houses a few times in the 1920s, the address where they seemed to have resided the longest was 19 Kosciuski Street. That house still stands, though it has obviously seen better days (Figure 1.4). The paint is peeling off the walls and windows and the house has been divided into flats, at least one of which was unoccupied when I visited it in 2017.

This, then, was Heniek's immediate family – grandparents,[28] parents, and seven uncles and aunts – all of whom lived in Włocławek as far as we know.

However, in Grabów, that small town to the south of Włocławek where Wolf hailed from, there were some other Tajfels, perhaps the most interesting of whom for our present purposes was Shlomo Tajfel's family. Shlomo was born there in 1902.

FIGURE 1.4 19, Kosciucki Street where Heniek lived as a child.
Source: Picture by the author, 2017.

His father was called Hersz Tajfel, as was his son, born in 1930. In Jewish families at that time it was common for children to be named after deceased relatives.[29] It is surely no coincidence that Heniek (birthname, Hersz) and this Grabów Hersz had the same first name. Wolf, Heniek's grandfather came from Grabów. Quite likely, then, he was Shlomo's uncle. Shlomo and his family managed to escape to Russia just after the Germans invaded in 1939. Whilst there, they ran into a Nachum Tajfel, 'one of our relatives from Wloclawek', as the younger Hersz told me.[30] This Nachum was probably Heniek's uncle, Wolf's fifth child. Indeed, Heniek's widow recalled that she remembered that her husband had once told her that an uncle of his ended up in Paris after the war, having come from Siberia where he had evaded the Germans. So, this Hersz Tajfel, who is still alive and living in the USA, is probably a second cousin of Heniek. Incidentally, he now goes by the name of Henry, the English version of the name that Heniek would later adopt (Henri).

On Heniek's grandmother's (Miriam Dyszel's) side there are still more relatives, two of whom are still alive. Although Miriam originally came from Lipno, some 25 km to the north of Włocławek on the other side of the Vistula, her mother (Estera) was born in Grabów and perhaps it was via that Grabów connection that Miriam met her husband Wolf. In any event, some of her siblings must have moved to Włocławek at about the same time as she did. One of them, Israel Dyszel, married Regina and they had six children. The oldest of these was called Hela and she and her husband lived in Włocławek and had two children, Svek and Ester, who later assumed a new name, Maria Lisiecka, to evade capture by the Nazis.[31] Israel and Regina's youngest was also called Ester (probably named after her grandmother) and she eventually married and had a little girl called Alina, born in the Warsaw ghetto in 1941. By my calculations, Maria and Alina were therefore also second cousins of Heniek Tajfel. They are both alive and living in the USA.[32]

Heniek's early years

What else is known about Heniek's early life and family? According to his widow Anne, he did not get on well with his father but was very fond of his mother.[33] There is but a single photograph surviving from his youth (Figure 1.5). This shows the young Heniek on the left of his mother and his younger brother, Milek, on her right.

As would have been common for a child from a Polish middle-class family, Heniek went to a gymnasium school (*gimnazium*). It is unclear whether he went to a State gymnasium or a private Jewish one (there were both in Włocławek). His Grabów namesake, whom I introduced above, came from a very similar background and went to a Jewish school in Łodz[34] and so it is entirely possible that Heniek did too. According to one account, the Jewish school in Włocławek was thought to be one of the best schools of its type in Poland.[35] For reasonably well off parents of a bright Jewish boy (as he proved to be), it would have been a natural choice of school. Certainly, his second cousin Ester Dyszel went to a Jewish school in Włocławek, which she described as 'prestigious' and 'expensive'.[36]

FIGURE 1.5 Heniek (on the left) with his mother Ruchla and brother Milek.
Source: Photograph courtesy of Anne Tajfel.

Wherever he went, he would have followed a standard curriculum that was introduced by the Polish government in the early years of the Second Republic. This would have covered the usual subjects, mathematics, sciences, humanities, and, in all probability, ample 'civic education', which seemed to have consisted of the instillation of much patriotic Polish sentiment, especially during the period of the very nationalistic Sanacja Regime (1926–1935), roughly corresponding to the period of Heniek's schooldays.[37] Even in the Jewish school, if that is where he went, there was a fairly broad curriculum.[38] It is also very likely that he would have learned French. Because of the strong political and cultural links between France and Poland during the Imperial era, French seems to have been quite widely used as a second (or third) language. Business and trade directories from the 1920s routinely gave the French word for each business sector underneath the Polish name (e.g., Rzeinicy (*boucher* – butcher), Skóry (*cuirs et peaux* – leather)). And a nineteenth-century souvenir postcard of 3 Maja Street, where some of the Tajfel family lived, is entitled 'Vue de la Grand-Rue de Włocławek'.

Heniek's first-known appearance in print may have been in 1927 when he was eight years old. In those days there was a well-known Jewish national newspaper called *Naszego Przegaldu*. Each week it carried a special supplement aimed at its younger readers, *Mały Przeglad* ('Little Review'). This section was edited by Janusz Korczak,[39] a well-known paediatrician, broadcaster, and writer of children's stories, some of which are still read to Polish children to this day. *Mały Przeglad* was full of stories and poems written by Jewish children. Every now and again, Korczak

FIGURE 1.6 First known traces of Heniek Tajfel in print, March 1927.

Source: 'Mały Przegląd, Pismo dla dzieci i Młodzieży', inside 'Nasz Przegląd', The Polish National Library, archival signature - mf. 59240, source: https://polona.pl/, copyrights - public domain (reproduced with permission).

would announce writing competitions in which he would invite his readers to participate, and then he would announce which schools had sent in the most entries, presumably to spur other schools to greater efforts the next time. We do not know the precise topic that Heniek wrote about, but whatever it was, it got a mention in *Mały Przegląd* in its issue on 25 March 1927, if for no other reason than that he had apparently forgotten to include his home address on the entry (Figure 1.6).

Against the xenophobic climate in Poland described earlier, it would not be surprising if Heniek experienced some anti-Semitic name-calling or bullying at school, although much would have depended on whether he went to a State or Jewish school. His Grabów namesake told me that he personally did not experience much discrimination because he lived in a predominantly Jewish neighbourhood and went to a Jewish school. Nevertheless, he did witness one horrific incident on his way home from school in the late 1930s. Here is how he described it:

> I used to come home from school the last few weeks before the war started. (Once) I remember coming – and where we lived was a Jewish neighbourhood, like mixed, but mostly Jewish – I remember two Polish kids – which I'll never forget, they're still in my mind – ran over to two Jews with long beards and they started yanking the beard, yanking to such an extent that they ripped the beard out with the skin, which started bleeding. This I remember, you know, that kind of made my stomach sick.[40]

Other sources confirm that anti-Semitism was rife in Polish schools at that time. One particularly vivid set of accounts was compiled by Alina Cala.[41] She analysed a collection of autobiographical essays written by young Jewish people, contributions to competitions organised by the Institute for Jewish Research (YIVO) based in Vilna, a city in the north-east of Poland. Here is what one student from Krakow wrote in 1939:

> I started primary school at the age of six. There were forty pupils in our class, among them four Jews. At that time anti-Semitism did exist, but not to the extent it does now. We Jews were up against it at every turn. The Christian pupils used to beat us up during every break, so that finally we never went out during breaks but stayed behind in the classroom. If we complained to the teachers, they only laughed at us, and later, during break, we would be in even worse trouble for having complained.[42]

Heniek's cousin, Ester Dyszel, experienced overt discrimination from her teachers in the state school she attended in Włocławek in the early 1930s:

> While the other children accepted me as one of their own – I went to their houses after school to play, and they came to mine – the instructors treated me like an outsider.
> I still remember one of my second grade teachers, a prim, middle-aged woman, pursing her lips and scrunching up her face in a sour, prune-like grimace whenever I made a mistake in my written work or said something that wasn't right. She'd tell me to stand up and humiliate me by pointing out how ignorant I was…. I never heard or saw her treat the other children in class that way.[43]

She reported that things only looked up when she transferred to the private Jewish gymnasium in Włocławek.

Although such anti-Semitism was common, the frequent daily contact between Jewish and Catholic students also sometimes resulted in cross-group friendships. Here is a boy from Sochazew, also writing in 1934:

> My best friend was a Catholic, Jósef Karpiński, whom I knew from school. We got on like brothers. We used to spend our afternoons and evenings together, talking and discussing books we had read.[44]

However, outside of school, relationships between young people of different faiths were not always easy. Korzen describes how young Catholic students from Włocławek as early as 1931 ran amok with anti-Semitic demonstrations, physical attacks on Jews, and vandalism of the synagogue, the Jewish gymnasium and private houses.[45] Over the next five years, such hate crime escalated in Włocławek and was accompanied by the closure of Jewish cultural organisations, sports clubs, and libraries. According to this same observer, the Jewish youth of Włocławek responded with various protest strikes.

Relationships with his peers inside and outside of school would not have been the only challenge that Heniek might have had to confront. Jewish adolescents growing up in Poland at that time often experienced identity conflicts as they sought to understand who they were and what their place in Polish society was or might be.

Some anecdotal reports capture those conflicts well. They are taken from the same YIVO archive referred to above.[46] Here is Abraham Rotfarb talking about growing up in Warsaw in 1939, a city which, at that time, might have consisted of 40% Jews:[47]

> There are more Jews than goyim. Because the janitor, the housemaid, and the workmen and other people performing 'menial tasks' were goyim, I ranked them very low. What do they know, these goyim? A goy knows nothing, a goy does not think, the only thing he knows how to do is to beat up Jews... My world was divided into Jews and goyim.[48]

Thus, for this boy, and perhaps for Heniek too, a simple bifurcation dominated his social life: Jews and *goyim*. However, such a binary categorisation would also have had to be reconciled with the strongly nationalistic flavour of civic education in Polish schools that I noted earlier. This was a country seeking to rebuild itself after its effective cultural annihilation by the nineteenth-century imperial powers, and the State considered it important to instil some patriotic pride in its future generations. So it would have been important to be Polish as well as Jewish. Here is that same Abraham Rotfarb, reflecting on the anguish of his own particular, but probably not unique, identity crisis:

> I am a poor assimilated soul. I am a Jew and a Pole, or rather I was a Jew, but gradually under the influence of the language, the culture, and the literature, I have also become a Pole. I love Poland. Its language, its culture, and most of all the fact of its liberation and the heroism of its independence struggle, all pluck at my heartstrings and fire my feelings and enthusiasm. But I do not love that Poland which, for no apparent reason, hates me.... Poland has brought me up as a Pole, but brands me a Jew who has to be driven out. I want to be a Pole, you have not let me; I want to be a Jew, but I don't know how, I have become alienated from Jewishness. (I do not like myself as a Jew).[49]

Ester, Heniek's cousin, evidently came from an assimilationist family:

> It was odd. Although I knew I was being mistreated because of my Jewish background, I didn't think of myself as Jewish. I knew I was Polish. I spoke Polish. Everyone in my family did. We were very assimilated. My parents used their Polish names, Herman and Hela. My birth name was Esther, but

everyone called me by my Polish nickname, Tusia. We were Polish patriots. When my parents heard the news that Piłsudski, the president of Poland had died, they burst into tears. They loved the great Polish leader.[50]

At this distance, it is impossible to know which identities the Tajfel family, and especially its younger members, espoused. Lichten suggests that there were several conflicting strands of opinion in the Jewish community in the new Polish republic.[51] One, perhaps the largest, was the Orthodox community, which, through its religious practices, languages (Yiddish or Hebrew) and dress codes, kept itself somewhat apart from mainstream Polish culture. Indeed, in cities with substantial Jewish populations, Włocławek included, Jews also tended to concentrate in a few neighbourhoods. Another important group were the Zionists who aspired to emigrate to Palestine. This group grew in popularity in the 1930s as the Depression bit and anti-Semitism grew, even though the opportunities for actual emigration (with a so-called Polish Alijah passport) became increasingly limited. There was also the Bund, an overtly left-wing labour and political organisation, which argued that Jews should stay in Poland and fight to establish socialism there. Then there were several 'assimilationist' organisations and political parties who, in differing degrees, advocated an identification with the new Polish State. Some of these, for example the Association of Unity Academic Youth (ZAMZ), were particularly active in the larger cities like Warsaw and Łodz and were aimed especially at young Jewish Poles. Lichten claims that ZAMZ was mainly popular amongst the Jewish middle class – professionals, business owners and artisans – and so it is possible that Heniek might have been affiliated to one of its branches. Although some of these organisations argued for full-blown assimilation, it seems clear that many of them were what we would now call 'dual-identity' in outlook since they wished to combine their Polish national identity with a retention of their ties with traditional Jewish culture.[52]

Given the variety of identities and value systems competing for the attention of the new generation of Polish Jews, it is not surprising that relationships between parents and their adolescent children in Jewish families were sometimes more than a little strained.[53] I noted earlier that Heniek seemed not to have got on well with his father; whether this was due to their conflicting personalities or owed something to clashing cultural values we shall never know.

With the benefit of hindsight, it is possible to comprehend the impact that growing up in such society, riven as it was by interethnic tensions, economic insecurity and many (contested) identities, would have on the adult Heniek's later intellectual preoccupations. Indeed, he acknowledged as much in an interview he gave later in his life:

> Having been brought up in Poland, I've always been felt a member of an extremely discriminated against minority which was the case with Jews in semi-fascist Poland before the war. It's nothing to do with religion but it is to do with social background. Everyone's social background is relevant to what they do.[54]

As we shall see, for most of his academic career he sought to understand the origins of intergroup conflict and the role that social identity processes play in its perpetuation and resolution.

But that is for later in this story. For now, we need just to record the fact that, faced with that increasingly hostile cultural and political climate and the difficulty of obtaining admission to a Polish university because of the 'numerus clausus' quotas, the decision was taken for Heniek to emigrate to France to continue his studies. Many years later, he recalled that decision:

> I was sent to study from my native Poland to France in 1936. My parents thought that whatever I did had to be 'practical' – the prospect of getting a job was as gloomy as it is going to be now, as it is now. And chemistry sounded practical.[55]

Thus it was that in 1936, at age 17, he set out on the first of many journeys that he would make throughout his life.

Notes

1 Davies (1981).
2 Davies (1981, 2001).
3 Davies (1972).
4 Fiddick (1973); Stachura (1998); Davies (1972).
5 Davies (1981), p. 293.
6 Davies (2001); Lukowski and Zowalski (2001).
7 Davies (2001), p. 107.
8 Stachura (1998), p. 62.
9 www.Sztetl.org.
10 Mendelsohn (1994).
11 www.Szetetl.org; www.searcharchives.jdc.org
12 www.Sztetl.org
13 Landau-Czajka (1994); Holzer (1977).
14 Rudnicki (2011).
15 Song of the Progressists, Members of the Society for Promoting Polish Industry and Trade 'Progress', founded in 1913 by right-wing extremists from National Democracy Party; original words in www.szetetl.org.pl; translation by Olga Kuzawińska.
16 Davies (1981); Rudnicki (2011).
17 Rudnicki (2011).
18 Korzen (1969).
19 Unearthing information about Jewish families in Poland in the early years of the twentieth century can be a frustrating business. While it is true that the international Jewish community has been remarkably assiduous in recording the names of its ancestors, the havoc wreaked in Poland by the Holocaust has meant that many records are lost forever. It is not just the scale of the slaughter which caused this obliteration – of approximately 3.3 million Polish Jews, only 369,000 (11%) survived the Second World War (Davies, 1981) – but many traditional repositories of Jewish genealogy, synagogues, and the like, were also systematically destroyed by the Germans. And those that were not deliberately

destroyed simply got lost in the chaos of war. From some assiduous fossicking in state archives and various genealogy sites, we have now reconstructed several of the relationships between the Tajfels from Włocławek and nearby towns.

20 Barbara Rubinstein, www.geni.com; Polish Genealogical Society: file 'Włocławek 8318–8338'; Torun State Archives.

21 Torun State Archives.

22 Yizkor books are public commemorations of Jewish communities in Poland and elsewhere. They record Jewish life and times in particular towns that had been decimated in the Holocaust, and often contain touching tributes by surviving family members to those who perished. The Włocławek Yizkor book is an impressive tome, half in English and half in Hebrew, and describes pre-war life in the town in painstaking detail (Biderman, 1969).

23 Biderman (1969), p. 133.

24 I am grateful to Darius Doliński for his assistance with the Włocławek town records.

25 I am also indebted to Darius Doliński for locating this photograph and for translating the shop sign.

26 Letter from Włocławek Register Office to Dariusz Doliński, October 2018.

27 A. Tajfel interview, September 2014.

28 We have definitive information only about his paternal grandparents. His mother's maiden name (Perle) has not yet surfaced in any genealogical investigations of Polish records. As a result, we know almost nothing about his mother's side of the family. The only tiniest clue comes from a letter that Heniek wrote to a Canadian colleague many years later about a possible shared family connection in Łodz. He mentioned that his aunt (his mother's sister) had been married to someone called Birnbaum, who owned a textile factory in Łodz (letter from Tajfel to Ian Lubek, 3 October 1977; WC, PSY/TAJ/7/6/12).

29 Francine Tajfel, personal communication. I am immensely grateful to Francine Tajfel for her tireless efforts in helping me to reconstruct Tajfel family trees. Alina Koren was also helpful in delineating the Dyszel family connections.

30 Henry Tajfel interview, November 2016.

31 Winkelman (2015).

32 Alina Koren, personal communication, May 2017.

33 A. Tajfel, personal communication, 2015.

34 Henry Tajfel, personal communication, 2016.

35 Korzen, in Biderman (1969), pp. 84–94.

36 Winkelman (2015), p. 18.

37 Cala (1994), p. 51.

38 Korzen (1969).

39 Actually, Janusz Korczak was only a *nom du plume*. His real name was Henryk Goldsmit.

40 Interview with Henry Tajfel, November 2016.

41 Cala (1994).

42 Cala (1994), p. 47.

43 Winkelman (2015), pp. 14–15.

44 Cala (1994), p. 48.

45 Korzen (1969), pp. 46–50.

46 Cala (1994).

47 Davies (1981).

48 Cala (1994), p. 45.

49 Cala (1994), p. 52.

50 Winkelman (2015), p. 16.

51 Lichten (1986).
52 Lichten (1986), p. 128. Many years later, Heniek wrote a letter to *The Times* describing these acculturation choices facing young Poles in the 1930s (see Chapter 7).
53 Cala (1994).
54 Cohen (1977), p. 298.
55 Cohen (1977), pp. 296–7.

2

FRANCE, GERMANY, AND AUSTRIA

1936–1945

The dream becomes a nightmare

What might the young Heniek have been thinking as he embarked on his journey westward? Probably he took the train, perhaps the Nord-Express, one of those great trans-continental trains that ran from Warsaw to Paris via Berlin, as it still does today. If so, the long journey would have given him plenty of time to wonder about his forthcoming French sojourn.

What a paradise France must have seemed to him. A country where, since 1799, Jews had enjoyed full political, legal, and social equality (at least in theory), rights which were becoming increasingly curtailed in the Poland he was leaving behind. A country which had the motto '*Liberté, Égalité et Fraternité*', three values that would have seemed impossible dreams in the oppressive, unequal and fractious country of his birth. A country which, in 1936–37, had a Jewish prime minister (Léon Blum), a *socialist* Jewish prime minister no less, an unthinkable idea in the deeply conservative and anti-Semitic Poland of the 1930s. A country where several famous Jewish intellectuals had lived and prospered – Bergson, Durkheim, Lèvy-Bruhl, and Proust, to name but four. And a country to whose capital writers and artists were drawn like moths to a flame – Hemingway, Scott Fitzgerald, Gertrude Stein, and Man Ray were among many hundreds of intellectuals who made Paris their home in the 1930s. For a young would-be Polish intellectual like Heniek, France must have seemed like the true embodiment of all ideals and ideas of the Age of Enlightenment, or '*Le Siècle des Lumières*', as I am sure he would have preferred to call it.

Heniek was not alone in making this journey. According to some estimates, in 1936 there were nearly 2.5 million immigrants in France, proportionately more than in any other country.[1] Of these, over 200,000 were Jews.[2] In Paris alone, the city where Heniek was to spend much of the next three years, there were probably

90,000 eastern European immigrants, of whom fully 50,000 were Polish and mostly Jewish.[3] And then, of course, since 1933 there was a steady migration of Jewish refugees from Nazi Germany – upwards of 25,000 in 1933[4] – which increased dramatically towards the end of the decade as the Nazis' anti-Semitic measures became ever more brutal. Indeed, there may have been as many as 180,000 refugees living in France by 1938.[5]

The impetus for the emigration from Germany in the 1930s seems obvious enough. But what of the tens of thousands of emigrants from Russia and Poland in those inter-war years? Joseph Roth, an Austrian journalist of Polish Jewish descent, sought to capture the motivation of these Jewish migrants thus:

> The Eastern Jew looks to the West with a longing that it doesn't really merit. To the Eastern Jew, the West signifies freedom, justice, civilisation, and the possibility to work and develop his talents. The West exports engineers, automobiles, books and poems to the East. It sends propaganda, soaps and hygiene, useful and elevating things, all of them beguiling and come-hitherish to the East.[6]

But, he warned,

> And so they leave, on foot, by train, on board ship, for Western countries where a different, somewhat reformed, though no less dismal, ghetto offers its own brand of darkness to the newcomers who have barely managed to escape the clutches of the concentration camps.

That warning, that the West might prove to be something other than the paradise dreamt of by those tens of thousands of eastern European émigrés, proved prophetic. In the mid to late 1930s, France was not an easy place to live in if you were a foreigner, especially if you were a Jewish foreigner. It still had not completely emerged from the great economic depression of the early 1930s and, as a consequence, unemployment was high and living standards were low. Alongside this harsh economic climate was the mass immigration from the East, as I have just noted. As often happens in times of hardship, these issues became causally linked in the popular imagination: immigrants were blamed for many of the economic ills of France.[7] By the late 1930s, anti-immigrant sentiment in general, and anti-Semitism in particular, were rife in sections of the French media and in right-wing political circles. There were occasional demonstrations against Jews in Paris, and foreigners were sometimes attacked on the streets.[8] Some politicians and leaders of professions called for the introduction of quotas ('*numerus clausus*') for certain occupations,[9] just as had been introduced in Poland a year or two before (Chapter 1).

Worse was to follow. As Hitler's territorial ambitions grew, with annexation of Austria in Spring 1938, the numbers of refugees from the East increased accordingly. The new French government – by then the left-leaning Blum administration had fallen – introduced a whole series of punitive decrees against foreigners.[10] There were restrictions on the right to work and on entitlements to housing; those whose visa documents were not in order, if indeed they had such documents at all, risked fines, imprisonment, and even repatriation. Then, in November 1938, a German diplomat was assassinated in Paris by Herman Grynzpan, a Polish Jew. The Nazis back in Germany were swift to exact revenge, resulting in the infamous *Kristallnacht* in which thousands of Jewish shops and synagogues throughout Germany were ransacked. Such events were to have ramifications in France, resulting in an intensification of the anti-Semitic atmosphere, especially in Paris.[11]

This, then, was the France that greeted Heniek on his arrival from Poland. According to his CV, Heniek first took his Baccalaureat (or '*equivalence*') in Paris in 1937, and then studied chemistry at the Universities of Toulouse and Paris (Sorbonne) between 1937 and 1939.

In various French army documents, Heniek lists three addresses in Paris (and one in Veretz, a small town near Tours, 250 km SW of Paris in the Loire valley[12]). Two of the Paris addresses were (and still are) in the heart of the student quarter in the 5th Arrondissement: 5, Rue des Carmes and 1, Rue de l'École Polytechnique, both near the Sorbonne where he was studying. Living there, perhaps he might not have been exposed to quite so much of the anti-Semitism that was swilling around the streets of Paris in the late 1930s. His third Paris address was 8, Rue des Immeubles Industriels in the 11th Arrondissement on the other side of the Seine. As the name of street implies, this is (now at any rate) a rather less fashionable part of town and is in what was then a predominantly Jewish neighbourhood.

Wherever he lived, though, he cannot have been unaware of the xenophobic rants in much of the popular press at the time. Here, for example, is *L'Action Francaise,* commenting after Grynzpan's assassination of the German diplomat:

> (was France destined to remain forever) the battlefield of all the métèques[13] of Europe and the entire world, and will we always have to pay the consequences for acts as heinous as the one that occurred yesterday? …..The great city of Paris is fed up with having to serve as the garbage dump for the entire cosmopolitan criminal underground.[14]

Among the many other thousands of '*métèques*' in Paris in 1938, was Albert Hirschmann (or Hirschman, as he was later known). Hirschmann was a German Jew, who had escaped from Nazi Germany, fought in the Spanish civil war, and was now freelancing as an economics teacher and writer. He was later to become a distinguished academic economist and philosopher at Harvard and Princeton. The reason for mentioning him here is that one of his books, *Exit, Voice and Loyalty,* was to prove influential in Heniek's own later work.[15] Also in Paris in 1939 was another Jewish man, a young PhD student from Harvard, Jerome Bruner, then travelling in Europe.[16] Bruner, too, would come to play an important role in Heniek's life.

I shall consider later the several identity journeys Heniek made after his emigration from Poland. For now, I just want to note that, at some point in his first two years in France, he changed his Polish first name from 'Heniek' to the more commonplace (in France) 'Henri'. This might be indicative of a desire to assimilate himself to the new society in which he was now living, although it is noteworthy that he did not attempt also to change his obviously eastern European surname, as did many other Jewish émigrés.

What was happening in the wider Jewish community in France in those fraught years leading up to the Second World War? Weinberg, in his seminal account of Parisian Jews in the 1930s, devotes an entire chapter to the nature of Jewish identification in that period. According to him, there were at least as many complex – and sometimes conflicting – strands of Jewish identity as there had been in the Poland that Henri (as we shall now call him) had just left. There was, first of all, a substantial 'settled' Jewish community, people who had emigrated in the nineteenth century and earlier. At the beginning of the twentieth century these might have numbered between 40,000 and 50,000 in Paris alone. Most of these Jews enjoyed full rights as French citizens and, partly as a result of this, many had become thoroughly assimilated into mainstream French culture, with much intermarriage and even some religious conversion.[17]

But then, in the 1930s, there was that huge expansion of the Jewish community due to emigration from Germany and further east. Many of these Jews, doubtless scarred by their recent experiences in their home countries, acculturated very differently. Quite a number were overtly 'separatist',[18] opting to maintain their Jewish traditions and often choosing to live in predominantly Jewish neighbourhoods in Paris and other French cities.[19] Indeed, just as Roth had prophesied, some Jewish intellectuals actively promulgated a 'return to the ghetto' as a self-defence against the growing threat of fascism from Germany.[20]

As the terrible events in Germany unfolded in 1938 and 1939, no Jews in France could have been left unaffected. The 'racial' definitions of Jewishness adopted by the Nazis, and the anti-foreigner (i.e., anti-Jew) decrees passed in the 1930s by the French Government in an attempt to limit the numbers of refugees seem to have created a strong common bond amongst the French Jewish community.[21]

Of course, we cannot know what the impact was of these events on Henri's own identity as a Jew or, indeed, what kind Jewishness he himself espoused. But it is reasonable to suppose that these years in France before the Second World War must have left a deep impression on him. One of his later abiding intellectual preoccupations was to understand the effects of changing intergroup contexts on the social identity of group members. It is hard to think of a more personally compelling demonstration of such phenomena than the experience of living in Paris as war loomed. And if that had not been a lesson enough, the next five years would have left even more indelible traces to shape his future thinking.

Behind barbed wire

Henri started out studying chemistry. By his own admission, he was not a very diligent student. In an interview later in his life, he recalled:

It [chemistry] was as indifferent to me as anything. I remember I failed the only exam I ever failed because I was interested in three things, one, the contemporary American novel, heaven knows why, two, the civil war in Spain, you can imagine on which side, and three, in playing poker.[22]

In the address at his memorial service in 1982, it was noted that he failed that examination in the summer of 1939 and decided to stay on to retake it instead of, presumably, returning home to Poland for his holidays. That examination failure and his decision to resit the paper were to save his life. For it meant that he was still in Paris when the Germans invaded Poland on 1 September 1939, followed soon after by the French declaration of war on Germany. Obviously, any trip to Poland was now out of the question; he was not to return there for another 27 years.

With war came military conscription. Some five million French citizens were mobilised immediately and sent for training or to the Maginot line on France's northern borders.[23] Foreigners, and particularly foreign Jews, were often at the head of the queue to enlist; it is estimated that of 100,000 foreigners who had volunteered or been drafted into the French army by May 1940, fully 30% were non-French Jews.[24]

Not that it was all plain sailing for these foreign volunteers. Many immigrants, particularly those from Germany, Austria, and Czechoslovakia, or who had had history of political dissent (especially (former) members of the Communist Party), were arrested by the French authorities and held in detention camps. One prominent example was Arthur Koestler, a Hungarian Jew and ex-Communist, who was arrested and imprisoned in October 1939.[25] Around 15,000 immigrants were arrested in the first days of September 1939.[26]

Fortunately, Henri was not amongst them, perhaps because of his Polish nationality. Nor was he among the first to enlist (or be conscripted). In his CV he notes that he was mobilised into the French army in November 1939, two months after war had been declared. He does not seem to have taken advantage of the offer of French citizenship that was available to foreign volunteers.[27] According to the French national archives, he was not naturalised as a French citizen until three years *after* the war, on 6 March 1948.[28]

We know nothing about Henri's military service, except that it was brief. Along with the rest of the French army, he would probably have passed six months of boring inactivity – the so-called 'phoney war' – between November 1939 and May 1940, when the Germans finally invaded France. Within weeks it was all over. In what is commonly regarded as one of modern military history's great catastrophes, the French army had capitulated by the middle of June, with the immediate loss of 124,000 French men and a further 200,000 wounded.[29] On 22 June 1940, Marshal Pétain, the newly appointed prime minister of France, signed an armistice agreement with the Germans – quite some 21st birthday present for Henri who, by then, was most likely already a prisoner-of-war (PoW), one of the 1,800,000 French soldiers captured by the Germans in those first six weeks after the invasion of France.[30] He would later remark to Judith Wilkes, the wife of his first research assistant:

Nobody can have any idea what it was like to be woken after a battle when you had crawled away into a wood to sleep, to be woken by a Nazi bayonet at four in the morning.[31]

To understand what life must have been like for Henri and his fellow prisoners, we are indebted to the French historian, Yves Durand, who has chronicled in some detail 'la vie quotidienne' of French prisoners of war (PoWs) between 1940 and 1945.[32] His meticulous work is based largely on first-hand testimony provided by prisoners after the war, and also on official French and German documents and photographs. Fortunately, there is much material in Durand's books referring specifically to the three camps where Henri was interred. In much of what follows, I draw on that material to paint a picture of Henri's five years in captivity.

After the surrender in June 1940, hundreds of thousands of French soldiers were rounded up by the Germans and marched for days, in some cases weeks, through northern France to Belgium and the Netherlands. Conditions were intolerable: it was mid-summer and very hot; rations, and especially water, were meagre in the extreme; the prisoners were forced to march for many hours each day, sometimes witnessing the dead bodies of other soldiers by the roadside. And it was not only their physical health that was affected. The shameful suddenness of the French surrender, the uncertainty concerning their own and their country's immediate future, and the inevitable shock of their abrupt transition from soldier to captive, left the soldiers feeling disoriented and demoralised. Here is how one of them described it:

I'm trudging like a sleepwalker. All accumulated weariness of these past days, the hunger and above all the thirst, and the emotion of the past hours, all this has emptied me of all my spirit.[33]

Henri himself was on one of these forced marches. In a rare mention of his wartime experiences, he described to David Milner, his first PhD student, how during the march northwards he slowly ate his Polish passport and any papers that might identify him as a Jew.[34] As we shall see, this episode was to assume profound personal significance for Henri for the remainder of his life.

Once the prisoners reached some embarkation points – usually railway stations in northern France, Belgium, and the Netherlands – they were herded into railway cattle trucks (and some onto canal barges) for their onward journey to one of the eighty or so PoW camps scattered throughout Germany, Austria, and Poland. If conditions on the route march had been bad enough, these train journeys must have been completely insufferable. There were sixty (or more) men packed into each wagon; there was no lighting and nor were there any toilet facilities; typically the trains would stop only once a day to allow the men to relieve themselves, so the air inside the trucks stank from those who had been unable to wait; it was oppressively hot and there was little to eat or drink; they had no idea where they were headed or what fate would befall them. Here is one poignant account from one of the incarcerated men:

Morale is at a new low. Everyone is wrapped up in his own miserable thoughts. Where are we going? What's going to happen? How will we be treated? How long will it last? It's the unknown, the start of a depressing adventure.[35]

Eventually, the trains arrived at the camps – 'stalags' for enlisted men, 'oflags' for officers – that would be their 'home' for the next five years. In Henri's case, he was in three stalags, one in Germany and two in Austria.[36] He arrived first at Stalag XIID, which was in Trèves (or Trier) close to the French-German border. This was on 10 February 1941, confirmed in *La Liste Officielle de Prisonniers Français* (No. 73) (Figure 2.1).

The entry reads:

Tajfel (Henri), 22–6–19, Wloclawek (Pol), 2e cl., 1er R. Pol. 180

This indicates that he was a soldier (second class) in the First Polish Regiment. The number 180 refers to Stalag XIID. This was a '*camp de triage*' where large numbers of prisoners arriving from France were held temporarily before being transferred to more permanent camps.[37] Indeed, Henri stayed there only three months before his transfer to camps in Austria.

It was a relatively large camp with around 24,690 prisoners held there in that month in 1941.[38] But this number is a bit misleading because the majority of prisoners notionally attached to a particular camp were actually working and living outside the camp in so-called '*Arbeitskommandos*' (work groups), or '*kommandos*' for short.

Amongst the many thousands of other prisoners who passed through the gates of Stalag XIID in 1941, was one Jean Paul Sartre.[39] It is theoretically possible that he and Henri met – their time in XIID overlapped by a month (February to March 1941) – although rather improbable given that there were more than 24,000 other prisoners in the camp at the time. Still, I like the fanciful thought that these two great twenty-century European intellectuals might actually have bumped into each other at the camp latrines one day.

On arrival at the camp, Henri would have had to undergo the degrading process of registration.[40] First, he will have been searched and any money and most personal possessions confiscated. He would have had to undress so that his clothing could be deloused. Then all his hair would have been shaved off, both from his scalp and the rest of his body. Following this depilation, he would have been painted all over with a delousing fluid and then pushed into a collective shower with several other men. After that, still completely naked, they were made to wait until their clothes were returned to them. Next came the process of 'matriculation'. He would have had to give some basic personal details on a registration card. A copy of that first registration document written in Henri's own hand is shown in Figure 2.2. It recorded the usual biographical stuff (date and place of birth), his occupation (student), his last address in Paris (5 rue de Carmes, Paris 5), his soldier rank (2nd class), the name

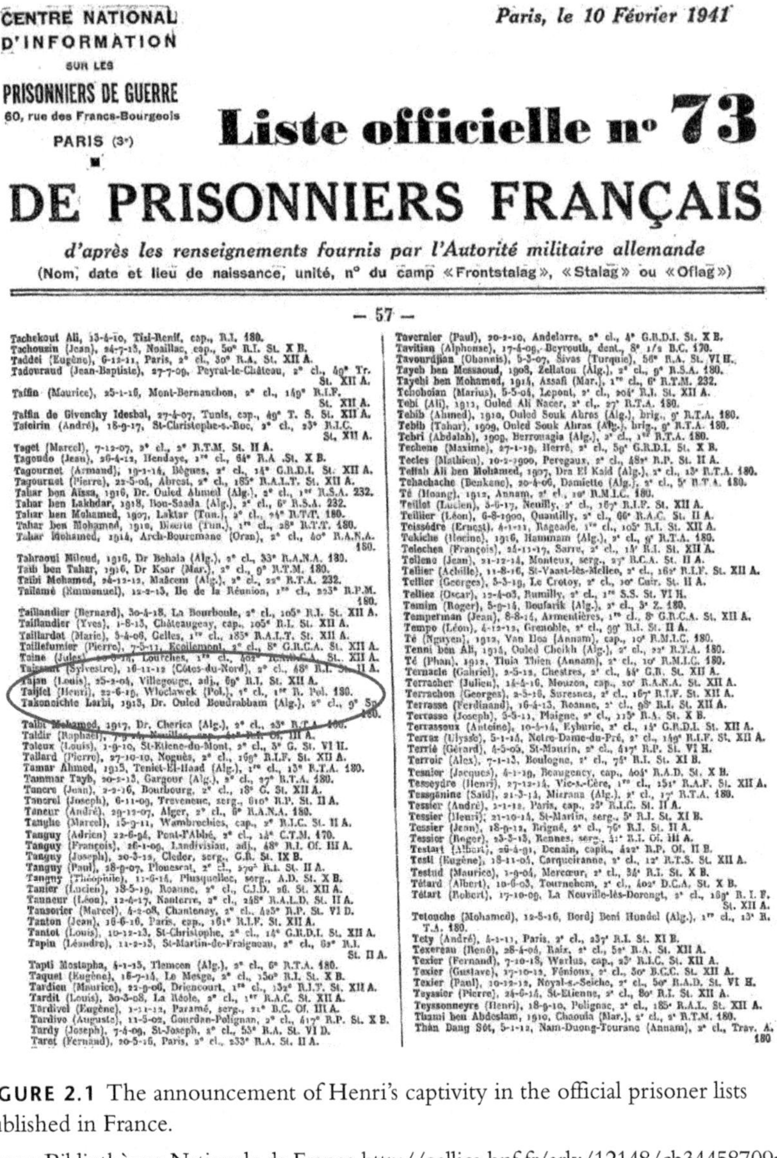

CENTRE NATIONAL D'INFORMATION SUR LES PRISONNIERS DE GUERRE
60, rue des Francs-Bourgeois
PARIS (3e)

Paris, le 10 Février 1941

Liste officielle n° 73
DE PRISONNIERS FRANÇAIS

d'après les renseignements fournis par l'Autorité militaire allemande
(Nom, date et lieu de naissance, unité, n° du camp «Frontstalag», «Stalag» ou «Oflag»)

— 57 —

Tachekout Ali, 13-4-10, Tizi-Renif, cap., R.I. 180.
Tachouzin (Jean), 24-7-13, Noaillac, cap., 50e R.I. St. X B.
Taddei (Eugène), 6-12-11, Paris, 2e cl., 30e R.A. St. XII A.
Tadouraud (Jean-Baptiste), 27-7-09, Peyrat-le-Château, 2e cl., 49e Tr. St. XII A.
Taffin (Maurice), 25-1-16, Mont-Bernanchon, 2e cl., 149e R.I.F. St. XII A.
Taffin de Givenchy Idesbal, 27-4-07, Tunis, cap., 49e T. S. St. XII A.
Tafoirin (André), 18-9-17, St-Christophe-s.-Roc, 2e cl., 23e R.I.C. St. XII A.
Taget (Marcel), 7-12-07, 2e cl., 2e R.T.M. St. II A.
Tagoudo (Jean), 26-4-12, Hendaye, 1re cl., 64e R.A. St. X B.
Tagournet (Armand), 19-1-14, Bègues, 2e cl., 14e G.R.D.I. St. XII A.
Tagournet (Pierre), 22-5-04, Abrest, 2e cl., 185e R.A.L.T. St. XII A.
Tahar ben Aissa, 1916, Dr. Ouled Ahmed (Alg.), 2e cl., 1er R.S.A. 232.
Tahar ben Lakhdar, 1918, Bou-Saada (Alg.), 2e cl., 6e R.S.A. 232.
Tahar ben Mohamed, 1907, Laktar (Tun.), 2e cl., 4e R.T.T. 180.
Tahar ben Mohamed, 1910, Bizerte (Tun.), 1re cl., 28e R.T.T. 180.
Tahar Mohamed, 1914, Arch-Bouremane (Oran), 2e cl., 40e R.A.N.A. 180.
Tahraoui Miloud, 1916, Dr Bohala (Alg.), 2e cl., 33e R.A.N.A. 180.
Taib ben Tahar, 1916, Dr Ksar (Mar.), 2e cl., 9e R.T.M. 180.
Taibi Mohamed, 24-12-12, Maâcem (Alg.), 2e cl., 22e R.T.A. 232.
Tailamé (Emmanuel), 12-2-13, Ile de la Réunion, 1re cl., 223e R.P.M. 180.
Taillandier (Bernard), 30-4-18, La Bourboule, 2e cl., 105e R.I. St. XII A.
Taillandier (Yves), 1-8-13, Châteaugeay, cap., 105e R.I. St. XII A.
Taillardat (Marie), 5-4-06, Gelles, 1re cl., 185e R.A.L.T. St. XII A.
Taillefumier (Pierre), 7-5-11, Ecoilemont, 2e cl., 8e G.R.C.A. St. XII A.
Taine (Jules), [illegible], Louches, 1re cl., 402e [illegible] St. XII A.
Taissant (Sylvestre), 16-11-12 (Côtes-du-Nord), 2e cl., 68e R.I. St. II A.
Tajan (Louis), 25-2-04, Villegouge, adj., 69e R.I. St. XII A.
Tajfel (Henri), 22-6-19, Wloclawek (Pol.), 1e cl., 1er R. Pol. 180.
Takoncichte Larbi, 1913, Dr. Ouled Boudrabbam (Alg.), 2e cl., 9e Sp. 180.
Talbi Mohamed, 1917, Dr. Cherica (Alg.), 2e cl., 23e R.T.A. 180.
Taldir (Raphaël), [illegible], Noaillac, cap., [illegible] Of. III A.
Taleux (Louis), 1-9-10, St-Etienne-du-Mont, 2e cl., 3e G. St. VI H.
Tallard (Pierre), 27-10-10, Noguès, 2e cl., 169e R.I.F. St. XII A.
Tamar Ahmed, 1915, Teniet-El-Haad (Alg.), 1re cl., 13e R.T.A. 180.
Tammar Tayb, 20-2-13, Gargour (Alg.), 2e cl., 27e R.T.A. 180.
Tancre (Jean), 2-2-16, Bourbourg, 2e cl., 18e G. St. XII A.
Tancrel (Joseph), 6-11-09, Treveneuc, serg., 610e R.P. St. II A.
Taneur (André), 29-12-07, Alger, 2e cl., 6e R.A.N.A. 180.
Tanghe (Marcel), 15-9-11, Wambrechies, cap., 2e R.I.C. St. II A.
Tanguy (Adrien) 22-6-94, Pont-l'Abbé, 2e cl., 14e C.T.M. 170.
Tanguy (François), 26-1-09, Landivisiau, adj., 48e R.I. Of. III A.
Tanguy (Joseph), 20-3-12, Cleder, serg., G.R. St. IX B.
Tanguy (Paul), 28-9-07, Plouescat, 2e cl., 270e R.I. St. II A.
Tanguy (Théophile), 11-6-14, Plusquellec, serg., A.D. St. X B.
Tanier (Lucien), 18-5-19, Roanne, 2e cl., G.I.D. 26. St. XII A.
Tanneur (Léon), 12-4-17, Nanterre, 2e cl., 248e R.A.L.D. St. II A.
Tansorier (Marcel), 4-2-08, Chantenay, 2e cl., 423e R.P. St. VI D.
Tanton (Jean), 16-6-16, Paris, cap., 161e R.I.F. St. XII A.
Tantot (Louis), 10-12-13, St-Christophe, 2e cl., 14e G.R.D.I. St. XII A.
Tapin (Léandre), 11-2-13, St-Martin-de-Fraigneau, 2e cl., 69e R.I. St. II A.
Tapti Mostapha, 4-1-13, Tlemcen (Alg.), 2e cl., 6e R.T.A. 180.
Taquet (Eugène), 16-7-14, Le Mesge, 2e cl., 150e R.I. St. X B.
Tardieu (Maurice), 22-9-06, Driencourt, 1re cl., 132e R.I.T. St. XII A.
Tardit (Louis), 30-3-08, La Réole, 2e cl., 1er R.A.C. St. XII A.
Tardivel (Eugène), 1-11-12, Paramé, serg., 21e B.C. Of. III A.
Tardivo (Auguste), 11-5-02, Gourdan-Polignan, 2e cl., 417e R.P. St. X B.
Tardy (Joseph), 7-4-09, St-Joseph, 2e cl., 53e R.A. St. VI D.
Taret (Fernand), 20-5-16, Paris, 2e cl., 233e R.A. St. II A.

Tavernier (Paul), 20-2-10, Andelarre, 2e cl., 4e G.R.D.I. St. X B.
Tavitian (Alphonse), 17-4-09, Beyrouth, dent., 8e 1/2 B.C. 170.
Tavourdjian (Ohannis), 5-3-07, Sivas (Turquie), 56e R.A. St. VI H.
Tayeb ben Messaoud, 1908, Zellatou (Alg.), 2e cl., 9e R.S.A. 180.
Tayebi ben Mohamed, 1914, Assafi (Mar.), 1re cl., 6e R.T.M. 232.
Tchoboian (Marius), 5-5-04, Lepont, 2e cl., 204e R.I. St. XII A.
Tebi (Ali), 1911, Ouled Ali Nacer, 2e cl., 27e R.T.A. 180.
Tebib (Ahmed), 1910, Ouled Souk Ahras (Alg.), brig., 9e R.T.A. 180.
Tebib (Tahar), 1909, Ouled Souk Ahras (Alg.), brig., 9e R.T.A. 180.
Tebri (Abdalah), 1909, Berrouagia (Alg.), 2e cl., 1er R.T.A. 180.
Techene (Maxime), 27-1-19, Herré, 2e cl., 59e G.R.D.I. St. X B.
Tecles (Mathieu), 10-2-1900, Peregaux, 2e cl., 482e R.P. St. II A.
Teffah Ali ben Mohamed, 1907, Dra El Kaid (Alg.), 2e cl., 13e R.T.A. 180.
Tehachache (Benkene), 20-4-06, Damiette (Alg.), 2e cl., 5e R.T.A. 180.
Té (Hoang), 1912, Annam, 2e cl., 10e R.M.I.C. 180.
Teillot (Lucien), 3-6-17, Neuilly, 2e cl., 167e R.I.F. St. XII A.
Teillier (Léon), 6-8-1900, Quantilly, 2e cl., 66e R.A.C. St. II A.
Teissédre (Ernest), 4-1-11, Rageade, 1re cl., 105e R.I. St. XII A.
Tekiche (Hocine), 1916, Hammam (Alg.), 2e cl., 9e R.T.A. 180.
Telechea (François), 24-11-17, Sarre, 2e cl., 14e R.I. St. XII A.
Tellene (Jean), 21-12-14, Monteux, serg., 27e B.C.A. St. II A.
Tellier (Achille), 11-8-16, St-Vaast-lès-Mellee, 2e cl., 162e R.I.F. St. XII A.
Tellier (Georges), 3-3-19, Le Crotoy, 2e cl., 10e Cuir. St. II A.
Telliez (Oscar), 12-4-03, Rumilly, 2e cl., 1re S.S. St. VI H.
Temim (Roger), 5-9-14, Boufarik (Alg.), 2e cl., 3e Z. 180.
Temperman (Jean), 8-8-14, Armentières, 1re cl., 8e G.R.C.A. St. XII A.
Tempo (Léon), 4-12-12, Grenoble, 2e cl., 99e R.I. St. II A.
Té (Nguyen), 1912, Van Hoa (Annam), cap., 10e R.M.I.C. 180.
Tenni ben Ali, 1914, Ouled Cheikh (Alg.), 2e cl., 22e R.T.A. 180.
Té (Phan), 1912, Thuia Thien (Annam), 2e cl., 10e R.M.I.C. 180.
Ternacle (Gabriel), 2-5-12, Chestres, 2e cl., 44e G.R. St. XII A.
Terracher (Julien), 14-4-16, Mouzon, cap., 20e R.A.N.A. St. XII A.
Terrachon (Georges), 2-5-16, Suresnes, 2e cl., 167e R.I.F. St. XII A.
Terrasse (Ferdinand), 16-4-13, Roanne, 2e cl., 98e R.I. St. XII A.
Terrasse (Joseph), 3-5-11, Plaigne, 2e cl., 115e R.A. St. X B.
Terrassoux (Antoine), 10-4-14, Eyburie, 2e cl., 14e G.R.D.I. St. XII A.
Terraz (Ulysse), 5-1-14, Notre-Dame-du-Pré, 2e cl., 149e R.I.F. St. XII A.
Terrié (Gérard), 4-5-05, St-Maurin, 2e cl., 417e R.P. St. VI H.
Terroir (Alex), 7-1-13, Boulogne, 2e cl., 74e R.I. St. XI B.
Tesnier (Jacques), 4-1-19, Beaugency, cap., 404e R.A.D. St. X B.
Tesseydre (Henri), 27-12-14, Vic-s.-Cère, 1re cl., 151e R.A.F. St. XII A.
Tessgânine (Saïd), 21-3-14, Mizrana (Alg.), 2e cl., 17e R.T.A. 180.
Tessier (André), 1-1-12, Paris, cap., 23e R.I.C. St. II A.
Tessier (Henri), 21-10-14, St-Martin, serg., 5e R.I. St. XI B.
Tessier (Jean), 18-9-12, Brigné, 2e cl., 76e R.I. St. II A.
Tessier (Roger), 23-3-13, Rennes, serg., 41e R.I. Of. III A.
Testart (Albert), 26-4-91, Denain, capit., 422e R.P. Of. II B.
Testi (Eugène), 18-11-04, Carqueiranne, 2e cl., 12e R.T.S. St. XII A.
Testud (Maurice), 1-9-04, Mercœur, 2e cl., 34e R.I. St. X B.
Tétard (Albert), 10-6-03, Tournehem, 2e cl., 402e D.C.A. St. X B.
Tétart (Robert), 17-10-09, La Neuville-lès-Dorengt, 2e cl., 189e R. I. F. St. XII A.
Tetouche (Mohamed), 12-5-16, Bordj Beni Hundel (Alg.), 1re cl., 13e R. T.A. 180.
Tety (André), 4-1-11, Paris, 2e cl., 237e R.I. St. XI B.
Texereau (René), 28-4-04, Raix, 2e cl., 52e R.A. St. XII A.
Texier (Fernand), 7-10-18, Warlus, cap., 23e R.I.C. St. XII A.
Texier (Gustave), 17-10-12, Fénioux, 2e cl., 30e B.C.C. St. XII A.
Texier (Paul), 10-12-12, Noyal-s.-Seiche, 2e cl., 50e R.A.D. St. VI H.
Teyssier (Pierre), 24-6-14, St-Etienne, 2e cl., 80e R.I. St. XII A.
Teyssonneyre (Henri), 18-9-10, Polignac, 2e cl., 185e R.A.L. St. XII A.
Thami ben Abdeslam, 1910, Chaouia (Mar.), 2e cl., 2e R.T.M. 180.
Thân Dang Sôt, 5-1-12, Nam-Duong-Tourane (Annam), 2e cl., Trav. A. 180

FIGURE 2.1 The announcement of Henri's captivity in the official prisoner lists published in France.

Source: Bibliothèque Nationale de France http://gallica.bnf.fr/ark:/12148/cb34458709m/date1941.liste (reproduced with permission).

of his unit (1 R.P.), and also a next of kin (Rosa Tajfel, Leszno 33, apartment 10, Varsovie (Warsaw), Pologne (Poland)).

Note, this matriculation card was not his official PoW identification document. For this, he would have been photographed (holding a card with his camp and prisoner number on it in front of him – in his case, XIID, 14988). This photograph was

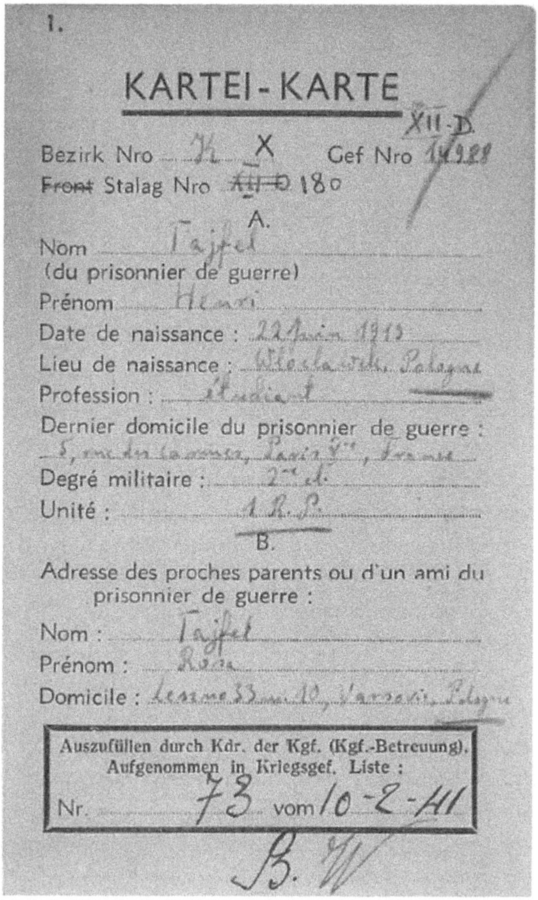

1.

KARTEI-KARTE

XII-D.

Bezirk Nro X Gef Nro

~~Front~~ Stalag Nro 180

A.

Nom Tajfel

(du prisonnier de guerre)

Prénom Henri

Date de naissance :

Lieu de naissance :

Profession :

Dernier domicile du prisonnier de guerre :

Degré militaire :

Unité :

B.

Adresse des proches parents ou d'un ami du prisonnier de guerre :

Nom : Tajfel

Prénom :

Domicile :

Auszufüllen durch Kdr. der Kgf. (Kgf.-Betreuung). Aufgenommen in Kriegsgef. Liste :
Nr. 73 vom 10-2-41

FIGURE 2.2 Henri's 'matriculation card' at Stalag XIID.

Source: Copy courtesy of Le Service historique de la Défense, DFA Caen, AC 22 P 3675 (reproduced with permission).

then transferred to another card which recorded further details, including his religion and a fingerprint. Finally, he would have been given a metal identity tag with his prisoner number engraved on it. For the remainder of his captivity, he would have been obliged to keep that metal tag about his person at all times. Thenceforth, in all the meticulous records maintained by his German captors over the next four years, his prisoner number would have remained a constant.

Henri, or prisoner 14988 as he now was, did not stay long at Stalag XIID. In May 1941 he was moved south to Austria, to Stalag XVIIIA, another large camp situated near Wolfsberg which is about 80 km south-west of Graz. Like many stalags, XVIIIA was divided into sections by nationality, in this case French, English and Russian. Despite the separation by nationality, some international fraternisation seems to have been possible. In my possession is a small photograph of Bill Briggs, a soldier from Glasgow in the Royal Signals Corps. On the reverse, he wrote the following note:

> Wolfsberg, Henri, may we never see the inside of a stalag again.
> Good luck,
> Bill Briggs

Two months later, Henri was on the move again. In July 1941 he was transferred to Stalag XVIIIC, another camp in Austria some 240 km away, where he was to spend the rest of the war. Stalag XVIIIC (or #317) was in a small town called St Johann in Pongau (although it is usually referred to as being in Markt Pongau), about 70 km south of Salzburg. The camp was located right beside the river Salzbach in a valley in the Austrian Alps. It was divided into two parts, North and South. Because he was an allied soldier, Henri would have been in the southern camp because the northern camp was reserved for Russian prisoners.[41] Not for the first time, his group membership, French/Polish not Russian, most probably saved Henri's life. The conditions in the southern camp, whilst pretty spartan (as we shall see), were nothing compared to what the Russian prisoners had to endure. Theirs can only be described as a death camp. Already starving and ill after long journey from the Eastern front, 30–40% of first group of Russian prisoners did not survive their first night in XVIIIC.[42] Thereafter, they received only starvation rations and were forced to undertake the hardest of labour, resulting in about 40 deaths per day. The memorial graveyard in the town cemetery grimly records the result of such maltreatment: of the 3782 PoWs buried there, 3709 are Russian (of a total of between 6000 and 7000 prisoners); just 15 are French (of around 8500 prisoners).[43] Here is how Erich Fried, an Austrian poet, depicted the camps in 1986:

Question Song

St Johann, St Johann in Pongau,
what path was that
you chose at a time
at which one will not speak?
What oath was
Which you then took?
You let grass cover it,
For who goes still to the graves?
To the right of the path
Prison camps were:
Englishman, Scots, Canadians –
Of them died only a few.
But to the left of the path
There they almost all still lie:
Yugoslavs, Russians, Ukrainians –

Nigh on 4000 dead.
Different the mortality
To the right and to the left of the path;
The ones that fed as it is right,
the others allowed to starve.
The dying finished off with spades.
St Johann, St Johann!
Your right hand did not know
What your left was about
Even today it still wants not to know,
St Johann in Pongau!
You have left grass grow
Over the grave-strewn path[44]

That such an arbitrary categorical detail as one's nationality could have such life or death consequences was a realisation that was to remain with Henri thereafter, an ever present undercurrent in his later thinking and research.

This camp was rather smaller than the camps Henri had been in hitherto. Its numbers varied considerably during his time there: in 1943 there were something over 8000 prisoners;[45] a year later these had apparently diminished to just over 5000, perhaps due to prisoners being repatriated back to France under the terms of the so-called 'Relève', a deal struck in 1942 between Pétain's Vichy Government and the Germans to allow some French PoWs to return home; but a year later the numbers were back up to 6000 as prisoners from camps further to the East were transferred ahead of the advancing Red Army.[46]

The camp seems to have been of a standard design (Figure 2.3): large wooden barracks with about 500 prisoners in each, divided into smaller dormitories, each containing about a dozen men sleeping in bunks or hammocks; sometimes there was heating; washing facilities seem to have been pretty primitive – according to one prisoner, there was just a single (manual) pump and two wells for the whole camp and there was often no running water during the day; latrines were 10 metre long trenches equipped with horizontal poles to sit on; there was little space between the barracks and the surrounding barbed wire, thus restricting the possibilities for exercise outside.[47]

The food was basic, and towards the end (in 1945), became more or less starvation rations – a bowl of thin soup, 250 grams of bread, three or four potatoes and a few grams of margarine and jam. As a result, most prisoners became quite thin and malnourished, some falling ill. Indeed, in an (undated) photograph of Henri and some of his fellow prisoners in Stalag XVIIIC, he is noticeably thin in the face[48] (Figure 2.4).

It is difficult to be certain about what privations Henri endured as a prisoner because the conditions just described only applied to those actually living in the camp. However, the vast majority (95%) of French PoWs were put to work *out-side* the camp in *kommandos*, often living in quarters attached to factories, mines or farms.[49] In fact, as the war progressed and the German army became embroiled in

FIGURE 2.3 Photograph of the barracks at Stalag XVIIIC.

Source: Mooslechner, M. (2014) Prisoner-of-war-camp STALAG XVIIIC, Markt Pongau. www.youblisher.com/p/1021823-PRISONER-OF-WAR-CAMP-STALAG-XVIII-C-Markt-Pongau/ (reproduced with permission of Michael Mooslechner).

fighting on several fronts simultaneously, the demand for military conscripts grew and the German economy became increasingly reliant on the million and a half French '*gästarbeiten*' held in stalags the length and breadth of the Reich.

There was great diversity in the kind of work to which *kommandos* could be put. Most (58%) were assigned to farms, but many worked in mines and heavy industries (28%), some in construction (4%), and transport, energy or communication (3%).[50] A colleague of Henri recalls him saying that he had mostly worked on farms during his period of captivity.[51]

Conditions in these work-places varied enormously. In many, the prisoners worked, ate, and slept alongside German workers. This was most typical of farm work where, occasionally, prisoners enjoyed reasonable food and had adequate shelter. However, even farm work was far from being a bucolic paradise. Here is how one prisoner from XVIIIC described his farm *kommando*:

> The surroundings are revoltingly filthy; guided by the fetid smell, the prisoners found decomposing entrails thrown near the place where the men washed themselves, not far from the kitchen, and on which a swarm of flies was feasting [...]. There was only one tap and five basins for 61 men. In addition, there was no light; one can imagine the chaos in the morning when all these men jostled each other in an attempt to reach the only tap. The latrines are primitive but clean. The men complain a lot about the food; no vegetables, except potatoes; no margarine; meat in minute quantities and of poor quality; finally, there were maggots in the cornmeal.[52]

FIGURE 2.4 Henri and some of his fellow prisoners at Stalag XVIIIC.

Source: Photograph courtesy of Anne Tajfel. Henri is 2nd from left, next to the man with the white shirt.

Because work on the *kommandos* took prisoners outside of the camp into Austrian farms and factories, it naturally brought them into contact with civilians, their fellow workers, and also with owners of the farms (usually women who were running things in the absence of their menfolk). Not infrequently, friendships – and occasionally romantic liaisons – grew out of these interactions. The common work predicament of civilian workers and French PoWs sometimes led to new alliances and collective solidarity. Sometimes, smaller *kommando* detachments to farms would even eat with the family around the kitchen table.[53]

However, such fraternisation between civilians and prisoners was strictly forbidden by the German authorities, on pain of imprisonment or death. In one stalag, each prisoner had to sign a document acknowledging the penalties for consorting with a German woman: talking with her, a fine of 10 marks; a kiss, one month in prison; sleeping with her, possible death sentence.[54] Nevertheless, despite the threat of such draconian sanctions, prisoners and civilian women continued to talk to each other (and more). At Stalag XVIIIA, where Henri had spent two months before being transferred to his more permanent 'home' at XVIIIC, a camp tribunal recorded 131 instances of such illicit liaisons in one year.[55]

Presumably, every so often the *kommandos* would return to their stalag. There, to relieve the daily drudgery of their existence, the prisoners organised many sporting, cultural, and religious activities. At XVIIIC there were Directors of Sport, Theatre and the Orchestra.[56] The latter was hardly a full symphonic ensemble, consisting as it did of two violins, three accordions, and two mandolins! Nevertheless, they held concerts every Sunday, sometimes with repeat performances during the week.[57] Given Henri's love of classical music and his utter disdain for '*la via sportive*', I suspect that he found these musical events much more to his liking than camp football tournaments. To attend to the men's spiritual needs, there were Catholic and Protestant priests, though it is highly unlikely that there were any rabbis to give succor to the many Jews in their midst.[58]

There were other diversions. Many camps had their own libraries. Some organised educational courses and seminars. At Wolfsberg, for instance, there was a 'Université du Stalag XVIIIA' run by some of the intellectuals in the camp, issuing their own '*certficats d'études*'. One could take language courses (German, Spanish, and Italian were offered, but not English, which was forbidden), also psychology, mathematics, physics, economics, colonialism, the family, and agriculture.[59] We do not know if there were similar offerings at XVIIIC but, given the presence of music, theatre, and a camp newspaper, it does not seem unlikely. If so, it is easy to imagine Henri being an enthusiastic participant in such activities.

However, we can be sure that there was one kind of activity in which he would *not* have taken part. These were the infamous '*cercles Pétain*', political groups set up in every camp and many *kommandos* from mid-1941 onwards to discuss and promulgate the policies being implemented by Marshal Pétain and his Vichy Government back home in France.[60] These were not just talking shops. Just as the Vichy Government was organising the capture and deportation of Jews from France, so too did some of these Pétain circles actively collaborate with their German captors. In one camp, a particularly enthusiastic French member of the Pétain circle in a camp successfully proposed that all Jewish PoWs should wear a yellow star. Ironically, it was the *German* camp commandant who rescinded this order on his return from leave a few days later.[61]

These Pétain circles declined in popularity as the war progressed and the prospect of a German defeat became more probable. At XVIIIC, in October 1942, the Pétain circle was said to '*marche très bien*'; less than a year later, in August 1943, it had '*très peu d'adhérents*'.[62] The demise of the ultra-nationalistic Pétain circles was not accompanied by any decline in patriotic feelings amongst the prisoners, however, quite the reverse. In a collective response that Henri would later write about at length, the constant repetition of being categorised together as '*prisonniers de guerre*', the years of shared privation behind barbed wire (a paradigmatic example of 'common fate'[63]), the ever-present German guards rendering hyper-salient the French-German group division, all conspired to inflate the prisoners' identification with France to bursting point. This patriotic fervour is movingly caught by one prisoner at XVIIIC, a Marcel Vuillamy, who saw a train full of young French men passing the camp one day in April 1943 (the railway line ran close to the barbed wire perimeter of the camp):

> I was in this camp where I dragged out my miserable existence, devoured by vermin and malnourished. Then one day, at the edge of the camp where there was a railway, as I was standing against the barbed wire which ran the length of this line, I saw a train arrive, packed with young Frenchmen, recruits for the STO (Service du Travail Obligitoire – see below). Seeing our khaki uniforms, they broke into a vibrant 'Marseillaise'. Imagine a thousand or fifteen hundred voices singing our national anthem. Deeply moved, a lump in the throat, eyes filling with tears, my comrades and I tried to sing in chorus with them. But we were so overcome at the recognition they gave us that no sound could escape us, and we were weeping like children as we saw the train fade into the distance.[64]

I like to imagine that Henri was there beside Marcel, listening to their fellow citizens bellowing out the *Marseillaise* from that train and being similarly overwhelmed by his feelings for his recently adopted homeland.

There is one other series of events that affected life and morale in many of the stalags containing French prisoners. These were labour exchange schemes negotiated by Pierre Laval, a senior Vichy minister, with the German Government in 1942 and 1943. The German Government was desperate for new manpower to keep the wheels of its industry turning as more and more of its citizens were deployed to the many battlefronts of the Reich. Naturally, Hitler turned his eyes to the occupied countries, of which France was the largest. The deal the Germans struck with the Vichy Government was that in return for hundreds of thousands 'volunteer'.[65] French workers coming to Germany – 250,000 in 1942 in the *Relève*, and a further 250,000 in 1943 in the *Transformation* – smaller numbers of PoWs would be released.[66] Some of these were repatriated back to France – for example, 90,000 prisoners returned home in the *Relève*; however, many more were 'released' from the stalags to work alongside Germans and the newly arrived workers from France under the terms of the *Transformation*. It is estimated that, in 1944, over 230,000 prisoners were released from stalags in this way.[67]

In Stalag XVIIIC, where Henri was held, some 2500 prisoners were '*transformés*' (out of a total of 5400). Those released under the *Transformation* scheme no longer had to wear their army uniform, they were paid the same as German and Austrian workers and, in principle, could move about freely in the towns in which they now lived (albeit displaying a distinctive badge that marked them out as French), exchanging their captivity under armed guard for surveillance by the civilian police and the Gestapo.

These repatriation or labour relocation schemes created some difficulties amongst the prisoner community. The choice of those to be repatriated lay mainly with the German commandants, consulting with the '*hommes de confiance*', those French soldiers who held some positions of authority in the camps. Naturally, only those prisoners who were not immediately 'useful' to the war effort (generally, the elderly and less skilled), or those who had been 'good' prisoners (often members of the Pétain circles) were let go. Although the prospect of rejoining their families must have been extremely attractive, the PoWs knew that they would be returning to a very different France from the one they had left so ignominiously in 1940 – a collaborationist anti-Semitic Vichy Government in the south, a German military occupied zone in the north. For those with the option of being relocated to German factories under the *Transformation*, the choice was not straightforward either. True, they would be escaping the strictures and privations of prison life but, in doing so, they would be abandoning their comrades, giving up what little protection the Geneva Convention offered them as soldiers, and assisting the German war effort to boot.

We do not know whether Henri was involved in any *Transformations* at Stalag XVIIIC, but I rather doubt that he was. I believe that his uncertain status as a French/Polish soldier, especially given his (probably hidden) Jewish identity, would have led him to resist being drafted into the German workforce as a civilian. In addition, he was far from being a 'model prisoner'. One informant related to me that Henri had told him that he had made 'several escape attempts' whilst a PoW, each time being recaptured.[68] The practical and moral dilemmas presented by the *Transformation* may have planted the seeds for some ideas that he would grapple with theoretically thirty years later, most notably in a paper inspired by Hirschman's book, *Exit, Voice and Loyalty*.[69] In this article and in some later writings,[70] Henri would discuss at length the problems confronting members of disadvantaged, stigmatised, or otherwise oppressed groups: should I abandon the group ('Exit'), or should I protest against the injustices of our existence ('Voice'), and what do both of these actions imply for my identification with the group ('Loyalty')?

Identities: shed, acquired, maintained and hidden

We have already seen that Henri had effected one significant change to his identity early in his time in France by changing his first name from Heniek to Henri. I want now to consider the several other identity transformations, both voluntary and enforced, that he underwent in the nine years between 1936 and 1945.

Let me start with his national identity as a Pole. We have precious little evidence to know what he thought of this in the first months in France. However, not one of my informants could remember him talking later in his life of his Polish origins or identity. Indeed, that particular identity seems subsequently to have become rather problematic for him. Two Polish colleagues who met him briefly at various times from the 1950s onwards confirmed to me that they always spoke together in English, not Polish.[71] In fact, one of them (Janusz Reykowski) went further. He explained how, at their first meeting (in 1959), he (Reykowski) wasn't immediately aware of Henri's Polish origins, perhaps due to his French sounding first name and the way he pronounced his second name (with the 'j' being apparent; this is unlike its Polish pronunciation). However, it soon became apparent that Henri was, indeed, from Poland and then, reported Reykowski, Henri explained why he was not speaking Polish. It was now, he said, 'impossible' for him to do so, not in a 'cognitive' sense (of lacking the linguistic capacity), but 'emotionally'. Subsequently, Henri explained that because of everything that had happened in Poland during the war, he was no longer able to use the language of his birth; it was simply too painful to do so. Another informant, Peter Robinson, later a colleague of Henri, related that Henri had once told him: 'I would never be ashamed of being a Jew but I am ashamed of being a Pole.'[72]

But the fact that being Polish had negative connotations for him later does not mean that he actively hid his Polishness before or during the war, as some have claimed.[73] As is clear from the first PoW registration document that he filled in, he gives his country of birth as '*Pologne*', his military unit as 1st Regiment Polonaise, and a next of kin address also in Poland (Figure 2.2). Moreover, he always retained his obviously eastern European surname. So, if he attempted to hide any identity, it was certainly not his Polish one.

Enlisting in the army in November 1939 gave Henri at least one new identity, '*soldat 2e classe (No. 8669A)*', albeit a temporary one. Within months, he had acquired yet another, '*prisonnier 14988*'. But this was not before the Germans had attempted to strip him of his former military identity, and perhaps of some of his humanity too. Remember the dehumanising process of travelling in cattle trucks to the first stalag and then the registration process at XIID: being stripped naked, shaved all over, forced into showers and then kept waiting (still naked) until his clothes were returned to him.

What of his Jewishness? Although he came from a Jewish family in Włocławek, Henri was never observant.[74] When asked by a journalist late in his life whether he went into social psychology to get away from a very religious or fundamentalist upbringing, he replied:

> No, I had my only religious crisis at the age of four or five. I never had a 'proper' religious crisis, which I suppose is very bad. I've always been happy to be an agnostic.[75]

Yet, it would have been surprising if his Jewish identity (in a cultural sense) had not become more salient to him in those first two turbulent years in France before war broke out. As we saw, anti-Semitism was widespread in Paris, especially as the 1930s drew to a close. With his Polish surname and accent – something he never lost, according to some native French speakers who knew him after the war – he would have been easily identifiable as a foreigner, if not a Jew, to his fellow students. And, of course, the growing numbers of Austrian and German Jews in Paris, fleeing Nazi persecution, would have been a visible reminder that members of his group were under threat elsewhere in Europe.

There is no doubt that his Jewish identity remained absolutely central to him throughout his life. Although he rarely wrote about it,[76] nearly every person I interviewed who knew him well insisted that his Jewish background was a mainspring in his professional and personal life. How much of his Jewish identity did Henri choose to reveal during the war, and especially to his German captors? This has been a matter much discussed by obituary writers and other commentators.

One view is that he did not attempt to hide his Jewish identity but, instead, chose to pass himself off as a *French* rather than a Polish Jew. Here, for example, is John Bamborough, in his memorial address at Linacre College:

> During the whole of that period of five years (captivity) there was constant danger that his captors would discover that he was Polish and not French; it says much for his resourcefulness, and not a little for the loyalty of his fellow captives, that this fact never emerged.

An anonymous obituary writer in an academic journal made a similar point.[77]

The revelation of his Jewishness (or not) is only implicit here. In another obituary, Hilde Himmelweit, a colleague who had known him well, is much more definite:

> For five years, until the end of the war he was in various German prisoner-of-war camps, always at risk for had the false identity, that of a French Jew which he had created for himself, been uncovered, as a Polish Jew he would have been shot.[78]

Similar views can be found elsewhere[79] and in the current Wikipedia entry for Tajfel:

> He faced a dilemma: whether or not to admit to the Germans that he was a Polish Jew. He claimed to be a French citizen but did not deny his Jewish identity. He reasoned that if he denied being Jewish and if the Germans found out later that he was Jewish, he would certainly have been killed. In the event, Tajfel survived the war in a series of prisoner-of-war camps.[80]

However, an earlier 2010 Wikipedia entry read a little differently:

> They never discovered that he was a Jew, so Tajfel survived the war in a series of prisoner-of-war camps.[81]

Checking the history of amendments to the Wikipedia entry, it is apparent that Michael Billig, one of Henri's first PhD students, was responsible for the amendment to that earlier version (on 19/11/2011).[82] He argued that Henri would have believed that his military uniform would protect him under the terms of the Geneva Convention which the Germans would have respected because of the many German prisoners held by the allies.[83]

There is some consensus, then, from these sources that Henri was more or less transparent about his Jewish, but not his national, identity during the period of his captivity. There is just that one dissenting view in the original (2010) Wikipedia entry.

My own view is that that original Wikipedia entry is closer to the mark than all the others and should not have been amended. Before presenting the evidence which supports this, it will be useful to review what we know about how Jewish PoWs in the French army were treated in the stalags. According to Durand, there was considerable variation. In some camps, those known to be Jewish were segregated from the other PoWs and put into separate huts ('*Judenbaracke*'). In some, but by no means all, camps they were forced to wear a yellow star or some other distinguishing badge and were frequently treated much more harshly than other prisoners. Thus, there was undoubtedly discrimination against Jews in some stalags, but this was far from being the general rule. Durand also reports that some German authorities in the camps treated Jewish soldiers similarly to other prisoners (more or less) protected by their uniforms under the terms of the Geneva Convention (to which Germany was a signatory).[84]

What did these different conditions imply for whether Jewish soldiers would admit or conceal their religion? Remember that the standard PoW identity card had a space for religion and so some answer would have been required (e.g., '*catholique*', '*juif* (or '*israelite*'), or '*none*'). Durand suggests that the more clear-sighted prisoners sought to hide their origins from the German authorities.[85] Presumably, they had the reasonable suspicion that they might be singled out for harsher treatment (or worse) if their Jewishness was known. This act of concealment was not without its risks and often depended on the discretion of one's fellow comrades in arms to maintain the fiction.[86]

Such solidarity could not always be relied upon. Serge Bac, taken prisoner like everyone else in early summer of 1940, describes how he and his companions had buried their identity papers so as not to be discovered as Jews. However, in the event, they were denounced to the Germans by some of their fellow soldiers to avoid reprisals. Nevertheless, and consistent with Billig's hypothesis above, he adds:

> Even though he was Jewish, he was protected by his status as a prisoner-of-war (under the Geneva Convention), whereas the Spanish were sent to Mathausen and Buchenwald.[87]

And, it seems, some Jews did voluntarily profess their faith to the Germans.[88]

These, then, were the *general* conditions faced by Jews as they entered the stalags; what of Henri's *particular* situation? Of one thing we can be sure: he did not attempt to disguise his Polish origins. Recall his registration card at Stalag XIID (Figure 2.2). There he clearly identifies himself as Polish, by his place of birth (in Włocławek), the address of his next of kin (in Warsaw), and his regiment (1st Polish). This information would have been transferred to PoW identity card, along with his photograph and fingerprint (unfortunately, this identity card has so far resisted all attempts to be traced). The presence of Polish soldiers (as well as several other nationalities) in Stalag XIIC, not far from XIID where Henri was first registered, was a commonplace and, in general, Polish soldiers were treated much the same as their French comrades.[89]

As to whether he was as open about his Jewishness, as some have claimed, here the evidence is less concrete but still, I believe, reasonably compelling. As we saw earlier, several people have suggested that Henri decided not to deny his Jewishness but, instead, chose to pass himself off as a French and not a Polish Jew. Yet we now know that he did not, in fact, hide his Polish nationality. A further argument offered in support of the surmise that he was open about his Jewish identity is that he believed that the consequences of any subsequent discovery of his Jewishness would have been more severe than if he declared it from the outset. Now it is true that the risk of discovery was ever-present, not least in that degrading registration process on arrival at Stalag XIID. At any point in that procedure, his (presumably) circumcised penis would have been in plain view and any of his German captors might have drawn the obvious inference.

Whilst I accept that this experience must have caused him considerable anxiety, could he have anticipated that he would be subjected to such exposure whilst on that long forced march after his capture during which, as we learned earlier, he ate all his documents? In my interview with David Milner, I asked him about how Henri had described this episode to him:

> This is according to him, and it may be embroidered, but what he told me was: he was captured soon after he enlisted in France. On a long route march through Germany he ate his passport, he ate his papers while all his family, friends, colleagues etc. back in Poland were being decimated… [and then he quotes Henri directly]: 'I've always felt guilty about this because at the same time as I was chewing my passport and pretending to be a Goy, they were getting murdered and it has driven me…'.[90]

Another interviewee, Marilynn Brewer, who spent three months visiting Henri in Bristol in 1980, partly confirms this account. I asked her if he ever spoke to her about his Jewishness:

> He felt that he had denied his identity. Was it his Polish identity or his Jewish identity that he felt he had disowned or hidden for self-preservation reasons that he did on occasion? I think what surprised or struck him was realizing that this was painful; that he felt so bad about it…
> [RB: when did he hide his identity?]
> It had something to do with an incident in France where he was asked about what his origins were, or where he came from, or…. I don't remember the details.
> [RB: and did he talk about this?]
> It was probably the only time we talked about some of the sources of his ideas and things, and the point he was trying to make was how painful it was to have been put in a situation to (have to) deny a group identity.[91]

Another informant, who had spent a sabbatical at Bristol the 1970s, spontaneously provided further confirmation that Henri had told him that he had 'concealed the fact that he was Jewish' during the war[92] as did his Oxford friend, Rom Harré.[93]

Here, then, are four independent accounts of conversations with Henri where he makes reference to hiding an aspect of his identity during the war. In three cases, he is explicit that he pretended not to be Jewish; in the other, it is more ambiguous but it seems to me most probable that it was his Jewishness and not his Polishness that he was referring to. As far as we know, the former was much more central to him than his country of origin.

One other detail supports the idea that he passed his period in captivity pretending not to be Jewish. On his registration card he nominates a 'Rosa Tajfel' as his next of kin (Figure 2.2). This is very curious. In the extensive genealogical research into his family in Poland that we have done, the name Rosa has come to light only once.[94] It is not an obvious Jewish name, as are all the names of his parents, uncles and aunts (see family tree in Chapter 1). So, who was this mysterious woman that he declared to the German authorities? One intriguing hypothesis has been put to me by Francine Tajfel, the daughter-in-law of Henri's American cousin, Henry Tajfel.[95] Perhaps 'Rosa' was code for 'Ruchla', his mother. As we shall discover in the next chapter, Henri's parents, Icek and Ruchla, and his brother Milek, moved from Włocławek to Warsaw some time after the Germans invaded Poland in 1939. Perhaps Henri may have known this and, while wishing his parents to know if anything were to happen to him, and yet not wishing to identify either them or himself as Jewish, chose a pseudonym for his mother.

Of course, at a distance of nearly eighty years, it is impossible to be certain of anything. However, in piecing together the above fragments of evidence at our disposal, I believe that the most probable conclusion is that Henri did, indeed, pass himself as a Polish (or French) non-Jew for at least some of his time in captivity. Whilst the full horrors of the Holocaust may not have been apparent to him in the early 1940s, he would have seen and heard more than enough on the streets of Paris, and perhaps from his family back in Poland as well, to realise that one's membership of the Jewish community had dreadful repercussions once it came to the notice of the Germans or, indeed, of the increasingly fascist Vichy regime in France. Nevertheless, as we saw in his remarks reported by Milner and Brewer, this subterfuge was to leave him with psychological scars that he bore for the rest of his life. But, at the same time, it provided him with a compulsion to understand how events like the Holocaust could have happened, and to apprehend the multifarious effects on people's identities and behaviours of belonging to a stigmatised group.

Notes

1 Marrus and Paxton (1981).
2 Lee (2014).
3 Weinberg (1977).
4 Caron (1999).
5 Marrus and Paxton (1981).
6 Roth (1926, 2001), pp. 1–2.

7 Marrus and Paxton (1981); Weinberg (1977).
8 Marrus and Paxton (1981), p. 40.
9 Caron (1999); Marrus and Paxton (1981).
10 Weinberg (1977).
11 Weinberg (1977).
12 This address in the Loire valley is quite mysterious. I have found no other information linking him to this area.
13 'Métèque' is an offensive term for foreigner, roughly equivalent to 'wog' or 'Paki' in English (Campbell, 2006). I am also grateful to Jean-Claude Croizet for assistance with this translation.
14 Quoted in Caron (1999), p. 275.
15 Tajfel (1975).
16 Bruner (1983).
17 Weinberg (1977), p. 48.
18 To use one of the four acculturation labels proposed by the cross-cultural psychologist Berry (1997).
19 Zuccotti (1993).
20 Weinberg (1977), pp. 189–96.
21 Caron (1999); Hyman (1998); Zuccotti (1993).
22 Cohen (1977), p. 297.
23 Zuccotti (1993).
24 Marrus and Paxton (1981); Zuccotti (1993).
25 Koestler (1941).
26 Zuccotti (1993).
27 Leroy (2012).
28 And *not* in 1946 as his Wikipedia entry currently claims (2017). Personal communication, Olivier Chosalland, Archives Nationales Pierrefitte, November 2016.
29 Judt (2008).
30 Durand (1980).
31 Interview with J. and A. Wilkes, February 2015.
32 Durand (1980, 1987).
33 Durand (1980), p. 55; translation by Sarah Carter.
34 Milner (2015), p. 99.
35 Durand (1980), p. 64; translation by Sarah Carter.
36 Personal communication from Alain Alexandra, Service Historique de la Défense, Centre Historique des Archives, Caen, France; 21 December 2016.
37 Durand (1980), p. 62.
38 Durand (1980), p. 96.
39 Gerassi (1989).
40 Durand (1980), pp. 65–6; Vinen (2006).
41 Mooslechner (2014).
42 Mooslechner (2014).
43 Durand (1987); Mooslechner (2014).
44 Reprinted from Mooslechner (2014), p. 12.
45 Durand (1980, p. 69).
46 Militaria1940 (2016).
47 Durand (1980), p. 155; Mooslechner (2015), pp. 6–8.
48 Although, on his medical discharge note (1945), it records his weight as 72 kg which, given his height of 1.70 m, would have given him a perfectly 'normal' BMI of 24.9.

Perhaps, between the time the photograph was taken and his release, he had had access to better rations.

49 Durand (1980), p. 96.
50 Durand (1980), p. 115.
51 Harré interview, October 2017.
52 Durand (1980), p. 105; translation by Sarah Carter.
53 Durand (1980), p. 405.
54 Durand (1980), p. 417; Vinen (2006).
55 Durand (1980), p. 417.
56 Militaria1940 (2016).
57 Durand (1987), pp. 184–5.
58 Durand (1987), p. 173.
59 Durand (1980), p. 293.
60 Durand (1980), ch. 16; Mooslechner (2014).
61 Durand (1980), p. 355.
62 Durand (1980), p. 362.
63 Lewin (1948).
64 Durand (1980), p. 361; translation by Sarah Carter.
65 'Volunteer' is something of a misnomer here. In reality, they were far from being volunteers. Under successive laws passed by the Vichy Government, especially the Service du Travail Obligatoire (STO), all French men between 21 and 23 years were liable to be dispatched to work in German factories.
66 Durand (1980, pp. 320–8).
67 Durand (1980).
68 Strickland interview, March 2017.
69 Tajfel (1975).
70 E.g., Tajfel (1978) and Tajfel and Turner (1979).
71 Grzelak, 2016, personal communication; Reykowski interview, April 2017.
72 Robinson interview, November 2016.
73 Bamborough, Oration at Henri's memorial service (1982); *British Journal of Social Psychology* (1982); Himmelweit (1982); Turner (1996).
74 Letter from A. Tajfel to Gustav Jahoda, undated.
75 Cohen (1977), p. 298.
76 For an exception, see Tajfel (1981b), ch. 1.
77 *British Journal of Social Psychology*, 1982, *21*, p. 185.
78 Himmelweit (1982), p. 288.
79 Stroebe (1982); Turner (1996).
80 *Wikipedia*, 31/1/2017.
81 *Wikipedia*, 13/10/2010.
82 He had made the change at the request of Anne Tajfel, Henri's widow, who had been upset by the original entry (Billig interview, October 2016).
83 Billig interview, October 2016.
84 Durand (1980), p. 354.
85 Durand (1980), p. 205.
86 Leroy (2012).
87 www.combattantrolontairejuif.org/57.html; translation by Sarah Carter.
88 Leroy (2012).
89 Vinen (2006), p. 186.
90 Milner interview, December 2016.

91 Brewer interview, November 2016.
92 Strickland interview, March 2017.
93 Harré interview, October 2017.
94 This was in an interview with Madelaine Hecht (25/10/16). Madelaine's father, a Solomon Tajfel, was born in Grabów in 1894 and emigrated in 1925. He had a daughter, born in Denmark in 1926, called *Rosa*. From there, they moved to Paris where Madelaine was born (in 1931). By a miracle, Madelaine and her father escaped from the round-ups in 1942, but her mother and her sister (Rosa) did not. They were deported to Auschwitz, where they perished. She (Madelaine) claims never to have heard of Henri. Given the age of Rosa (14 in 1940), and the fact that she was living in Paris, it is impossible that this is the 'Rosa' that Henri nominated as his next of kin on his prison registration document.
95 Personal communication, January 2017.

3

FRANCE, BELGIUM, AND GERMANY

1945–1951

Liberation and return to France: paradise regained?

The first few months of 1945 saw the last act of the Second World War in Europe. As the Allied armies from the west and the Red Army from the east converged on Berlin, one by one the stalags and oflags were liberated, along with the concentration and death camps in Germany and Poland. Stalag XVIIIC was in southern Austria, somewhat out of the way of the advancing armies and, as a result, was one of the last camps to be liberated. Henri's PoW registration card indicates that he was not actually repatriated until 7 May 1945, just one day before the Germans had unconditionally surrendered and the war in Europe was over.

After their initial elation on seeing Russian, American or British tanks at the gates of the camps, prisoners experienced a frustrating limbo period whilst they awaited repatriation. The rapidity with which the advancing armies swept through Germany and Austria created an enormous logistical challenge for the victorious powers. Over two million displaced persons (DPs) were already on the move in May 1945, a number that subsequently swelled to over eleven million.[1] These were liberated prisoners of war (PoWs) like Henri, forced labourers from Poland, Holland and France and, of course, hundreds of thousands of German civilians fleeing from the advancing Russian army or made homeless by the carpet bombing of German cities. All these people had to be fed and sheltered and, where possible, repatriated to their homelands. Repatriation was to prove a particular headache, for many of these displaced persons literally had no home to go to. For the few survivors of Dachau, Buchenwald, and Bergen Belsen, nearly all of their relatives had been murdered and their homes stolen or destroyed. Indeed, so severe were the difficulties posed by this enormous number of refugees that they were still being tackled five years after the end of the war.

Henri's return to France seems to have been relatively straightforward. Probably, like most of the PoWs from Austria, he made his way back to France via Italy. He arrived in Paris, as he was later to note,[2] at the Gare d'Orsay, one of the dozens of reception centres in France that had been hurriedly established to deal with the two million returning French soldiers and forced labourers (STOs).[3] These reception centres struggled to cope with the enormous human traffic that came through their doors; some were processing as many as 55,000 people a day.[4] Typically, the soldiers were divided into groups according to the area of France they came from. Then, in a process strangely reminiscent of their registration in those first German triage stalags five years before, each person was fingerprinted, photographed, screened by the Securité Nationale, and given a medical examination, including an X-ray, urine analysis, immunisation injections, and a dental check up. In Henri's case, his discharge medical certificate declares his general health to be '*bon*', the only problem noted being '*mauvaise dentition*' (bad teeth).[5]

All being well, each soldier (or forced labourer (STO)) was offered a haircut, a new set of clothes, 1000 Francs, a second-class rail ticket home and an address for a local 'Maison du prisonnier', group hostels where returnees could stay (free) for a few days before returning home.[6]

For a great many of these returnees – PoWs and STOs alike – the return to their homeland proved something of a disappointment, a far cry from what they might have imagined in the first heady days after liberation.[7] France was greatly changed from how it had been five years before. There were serious food shortages and prices were astronomically high. Their 1000 francs would not have lasted them long. Although Paris had mercifully escaped serious bomb damage, the physical evidence of the German occupation was still plain to see.[8] But an even more striking difference from the pre-war era was the social climate. Summary justice was meted out in the streets – those suspected of active collaboration or sexual cohabitation with the Germans were often shot, beaten up or publicly humiliated (women thought to have slept with Germans – so called '*collaborateurs horizontals*' – were often stripped, had their heads shaved and put on public display[9]).

But perhaps the biggest source of disillusionment for the returnees were the rather ambivalent attitudes of the French public towards them.[10] PoWs like Henri were not exactly viewed as returning war heroes. After all, the French army had ignominiously capitulated to the Germans in a matter of weeks in the '*debacle*' of May and June 1940, hardly something to celebrate, or so many French people thought. The STOs were also regarded with ambivalence in some quarters; hadn't they volunteered to assist the German war effort (a view which overlooked the fact the majority of STOs had actually been press-ganged into working in Germany)? The few Jewish deportees who managed to survive the concentration and death camps also met a somewhat equivocal reception.[11] In their case, public reaction seems to have been an uncomprehending horror at what they had experienced, coupled with a degree of shame at the complicity of the Vichy Government (and many ordinary French people) in their deportation in the first place. Moreover, most Jewish homes and possessions had been expropriated by members of the French public during the five long years of the war and now there were awkward questions of restitution and reparation to be answered.

In Memory

Of my beloved Mother **BAJLA**
(born **Warszawska**) **WLOCLAWSKA**
of my Brothers **SALLY & ABRAHAM**
and Sisters **HELENA & ANDZIA**
my **Nieces and Nephews** who deceased and perished during the
German occupation of Poland.

Ester-Edja Jacobson (Wloclawska)
Larchmont, N. Y.

In Memoriam

My Father **ABRAM TREMBSKI**
died in 1909
and Mother **HYNDA TREMBSKA**
perished in ghetto of Warsaw
My **BROTHERS** and **SISTERS**
who perished in the ghettos of
Warsaw & Lodz and in

In Loving Memory of

My Father **ICEK HENYNE**
and my Mother **RUCHLA**

and Brother **MILEK TAJFEL**
who perished in the ghetto of
Warsaw

Heniek Tayfel, Bristol, England

FIGURE 3.1 In Memoriam notice in Włocławek Yizkor Book, 1967.
Source: Biderman (1969), p. 245.

For Jews returning to France, whether ex-PoWs like Henri or survivors from the concentration and death camps, readjustment to 'normal life' was particularly problematic. Not only had many of them lost their homes, but most of them had to cope with the realisation that they had lost their entire families as well. Henri was no exception. In a poignant In Memoriam notice that he was to publish twenty years later in the Włocławek *Yizkor Book*, he recorded the tragic loss of his mother, father and brother in the Warsaw ghetto (Figure 3.1).

It is not known how Ruchla, Icek, and Milek died. It will be recalled from Chapter 2 that Henri listed a 'Rosa Tajfel' at Leszno 33 (apartment 10) in Warsaw as his next of kin, someone I believe to be a pseudonym of his mother Ruchla. An exhaustive search for the occupants of that apartment has revealed no traces of any Tajfels living there in 1940 or 1941. There was, however, a family of Kunins in that apartment and, as it happens, Jackub Kunin is listed in a Polish Trade Directory of the time as owning a leather business. Icek Tajfel, like his father and one of his brothers, was also in the leather business. It seems likely, then, that the Tajfels moved to Warsaw from Włocławek after the Germans invaded Poland, as many Jews from outlying towns did. They probably stayed as house guests of the Kunins, whom they may have known through business connections.

That part of Leszno Street was right in the heart of the Jewish ghetto that the Germans had created in 1940. Even when the Germans compressed the ghetto in 1942, the 'small ghetto' boundary was just outside number 33, just along from the cinema, Kino Femina next door, an important venue for various cultural events in the ghetto in those war years. The original building of Leszno, 33 is no more. Along with the rest of the Warsaw ghetto, it was destroyed by the Germans as they razed the whole area to the ground after the ghetto uprising in 1943.[12] The ground floor of the building which has been constructed on the site of the old number 33 is now a shop called 'Rosa Drogeria'. So 'Rosa' lives on at that address, a ghost of one of its former occupants.

How Henri's parents died is nowhere recorded. If they survived the daily random beatings or shootings on the streets of the ghetto, they most likely died of the cold, starvation or illness. Typhus was rife in the ghetto as the overcrowding became oppressive – an average of seven people per room, according to some estimates.[13] And if those conditions did not kill them, they will have perished in the 'blitzkrieg' of April 1943 which left scarcely a building standing (although, the Kino Femina next door somehow was unscathed; it is now a supermarket with the same name). Of the 400,000 Jews living in the ghetto in 1940, it is thought that less than 3% had survived by 1945.[14]

It was not just Henri's immediate family who perished in the Holocaust. From the family tree I presented in Chapter 1, in addition to his parents and his brother (and probably his grandparents), he lost two aunts and an uncle from Włocławek, at least nine members of the Grabów Tajfel family, and at least eight from the Dyszel side of the family (of whom only Ester and Alina survive). These are almost certainly underestimates. Henri once told one of my informants that over forty members of his family died in the Holocaust.[15]

An orphan amongst orphans

So it was in May 1945 that Henri, now orphaned at the age of 26, found himself on the streets of Paris, homeless, jobless, and stateless (he was not to obtain his French citizenship for another three years). A former colleague of his remembered Henri telling him how devastated he had been to return to France amidst all the victory celebrations:

> He'd lost all his family as far as he knew. He had no relatives left in the world and he was an isolate, and that was it.[16]

Henri was not quite 'down and out in Paris' as George Orwell[17] had been some years previously, but his current situation and future prospects were precarious nonetheless. He had barely more than the clothes he stood up in and still possessed no formal academic qualifications. He soon set about to remedy the latter by resuming his interrupted studies at the Sorbonne, but this time in Psychology not Chemistry. His CV records that he enrolled for a Certificat de Psychologie Generale, thanks to a grant awarded by the French Government in 1945 to returning prisoners of war.[18] He must have pursued this course part-time, or at least by 'distance learning', because he was soon to obtain a full-time job.

This was as an 'educateur' (teacher) in a Jewish orphanage, Villa Essor, a large house in Collonges-au-Mont d'Or near Lyon. This orphanage was one of several such institutions set up in France by *Oeuvre de Secours aux Enfants* (OSE), an NGO that originated in St Petersburg in 1912 with the aim of providing practical assistance and health care for Jews excluded from the Russian health system, and also for caring for children affected by the anti-Jewish pogroms of those times.[19] After the Russian Revolution, OSE was transferred to Paris in 1933. Here it quickly established itself as one of the primary organisations to provide support for the large number of Jewish refugees arriving in France from Germany and Austria. During the war, it played a leading role in hiding Jewish children, both in the northern Occupied Zone and in the Vichy area.[20] After the war, there was an even greater need for OSE's services. In addition to the thousands of 'hidden' children in France ('enfants cachés'), most of whose parents had been killed in the Holocaust, there were also over four hundred children who had somehow survived the camps and who needed looking after.[21] Most of these 'children of Buchenwald' were also orphans and, for the most part, were not of French origin but were Hungarian or Polish. As a result, they spoke little or no French when they arrived at the orphanages.[22]

'*Réparer, telle est la mission de l'OSE après la geurre*' ('to repair, this was the mission of OSE after the war'). This was how Katy Hazan, the official historian of OSE, encapsulated the goal of the organisation in those difficult post-war years as Europe struggled to come to terms with the horror of the Nazi war crimes and the enormity of the task of rebuilding people's lives in the aftermath of humanity's bloodiest ever conflict.[23] Not for nothing was 1945 known in Germany as '*Die Stunde Null*' (The Year Zero), the year when the whole world had to start all over again.[24] OSE's role in this reconstruction process was to provide shelter and succour to several thousand Jewish children in France whose young lives had been cruelly interrupted by the war. To this end, OSE opened twenty-five homes throughout France, and one in Switzerland. From the outset, these homes aimed to provide for far more than just the children's physical needs. Aware that many of the children had been traumatised by the separation from and loss of their parents, the 'directeurs' and 'educateurs' of OSE homes sought to create a family environment where they could repair the damage done. Above all, they looked to '*créer ou recréer une identité*' ('create or recreate an identity') for the children.[25]

Villa Essor (Collonges), where Henri found himself in the summer of 1945, was run by Hugo and Émilie Hanau, two German emigrés. His exact start date at Collonges is not certain. Curiously, a later letter of reference for him, written by Mr Job, an administrator at OSE, states that he started in January 1945. This would have been rather difficult since he was still a PoW in Austria then! Villa Essor was quite a large mixed-sex home, housing over forty children of ages varying from under ten to over twenty years, at least to judge from a contemporary photograph.[26]

This was the perfect place for Henri to begin his pedagogic career and the children certainly seem to have appreciated him. Here is how Ossie Goldstein and Maurice Borenstein, two of the boys at Villa Essor, remembered their time there:

> We would not want to finish without thanking those who have contributed so much to the formation of our large family. To you, Hugues and Milli

[the Hanaus], to whom we are grateful for everything you have done for us, despite our arguments, often so long. Forgive us for having behaved badly towards you sometimes, but you were always there for us as you wanted to be. And you Henri, how can we forget you? Were you not a living part of the Essor spirit? We won't say 'adieu', you will remain with us, 'our Henri…'. For us the big family is not dead and will never be: for us Collonges will be a beautiful memory.[27]

The boys' feelings for Henri were reciprocated by him. In October 1945, he wrote a long and affectionate letter to Pierre Vormus, a boy who had recently left Villa Essor to study in Avignon. The very fact that Vormus retained this letter for seventy years (he gave it to me in 2015), is testament itself to the enduring affection he felt for Henri throughout his life. I have reproduced it in full[28] (Figure 3.2) because it reveals Henri to have mastered almost perfect French at this point in his life, just eight years after his arrival from Poland, but also because his occasional use of very formal salutations, so out of place in such an informal letter to a teenager, conveys something of his sense of humour. Notice how he begins and ends the letter – 'I humbly and officially apologise'… 'please accept sir the assurance of my highest consideration'. Such phrases would not be out of place in a letter to one's lawyer or bank manager! The first paragraph is interesting because it reveals something of his work at the home – trying to find schools and apprenticeships for the boys in his care – and also that he has already commenced his studies in psychology at the Sorbonne. In the third paragraph that we can discern elements of his enthusiastic pedagogic style that would remain with him for the remainder of his career. In that long and eclectic reading list he recommends to Pierre, his thirst for knowledge is obvious, as is his passion to grapple with the problems of the world. Perhaps, too, we can detect his own nascent intellectual ambitions in the final sentence of that paragraph: 'Only the man who begins to want to understand at an early age becomes a great man.'

Henri obviously had some success with his new-found vocation because, in September 1946, he took charge of his own orphanage at Le Vésinet, a small town just 18 km to the west of Paris, nestling inside one of the many sinuous bends that the river Seine makes on its way out of the city. The house that OSE had acquired was a large three-storey villa at 14 Boulevard Carnot (now Boulevard du Maréchal Foch). The home was called Foyer Pauline Gaudefroy – or FOPOGO, as the boys called it – named after the famous French resistance fighter who had been shot in 1944. FOPOGO was quite different from Villa Essor: it was smaller and single-sex – just twenty-two boys – and these young people had been specially selected as having shown above average academic aptitude in their schooling. It seems that the idea for this new home came from Henri himself,[29] presumably with the idea that working with a smaller and more select group of boys would ultimately be more beneficial for their education and well-being. From being a mere '*educateur*' at Collonges, Henri was now '*directeur*', with sole responsibility not only for the boys' welfare but also for the day-to-day running of the home.

Œuvre de Secours aux Enfants

O S E

MAISON D'ENFANTS

"VILLA ESSOR

COLLONGES-AU-MONT-D'OR

(RHONE)

TÉL. 121 COLLONGES

Le　20 .Octobre 46

　　Mon cher Pierrot

　　Avant de commencer cette lettre je te présente mes excuses les
plus humbles et les plus officielles. Il est vrai que j'aurai dû
t'écrire depuis pas mal de temps déjà et que ton indignation dont m
m'a parlé Roger est tout à fait justifiée. Mais je te prie de m'a-
ccorder quelques circonstances atténuantes. Depuis que je suis de r
retour à Collonges je suis vraiment terriblement occupé. Tu sais
que c'est maintenant la période où il faut placer tous les garçons,
~~où il faut leur trouver ou un apprentissage ou une école et je passe~~
mon temps à courir Lyon dans tous les sens pour trouver des "boîtes"
convenables. A part ça j'ai beaucoup de travail personnel, tu sais
que j'aurai voulu me présenter à un examen à la Faculté des Lettres
au mois de Février ou peut-être même Janvier et le temps presse.Tu
n'es pas le seul,dans ces dernières semaines j'ai négligé tout mon
courrier. Il fallait vraiment une occasion spéciale pour que j'é-
crive à Roger pendant qu'il était chez toi.
　　J'espère que mes excuses étaient suffisamment plates pour apai-
ser ton juste courroux.Et pour me prouver que tu ne m'en veux plus
tu me répondras très vite et par une lettre qui sera plus longue que
toutes celles que tu as l'habitude de m'écrire.
　　J'espère que ta maman va déjà mieux. Je voudrais aussi que tu me
dises en détail en quoi consiste ton travail maintenant;si tu es content,si tu as des copains intéressants ou du prends goût à tes études,quelles sont tes intentions pour l'avenir le plus immédiat,
quelles sont actuellement tes lectures etc. Il m'a semblé lors de
la dernière conversation que nous avions à Paris que tu commences
à t'intéresser à des certains problèmes très graves et très diffici
les,mais que tu le fais avec beaucoup de bon sens. Et il m'a semblé
aussi te voir comprendre qu'avant d'aborder quoi que ce soit il
faut avoir une préparation sérieuse,qu'il faut comprendre avant de
juger.A ton âge le meilleur moyen de comprendre,c'est lire avec
discernement. Je te conseillerais,si tu as le temps,d'attaquer un
peu les romans de Duhamel,Kipling,Romain Rolland,Dickens,Wells,
Malraux,Alexis Tolstoï,Dreiser,Stefan Zweig,Maurois,Upton Sinclair,
Demaison,Joseph Conrad,Stevenson,Wasilewska,Bojer etc. Tu as
certainement remarqué que je te cite pêle-mêle les noms des écri-
vains français,anglais,russes,américains,allemands,scandinaves,
polonais...C'est parce que j'estime

FIGURE 3.2　Letter to Pierre Vormus in October 1945.

Source: Letter courtesy of Pierre Vormus (reproduced with his permission).

Of the twenty-two FOPOGO boys – actually, 'boys' is a misnomer since they
were really young men, aged between seventeen and twenty-one years[30]– I want to
mention nine in particular because they seem to have played especially important
roles in the life at the home and, perhaps because of that, they were particularly close
to Henri. Five of them also provided me with invaluable eye-witness testimony

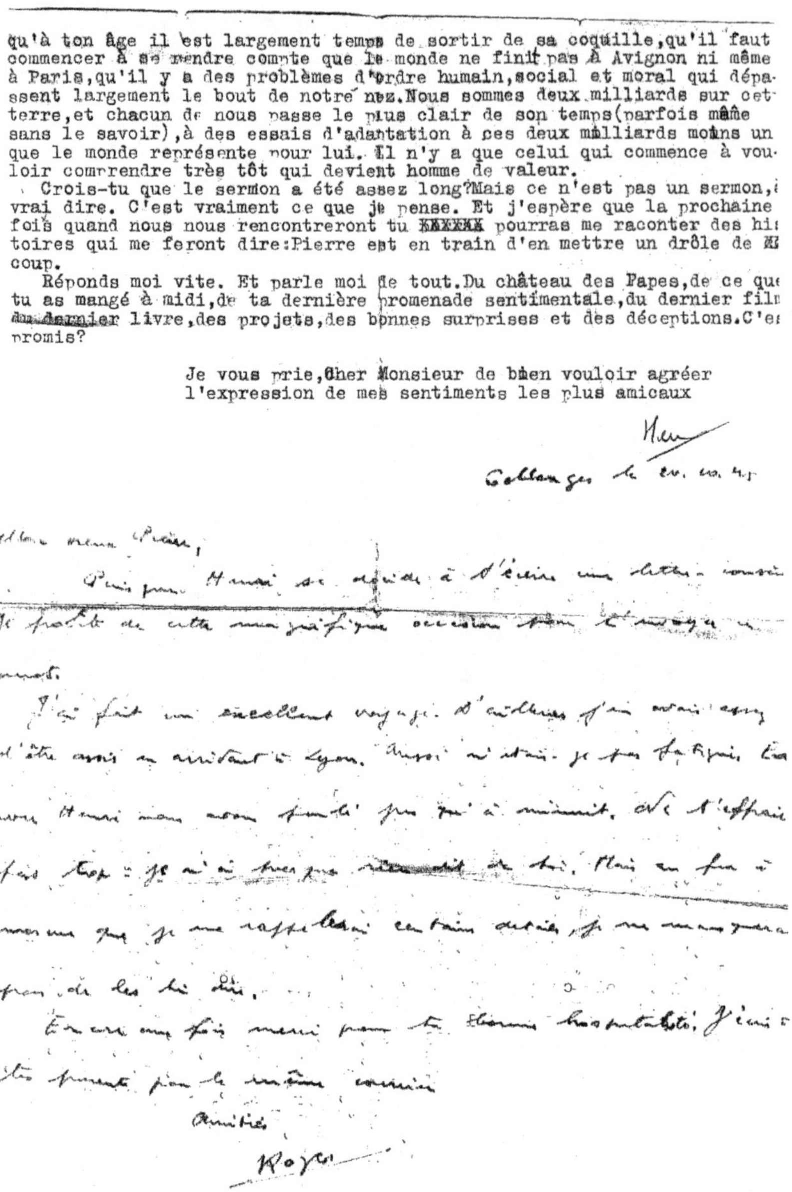

qu'à ton âge il est largement temps de sortir de sa coquille,qu'il faut
commencer à se rendre compte que le monde ne finit pas à Avignon ni même
à Paris,qu'il y a des problèmes d'ordre humain,social et moral qui dépa-
ssent largement le bout de notre nez.Nous sommes deux milliards sur cet-
terre,et chacun de nous passe le plus clair de son temps(parfois même
sans le savoir),à des essais d'adaptation à ces deux milliards moins un
que le monde représente pour lui. Il n'y a que celui qui commence à vou-
loir comprendre très tôt qui devient homme de valeur.

   Crois-tu que le sermon a été assez long?Mais ce n'est pas un sermon,à
vrai dire. C'est vraiment ce que je pense. Et j'espère que la prochaine
fois quand nous nous rencontrerons tu pourras me raconter des his-
toires qui me feront dire:Pierre est en train d'en mettre un drôle de
coup.

   Réponds moi vite. Et parle moi de tout.Du château des Papes,de ce que
tu as mangé à midi,de ta dernière promenade sentimentale,du dernier film
du dernier livre,des projets,des bonnes surprises et des déceptions.C'es
promis?

                Je vous prie,Cher Monsieur de bien vouloir agréer
                l'expression de mes sentiments les plus amicaux

FIGURE 3.2 (continued)

about their time at FOPOGO. In alphabetical order, they are: Pierre Aron, Victor
Graimont, Oskar ('Ossie') Goldstein, Maurice Michower, Jacques Schlaf, Roger
Waksman, Maurice Weksler, and two 'Buchenwald boys', Juchka and Pirochka (sur-
names unknown). Some of these had come from Collonges where they had been
with Henri at Villa Essor; others came from homes at Champigny and elsewhere.

During term time, Henri's main job was to ensure that the boys got off to school, either the local lycée or a technical college, did their homework and so on. He also had to manage the practical aspects of life in the home, organising with the cook the arrangements for feeding hungry teenagers at a time in France when there were still food shortages. Fortunately, there was space in the garden to raise animals – two pigs by the name of Adolf and Bartholo were recalled by one former resident[31]– who were occasionally slaughtered to supplement the otherwise meagre rations.

The young men slept in dormitories in attic rooms at the top of the house. Henri's office was on the second floor which also served as a music room where re-cords could be played. During the evenings and at weekends, FOPOGO was a hive of activity. There were political debates, theatre productions, musical performances (two of the young men were gifted musicians), sporting activities of various kinds (they had a particularly good basket-ball team), and, not least, parties and dances involving girls at a nearby OSE home.[32] In all these activities (except for the sport – never really his thing), Henri was a constant presence, cajoling, encouraging, and arguing with the boys.

One anecdote, related to me by one of the ex-residents at FOPOGO, nicely cap-tures the enquiring zeitgeist he seems to have engendered. Apparently, one evening, he and some of the boys were visiting someone's house in town for dinner. One of the boys, a precocious chemist (later to be Professor of Chemistry and Physics at Limoges University), proposed to those present a startling hypothesis: that the ash from a cigarette would weigh more than the original cigarette itself. Henri, already a heavy smoker, but also a budding scientist, instantly suggested that they put this idea to the test. A set of scales to weigh letters was summoned from their host and the experiment was performed there and then on the dining room table. As one of the former FOPOGO residents put it to me, 'He gave us the desire to continue to educate ourselves.'[33]

In addition to these day-to-day activities were various holiday excursions to Belgium, hiking in the Pyrenées, camping at Lake d'Annècy, and fruit picking at Saint-Antonin.[34] One such trip was to prove momentous for Henri. In 1947, he took a small group for a week-long visit to London. Apparently, the cook at FOPOGO knew someone who owned a house in Highgate in North London which had a Jewish family as tenants and who also had a spare flat upstairs where Henri could stay. This family had emigrated from Hamburg in the 1930s with their two daughters. One of these, Anne, aged 23 and studying French at Edinburgh University, was deputed to look after the young visitor from France who, at that point spoke only Polish and French (and a smattering of German from his time in the stalags).

Henri took an instant shine to Anne, so much so that on one of their frequent walks on Hampstead Heath he proposed to her, this after knowing her for just three days! Although she did not accept then, their love affair blossomed over the next year. Henri would visit her in Edinburgh and they would stay in guest houses in the Borders, posing as a married couple. And she visited several times at FOPOGO, necessitating some re-arrangement of the boys' sleeping quarters so they could

FIGURE 3.3 Henri and Anne in Paris, 1947.

Source: Picture courtesy of Maurice Michower and OSE/CDJC mémorial de la Shoah.

share a room together – the 'great exodus' as the boys came to call it. A photograph taken on one of her visits to France shows them walking somewhere in Paris on a day out from Le Vésinet (Figure 3.3).

Meanwhile, Henri's work at FOPOGO continued. I have already mentioned his constant stimulating presence in the lives of the boys. But, above all, he sought to create '*une grande famille*',[35] to replace the family life that they had had so cruelly wrenched from them by the war. In this, he was strikingly successful. In my interviews with four former FOPOGO residents, they constantly referred to the warmth and the empathic nature of his relationships with them.[36] Doubtless due to the small age difference between them – he was only six years older than some of the oldest boys – he was as much a friend or an older brother as he was '*directeur*' of an orphanage.

The feelings he engendered in this group of adolescents are perfectly captured in a long letter I received from one of them, Pierre Aron, written over sixty years after leaving FOPOGO. He began by describing the atmosphere in the home:

> twenty individuals, at a difficult age, barely out of adolescence, on the threshold of adulthood … [who had already undergone the ordeal of the war years with the] constant fear of death, false identities, (for some) sudden arrests

and the horror that went with it, the murder of fathers, mothers, often both, not to mention the disappearance of brothers, sisters and friends, hunger, all of which undoubtedly left permanent scars …. and the person who ensured that our communal life was well organised, the one who was responsible for our well-being, our confidant in difficult times, the mediator when tensions between us arose, the person responsible, let us not forget, for the material needs, even the food in this little world? A young man called Henri Tajfel.

The most astonishing thing for me is that if I am asked what precise memory I have of him at any given moment, I must admit I don't have any. He was there, among us, a friend among friends, wielding an authority that was so well accepted that it went unnoticed, at least by me. The only thing I remember is the friendship I felt for him and, no doubt, he for me, and this friendship lasted long after the home was closed.[37]

Then he went on to recount a particular episode at the home involving the two 'Buchenwald boys':

The daily fight for survival in an environment of extreme brutality such as the concentration camp had turned these boys into 'savages' which posed an enormous challenge for the educateurs in charge of readjusting them to 'civilised' society. Two of these boys, among the most difficult, were sent to FOPOGO to live with boys they had nothing in common with, neither origin (they came from Hungary) nor language, interests, education level. So they came to us, Jushka, short, stocky, herculean and Piroshka, a tall red head, both rather off-putting, uncouth if I may say so. And a miracle occurred. In a relatively short time, they were integrated in the group and turned out to have a golden heart and when they left us to emigrate to the US or Australia we had become friends.

As I said before, I don't remember the role Henri played in this success but there is no doubt this rapid and complete recovery owes a lot to him. Once more, his tact and efficiency had worked wonders.

He concluded his letter with this touching tribute:

At a small reunion of the 'old boys' of the Pauline Gaudefroy House, Katy Hazan, the historian of OSE, asked each of us which was our worst and our best memory of our communal life. I had to admit, I couldn't answer the second question but my worst memory was on the day they closed the house, the day we were separated, the end of two years of stable, rich, happy life which we owe in great part to HENRI TAJFEL.

Pierre's reference to occasional conflicts amongst the boys may have been prompted by memories of the cliques that developed at FOPOGO in the two years of its existence. There were several such groups: the 'intellectuals' and the

FIGURE 3.4 Henri (centre) with most of the boys from FOPOGO, the home at Le Vésinet.

Source: Picture courtesy of Maurice Michower and OSE/CDJC mémorial de la Shoah. Original image by Limot.

'monkeys', presumably referring to the more and less academically inclined of the boys; 'the enemy brothers', Pierre and Thomas Aron, on account of their perpetual squabbling; 'the Little Swiss', a group that had come from Geneva; 'the mopistes', the boys that had come with Henri from Villa Essor, especially Ossie Goldstein and Roger Waksman; the 'zouzas', two musically gifted boys; and, of course, Youska and Piroska, the two Buchenwald survivors.[38] Most of these boys can be seen in a photograph taken in 1946 at FOPOGO (Figure 3.4). Was Henri's later fascination with the power of groups to shape human behaviour kindled there at FOPOGO in his daily efforts to help teenagers rebuild their lives?

FOPOGO hosted many events – musical soirées, parties involving nearby orphanages, and occasional individual visitors. One such guest, in 1947 or 1948 – she cannot recall the precise year – was Erika Apfelbaum, a young Jewish teenager who was taken there by Aline Buchenwinder, her scout leader.[39] It seems that Aline had fallen in love with one of the FOPOGO boys, Stéphane Ehrlich, and had used the visit to Le Vésinet as a pretext to see him again. Thus began a chain of coincidences. Erika herself studied psychology at the Sorbonne, went on to become a distinguished social psychologist in her own right,[40] and came to know Henri well later in her career. At the Sorbonne she was taught statistics by Ehrlich who, in 1970, co-authored a statistics text-book with Claude Flament, a mathematical psychologist at Aix-en-Provence. As it happens, the same Flament devised a measure of intergroup discrimination that Henri employed in one of his most famous experiments (Chapter 6).

'Par les jeunes, pour les jeunes'

Perhaps Henri's most signal achievement in his time working for OSE was the foundation of *Lendemains: par les jeunes, pour les jeunes* (The next days: by the young, for the young). This was a monthly magazine written by and for the residents of the twenty-five OSE homes. The idea for such a journal had been mooted at another home near Lyon, L'Hirondelle,[41] but Henri became its prime mover and editor for two years between 1946 and 1948. Fourteen editions came out, all professionally printed, and they were distributed to all the homes under OSE's jurisdiction. Henri persuaded over 300 children to write for this journal. These were an extraordinary mix of contributions: personal reminiscences and stories, poems, film and music reviews, political and philosophical polemics, reports of sporting contests, usually involving different orphanages, crosswords and other quizzes, and, interspersed amongst this potpourri of adolescent self-expression, a few humorous remarks by '*La Redaction*', Henri's nom du plume as editor.

His chosen title, *Lendemains*, is significant. Consistent with OSE's philosophy of seeking to reconstruct these children's lives so that they could have happier futures than their tragic pasts, he sought to encourage them to look forward rather than back. In the conclusion to his opening editorial in June 1946, Henri makes this clear:

> We would like to dedicate the first of our Lendemains to those who, during the tragic years, never ceased daily to flirt with death to save the children, always more children. For, without them, there would be no Lendemains, there would be no homes which live, work and sing, there would be no young people who, without forgetting the past, are taking a decisive step towards the future.[42]

It is worth pausing here to review the content of that first issue of *Lendemains*. Running to 65 pages, it contained 54 articles written by boys and girls from 17 different homes, including two short editorial pieces by Henri himself. There were: poems, an essay on friendship, short accounts of some of the children's experiences in the homes, a review of Beethoven's Ninth Symphony and Mozart's work, a book review (of something by Stefan Zweig), and a sports section. A recurring theme was the nature of Jewish identity and the children's experiences during the war, some written originally in Yiddish or Polish, presumably by survivors from the camps. It is difficult to do justice to the richness and variety of the contributions to this inaugural issue of *Lendemains* but perhaps three examples will suffice to illustrate its tenor.

The first is a piece by Pierre Vormus, the same boy to whom Henri had written so affectionately the year before. He writes nostalgically of his time at Villa Essor, a period he describes as being formative for his physical and moral development, where he understood for the first time the *'grands problèmes'* that life presents us with and the importance of looking 'beyond the end of one's nose'.[43] For him, Villa Essor was 'a point of departure for his life'.[44]

The second is an essay on being a Jew in France. It was written by another boy from Villa Essor, Roger Waksman, who thirty-six years later would read a short address at Henri's funeral. The title of his article says it all: '*La vie Juive et nous: vers où? Vers quoi?*' (Jewish life and us: towards where? Towards what?). In the piece, Roger confronts the big questions that were hotly debated in the Jewish community in France after the war. What is the future for French Jews? Communism? Zionism? Assimilation? He alludes to his parents' arrest in *'les rafles'* (round-ups of Jews in the early years of the war), and his own miraculous escape, and the five years of his clandestine existence with a French family. Throughout, he grapples with several contradictory ideas: his love of French culture and literature (Voltaire, Hugo, Beaudelaire), his attachment to the French countryside (waterfalls in the Vosges, basalt cliffs of the Auvergne), his knowledge that some of their French neighbours may have betrayed his parents to the Nazis, and the post-war lure of Palestine, pulling him away from the country of his birth.

The third was written by Joseph Nichthauser, a young Polish boy. Entitled, '*Les ombres du passé et notre Liberté*' (the shadows of the past and our freedom), it is a moving memoir of his life in a concentration camp and his hopes for the future. He contrasts their life in the camp, 'in dark barracks surrounded by barbed wired, the hard work and the famine … the nostalgia, pain and cries in the heart … the cries of a soul innocently tortured', with that on the other side of the wire, where 'free men savour springtime, enjoying its flowers and sunshine … where there are no Jews, we who are no longer men …., for a dog running in the street is happier than us'.

But the article ends on a note of redemption:

> These are the young who have a past, but who also today have a new energy, a renewed faith in life. We, the debris of our people, begin to build on the ruins victoriously to approach our destination.[45]

These lines must have been particularly poignant to Henri, fresh in the knowledge that his own family had perished in Poland and conscious that he, too, was having to rebuild his life on the ruins of the past.

Not that one could guess this from his final editorial comments in that first issue of *Lendemains*. After a long list of apologies – for the tardiness of the issue, for not having been able to publish all the articles he had been sent, for not including any drawing from the children, for not having replied to all the letters he had received – in a wonderful echo of Janusz Korczak's children's essay writing competitions in a Polish newspaper in the 1920s (Chapter 1), where he would publish detailed statistics of the essays he had received from different towns, Henri concluded with some statistics of his own:

Journal des Enfants de l'O.S.E.
(Juin 1946 - Avril 1948)
Recueil comprenant les tomes I et II de l'édition 2012

LENDEMAINS

Par les jeunes, pour les jeunes

FIGURE 3.5 Cover of collected edition of *Lendemains.*
Source: Lendemains is published by OSE. Original image is by Limot.

Qui fait mieux? (who did the best?)
Saint Germain: *8 articles dont 7 publiés* (8 articles, of which 7 were published)
Boucicant: *7 articles dont 7 publiés*
Collonges: *7 articles dont 5 publiés.*[46]

From the beginning, it is clear that Henri saw *Lendemains* as something of a therapeutic intervention for the hundreds of Jewish children scattered throughout France in OSE homes. He wanted to provide them with an outlet where they could freely express their anxieties about the past but, above all, their hopes for the future. For those involved with its actual editing and production – primarily the boys at FOPOGO – it also gave them an invaluable lesson in the excitement and frustration of teamwork. Figure 3.5, the photograph that now adorns the collected edition of *Lendemains* (all fourteen numbers), shows his editorial committee at work: Henri is at its centre; a boy opposite is typing some material; and the other eight are all intent on various aspects of the publication process. Maurice Michower, one of my principal informants from FOPOGO, is second from the left.

It is impossible to convey here the extraordinary range of articles that appeared in *Lendemains* in the two years of its existence. From the beginning, it was always a mix of accounts of children's daily lives in their homes (of the 'what we did on our holidays' variety) and more profound political essays. With the move of Henri to Le Vésinet in 1946, the stamp of the editorial collective he assembled becomes more obvious. There are still reports of sport matches, crossword puzzles and the like, but the writing becomes more ambitious in its scope: enquiries into the advantages and disadvantages of communal living are launched, including interviews with senior OSE officials (January 1947 issue); moving accounts of some of the residents' experiences of the Holocaust – Maurice Michower's story about losing his parents and two sisters in one of the 'round ups' is particularly harrowing,[47] as are first-hand reports from survivors of Auschwitz[48] and the Warsaw ghetto.[49] By January 1947, wonderful line drawings (by Paul Kornowski, one of the FOPOGO group) and occasional photographs enliven the text. And there are thoughtful pieces on whether OSE homes should be mixed sex, on the origins and cures of anti-Semitism, and much more besides.

One essay on anti-Semitism particularly caught my eye. It was written by Stéphane Ehrlich, who would go on to be a professor of psychology at the Sorbonne[50]. It contains some interesting observations on whether 'assimilation' can offer a solution to the difficulties faced by Jews in an anti-Semitic world. While he acknowledges the possible advantages that this strategy can offer individual Jews, he notes that fundamentally nothing will change since anti-Semitism is, at root, an intergroup problem – a weak minority oppressed by a powerful majority. Thirty-seven years later, Henri himself would develop similar arguments in his theorising on social identity and intergroup relations (Chapter 7).

But all good things come to an end. In November 1947 (Issue No. 12, p. 3), the editorial team warns its readers of 'immense difficulties' in producing the journal. It refers obliquely to a 'new situation' that the FOPOGO home was facing, a hint about its imminent closure, subsequently confirmed in an announcement two months later (Issue No. 13, p. 8). The demise of *Lendemains* in April 1948 was undoubtedly occasioned by the decision to close the home at Le Vésinet. Henri's indefatigable fellow would-be journalists were all now of an age when they needed to strike out on their own. Several went to university and ended up as businessmen, doctors, academics, or lawyers; others secured apprenticeships and pursued successful careers in industry. With their departure, the closure of the home was inevitable. Many other OSE homes closed at about the same time as the children they served gradually became integrated into French society or emigrated to the USA or Israel.[51]

'D'un home à l'autre'

Thus it was that on 15 June 1948, one week before his twenty-ninth birthday, Henri found himself out of work again. Newly engaged to Anne, he was sorely in need of a job. Nothing suitable can have been available in France, otherwise he would surely have stayed in the country of which he had so recently become a citizen (in March 1948[52]). So he was forced to seek a position elsewhere.

He did not leave France that summer completely empty-handed. Not only had he acquired three valuable and fulfilling years of humanitarian work experience, something for which for which he had proved himself so well suited, but he

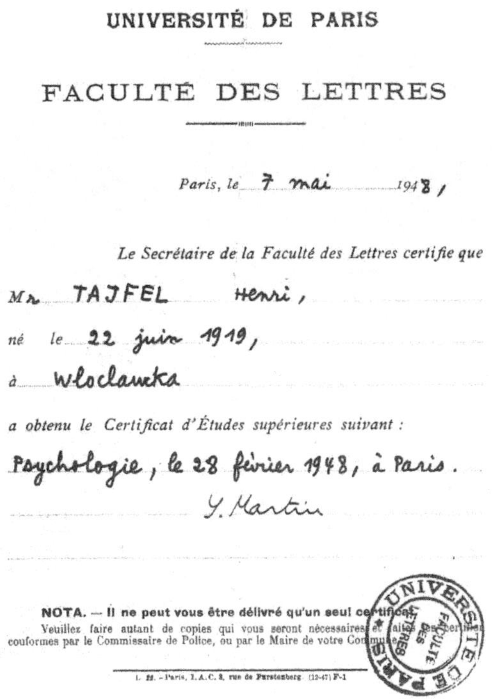

UNIVERSITÉ DE PARIS

FACULTÉ DES LETTRES

Paris, le **7 mai** 1948

Le Secrétaire de la Faculté des Lettres certifie que

M. **TAJFEL** Henri,

né le **22 juin 1919**,

à **Wloclawcka**

a obtenu le Certificat d'Études supérieures suivant :

Psychologie, le 28 février 1948, à Paris.

Y. Martin

NOTA. — Il ne peut vous être délivré qu'un seul certificat.
Veuillez faire autant de copies qui vous seront nécessaires et faites certifier
conformes par le Commissaire de Police, ou par le Maire de votre Commune.

I. M. – Paris, I.A.C. 2, rue de Furstenberg (12–47) F-1

FIGURE 3.6 Henri's first academic qualification.
Source: Courtesy of Anne Tajfel.

now also possessed his first formal academic qualification. The exams of which he had written to Pierre Vormus three years earlier had evidently gone better than the chemistry exams he had taken (and failed) in 1939. On 7 May 1948 he was awarded a '*Certificat d'Études Supérieures*' in Psychology by the University of Paris (Figure 3.6).

Fortunately, he was not unemployed for long. Thanks to the many connections he had made through *Lendemains* and from holiday excursions with his boys, he soon found himself a job as Directeur of a Belgian orphanage, Villa Miravalle, in Boitsfort, a leafy suburb to the south-east of Brussels (Figure 3.7). Miravalle was one of thirteen homes for orphaned Jewish children that were opened in Belgium in 1945 by *L'Aide aux Israélites Victimes de la Guerre* (AIVG). AIVG was a similar organisation to OSE. Like OSE, it saw itself as providing homes for Jewish children who had been hidden during the war and who had mostly lost their parents and relatives in the death camps in Poland. Its aim was to rebuild these children's lives by providing them with the resilience to confront and overcome the trauma of parental separation and loss. There was no single set of pedagogic principles that guided the running of AIVG homes although apparently the work of Janusz Korczak, the Polish writer and paediatrician (Chapter 1), was influential in some.[53]

FIGURE 3.7 Henri's Belgian identity card, showing his new job as *Directeur* at Miravalle.

Source: Courtesy of Anne Tajfel.

Villa Miravalle was a large nineteenth-century mansion. Its house and gardens were ideally suited for an orphanage: there were many rooms of different sizes inside the house that were used as dormitories, dining room, games rooms, and so on; and outside there was a tennis court, football pitch, basket-ball court and extensive grounds and woods, a perfect space for adolescent boys to amuse themselves in.[54] AIVG opened the home in 1945 and quickly placed around thirty boys there, mostly '*enfants cachés*' (hidden children) but also including at least four children who had survived concentration camps in the east. Marcel Frydman, one of the first cohort of boys at Miravalle, went on to be a clinical psychologist specialising in childhood trauma. Commenting later on the psychological condition of '*enfants cachés*' (as he himself was), he noted that many of them suffered a unique double form of trauma.[55] Not only had they experienced the anxiety consequent on being separated from their parents at an early age, but they also had to undergo a complete forced change of identity, many of them having had to assume more typical Belgian names and being brought up as Catholics instead of Jews. Moreover, for many, secrecy during their years in hiding was of the essence – they were unable or forbidden to talk about their former life. These problems were often compounded after the war, either by their uncertainty over the fate of their parents or by the definitive news of their death in the camps. As a result, several of the children at Miravalle (and other homes) manifested behavioural problems of various kinds (usually aggression), found it difficult to form new relationships, and were often unprepared and ill-suited for communal living.[56]

The repercussions of the trauma experienced by these young victims of the Holocaust were often long-lasting. In a commemorative volume dedicated to AIVG homes, there is a moving chapter entitled, '*D'un home à l'autre*', in which former children and staff from AIVG homes after the war share their memories.[57] One of these, Robert Fuks, another former resident of Miravalle, describes how he was six years old when his father was arrested and taken to Auschwitz. He spent the next three years in no fewer than six different locations. He remembered how he never cried much in those awful years of his childhood nor, indeed, for forty years after. Only much later, at a reunion of residents of one of the homes he had stayed in, did the tears return: '*j'ai réappris à pleurer*' (I had learned how to cry again).[58] These, then, were the kinds of children who had been living at Miravalle for three years before Henri's arrival.

The situation Henri faced as Directeur was very different from how it had been at FOPOGO. There he had set up the home from scratch, bringing with him several of the boys from Collonges; the remaining boys had been selected as being more academically inclined. So, he was able to create exactly the social environment that he wanted. At Miravalle he inherited an academically more heterogeneous group of boys who had experienced an unhappy start to their post-war recuperation. Moreover, the previous directors had not been a conspicuous success.[59]

Fortunately, he got off on the right foot. The boys at Miravalle had already heard of him and his '*remarkable success*' at FOPOGO.[60] Perhaps they had been told something by Guy Mansbach, one of the directors at AIVG, who had received a most flattering reference letter from Mr Job, the Secretary General of OSE. Mr Job recommended Henri warmly for the position, noting his 'pedagogic qualities and the interest which he never failed to show in the young people in his care' and his 'signal services to the cause of children, victims of war'.[61]

From the beginning, Marcel Frydman told me, it was obvious that Henri knew what to do. He immediately set out to reduce the social distance between himself and the boys. He insisted that they call him 'Henri' and use 'tu' when speaking with him. Soon after his arrival (in the summer of 1948), he set up a 'council' of five boys and himself who took all the major decisions over the running of Miravalle. This was no sham exercise in democracy; even when he disagreed with the majority, Henri accepted and implemented their decisions[62]. Henri encouraged them to continue with their house journal, *Reflets*, a rather poor relation to *Lendemains* that he had founded in France. He was apparently particularly keen to develop the boys' appreciation of film. There were weekly visits not only to the local cinema but also to cinemas in Brussels. The films were followed by intense discussions of what they had seen (Henri was to retain a life-long love of cinema, being particularly keen on Russian and Polish directors, especially Sergei Eisenstein and Andrzej Wajda[63]). He subscribed to French weekly magazines like *L'Observateur* and organised regular discussions of current affairs – the Cold War, the situation of Blacks in the USA, independence struggles of colonised peoples, and psychoanalysis

FIGURE 3.8 Henri and Anne on their wedding day.

Source: Picture courtesy of Anne Tajfel.

were among the many topics discussed[64]. Together with the educateur in the home, Jacques Lévy, they put on courses in Hebrew and Greek philosophy, and invited speakers to address the boys – the Grand Rabbi of Belgium and a professor of genetics from Brussels University were particular highlights. These activities not only reveal Henri's remarkable gift for inspiring young people, but also are indicative of his already well developed keen interest in social and political affairs.

Not long after his arrival at Miravalle, Henri returned to London to marry Anne. The wedding took place at Golders Green Registry Office on 6 October 1948 (Figure 3.8). Two days later, they were back in Brussels, staying in a small cottage attached to Miravalle.

Although Henri was obviously a breath of fresh air at the home, especially in comparison to his predecessors, he did not enjoy quite the same unalloyed affection from the boys as he had at FOPOGO. Marcel Frydman explained to me that some of the boys felt he had his favourites, tending to be more interested in the 'intellectual and academic' children rather at the expense of the others.

A third factor which increasingly distracted Henri's attention away from the boys' activities at Miravalle was his new found enthusiasm for academic study. Soon after his arrival in Belgium, he enrolled at the Université Libre de Bruxelles in the School of Educational Sciences. Armed with his certificate from the Sorbonne (which probably exempted him from some of the curriculum) and a glowing testimonial from Mr Cohn, head of the Pedagogic Service at OSE, Henri registered for a wonderfully eclectic array of courses:

Introduction to philosophy and logic
History of civilisation
Elements of general biology
Individual hygiene
Social hygiene
General Psychology
Experimental pedagogy
Moral philosophy
Introduction to the history of modern literature
Human physiology
School hygiene (including infant mental hygiene)
Psychology of the child and adolescent
History of pedagogy
Organisation of teaching
Comparative scholastic legislation
General methodology
Statistical methods and graphs in pedagogy
Legislation for the protection of the child.[65]

Faced with the daunting prospect of following eighteen courses simultaneously, little wonder that Henri did not always seem wholly focussed on his work as Directeur. Siegi Hirsch, who worked for a few weeks as an Educateur at Miravalle under Henri, recounted how, in previous AIVG homes where he had worked, he would frequently have discussions with the director about the work they were doing, the activities they should organise. He could not recall a single such discussion with Henri. Instead, he (Henri) stayed in his office and simply left him to get on with his work by himself.[66]

In this, his third university experience, Henri can hardly be described as a star student. In his formal Candidate Certificate, granted by Brussels University in July 1949, he achieved only a 'satisfactory' grade. In the Belgian system, 'satisfactory' (60% on average) was just one step up from 'fail', and below 'Distinction' (70%), 'Grande Distinction' (80%) and the acme, 'La plus grande Distinction' (90%).[67] At that time, university training in Belgium was divided into two cycles of two years, 'Candidature' and then 'Licence'. Candidature, then, was something akin to a diploma, a precursor to the full Licence degree with which, as psychologist, you were allowed to practise.

He never completed his Licence. In May 1949, during one of the routine inspection visits by a Mr Roger DeWilder, a local school teacher appointed by AIVG to monitor their homes, there was a heated argument between him and Henri about how Miravalle was being run. Mr DeWilder was rather 'old fashioned' in his views and also seems to have been a stickler for cleanliness and order. Siegi Hirsch,

Henri's successor as Directeur, noted that visits by Mr Dewilder were particularly feared in case he found grease stains on the required written reports.[68] Moreover, as he explained to me, there was something of a culture clash between the two men – Henri, the Paris intellectual, versus Dewilder, the staid Belgian bureaucrat.[69] Doubtless, too, Henri's rather progressive way of running the home with the help of his Council of five 'wise boys' will not have sat well with Mr Dewilder's more conventional pedagogic approach. Whatever the source of the conflict, it was sufficiently serious to result in Henri's dismissal from his post. Marcel Frydman recalls the moment when they learned that Henri was going:

> It was not without emotion that, at the last meeting of Council, we learned following the reading of the exchange of letters with AIVG, the reasons for his departure, that I bitterly regretted and I was not the only one.[70]

Henri's successor was Siegi Hirsch.[71] This proved to be an inspired recommendation. Mr Hirsch remained as Directeur of Miravalle for the next six years until its closure in May 1955. Although he did not work with Henri long enough to know him well, he offered this fitting tribute to Henri's work at Miravalle:

> *Maybe through his attitude he helped you develop your creativity....*
> *and make your mistakes....and (then) make better mistakes the*
> *next time.*[72]

Return to Germany

The unfortunate incident with Mr De Wilder which led to Henri's dismissal from Miravalle could not have happened at a worse time. He was unemployed again and the chances of obtaining another position in a children's home were remote. He had blotted his copy-book with AIVG and, in any case, organisations like AIVG and OSE (in France) were winding down their operations as the Jewish children they were looking after grew up and attained independence. He still had no university degree and continuing at Brussels University was no longer feasible without some means to support himself. And, to cap it all, Anne was three months pregnant with their first child.

So, the need to find a new job was rather urgent and fortunately it was not long before he obtained one. An acquaintance of Anne from Cambridge, where she had lived during the war, told them of a vacancy with the International Refugee Organisation (IRO) to work as a Rehabilitation and Vocational Training Officer in one of the several rehabilitation centres that the IRO had established in Germany, Austria, Italy, and Switzerland after the Second World War.[73] Quite what qualifications or experience Henri possessed for such a position is not clear and perhaps it is a mark of his resourcefulness and powers of persuasion that he managed to convince someone in the IRO that he was the right person for the job (although the acute shortage of IRO staff in the late 1940s might also have played a part[74]). Thus it was embarked on his new career as in vocational guidance and rehabilitation in December 1949, earning the not inconsiderable annual salary of US$3100 (+ $400 dependents' allowance).[75]

Before he started work in Germany, their son Michael was born in London in November 1949. Like many expectant fathers before and since, Henri awaited the birth in a state of considerable agitation. One of the former FOPOGO 'boys', Pierre Aron, happened to be visiting at the time and he described the episode in vivid detail:

> I do remember visiting him in London. It was cold and almost dark as we were walking along the Thames, not far from the hospital where his wife was giving birth to their baby. For some reason, which I forget, he had not been allowed to stay with Anne and I remember his anguish while we were pacing in front of the hospital, an overwhelming anguish as if he had been in labour himself instead of his wife.[76]

Henri soon had to leave his new family in London to start his new job and hence saw little of his son in the first weeks of his life. A few months later Anne and Michael joined him in Germany (Figure 3.9).

The IRO, Henri's new employer, was the successor to the United Nations Relief and Rehabilitation Administration (UNRRA), an organisation set up at the instigation of the American Government during the war in anticipation of a predicted

FIGURE 3.9 Anne, Michael, and Henri in Germany.
Source: Picture courtesy of Anne Tajfel.

refugee crisis at the war's end. This prediction proved to be well founded. After the surrender of Germany in 1945, as many as seven million displaced persons (DPs) became the responsibility of the Western Allies, with perhaps a similar number under the jurisdiction of the Soviet Union.[77] In a remarkable feat of logistical organisation, the UNRRA succeeded in repatriating most of these refugees by the end of 1946. However, its operations were severely hampered by the increasingly frosty relationship between the Western powers and the Soviet Union. Moreover, UNRRA was effectively under the control of the Allied occupying powers in Germany and elsewhere, whose primary concern was to resettle the millions of DPs as quickly as possible so that they would no longer be a drain on those governments' resources.[78]

By 1947 there were still over one million DPs living in camps in Germany, Austria and Italy, the so-called 'hard-core' of refugees who had, for various reasons, resisted UNRRA's efforts at repatriation.[79] The IRO came into existence in 1947 to deal with this 'last million'. Several features of the IRO distinguished it from its predecessor.

First, written into its constitution was a broader definition of what counted as a refugee. Now, for the first time, a DP's refusal to return 'home' could be legitimately based on 'persecution, or fear, based on reasonable grounds, of persecution because of race, religion, nationality or political opinions'.[80] This anticipated the definition of a refugee that was subsequently adopted (in 1951) by the United Nations High Commission on Refugees, a definition that it uses to this day.[81] This meant that the IRO could be sympathetic, at least in principle, to the hundreds of thousands of Poles, Ukrainians, and Yugoslavs who feared the prospect of returning to their home countries.

Second, although the IRO, like the UNRRA before it, was predominantly American funded, it was permitted to operate outside the auspices of the UN and had its own budget and personnel division. This gave it a degree of autonomy in its staff recruitment and in its dealings with the new German civic authorities and the various refugee receiving countries which its predecessor had never enjoyed.

Third, from the beginning IRO was concerned with the training and rehabilitation of refugees, so that they could pursue independent lives wherever they happened to end up. In 1948, it set up a social Division of Employment and Vocational Training with an initial budget of $13million. The need for rehabilitation and training was unquestionable. The war had exacted a terrible toll on the peoples of Europe. Over and above the many millions who had died, countless others were left severely handicapped by various physical and other disabilities. Even as late as 1948, an IRO survey found that 26,000 DPs were physically handicapped, over half due to pulmonary tuberculosis. In addition to these physical disabilities, survivors of the war – former forced labourers, PoWs or concentration camp prisoners – carried many psychological scars, leaving them ill-equipped, and sometimes ill-motivated, to resume their former occupations. And even those whom the war had left physically or psychologically unscathed faced considerable difficulties finding work. A combination of the dire economic situation in Germany and Austria (high unemployment and low pay) and not infrequent discrimination by German employers meant that refugees' idleness was as often enforced as it was unwanted.[82]

Although there is no doubt that the IRO was driven primarily by humanitarian concerns, the motivations of its funders (the victorious Allied powers)
were not entirely altruistic. The war had left many of their economies in a par-
lous state and there was a desperate shortage of labour as they sought to get the
wheels of industry and agriculture moving again. Thus, the hundreds of thousands of able-bodied men and women languishing in DP camps in Austria and
Germany were a tempting prospect for the ministries of labour of the western
governments. Accordingly, they dispatched teams of selectors to the DP camps
to recruit workers who looked best able to fill the vacancies in the factories,
farms and hospitals back home. The refugees were medically and occupationally
tested and those who passed muster were offered the opportunity to emigrate.
In this way, more than a million refugees were resettled by the IRO between
1947 and 1951,[83] causing one commentator to describe it as little more than 'an
international employment agency'.[84] Somewhat less kindly, but perhaps just as
accurately, another likened the selection process in the DP camps to a farmers'
market where refugees were chosen 'like good beef cattle'.[85]

Given this pressure from its funders to provide workers with useful skills, the
IRO established sixteen Rehabilitation and Vocational Training Centres in the
occupied countries. One of these was at Eversburg, a suburb of Osnabrück, a town
of around 100,000 inhabitants in the north-west of Germany. Osnabrück contained a very large DP camp, using the same premises as a former German PoW
camp, Oflag VIC. By the end of 1946, there were still over 5000 DPs living in
this camp, according to a local historian.[86] It was to the Eversburg Rehabilitation
Centre that Henri was sent at the end of 1949, and where he was to spend most
of the next two years. This Centre was easily the largest in Germany and Austria.
In January 1950, just after Henri arrived, it housed 300 refugees, well over twice
the number at any other IRO centre.[87] Many of these refugees were quite severely
disabled, at least to judge from one document compiled by the Eversburg medical
officer in December 1950.[88] Listed there are 42 refugees and their various disabil-
ities: amputated leg (12), amputated arm (4), syphilis (2), and a miscellany of other
ailments.

What were Henri's duties? These were described by the IRO Personnel Officer
on Henri's service record:

> His duties have been the organisation and supervision of vocational training
> courses set up for handicapped Displaced Persons/Refugees. He has, in con-
> junction with Medical and Welfare staff, selected trainees for specialised
> courses; checked the progress and suitability of courses; checked and super-
> vised the progress of individual students and their eventual discharge upon
> completion of the training course. Mr Tajfel was also responsible for ensuring
> adequate accommodation for trainees, and that all necessary supplies were
> available for the students' use. The nature of Mr Tajfel's duties were such that
> close co-operation and liaison with Medical, Welfare and Resettlement offi-
> cials was at all times essential.[89]

That rather dry job description was elaborated by a Mr Chamberlin who was Henri's boss at Eversburg. In a testimonial letter for Henri, written shortly before his departure from Germany, he wrote:

> During this time he (Tajfel) has been in charge of the Vocational Training aspect of this large IRO Centre, whose purpose is to prepare disables [*sic*] Displaced Persons for employability either in the German economy or in other countries.
>
> He has a good understanding of the problems involved in managing personnel, programs and equipment necessary for the operation of a school of this size and character. His teaching staff has been 40 persons and the school has averaged 420 trainees. Both staff and trainees represent a variety of nationalities. Mr Tajfel has shown himself especially capable in directing the testing of skills required in our school courses. He has worked closely with IRO and German testing teams, to provide certificates of competence as different levels of skill are attained.
>
> Eversburg is one of the largest Rehabilitation Centres in the world, certainly the largest in Europe. In supervising the program here, we have all become (through daily experience) very well versed in problems of the disabled – especially amputees.
>
> I consider Mr Tajfel a capable educational administrator. He is sympathetic in handling individual problems of human relationships; yet objective in evaluating the progress and results of a complete training program. His written reports are direct, lucid and effortless.
>
> As a member of our team he is friendly, good-humoured and popular. I think he will fit into any group very naturally.[90]

Several things about Henri stand out from this letter. One is his obvious versatility. His previous four years had been spent working in and then directing children's homes with responsibility for perhaps thirty adolescents and two or three staff. Now he had a staff of forty and several hundred mostly disabled refugees to worry about. It is interesting that Mr Chamberlin comments specifically on his writing ability. Henri had been speaking English only for three or four years at this point (since he met Anne) and yet he is now writing reports that are 'lucid and effortless'. His human qualities are also evident. We already know from his time in the orphanages in France and Belgium that he formed life-long affectionate friendships with several of the boys he looked after. That same ease in making and sustaining relationships was noted by Mr Chamberlin. In other words, he was, as Italians would say, *un simpatico*. It is also apparent what a good manager of people he was.

It is all the more remarkable that he was such a success in this new vocation given that it was achieved in Germany, the country where he had spent five unpleasant years as a PoW and whose Nazi leaders had been responsible for the murder of almost his entire family (along with millions of other Jews). It cannot have been easy for him to have had daily dealings with other victims of the war and to be back living among Germans again.

Not that he and Anne would have had much contact with German people in those two years. They lived at Nienburg, a town over 100 km and a two-hour drive from Osnabrück, where they were housed in military accommodation that had been requisitioned by the British army. They were strongly discouraged – if not prohibited – from fraternising with German nationals, and their only social contacts were British officers, the people who cleaned their house (paid for by IRO), Henri's chauffeur (likewise) and, of course, his fellow IRO colleagues and the refugees at the Eversburg Centre.

The IRO, and hence Henri's job, was never intended to be permanent. In June 1947 it had responsibility for 700,000 DPs; by 1950, that number had dwindled to 248,000; and by June 1951, only 51,000 DPs were still under its care.[91] As a consequence, the number of IRO Rehabilitation Centres also declined, from sixteen in February 1950 shortly after Henri started work, to just three by July 1951.[92] Thus it was that, on 30 June 1951, Henri's job with the IRO came to an end. His service record noted tersely: 'Reason for termination of service: reduction in force.'

Notes

1 Shephard (2010).
2 Tajfel (1981b), p. 1.
3 Quinn (2007).
4 Shephard (2010).
5 Fiche Medicale, 1945; Archives Nationales, Service Historique de la Défense, Caen.
6 Durand (1980); Quinn (2007).
7 Auslander (2005); Quinn (2007).
8 Beevor and Cooper (1994).
9 Beevor and Cooper (1994); Lowe (2012).
10 Quinn (2007); Shephard (2010).
11 Auslander (2005).
12 Ester Dyszel, Henri's cousin, who was by then living in hiding outside of Warsaw, witnessed the conflagration: '*Because the house was on top of a hill, we could see all the way into the city. The sky was red with fire and huge clouds of smoke billowed into the air. It was the ghetto burning*' (Winkelman, 2015, p. 70).
13 United States Holocaust Memorial Museum.
14 United States Holocaust Memorial Museum.
15 Speltini interview, June 2016.
16 Robinson interview, November 2016.
17 Orwell (1933).
18 '*Bourses d'enseignement supérieur accordées pour faits de guerre (1945–1958)*'; Olivier Chosalland, Archives Nationales, November 2016.
19 Guthmann (2012).
20 Guthmann (2012).
21 Guthmann (2012).

22 Veil (2012).
23 Hazan (2012), p. 6.
24 Buruma (2013); Giles (1997).
25 Hazan (2012), p. 6.
26 Hazan (2012), p. 43.
27 *Lendemains*, 1946, No. 4, p. 13 (my translation).
28 Its translation (by Ginette Herman, Sarah Carter and the author):

> My dear Pierrot
>
> Before beginning this letter, I wish to offer you my most humble and formal apologies. It is true that I should have written to you a long time ago and that your indignation which Roger told me about is quite justified. But I beg you to recognize some mitigating circumstances. Since I came back to Collonges, I have really been terribly busy. You know that this is time when we have to place all the boys, to find them an apprenticeship or a school and I spend my time running hither and thither around Lyon to find suitable 'slots' (slang for schools) for them. Apart from that, I have a lot of personal work; you know that I am hoping to take an exam next February or even January in the Faculty of Arts and time is running out. You are not alone, during the past few weeks I've neglected all my correspondence. I really needed a special opportunity to write to Roger while he was at your place.
>
> I hope that my excuses are enough to appease your justifiable anger. And to prove that you don't hold it against me, reply very soon, and with a longer letter than you usually write to me.
>
> I hope that your mother is getting better. I would also like you to tell me in detail what your work is about now. If you are happy, if you have interesting friends, if you are finding your studies to your taste, what are your plans for the immediate future, what you are reading nowadays. It seemed to me after our last conversation in Paris that you are starting to become interested in some very serious and difficult issues, but you are doing so with common sense. And I think I was also able to make you understand that before embarking on whatever it may be, you have to prepare seriously, to understand before forming a judgment. At your age, the best way to understand is to read with discernment. I would advise you, if you have time, to tackle the novels of Duhamel, Kipling, Romain Rolland, Dickens, Wells, Malraux, Alexis Tolstoï, Dreiser, Stefan Zweig, Maurois, Upton Sinclair, Demaison, Joseph Conrad, Stevenson, Wassilewska, Bojer etc. You notice that I have listed pell-mell the names of French, English, Russian, American, German, Scandinavian, Polish writers… It is because I believe that at your age, it's a matter of coming out of your shell, that one must start to realize that the world does not end in Avignon, or even Paris, that there are wider human, social, ethical problems beyond the end of our nose. We are two billion people on earth, and each of us spends most of his time (sometimes without even being aware of it) to try to adapt to these two billion minus one which the world represents for him. Only the man who begins to want to understand at an early age becomes a great man.
>
> Do you think that this sermon has gone on long enough? To tell the truth it is not really a sermon. It is truly what I believe. And I hope that the next time we meet, you will be able to tell me stories that would me make to say: Pierre is making a great deal of effort.
>
> Answer me quickly. And tell me everything. About the Chateau des Papes (sic: it is usually known as the Palais de Papes at Avignon), what you had for lunch, your last romantic walk, the last film you saw, your last book, your projects, pleasant surprises and disappointments. Promise?
>
> Please accept sir the assurance of my highest consideration,

29 Letter from J. Cohn (OSE), 11 May 1949.

30 Hazan (2012), p. 56.

31 Hazan (2012), p. 56.

32 Hazan (2012), p. 56.

33 OSE interviews, April 2015.

34 Hazan (2012), p. 57.

35 Hazan (2012), p. 56.

36 OSE interviews, April 2015.

37 Personal communication to the author. Translation by Hélène Rozenberg, Sarah Carter and the author.

38 Hazan (2012).

39 Apfelbaum interview, April 2017.

40 Apfelbaum (2009).

41 Hazan (2012), p. 9.

42 La Redaction, *Lendemains*, 1946, No. 1, p. 2; my translation.

43 A phrase that Henri had used in his letter to him of October 1945 – Figure 3/2.

44 *Lendemains*, 1946, No. 1, p. 14.

45 *Lendemains*, No. 1, pp. 40–1; my translation.

46 *Lendemains*, 1946, No. 1, p. 65; the three places refer to different OSE homes.

47 *Lendemains*, No. 7, pp. 39–40.

48 *Lendemains*, No. 7, pp. 36–8.

49 *Lendemains*, No. 10, pp. 28–9.

50 *Lendemains*, No. 7, pp. 22–4.

51 Hazan (2012).

52 Archives Nationales Pierrefitte, November 2016.

53 Nysenholc (2004), p. 23.

54 Frydman (2014).

55 Frydman (2014).

56 Frydman (2014).

57 Nysenholc (2004).

58 Nysenholc (2004), p. 42.

59 Frydman (2014).

60 Frydman (2014), p. 108.

61 R. Job, letter, 26 May 1948; my translation.

62 Frydman interview, January 2015.

63 A. Tajfel letter to Gustav Jahoda, undated.

64 Frydman interview, January 2015; Frydman (2014).

65 Letter from H Waterlot, L'Adjoint au Secretariat, Université Libre de Bruxelles, September 1949.

66 Hirsch interview, January 2014.

67 Olivier Klein, personal communication, May 2017.

68 Hirsch (2004), p. 33.

69 Hirsch interview, January 2015.

70 Frydman (2014), p. 110; my translation.

71 Siegi Hirsch is an extraordinary man. Deported to Poland as a teenager, he is a survivor of Auschwitz and Buchenwald. In Auschwitz he had made a promise to one of his fellow prisoners that, if he ever made it out alive, he would dedicate himself to the children of the Holocaust. After his miraculous survival, he made good on that promise, working in various AIVG homes for thirteen years. He explained how his philosophy in working with Jewish orphans stemmed from his time in the camps. The one thing he forbade in the homes was any discussion about the past:

(in the camps) you couldn't speak about the past because then you went down ... you could speak about the past when you had a basic security and you were feeling good, secure. Then you could remember. I think there's a law: you have to forget, and not just to forget, but you have to forget that you have forgotten

Hirsch interview, January 2015

Anne Tajfel told me that she and Henri adopted a similar maxim. They never talked about the Holocaust or their past lives before the war, and they never talked to their children about them either.

72 Hirsch interview, January 2015.
73 Holborn (1956).
74 Holborn (1956), p. 283.
75 The dollar-pound exchange rate in 1950 was about 2.8 so this gave him a salary of £1250. Given that United Nations employees, as IRO workers were, did not pay income tax, this was a tidy sum indeed, easily putting Henri in the top 10% of earners in Britain at the time (A. Newell, personal communication, 2017).
76 Letter to the author from P. Aron, March 2015; translated by Hélène Rozenberg and Sarah Carter.
77 Marrus (1985).
78 Marrus (1985).
79 Holborn (1956); Lane (1952); Marrus (1985).
80 Holborn (1956), p. 585.
81 UNHCR (2010).
82 Holborn (1956).
83 Marrus (1985), p. 344.
84 Proudfoot (1956).
85 Shephard (2010), p. 341.
86 Ordelheide (1982).
87 Holborn (1956), p. 310.
88 Bad-Arolsen ITS archive, www.dpscampinventory.its-arolsen.org).
89 IRO Certificate of Service, June 1951.
90 Charles D. Chamberlin, Cultural Exchanges Branch, HICOG, Frankfurt; February 1951.
91 Proudfoot (1956).
92 Holborn (1956).

4

LONDON AND DURHAM

1951–1956

A student again

The end of Henri's IRO job was not unexpected; he and Anne had been discussing various career options for some time. Early on in their relationship he had expressed a wish to emigrate to the newly created state of Israel but she was unwilling to uproot herself again and insisted that they live in Britain. So, a job in Britain it had to be. Henri once had an idea to go into journalism but the prospects of a foreigner who had only recently acquired English obtaining a job in a British newspaper did not seem very bright. He had also toyed with the notion of finding work in publishing, even going so far as getting an interview with a French publishing house, but that came to nothing. In the end, they decided that completing his university education would be necessary for whatever career path he eventually chose, and so he sought entrance to the University of London, Birkbeck College, to read for a degree in Psychology, the subject he had studied in Paris and Brussels without ever graduating.

This did not turn out to be a straightforward matter. At the time, British universities did not recognise educational qualifications from other countries as they do today. Thus, his Polish secondary school leaving certificates counted for nothing, nor did his '*Certificats*' from the Sorbonne or the Université Libre de Bruxelles. So, he was obliged to pass some British examinations before Birkbeck would consider him. This he duly did, flying back to London (at IRO's expense) in 1950 to take the necessary exams ('Special University Entrance Examination'). All went well and he was accepted for a BA in Psychology at Birkbeck, a degree course that he began in October 1951.

A distinctive feature of Birkbeck was that it catered mainly for part-time students (as it still does), running classes in the evenings so that students could work during the day. This was necessary for Henri because, with the demise of his IRO job and now with a family to support, he needed something to pay the rent and put food on the table. His first job in Britain, which he started in October 1951, was as a shipping clerk at Baker, Britt and Company Ltd, Shipping Agents and Wharfingers, Haulage Contractors and International Carriers, whose offices were in the east end of London. This was not the most obvious line of work for a would-be intellectual, as I suspect he now saw himself, but needs must. Perhaps he got the position via his father-in-law who was in the import–export business himself and who had promised to help Henri find work when he had announced his engagement to Anne two years before.[1]

For a person of his talents, such a job seems unlikely to have been very taxing or stimulating but it did at least give him plenty of time for his studies. It did not last long, however: seven months later, his services were dispensed with 'owing to a decline in trade', as his employer's reference letter put it. The same letter went on to remark that they had always found 'his work satisfactory and him conscientious and willing'.[2]

If that first job in his newly adopted country was not exactly stimulating, his second at least found him back in an educational role. Somehow or other, he landed a job as a school teacher at North Bridge House School, a (private) preparatory school in St John's Wood in London.[3] There he taught French and General Studies, two subjects for which he was admirably qualified, and considerably more so than for his additional duties which included supervising games of cricket on Hampstead Heath. Somehow, the image of Henri, a chain-smoking French intellectual and one of the least athletically inclined people I ever knew, overseeing young boys playing that most quintessentially English of games, I find irresistibly funny. Perhaps it was to those extra-curricular activities that his head-teacher was referring when he wrote to Henri on his departure from the school:

> I should like to thank you for all your efforts – it can have been no easy matter to work here – and I hope we shall continue to keep in touch. We shall always be glad to see you.[4]

Henri's tenure as a school teacher lasted only a year. At some point in 1952–1953 he had applied for a State Scholarship from the Ministry of Education. Part of the application process for this involved the submission of an essay. Henri's chosen topic for this was *Prejudice*. Doubtless this choice was inspired by his life experiences to this point and probably also by some of the material that he was already studying for his degree. Whatever his motivation, it proved to be a prophetic choice: for the entirety of his career, Henri was to be concerned, one way or another, with trying to understand the psychological origins and functions of prejudice.

Although no copy still exists of this early analysis of prejudice, it was sufficiently impressive to convince the Ministry of Education to award him a State Scholarship for Mature Students for the remainder of his degree. Not only did it cover his fees, but it also paid him a grant of £359 per year.[5] This scholarship was triply welcome to Henri: it provided him with the first official recognition of his talents as a scholar, a much needed fillip after his earlier indifferent achievements at the Sorbonne and Brussels; it also meant that he could give up his school-teacher job since he now had a small income which he and his family could live on; and thirdly, and no less importantly given Henri's age (he was already thirty-four), it meant that he could now study psychology full-time instead of part-time, thus shortening his degree from the usual four years to three.

The department at Birkbeck at that time was called the Department of Psychology and Philosophy. Its head was C.A. Mace, a Cambridge philosopher (and student of Bertrand Russell), who later became influential in the then burgeoning field of occupational psychology.[6] Alongside him was another philosopher, R.S. Peters, once described as the founding father of British philosophy of education.[7] Another key figure in the department was Brian Foss, who would also go on to work in educational psychology but who, at the time, had a rather eclectic range of interests, including consciousness, neurophysiology, and animal behaviour (apparently, he kept mynah birds in his office[8]). Other faculty included John Cohen, Peter Dodwell, Thelma Veness, Alec Rodger, and Harry Hurwitz, all of whom were later to occupy chairs at various universities in Britain or North America.

The students were mostly, if not all, mature students like Henri in their thirties or older – school teachers, engineers, retirees and the like (Figure 4.1). As a result, many of them were older than their lecturers which probably meant that relations between staff and students were probably more egalitarian than would have been the norm at other British universities in that era. The psychology syllabus was both broad and idiosyncratic since each College of the University of London (as Birkbeck was) could decide for itself what was taught. There was no straightjacket such as exists today via the British Psychological Society's curriculum. Because Behaviourism was then in its heyday, there was considerable material on animal learning to be studied, but there was much else besides. Social psychology, Henri's subsequent specialty, was taught by Veness, supplemented by lectures on personality by Foss and Hurwitz.[9] Apparently, these lectures covered such topics as The Authoritarian Personality, Lewin and others of the Gestalt School, Frustration-Aggression Theory, and the nascent field of social perception, all of which were active research areas in the early 1950s.[10]

What kind of impression did Henri make on his lecturers in this his fourth venture into university education? Harry Hurwitz, a newly appointed lecturer at Birkbeck and someone who subsequently became a close friend of Henri, described one of his first meetings with Henri:

> [he was] odd … very, very insecure … almost deferential, though that changed later on. He knew how to ingratiate himself and my colleagues were sensitive to it and rejected it for the most part. It's not part of the British tradition.

FIGURE 4.1 Henri with some of his fellow Birkbeck students. Henri is lying down at the front. One of his lecturers, Harry Hurwitz, is third from the left in the back row.

Source: Photograph courtesy of Harry Hurwitz.

He also noted Henri's sense of being an 'outsider':

> He was sensitive to the fact that he was a foreigner – and I must make this as a commentary because I faced that problem myself [Hurwitz was an emigré from Germany via South Africa]. To have a foreign accent was a big negative….You weren't allowed to talk about whatever part of England you came from. You went into an interview with a foreign accent and you were lost….. on average it didn't go down well.

But he quickly recognised Henri's intellectual gifts:

> he was brilliant … much more broadly educated than most. He showed his European background. He had interests in literature, politics … .everything

UNIVERSITY DEGREES AND POSTGRADUATE DIPLOMAS OBTAINED BY STUDENTS OF THE COLLEGE DURING THE SESSION 1953-54

FACULTY OF ARTS

Ph.D.

Internal	Bauer, Josephine, M.A. (Wash.)	English
	McGurk, Patrick M. J., B.A.	History
	Ashby, Ronald W., B.A.	Philosophy
	Nidditch, Peter, M.A.	Philosophy
	Jackson, Frederick H., M.A.	Mathematics
	Crawford, Sheila S., M.A. (N.Z.)	Geography
	Gately, Grace M., B.A.	Psychology
	Mangan, Gordon L., M.A. (N.Z.)	Psychology
	Morgan, Griffith A. V., B.A. (Cantab.)	Psychology
	Pawlik, Wladyslaw, M.A. (Edin.)	Psychology
	Shearn, Martin C.E., B.A.	Psychology
	Thiele, Harold W., M.A. (Q'ld.)	Psychology

M.A.

Barber, Frank, B.A.	Classics
Charlesworth, Dorothy A., B.A.	Classics
O'Donnell, Eunan P., B.A., (N.U.I.)	Classics
*Chandler, Edmund R., B.A.	English
Spear, Hilda D., B.A.	English
Königsberg, Isidore, B.A.	French
Rhodes, Frederick V., B.A.	German
Taylor, Roy, B.A.	History
Simms, Alfred G., B.A. (Nott.)	Mathematics
Rigg, John B., B.A.	Geography
Short, Joseph P., B.A.	Geography
Greaves, Mary E., B.Sc. (Econ.)	Psychology
Phillipson, Herbert, B.A.	Psychology

* *Awarded a Mark of Distinction*

B.A.

Honours　　　　　FIRST CLASS

Internal	Cook, David J.	English
	Hall, Norma	French
	Megson, Brenda M.	French
	Price-Williams, Douglass R.	Psychology
	Tajfel, Henri	Psychology

FIGURE 4.2 Announcement of Henri's degree in the Birkbeck College Annual Report, 1954.

lay in his field of interest.... It was difficult to understand him because of his accent but once he sat down to write anything, it was excellent. His essays were exemplary.[11]

Hurwitz believes Henri did his undergraduate dissertation under the supervision of Brian Foss. He thinks that it may have been something on psychophysical judgement. If so, this would help to make sense of Henri's early scientific interests which would be concerned with such issues as people's estimates of weight, coin sizes, and line lengths.

One of Henri's contemporaries and close friends at Birkbeck was Douglass Price-Williams, later to become a famous cross-cultural psychologist.[12] Although their backgrounds could not have been more different – Price-Williams was a product of the English public school system and an ex-Merchant Naval officer – they got on well, collaborating on their preparation for essays and other academic work. Like Henri, Price-Williams was an exceptional student and they both graduated in due course with First Class degrees, the only two in Psychology to do so (Figure 4.2). Another of his classmates was Irene Freud, grand-daughter-in-law of the famous Sigmund (she was married to W. Ernest Freud, Freud's eldest grandson).

It was not all work for Henri at Birkbeck, however. Because Birkbeck students were close in age with their lecturers and professors, there was frequent socialisation between them in the refectory before and after classes. Henri also used to inveigle Hurwitz into watching matinee performances at a cinema in Belsize Park. Henri was a great cineaste, an interest born and nurtured in his years in Paris before and after the war. Even so, Henri would often walk out of the film early if it threatened to go on beyond the time he had allotted himself for the cinematic excursion.[13] Every year the department staged a Christmas party which usually included a musical composed by Foss. On one occasion, Foss cast Henri as 'Dr Freud', a choice no doubt prompted by Henri's pronounced foreign (though not Austrian!) accent. It seems that this required Henri actually to sing a number, which Hurwitz described it as a 'tour de force', although unfortunately we have no record of the lyrics.[14]

A new job and *The New Look*

By the time Henri settled in Britain in 1951, he was already a well-travelled man. At thirty-two, when he moved to London from Germany, he had lived in no fewer than six different countries – Poland, France (twice), Germany (twice), Austria, Belgium, and Britain – and had had two nationalities (Polish, French). Obviously, some of those sojourns were hardly of his choice but they did establish a pattern that was to persist for the remainder of his life: Henri loved to travel.

This is evident from the visa stamps in his French passport of the mid 1950s. In the two years between January 1954 and February 1956 he made four trips to the Continent, including short visits to Belgium and Germany, possibly on business for his father-in-law, and holidays with Anne and Michael in France and Italy. Given that travel in those days was considerably more expensive and less easy to arrange than it is today, this seems to be quite remarkable, the more so since the first two journeys were made whilst he was still a student.

It is 1954 and Henri finally has a university degree to his name at the age of thirty-five. His three years at Birkbeck were clearly decisive for his choice of career as an academic and now he needed a job. If Henri had been asked in that summer of 1954, I very much doubt that Durham would have been anywhere near the top of his wish-list as a place to live and from where to launch his career. Originally a fortified city with its own cathedral and bishop, it had become a small market town and county seat in the Durham coalfield, itself blighted by pre-war mass unemployment and current decline due to unfavourable geology.[15] It was also a long way (over 250 miles) from London and the world he had known since emigrating to Britain three years earlier. Durham University, although quite old (established in 1832), was not exactly thriving in the 1950s, according to Jerry Ravetz, a mathematician who went there at about the same time and who befriended the Tajfels.[16]

The staff in the Durham Psychology Department in 1954 were not an obvious fit with Henri's developing interests in social psychology. The Head of Department was an eccentric Australian by the name of Frederick Viggers Smith, usually known as 'Fred'. Smith had got his Chair on the strength of two review papers in the 1940s and his book *The Explanation of Human Behaviour* (1951), an astute appraisal of some of the popular psychological theories at the time. Interestingly (from Henri's point of view), that book contained chapters on William McDougall, Kurt Lewin, and Gordon Allport, who were among the most influential social psychologists of that era. There was also a chapter on Clark Hull, whom Henri had read as an undergraduate and who would be the subject of one of his first academic publications.

Also on the Durham staff then were: Wladek Sluckin, like Henri a Polish emigré, who also had rather wide-ranging interests (cybernetics, industrial incentives, imprinting in domestic fowl); Ian Howard, who was to become Henri's brother-in-law and subsequently had a distinguished career as a vision scientist; and Douglas Graham who published little on his own until much later in his career, when he also 'moonlighted' as a translator of French academic monographs.

Henri was originally hired as a personal research assistant to Fred Smith to help him with the revision of *Explanation of Human Behaviour*.[17] This had been published three years before and the second edition came out in 1960. The story of how he obtained this position bears the telling.

Apparently, Smith was down in London on business. Henri had been tipped off that he was looking for an assistant, probably by one of his Birkbeck lecturers since Smith had some connection with Birkbeck. So Henri invited him to dinner in their tiny basement flat in Belsize Park where Anne cooked them a nice meal and where much wine was consumed. According to Anne, Smith (who was partial to a drop[18]) got 'as drunk as a lord', so much so that at one point he asked Anne if she had a sister[19] because he was looking for a wife.[20] Anyway, inebriated though he might have been, Smith seems to have used the dinner as a job interview and was sufficiently impressed with Henri to offer him the job. And, although it cannot have been quite what he had envisaged for his first academic post, since beggars can seldom be choosers, Henri felt obliged to accept. Before long, after a holiday in France and Italy that summer, he, Anne and Michael moved to Durham in the autumn of 1954.

The two years they spent at Durham were not happy ones for Henri and Anne, however fruitful they eventually proved to be professionally for Henri. He hated the town ('Northern and grey'), not least because there were no decent bookshops or restaurants.[21] Ravetz, who got to know Henri quite well at Durham (they were both junior faculty), described Henri as 'in every way a fish out of water there' and recalled that he was particularly frustrated by the impossibility of finding the brand of (Continental) cigarettes that he favoured.[22] They lived in a small downstairs flat in a large house in Vincent Terrace near Durham station. Anne, too, must have found life hard, now living so far away from her friends and family and virtually looking after Michael single-handed. Perhaps a further factor contributing to her isolation was that she was pregnant with their second child when they moved to Durham. Paul was born in April 1955.

Ravetz, an American also with a Jewish background, had clear recollections of Henri whilst they were at Durham:

> He came across as very brilliant….(after) just three minutes talking to him, but with all the arrogance of a French intellectual.

He went on:

> He was very much the outsider, in every way…. I still remember him being rather cross with everything, smoking yet another continental cigarette … but, in his way, I could see a very warm and wonderful person … with a lot of tragedy.[23]

Ravetz remembered something else about Henri at Durham which, with the benefit of hindsight, seems somewhat prophetic. It seems that he did not have very progressive attitudes about women. Apparently, he once angered Ravetz's then wife, a strong feminist, with some rather antediluvian remark about women's capabilities. Here is how Ravetz related the incident:

> He did seem to have, along with all his other sorts of arrogance, […] about women…. He made some comment, which one would take as standard for French intellectual at the time, but my wife Alison took exception to it. He said something like, 'Oh, women can't make good academics', and she was livid.[24]

Ostensibly, Henri was appointed to assist Smith with research for his book but, according to Anne, his collaboration with Smith was fairly minimal, although Smith was unfailingly kind and helpful to Henri during their time together. As she put it, 'improvising like mad', Henri pretty much did his own thing in his two years at Durham. What exactly was 'his own thing' in that period? A clue can be gleaned from a letter he received in November 1955 from a Dr Lacy at Trinity College, Connecticut (USA), presumably in response to a letter that Henri had written to him.

> Dear Dr Tijel [*sic*]:
>
> The obscene words, in case you are interested, were:
>
> | | | |
> |------|-------|------|
> | Cock | pussy | twat |
> | fuck | tits | turd |
> | cunt | puke | ass |
> | fart | piss | crud |
> | shit | crap | snot |
>
> I shall be grateful for copies of any published or unpublished research you may have done or are doing in this area. At the present time, we are undertaking further studies in this line of investigation here at Trinity.
>
> Very cordially yours,

What was this line of investigation that Dr Lacy was pursuing that involved such sexually and scatalogically explicit material? Almost certainly, Henri's letter had been prompted by a publication of Lacy's two years earlier: 'Foreknowledge as a factor affecting perceptual defense and alertness'.[25] This was a report of two experiments which involved measuring the recognition thresholds of fifteen taboo and non-taboo words under various presentational conditions. The authors list the non-taboo words but, presumably mindful of their readers' sensibilities, did not publish the taboo ones, merely noting that they were 'readily recognizable Anglo-Saxon obscene words....13 of four letters, 1 of three letters, and 1 of five letters'.[26] Such a description corresponds exactly to the fifteen words in Lacy's letter to Henri.

The phrase 'perceptual defense' in the title of Lacy's paper refers to the phenomenon in which certain classes of words – typically taboo or emotionally laden ones – take longer to be recognised than equivalent neutral words. In an early demonstration of this effect, recognition thresholds for taboo words were 45 ms higher than for non-taboo words (this was approximately replicated in the Control conditions of Lacy's experiments).[27] Although the concept of perceptual defence owed much to the psychoanalytic idea of 'defence mechanism' in which the *ego* is thought to be capable of protecting the self from psychologically 'harmful' material, its first appearance in the experimental psychology literature was in a paper by Postman, Bruner, and McGinnies.[28] In that paper, Postman and his colleagues linked perceptual defence to two other phenomena – 'selective sensitization' and 'value resonance'.

Sensitisation is the *enhanced* ability to recognise or respond to certain classes of words, especially those that are consonant with a person's values, preferences or immediate concerns – the opposite, in other words, of perceptual defence. An auditory example of this might be the so-called 'cocktail party effect' in which we seem to be sensitive to hearing someone using our name across a noisy room.[29] Value resonance refers to the tendency for people's guesses about the identity of a very briefly presented word to be semantically associated in some way with the stimulus word, especially if that word has some personal relevance. An analogue of this in the visual domain would be the unfortunate tendency of some police officers to misperceive a harmless object in the hand of a Black person as a gun, as apparently happened in Sacramento in 2018 when an African American man was shot by police, thinking he was armed. He turned out to have on his person nothing more dangerous than a mobile phone.[30] What may happen in these cases is that the officers in question may hold (stereotypical) hypotheses that Black people are more likely to be armed than White people which, under conditions of poor visibility or the stress of a perceived emergency, get 'confirmed', resulting in their decision to shoot first and ask questions afterwards.

What was exciting – and controversial[31] – about these claims of Postman and his colleagues was that they seemed to imply the existence of psychological processes operating outside of conscious awareness, which serve to inhibit or sensitise people's responsiveness to the world around them. As Simon and Garfunkel might have sung in their famous song 'The Boxer', 'A man sees[32] what he wants to see and disregards the rest'. For some, that presented an insuperable (psycho)logical paradox: that somehow a person must be able to know something of a stimulus in order to resist (or be interested in) knowing it.

Despite his correspondence with Lacy, Henri never published any research of his own on perceptual defence. However, perceptual defence was emblematic of a radical new approach to perception and cognition in the 1940s and 1950s that came to be known as *The New Look*.[33] It was this perspective that clearly fired Henri's research interests, both in his two years at Durham and for the decade after. To understand the significance of *The New Look* and why it so captured Henri's imagination, it is instructive to consider some of the experiments that provided the empirical foundations of this radical new way of understanding perception.

Bruner and Goldman presented ten-year-old children with coins of various denominations (1, 5, 10, 25, and 50 cents) and, by means of a special apparatus, asked them to adjust the size of a projected disc of light so that it seemed to be the same size as each coin.[34] They repeated the procedure with another group of children, but, this time, instead of coins, they were asked to estimate the size of cardboard discs (exactly equal in size to the five coins). As a visual perception task, the two procedures are identical – to estimate the size of some circular objects. The children presented with the cardboard discs were approximately accurate: their estimates were +/- 5% of the actual size of each disc. Yet, those judging the sizes of coins consistently *over*estimated their size – by between 15% and 40%. And the more valuable the coin, the larger the errors (although this tendency did not extend to the 50 cent piece, which was judged as inaccurately as the 'quarters'). Still more curiously, when the children in the 'coin condition' were divided according to their social-class background, the better off middle-class children made smaller errors (between 10% and 25% overestimation) than the poorer working-class children (between 20% and

55%). Here, then, was an early demonstration that the process of visual perception was not wholly determined by the objective properties of the stimulus to be perceived (i.e., the diameter of the circular objects): instead, it seemed to depend both on the nature of objects (valuable or not) and on the people doing the perceiving (rich or poor).

A similar point was made a year later in another experiment by Bruner and Postman.[35] Again, the experiment involved estimating the size of some circular discs. Some discs had a dollar sign printed on them, others had a swastika. There were also some neutral discs with a rectangle and its two diagonals printed on them. This time, the people's estimates (the participants were students) were all somewhat astray, with greater errors for the larger discs. However, the discs with cultural significance to the participants (those with the swastika or dollar) were overestimated more than neutral discs: the 'dollar discs' were seen as biggest of all, followed by the 'swastika discs' (though it is doubtful whether this was a statistically reliable difference). Once more, from a purely psychophysical point of view, whatever was printed on each disc should not have affected how large it was seen. Yet it did.

It was not just the visual sense that seemed prone to overestimation effects. Dukes and Bevan asked six-to-ten-year old children to estimate the weights of some glass jars.[36] Some of these jars were filled with sawdust and sand and varied in weight between 176 gm and 224 gm (in 6 gm intervals). Other identical jars were filled with sweets and varied in weight exactly as had the sawdust-sand jars. The children's task was to say whether each 'stimulus' jar was heavier (or lighter) than a 'standard' jar (which always weighed 200 gm). In reality, there were always eight jars that were heavier and eight which were lighter than this 'standard'. What varied in the experiment was the nature of the 'standard' and the 'stimulus' jars. Sometimes they were the same (both filled with sawdust and sand, or both filled with sweets), sometimes they differed (the 'standard' being sawdust and sand and the 'stimulus' being sweets, or vice versa). The latter trials were of particular interest to the researchers since they expected that the children faced with estimating the weight of a jar of sweets (as compared to a jar of sawdust/sand) would overestimate that weight or, in the inverse condition, would underestimate it. So it turned out. In the condition where jars of sweets were compared to the jar of sawdust and sand, an average of over ten jars were thought to be heavier than the standard (remember, the correct answer is eight); in the reverse condition fewer than seven jars were thought to be heavier. When the standard and stimulus jars were the same, the children were remarkably accurate. Once again, the association of a stimulus dimension (weight) with something 'valued', as sweets surely were to young children, changed the perception.

Another line of enquiry in this emerging *New Look* tradition was the influence of our prior expectations on what we perceive. Most famously this was shown by Bruner and Postman who showed their participants playing cards under very brief exposure conditions.[37] On each trial, starting with a 10 ms exposure and gradually increasing it until the card was correctly described, the participant was instructed 'to report everything he saw or thought he saw'.[38] A simple enough task one might think, were it not for a piece of trickery by the experimenters. Every so often in each series of presentations, one or more of the cards shown would have something incongruous about them. For example, the three of hearts would look just like a normal three of hearts except that the three symbols would be black instead of their more conventional red. Similarly, the six of spades would be coloured red (instead of black) and the ace of diamonds black (instead of red). The first result of note was that these 'trick' cards took over four times longer to describe correctly than the normal playing cards (114 ms vs. 28 ms). What was even more interesting was the nature of the errors that participants made on the trials leading up to the correct perception. Very often they simply mis-described the trick card, calling the red six of spades simply 'the six of spades' or sometimes 'the six of hearts'. In other words, their expectancies, based on many years of playing snap, rummy, bridge, or poker, led them to 'see' (incorrectly) a black six of spades or a red six of hearts.

From these few examples of *New Look* research it is possible to discern some common themes. People (or 'organisms', as papers of that era quaintly described them) are seen as active agents, creating, confirming, and (sometimes) falsifying hypotheses about the world around them. Those constructive processes are seldom open to introspection but usually seem to operate without conscious awareness or, as we would say nowadays, 'implicitly' or 'automatically'.[39] Their perceptions and cognitions about any situation are not driven wholly by stimulus features of that situation but are also influenced by prior expectations, their personal values and motivations, or by their wider social background (or all of these). Perceptions, in other words, 'go beyond the information given', to borrow from the title of Bruner's influential later book.[40]

This vision of human psychology was quite at odds with several of the prevailing orthodoxies of the 1940s and 1950s.[41] It did not sit well with the Gestaltists who believed that perceptions – of shape, colour, movement, or whatever – were driven by various inherent features of the objects to be perceived and their configurations – so called 'gestalts' (whole shapes or forms[42]). For a similar reason, it was inconsistent with Ecological psychology which held that perceptions were entirely determined by the stimulus properties of the environment, thus obviating the need to posit any kind of internal hypothesis testing or matching.[43] It was also a challenge to the rather mechanistic conceptions of traditional experimental psychophysics which dealt only with the objective properties of stimuli (e.g., in terms of lumens of light illumination or decibels of noise), their physical impact on the organism's sensory apparatus (the receptors in the retina or the cochlea), the neural pathways to different parts of the cortex and the resulting 'percept'.[44]

None of these perspectives seemed able to explain why, in Bruner and Goodman's experiment, a 24 mm diameter disc might be seen by normal ten-year-old children as having a diameter of nearly 33 mm (or 36 mm if they were from a working-class background) if that disc happened to be a 25 cent coin, and yet as having a more veridical diameter of 24.5 mm if it is made of plain cardboard. The physical properties of the object (its size and circularity) are the same in both cases. Presumably the children all had normally functioning visual systems. And yet their perceptions differed according to the cultural value of the object (a coin or a worthless piece of card) and the cultural background of the child (working-class or middle-class).

The New Look was also an anathema to one of the other 'big beasts' of the psychological world at the time, Behaviourism.[45] Behaviourists, in their search to explain everything in terms of observable stimuli and learned behavioural responses, eschewed completely any reference to internal 'mentalistic' concepts like 'cognitive hypotheses' or 'personal values'. While it might have been possible to explain some of the surprising *New Look* discoveries in terms of learned (or inhibited) responses – for example, people's 'perceptual defence' against seeing or naming taboo words in could have been the result of a history of negative reinforcements associated with uttering swear words – it was much less obvious how the over-estimation of coin sizes could be similarly explained.

Beyond these intellectual challenges that the *New Look* posed to mainstream psychological theorising of the day, it also offered the promise of explanations that would be more relevant to the problems of everyday life. At that time there seems to have been a growing dissatisfaction with the rather reductionist accounts of human behaviour provided by traditional psychology, derived as they were from sterile conditions of the laboratory where all external factors had been eliminated or controlled. As Bruner and Goodman wittily observed:

> Given a dark room and a highly motivated subject, one has no difficulty in demonstrating Korte's Laws of phenomenal movement. Lead the subject from the dark room to the market place and then find out what he [*sic*] sees moving and under what conditions, and Korte's Laws, though still valid, describe the situation about as well as the Laws of Color Mixture describe one's feelings before on EL Greco canvas.[46]

In other words, advocates of *The New Look* sought to contextualise perception and cognition by deliberately introducing – rather than excluding – social, personal, and motivational factors into their theories and experiments. In this way, they hoped not only to provide more complete explanations of people's everyday perceptual experiences, but also to open up the possibility of linking cognitive processes to phenomena such as people's perceptions of and attitudes towards social groups. In this regard, it is not insignificant that Bruner, the main architect of *The New Look*, had been a PhD student of Gordon Allport, one of the most famous social psychologists of that time and the subsequent author of an influential book on prejudice.[47]

It is not difficult to see why Henri would have been seduced by this radical new vision of human psychology. His own personal history would surely have sensitised him to the possibility that cultural, political and historical events could have an influence on people's world views. We know that he had an early interest in prejudice (recall the scholarship winning essay he wrote to support his studies at Birkbeck). We know, too, from the 'boys' he looked after in the children's homes, from someone who taught him as a student (Hurwitz), and from a friend and colleague at Durham (Ravetz), that he had long cultivated an intense interest in culture and politics and had a restless enquiring mind – he was an intellectual to the bone. What, then, could be more exciting than to align himself with these revolutionary new thinkers who were threatening to upset the apple cart of conventional psychological theory and research?

Into print

Henri may not have been very happy living in Durham but he certainly made the most of the experience professionally. With the help of a grant from the Durham Colleges Research Fund, he conducted a series of experiments on perceptual over-estimation which aimed to refine methodologically one of the *New Look* studies I described in the previous section. At the same time, he was hard at work theoretically, seeking to synthesise several of the perceptual over-estimation effects reported by Bruner and others into a single explanatory framework. And if all this was not enough (for someone supposed to be a research assistant working full-time on someone else's project), he maintained contact with one of his former Birkbeck teachers, a collaboration which resulted in a publication on the philosophy of science.

Henri's first foray into research was squarely located in the *New Look* tradition. Inspired by the Dukes and Bevan study on the overestimation of the weight of jars of sweets, Henri conducted four experiments that were methodologically more sophisticated and also promised to offer a more general explanation of the effects of value on perception. He designed an ingenious piece of apparatus which consisted of a balance beam which protruded through a screen so that the weights (tin cans filled with lead shot) were on one side, with a knob for the participant to press down on the other (in order to judge the weight of each can). This way, visual cues were eliminated from the task. To associate 'value' with the stimuli, Henri arranged for small monetary tokens (worth three old British pence) to be given to the participant in some of the practice trials (where they were not required actually to give any weight estimates, but merely press down on the knob so they could feel the weight of the hidden cans). Depending on the experiment, these tokens arrived either after the *heaviest* weight had been presented (Experiment 1), or after the *lightest* weight (Experiment 2), or *haphazardly* (Experiment 3). In a fourth experiment, the tokens were worthless pieces of paper. After these practice trials, the weight estimation trials proper took place, but this time with no tokens being presented. The purpose of the practice trials was thus to establish in the participant's mind a systematic association between weight and value, at least in Experiments 1 and 2. In Experiments 3 and 4 (the 'control' experiments), no such association was established. On each trial, the participant simply had to estimate the weight of the can on the other side of the screen on a 1–7 scale. The next day the procedure was repeated but with no tokens being presented in the practice trials. This was the 'neutral' (or no value) condition.[48]

As might be guessed, Henri's principal interest was in comparing people's weight estimates in the 'value' conditions of Experiments 1 and 2 with their estimates in the corresponding 'neutral' conditions (formally equivalent to the comparison of estimates of the jars of sweets versus the jars of sand and sawdust in the Dukes and Bevan experiment, or the comparison of coins with cardboard discs in Bruner and Goodman's study). But his hypothesis was more subtle than the simple 'over-estimation' prediction in those earlier studies ('valued' stimuli being perceived as heavier or larger than 'neutral' stimuli). Instead, he predicted an 'accentuation' effect so that the weights in the 'value' condition would be perceptually differentiated to a greater extent – *at both ends of the weight continuum* – than the weights in the 'neutral' condition. So it proved. In the 'value' conditions of Experiments 1 and 2, the heaviest weights were judged a little heavier and the lightest weights a little lighter than the exact same weights in the 'neutral' conditions. As a result, the range of weight estimates (heaviest minus lightest) was reliably larger in the 'value' conditions than in the 'neutral' conditions. In Experiments 3 and 4, where there were no consistent associations between value and weight, the participants' estimates in the 'value' and 'neutral' conditions were indistinguishable.

Notice what a classic piece of *New Look* research this series of experiments was. In all conditions in the experiments, the perceptual task was identical – to estimate the weights of some hidden objects. Yet, simply by establishing a prior association between the stimulus dimension (weight) and some external value (money) in two of the experiments, he succeeded in systematically distorting participants' perceptions. Henri's explanation for the enhanced perceptual differentiation that he had observed went beyond the accounts that been offered hitherto. Bruner and Goodman had speculated that 'valued' stimuli in their coins experiment became perceptually accentuated because they are seen as somehow more 'vivid' and hence have greater 'clarity', 'brightness', or apparent size. Instead, Henri argued that the external imposition of value on an ordered series of stimuli (different weight tins in his case), meant that it was instrumental or functional for the participants to distinguish more sharply between the lighter and heavier weights; note that the perceptual biases occurred at *both* ends of the spectrum. This was the first of several empirical demonstrations of perceptual 'accentuation of differences' that Henri would publish over the next ten years.

Whilst conducting these experiments, Henri was also busy writing a theoretical paper in which he sought to bring together many of the previously published *New Look* perceptual bias experiments and explain them via an accentuation hypothesis[49]. In this article, he begins by noting that perceptual overestimation studies in the *New Look* tradition typically were of two kinds: those where the dimension of value was correlated with the stimulus dimension to be judged, and those where the value and stimulus dimensions were unrelated. Bruner and Goodman's coin experiment was an example of the former type (more valuable coins were also larger); Bruner and Postman's experiment involving discs with swastikas or dollar signs was an instance of the latter variety (the swastikas or dollar symbols, whilst 'value laden', were not systematically related to the size of the discs on which they were super-imposed).

In a careful analysis of these two kinds of experiments, Henri showed that the estimation biases in the first group tended to be in a form in which perceived differences *within* the 'value' series of stimuli were accentuated (relative to the differences within the 'neutral' series). He himself had shown this in his weight estimation experiments just described. He argued that such perceptual biases were 'good errors' in the sense that 'minimising the differences entails a risk of confusion; accentuating them is an additional guarantee of a successful response'.[50] On the other hand, where the 'value' dimension is uncorrelated with the stimulus dimension, then the most likely (and most functional) response errors will be to exaggerate the differences *between* the 'value' stimuli taken as a whole and the 'neutral' stimuli as a whole. The same accentuation principle is at work but this time it should not cause a consistent over- (or under-) estimation, merely a systematic perception of difference between the two groups of stimuli in whatever direction would distinguish them the most clearly. Although Henri's first experiments focussed on the first kind of accentuation (*within* a series), it was the second type of (*between* series) accentuation that was to preoccupy him subsequently since it had the more obvious implications for social psychology.

Henri had been scrupulous in his first empirical paper not to speculate about the wider implications of his results, but in this theoretical piece he took two paragraphs towards the end of article to extend his accentuation thesis to *social* perception. He quotes from a chapter by the vision psychologist Julian Hochberg who had speculated that:

> If a group of individuals is perceived as different from the non-group individuals, the perceived differences between those within the group and those outside the group will automatically be sharpened, and the differences perceived between members of the group (e.g., intragroup differences), and between those outside the group will be lessened'.[51]

In support of this hypothesis, Henri cites a study by Secord, Bevan, and Katz which had just been published as he was writing this paper.[52] In that study, (presumably) White[53] teenagers were asked to judge both the 'negroidness' and the likely stereotypic attributes of a series of ten Black and five White photographs. These fifteen photographs had been pretested to vary physiognomically in how typically 'Black' they appeared (in an ordered series from 'most Black' to 'most White'). The result from this experiment that Henri latched onto was that more prejudiced participants judged the 'Black' photographs to be 'blacker' than did the participants who were less prejudiced. He concluded that the former group had 'sharpened the differences' between the two groups of photographs, just as others might exaggerate the frequency of crimes among various social groups, especially if they had 'an axe to grind'.[54]

Henri's choice of the Hochberg quotation and the Secord experiment is revealing since it is the first published indication of his scientific interest in prejudice. Indeed, the hypothesis advanced by Hochberg would be tested by Henri in several of his later papers. Nevertheless, despite his brief description of one of the results of the Secord experiment, it is curious that he did not make more of two other findings that it yielded. One of these was the observation, specifically noted by Secord and his colleagues, that the stereotypic attributes associated with the ten 'Black' photographs did not vary much as a function of how 'black' physiognomically the photographs were. In other words, the members of the same category were perceived to be rather homogeneous in their possession of the dozen or so personality traits that comprised the stereotype measure. This is just what Hochberg had predicted. The second finding of interest, unremarked on by Secord and his colleagues or by Henri, was a discernible shift in the stereotypic ratings of the palest 'black' face and the darkest 'white' face – i.e., at the category boundary. This would appear to be a very nice example of the between-groups accentuation principle that Henri had spelt out earlier in the paper and so it is quite surprising that he did not make anything of it.

This first paper of Henri's appeared in *Psychological Review* then, as now, the premier journal for new theoretical ideas in psychology. In the same issue were articles by such luminaries as: S.S. Stevens, probably the most famous psychophysicist of his generation, proposing his famous 'power law' – that the relationship between one's sensation and properties of the stimulus that gave rise to it obey a power function; Frank Restle, an early pioneer in mathematical psychology, providing a formal description of learning via reinforcement; and Donald Broadbent, sketching out his famous model of selective attention and short-term memory for the first time. This was undoubtedly an auspicious start to Henri's publication career.

His second article was also a theoretical piece and was co-authored with R.S. Peters, a philosopher who had taught him at Birkbeck.[55] Entitled, 'Hobbes and Hull – metaphysicians of behaviour', it was a coruscating attack on reductionism in psychology, as represented by Hobbes, the seventeenth-century philosopher and scientist, and Hull, one of Behaviourism's leading lights. According to Peters and Henri, both Hobbes and Hull sought to provide a mechanistic psychological theory in which *all* human behaviours, be they individual actions, the activities of groups, or the workings of society, can be explained by and reduced to the operation of a few basic principles – the 'motions' of objects in Hobbes's case, stimulus–response associations and consequent physiological activity in Hull's.

Peters and Henri argued that this ambition of Hobbes and Hull was a 'pipe-dream', not just because of the enormous complexity of human behaviour but principally for logical reasons. So much of human activity, they argued, is 'rule governed' – that is, determined by norms and conventions – and it is to these rules, rather than to some underlying mechanistic processes, that scientists should look to understand and explain it. While the creation and workings of social norms necessarily depended on the physical existence and functioning of human brains, they could not be derived from them; they operated at logically different levels. Peters and Henri employed some telling and colourful analogies to make their case. Here are two of my favourites:

> In what sense can a physiological theory of the brain be said to *explain* a geometer's conclusions or a move at a game of chess?[56]

> To say that sensation and the conceptual processes are *nothing but* motions is rather like saying that kissing is simply the mutual movement of lips or that work is moving lumps of matter about.[57]

Although not mentioned in their article, it is interesting that, five years before, Solomon Asch had employed rather similar arguments against Floyd Allport, one of the doyens of (social) behaviourism.[58] Allport had sought to reduce all group behaviours to the actions (and interactions) of individuals – 'There is no psychology of groups which is not essentially and entirely a psychology of individuals', as he is famously remembered for saying.[59] On the contrary, argued Asch, in a way of which Peters and Henri would surely have approved, groups, though comprised of individuals, possessed a separate reality and often behaved in ways that could not be inferred from the characteristics and actions of those individuals.[60]

Henri's article with Peters was the first of many that he would publish that sought to combat reductionist thinking in psychology. Indeed, he devoted much of the latter part of his career to the establishment of a distinctively new social psychological approach, one that did not facilely reduce social phenomena to the behaviour of 'atomised' individuals, divorced from their group, intergroup, and societal contexts.

Notes

1 A. Tajfel interview, September 2014.
2 Letter from Baker, Britt and Co., June 1952.
3 This school still exists and has greatly expanded since Henri's day. It now offers co-educational education from nursery through to sixth form secondary, obviously catering for the well-to-do of London – in 2017 preparatory school fees were £5780 per term (www.northbridgehouse.com).
4 Letter from K. Warwick James, August 1953.
5 Letter from Ministry of Education, Curzon Street, June 1953.
6 www.bbk.ac.uk/psychology/ow-research/our-history
7 *Times* obituary, 27 January, 2012.
8 Pickersgill (1998).
9 Hurwitz personal communication, July 2017.
10 Jones (1998).
11 Hurwitz interview, July 2017.
12 E.g., Price-Williams (1978).
13 Hurwitz, interview, July 2017.
14 Hurwitz interview, July 2017.
15 www.durhamrecordoffice.org.uk
16 Ravetz interview, May 2017.
17 A. Tajfel interview, September 2014.
18 Ravetz interview, May 2017.
19 As it happens, she did. But she ended up marrying one of Smith's colleagues (Ian Howard) not him!
20 A. Tajfel interview, September 2014.
21 A. Tajfel interview, July 2017.

22 Ravetz interview, May 2017.

23 Ravetz interview, May 2017.

24 Ravetz interview, May 2017.

25 Lacy, Lewinger, and Adamson, 1953.

26 Lacy *et al.* (1953), p. 170.

27 McGinnies (1949).

28 Postman, Bruner, and McGinnies (1948).

29 Moray (1959).

30 www.nytimes.com/2018/03/28/us/sacramento-stephon-clark.html; Plant and Peruche (2005).

31 Howes and Solomon (1951); McGinnies (1950); Luchins (1950); Howie (1952).

32 'Hears' and 'hear' in the original 1970 song.

33 Krech (1949).

34 Bruner and Goodman (1947).

35 Bruner and Postman (1948).

36 Dukes and Bevan (1952).

37 Bruner and Postman (1949).

38 Bruner and Postman (1949), p. 210.

39 E.g., Wegner and Bargh (1998).

40 Bruner (1973).

41 For a witty account of the challenge that the *New Look* posed to orthodox psychology at the time, see Bruner (1983), chs 6–7.

42 E.g., Koffka (1935).

43 E.g., Gibson (1950).

44 E.g., Stevens (1951).

45 E.g., Hull (1952).

46 Bruner and Goodman (1947), p. 33.

47 Allport (1954).

48 The order of presentation across the two days of the experiment was counterbalanced.

49 Tajfel (1957). The footnote to this paper has an acknowledgement to Bruner (amongst others), thanking him 'for encouragement and advice'. Therein lies a tale: It seems that Henri had, indeed, sent Bruner a draft of the paper for comment. Bruner had replied, saying that the paper was fine, except that Henri should add Bruner's name a co-author. To Henri's credit, he did no such thing (Robinson interview, November 2016).

50 Tajfel (1957), p. 197.

51 Hochberg (1958) cited in Tajfel (1957), p. 202.

52 Secord, Bevan and Katz (1956).

53 Though the paper does not actually specify the ethnicity of participants.

54 Tajfel (1957), p. 203.

55 Peters and Tajfel (1957).

56 Peters and Tajfel (1957), p. 43; emphasis in original.

57 Peters and Tajfel 1957), p. 41; emphasis in original.

58 Asch (1952).

59 Allport (1924), p. 6.

60 See Brown and Pehrson (2019), ch. 1, for a fuller discussion of this debate.

5

OXFORD

1956–1966

'A city of perspiring dreams'

Henri's research assistantship at Durham was always only a temporary position. Even if it hadn't been, he would have been eager to move. As a place to live, it was never much to his taste and was far from the centre of gravity of British academia – the so-called 'golden triangle' of Cambridge, London, and Oxford. So he started applying for jobs. Anne remembers applications to Exeter and the London School of Economics, but they came to nothing.[1] Then a vacancy at Oxford came up. This was at an institution called the Delegacy for Social Training, based in Barnett House, Oxford.

Barnett House had been founded in 1914 with the help of some wealthy businessmen and philanthropists. Named after Canon Barnett, a Christian social reformer who had run Toynbee Hall in East London for many years, its aims were to provide adult education (especially in social work), and to be a centre for social and economic research and, crucially, *social action*.[2] In other words, it was far from being a conventional Oxford academic department with its well-heeled under-graduates, and staff devoted to a life of detached scholarly study.

Also, it was not a proper university department at all but a 'Delegacy'. In the labyrinthine structure of Oxford University, with its colleges, faculties, and depart-ments, delegacies occupied a rather peripheral position. Although they were over-seen by committees comprising senior Oxford academics, and received grants from the university, they sat outside the formal university structure[3]. Their staff members and students were not typically members of colleges with all the perks and status that such memberships entailed.

In 1956 the Director of Barnett House was Leonard Barnes, a decorated First World War veteran (Military Cross), former Colonial Office civil servant, one-time South African farmer, published poet, once a Parliamentary candidate for the Labour Party, and a member of PEN, an organisation of writers championing freedom of expression and opposing censorship.[4] Anne described their first meeting with him, a day or so before Henri's formal interview:

> We both came down. And Leonard Barnes invited us to their wonderful place outside Oxford (Water Eaton Manor). And he was simply amazed and enchanted by Henri because, for one thing, Henri couldn't care less about colleges and he was interested in what he was doing. He didn't care whether they were rich or poor, whether they had a name or not. We had the most wonderful weekend there. And he got the job.[5]

Henri's unusual background, with his experience of rehabilitating young people and displaced persons after the war (Chapter 3), probably told in his favour for a teaching position that was primarily concerned with the education of social workers and probation officers. And I am sure that his interest in socially engaged research, one of the cornerstones of the Barnett House ethos, would have come across in his conversation with Barnes. Whatever the reason, he received a letter from Barnes in April 1956, offering him a 'tutorship in social psychology'.

Although it must have been a relief to have obtained a permanent position, and at Oxford no less, I suspect it was not long before Henri started to feel somewhat irked by his marginal status in the university, especially as compared to colleagues at the prestigious Institute of Experimental Psychology, one of the leading psychology departments at the time, headed by Carolus Oldfield. Amongst those colleagues were Michael Argyle who had been appointed to a lectureship – *not* a tutorship! – in social psychology as early as 1952, and Brian Foss, his former lecturer at Birkbeck, appointed in 1957.[6] Several of these fully fledged lecturers would also have been fellows of an Oxford colleges, which usually entitled them to an additional stipend and various other benefits (e.g., free college dining). In Oxford parlance, such college fellows were 'Dons', and those without fellowships were 'non-Dons'.[7]

The first year or two at Oxford were not the easiest times for the Tajfels. Anne described it as a 'very awkward time', caused mainly by what she regarded as some Oxford snobbery. For example, they were never invited to Argyle's parties, only to those of the staff at Barnett House.[8] To Henri, already feeling himself to be something of an outsider, such formal and informal exclusions must have been keenly felt. As a family, the Tajfels moved to a new house in Bainton Road, a semi-detached house on the north side of Oxford overlooking some playing fields and sandwiched between the Oxford canal to the west and the busy Woodstock Road to the east. Meanwhile, Henri's relationships with his two sons continued to evolve. He had always had a somewhat troubled relationship with Michael; his relationship with Paul, on the other hand, was much easier. Dick Eiser, who was taught by Henri as an undergraduate, was later a colleague and got to know the family well, described Henri's relationship with the two boys:

They were very different. Henri seemed ashamed of Michael, clearly ashamed, not just embarrassed… [but] Paul could do no wrong. … It was so polarised, each was excessive…. He wanted to see his boys as an extension of himself and, in the end, neither was.[9]

Soon after their move to Oxford, there was a further significant development for Henri – he acquired British citizenship by naturalisation on 21 January 1957.[10] This was his third nationality in this his fourth decade. According to Anne, this decision to apply for citizenship may have been partly prompted by the Algerian War of Independence in the mid-1950s. In the time-honoured fashion of colonial powers, France attempted to suppress the rebellion by dispatching around 500,000 troops to Algeria, many of whom were conscripts.[11] Since Henri was a French citizen, technically he may have been liable to have been called up, not a very attractive prospect for someone with a young family at the beginning of his career, and especially for someone with his left-wing and anti-colonialist sympathies.

If Oxford's dreaming spires[12] were not quite as Henri himself might have dreamed of them, at least his colleagues at Barnett House were collegial and the atmosphere there congenial to research. In addition to Henri, there were four other staff: Peter Collison, author of a famous book on the Cutteslowe Walls in Oxford;[13] John Vaizey, later a distinguished economist; and Una Cormack and Dorothy Jackson, both tutors in social work (Figure 5.1). Henri, himself, lost no time in pursuing his research and writing.

In 1959, he had two papers published in the *British Journal of Psychology*. The first I have already described in the previous chapter.[14] The second was a purely theoretical paper, elaborating the ideas that he had presented in his *Psychological Review* article.[15] While in the latter he had been scrupulous in restricting his argument to biases in physical judgements, allowing himself just two paragraphs at the end to speculate on its implications for *social* perception, in this new paper there is a clear statement of intent from the outset, both in its title ('Quantitative judgement in social perception'), and in its first sentence:

The main concern of the study of social perception is with the ways in which people perceive, judge, and interpret the social objects and events which together amount to what is called their 'social environment'.[16]

The whole thrust of this paper was to argue that many of the accentuation effects that he and others had observed in the realm of estimating the size of coins or the weights of jars of sweets could be found in judgements of people, especially *groups* of people. Indeed, the main contention of the paper was that the same psychological principles could be used to explain all such accentuation effects. The article is replete with references to some of the leading social psychologists of the time: Asch, Pettigrew, Allport, and Secord.[17] In other words, for the first time, we

FIGURE 5.1 Barnett House Group, staff and students, Trinity Term 1960. Henri is second from left seated. Barnes is seated in the centre and Peter Collison is on the right of Barnes.

Source: Reproduced with permission from Barnett House's jubilee year publication, Old Students' Association: Barnett House, 1914–1964.

see Henri clearly expressing an interest in some important questions in the field of stereotyping and prejudice.

In the body of this second 1959 paper, Henri formally defines a number of perceptual situations in which a judgement dimension is (or is not) correlated in various ways with another attribute of value, and where an arbitrary classification is (or is not) superimposed on the original dimension. For example, suppose we are asked to make judgements of physical length about a number of lines, each of which differs systematically in length from its neighbours. Such a task poses no special perceptual difficulties and will be performed more or less accurately. But now suppose an arbitrary category division (A/B) is superimposed on the series so that the shorter lines all happen to fall into category A, and the longer lines into category B. Henri's prediction was that the addition of this classification would instigate a perceptual accentuation effect, such that the shorter lines would be seen as a little shorter and the longer lines a little longer. From his *New Look* functional perspective, to which he was now firmly wedded, such a bias makes sense since it is facilitating – making more efficient – our perceptual judgements. Our brain can draw on the additional information provided by the A/B classification to make a more rapid, even if slightly erroneous, judgement about the line lengths.

Other articles quickly followed. He replicated Bruner and Goodman's coin estimation study with a much larger sample of British adults using, instead of cardboard discs as control stimuli, rare British and South African nineteenth-century coins.[18] Broadly similar results emerged: the sizes of the current and familiar British coins were overestimated more than the sizes of the rare and unfamiliar coinage. He also re-analysed some data from a team of Canadian social psychologists which had shown that Canadian participants' evaluations of voice recordings of the same bilingual speakers depended both on the language in which they spoke (French or English) and the preferred language of the participant (francophone or anglophone).[19] The Canadian researchers had reported that anglophone listeners generally preferred speakers talking in English, a form of linguistic ingroup bias. However, the francophone listeners also preferred the English speakers, apparently a form of *outgroup* bias. In a careful analysis of the data, Henri showed that both these phenomena were examples of category accentuation, in line with his predictions. This commentary presaged, by nearly twenty years, some arguments that he would later make about intergroup relations between different status groups.

It was also apparent that Henri was taking seriously his new pedagogic responsibilities at Barnett House. Within a year of his arrival there, he wrote an article for the *Bulletin of the British Psychological Society* (the 'house journal' for Society members) on the problems of teaching psychology to social workers, probation officers, community organisers, and the like.[20] Rejecting the type of psychology that such students were typically taught (usually a heavy dose of psychoanalysis), Henri argued forcefully for a rigorous 'evidence-based approach' focussing on cognitive, motivational and developmental processes and 'a consideration of the individual in relation to the society in which he [sic] lives'.[21] That final phrase encapsulates Henri's developing perspective on social psychology, one which he would articulate at greater length in his later writings.

Perhaps the phrase 'taking seriously' in the previous paragraph is a slight exaggeration. According to Juliet Cheetham, who was taught by Henri and who subsequently became his colleague at Barnett House, Henri was not the most conscientious teacher:

> He wasn't an easy tutor to have and when you were having a tutorial with him he was always doing other stuff when he should (allegedly) be listening to you… he was a bit of a laughing stock to be honest, and girls particularly would say, 'Oh, you don't get much teaching.'[22]

From Oxford to Cambridge (Mass.)

Henri had been at Barnett House only a year or so when he began to make plans to leave, even if only temporarily. Whilst at Durham, he had written to Bruner, the king-pin of the *New Look* movement (Chapter 4), who was spending a sabbatical year at Cambridge. In his letter, he mentions his experiments on the role of value in biasing judgement and notes the congruence of his results with Bruner's own work.[23] Henri was planning to go to London (to attend some lectures by Jozef Nuttin), and he asked Bruner for a meeting. Bruner agreed and arrangements were made for the two of them to meet on 1 December in a seminar room in University College London. This, to steal that famous last line from the film *Casablanca*, was the beginning of a beautiful friendship.

From the start, the two men obviously hit it off. In an exchange of letters over the next few days, they were soon discussing ideas for new experiments, including the naturalistic replication of Bruner and Goodman's famous coin estimation experiment that I described above,[24] and arranged to meet again. At this stage, their relationship, whilst obviously cordial, was still quite formal, at least to judge from the salutations in their letters ('Dear Professor Bruner', 'Dear Tajfel').

There is then a frustrating gap in their correspondence (between late 1955 and early 1958), but they must have been in regular contact because, by January 1958 Henri was discussing a year's leave of absence to visit Bruner in Harvard. This was no easy matter. One of his Barnett House colleagues had also applied for leave in the same period and, understandably, his department was unhappy over the prospect of losing two colleagues for a whole year. Bruner had seemingly offered Henri the prospect of paid employment at Harvard for 1958/59; the problem was how to convince Oxford to let him go. He had the support of Oldfield, but others on the relevant committees were proving recalcitrant. In an amusing postscript to his letter to Bruner (now 'Jerry'), Henri likens these machinations to life in Renaissance Italy:

> Suggested question for an examination in modern history: Discuss the similarities between Oxford of mid-twentieth century and some aspects of Italian political life at the beginning of the Renaissance.[25]

Nevertheless, over the next months, Henri managed to circumvent all the obstacles that Oxford had placed in his path. He persuaded one of his Durham colleagues (Douglas Graham) to take over his teaching for the year; Bruner's offer of work, a Research Assistantship for nine months (salary $6000), was firmed up; and he began pursuing a Fulbright grant to defray travel expenses. Perhaps his case was also helped by the news that he had just been awarded a £3000 British Government grant (from the Department of Scientific and Industrial Research (DSIR)) to investigate various effects of categorisation.[26] It says something about Henri's chutzpah and powers of persuasion that, as a still largely unknown academic, he managed to persuade a senior American academic to take him on as a visiting researcher, a government fund to release a sizeable sum of money (probably worth over £150,000 at today's prices), and his new employer to give him a whole year's leave of absence after being in post for only eighteen months or so. But persuade them he did and, on 5 September 1958, the Tajfel family set sail from Southampton on the ocean liner *The Haseatic*[27] (Figure 5.2).

The choice of Harvard as a place to spend his fellowship is not hard to fathom. In 1958, Harvard was something of a 'Mecca' for budding psychologists since it was home to many of the most eminent figures in the discipline, as well as some of its 'rising stars'. In no particular order, on the Harvard faculty at the time were: B.F. Skinner, the doyen of Behaviourism; Henry Murray, a clinical psychologist

FIGURE 5.2 Henri and Anne en route for America in 1958.
Source: Photograph courtesy of Anne Tajfel.

and originator of the famous Thematic Apperception Test; David McClelland, later author of an influential theory of motivation; the cognitive psychologists, George Miller and George Mandler, well known for their discoveries in human memory and psycho-linguistics; S.S. Stevens, one of the founding fathers of experimental psychophysics; Gordon Allport, then at the height of his influence in social psychology after his seminal book on prejudice; his PhD student, Stanley Milgram, the future originator of controversial experiments on obedience; Robert Bales, a pioneer in the study of small group dynamics and leadership; Tom Pettigrew, already starting to make his name in the psychology of racism; Roger Brown, who would go on to write one of the most widely read social psychology textbooks in the 1960s; and, of course, most significantly of all from Henri's point of view, Jerry Bruner, a polymath who straddled cognitive, developmental, and social psychology, and with whom he had now struck up a warm professional and personal relationship.

I suspect that Bruner must have been an irresistible role model for Henri. They were of the same generation (Bruner was just four years older), both had a (secular) Jewish background, and both had experienced the Second World War, albeit in very different ways – Henri as a PoW for five years, Bruner as an American army intelligence officer, eventually being posted to Paris after the liberation of France in 1944.[28] But while the war and its aftermath had so cruelly disrupted

Henri's university education and early career, it seems hardly to have made a dent in Bruner's. He published his first papers – on rat behaviour – before he had even begun his PhD with Gordon Allport. His third paper, a historical review of social psychology, was published a year later,[29] and throughout the war and after it he published a string of book reviews and articles on the measurement of public opinion. By 1945 he had obtained a coveted tenure-track position at Harvard, from where he initiated the *New Look*. By 1958, the year Henri joined him at Harvard, he had published over fifty pieces, which included two co-authored books and one edited volume. Henri had published just three articles by then.

The range of Bruner's early publications is astonishing. In this period, he published no fewer than *four Psychological Review* papers, including perhaps his most influential paper of those two decades, 'On perceptual readiness'.[30] In this article, Bruner attempts to summarise and integrate all the discoveries of the *New Look* movement with the help of two concepts, 'accessibility' (the sensitivity of perceivers to certain kinds of stimuli because of their personal histories or current needs), and 'fit' (the functional utility of certain cues in people's environment). It also contains the arresting sentence:

> All perceptual experience is necessarily the end product of a categorisation process.[31]

This was a dictum that Henri himself took to heart in his own thinking over the next few years.

In addition to these theoretical articles, Bruner published dozens of experimental studies on perception, all promulgating the *New Look*, but also papers on animal behaviour, Freud, public opinion and sociometric choices. Clearly, Bruner was a man with a prodigious intellect and an impressively catholic array of research interests, just the kind of scholar that Henri would soon aspire to be himself.

Any awe (or envy) that Henri might have experienced in becoming better acquainted with Bruner at Harvard did nothing to stop a close friendship blossoming between the two men, a relationship that would endure for the next twenty years or more. In his autobiography, Bruner would later write:

> Perhaps I am a natural wanderer,[32] although the record may conceal it, for in my academic career I served twenty-seven years at Harvard and eight at Oxford, which, I realize, is not a flighty career. But for all that, I have an attachment for friends in distant corners of the world that I have kept alive not only by correspondence but by visits. There was, for example, Henri Tajfel, whom I knew first when he was a young don at Durham in the north-east of England. He came to visit me to talk shop at Cambridge, England, in the mid 1950s and, if I remember rightly, a year never passed after that in which we did not visit. In some ways we were brothers. He was one of the people in the world with whom sharing was essential.[33]

My interview with Bruner, two years before he died, was also suffused with the warmth of his feelings for Henri:

> It was far more than a collegial relationship; we got to be good friends …. he was great fun, because, if we disagreed, he would say, 'I wonder how we came to these different views', and took us as two scholars and friends working on (and) coming to the task with quite different backgrounds. It made for a good relationship…. We used to go on long walks together and talk about the sad state of psychology and how we could somehow bring it to the point where it would deal, not only with the 'inside out', so to speak, the personal, but also what the effects of membership in a cultural group (would be). And we found that a strong link together – we both believed it. And he had a combination of being well read and knowledgeable but, at the same time, having a marvellous intuition…. We must have shared some very deep views about the relationship between cultural pressures and internal personal pressures … and he had a wonderful sense of humour. His interest in psychological phenomena did not stop when you got out of the lab. He was a generalist. A charming guy.[34]

Nearly all Bruner's memories of Henri's time at Harvard were of this kind – affectionate anecdotes about conversations they had had together. He rarely mentioned any actual collaborative research that they did together, despite the fact that a substantial article did appear under their joint names just two years later, based on experiments that had been designed and conducted in Henri's year at Harvard. This paper was an investigation into individual differences in the breadth of people's judgement categories.[35] They believed this topic to be important for several reasons. People may use narrow or broad categories depending on the risks associated with over-exclusion in any particular situation. A sentry on the lookout for potential enemy soldiers might be wise to adopt a broad category of 'foe' (better safe than sorry), while an inspector carrying out quality control checks on parachutes should use a rather narrow definition of 'safe', given that the consequences of overlooking a faulty parachute are likely to be severe. In addition, people's general preferences for narrow (or broad) categories were thought to be related to personality factors. People high in authoritarianism, for instance, might typically use narrow categories in their moral or social judgements. Bruner and Henri's hypothesis was that 'narrow' categorisers should, in general, be more sensitive to situational changes since they are more concerned about being right than 'broad' categorisers are worried about being wrong. This was what they found in three experiments involving young children making estimates about the number of dots presented briefly in slides.

This early interest of Henri in individual differences in categorising is curious, given his later vociferous disparagement of individual differences approaches in social psychology.[36] Still, curious or not, he went on to publish three other papers on this topic.[37]

Part of the arrangement for Henri's visit to Harvard seems to have been that he would teach a junior-year tutorial on Social Perception for Social Relations

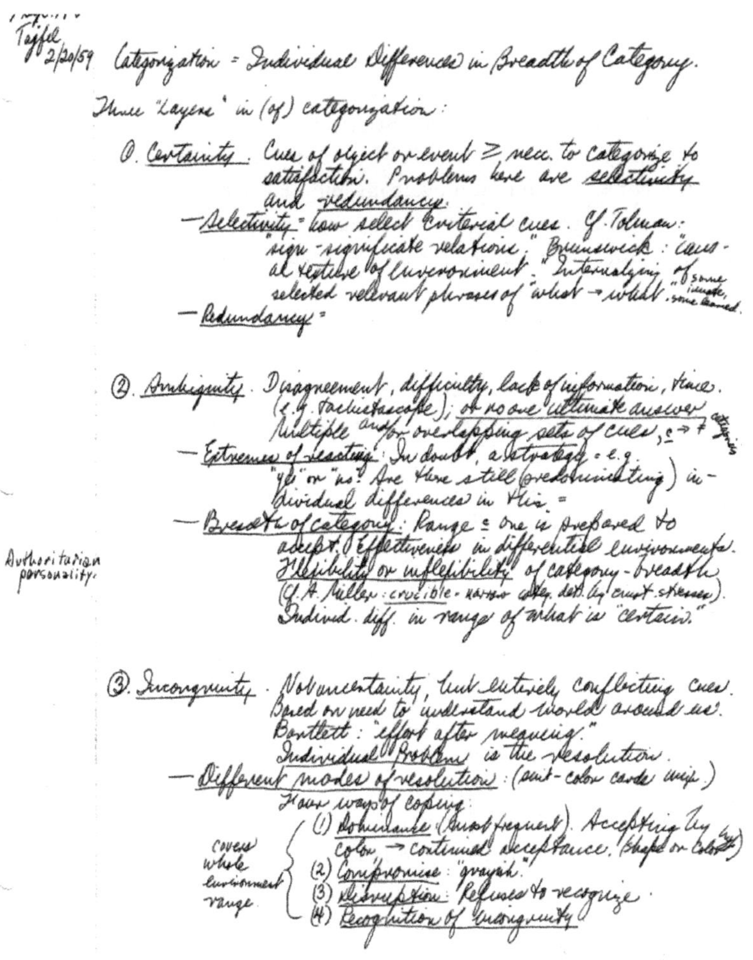

Tajfel 2/20/59 Categorization = Individual Differences in Breadth of Category.

Three "Layers" in (of) categorization:

0. Certainty. Cues of object or event ≥ nec. to categorize to satisfaction. Problems here are selectivity and redundancy.
—Selectivity: how select criterial cues. Cf. Tolman: "sign-significate relations." Brunswick: "causal texture of environment." Internalizing of some selected relevant phrases of "what → what." (some innate, some learned)
—Redundancy:

(2). Ambiguity. Disagreement, difficulty, lack of information, hence (e.g. tachistoscope); or no one ultimate answer. Multiple and/or overlapping sets of cues; c → ? categories
—Extremes of reacting: In doubt, a strategy: e.g. "yes" or "no." Are there still (predominating) individual differences in this =
—Breadth of category: Range ≤ one is prepared to accept. Effectiveness in differential environments. Flexibility or inflexibility of category-breadth (cf. A. Miller: crucible - narrow categ. det. by ... stresses). Individ. diff. in range of what is "certain."

Authoritarian personality

(3). Incongruity. Not uncertainty, but entirely conflicting cues. Based on need to understand world around us. Bartlett: "effort after meaning." Individual Problem is the resolution.
—Different modes of resolution: (suit-color cards exp.)
Have ways of coping:
(1) Dominance (most frequent). Accepting by color, → continued acceptance. (Shape or color)
(2) Compromise: "grayish."
(3) Disruption: Refuses to recognize.
(4) Recognition of incongruity

covers whole environment range

FIGURE 5.3 A student's notes of one of Henri's Harvard lectures.

Source: Notes courtesy of David Winter.

students, as well as giving guest lectures in other courses (e.g., Bruner and Miller's course on cognition). David Winter, who would go on to become a prominent political psychologist, attended those tutorials and lectures as an undergraduate. One of the lectures was devoted to the very topic of that Bruner and Tajfel paper I have just presented. Winter's notes from that class are shown in Figure 5.3, where some of the issues discussed in Bruner and Tajfel paper are clearly legible (especially under section 2 of his notes). Also of interest is Henri's discussion of the Bruner and Postman's playing card experiment (Chapter 4).

Even though Winter was only an undergraduate, he and Henri became friends, perhaps because Winter was one of the more interested members of that tutorial class. He had written a paper about Henri's *Psychological Review* article and then had responded positively when Henri had asked someone from the class to help him with a new experiment he was planning. Here is how he remembers Henri:

> This Tajfel guy was kind of interesting. He had a kind of effervescent, bubbly personality. He was enthusiastic. He would sort of lean forward in his chair. He was constantly in motion verbally and maybe even physically. (He said) he was developing a theory and he had this experiment he wanted to run and maybe somebody from our group would like to work with him.[38]

The experiment he had designed was a replication and extension of an early size over-estimation study which had appeared to contradict one of his key hypotheses in his *Psychological Review* paper.[39] The new experiment seemed to resolve the contradiction and resulted in Winter's first publication.[40] Although, in truth, Winter had been little more than an assistant running the experimental sessions, it was not untypical of Henri's generosity when it came to co-authorship that he added Winter's name to the paper, telling him he was 'too tall for just a footnote'.[41]

Winter also commented on the relationship that had developed between Henri and Bruner that year:

> I gathered that he and Bruner did not always see eye to eye. And he (Henri) made some joke about it, 'Well, it's not Tajfel *and* Bruner, it's Tajfel *versus* Bruner (or the other way around)'. In any case, there was the sense of, I would say, not animosity, but fairly profound intellectual divergence.[42]

The Tajfels lived in a flat on Sacramento Street in Cambridge, a typical tree-lined Cambridge street, a comfortable 15 minute walk from Bow Street, where Bruner had his laboratory and where Henri worked during his year at Harvard.

It seems to have been a sociable time for Henri and Anne. There were Wednesday parties to which the faculty wives were invited. Anne remembers meeting Gordon Allport, Roger Brown, and George Mandler. Henri also played poker with some colleagues, although Anne had to impose a strict limit on his gambling because of the modest nature of Henri's salary. One of the leading lights of the poker school was Frederick Mosteller, the famous game theorist.[43]

There can be no doubt about the significance of Harvard for Henri. It introduced him to the 'great and the good' of twentieth-century psychology, with some of whom he was to develop lasting friendships (especially Allport, Bruner, and Mandler). It was also a very productive period for him: he conducted several experiments that led to two publications;[44] he also wrote a fifty-page chapter entitled 'Social Perception' for a book by his Oxford colleague, Argyle.[45] This chapter was a lucid and up-to-date review of the field and a practical guide for conducting experiments on the topic. The influence of his Harvard experience in this chapter is obvious: it includes extensive accounts of experiments by two of his Harvard colleagues, Roger Brown and Bruner, as well as a reference to his unpublished correspondence with Stanley Milgram. The chapter locates Henri squarely within social psychology, discussing such topics as conformity, stereotyping, prejudice, and impression formation. There are also glimpses of the theoretical issues that would come to preoccupy him later in his career. Discussing the importance of the social environment for human cognition, he wrote:

'It is an extremely complex environment, and in order to make sense of it we must simplify, classify and label. *An individual may be of interest to us either as a member of a special gang or class of people, or in his unique capacity.*[46]

Elsewhere in the chapter, he notes how the famous Katz and Braly experiments[47] on national stereotypes had so successfully eliminated all information about specific members of national groups that they were 'in a sense, experiments in a vacuum'[48] (Chapter 6). And, finally, whilst discussing the role of emotional involvement of the perceiver on the use of stereotypes he takes a swipe, *en passant,* at the idea that prejudice and stereotyping can be understood as a problem of individual personality type:

It can hardly be assumed that a majority of people living in a country, a district, or a city have suddenly acquired a personality structure described by Adorno et al. (1950) as 'authoritarian', or that a majority of them are latently authoritarian, waiting only for an occasion to demonstrate these latent tendencies.[49]

Above all, though, Henri's year at Harvard provided a powerful affirmation of his nascent identity as an experimental social psychologist. As Anne put it:

It was where he blossomed … he immersed himself in it. (And his colleagues there) didn't care about his lack of PhD, which college he went to etc. They treated him as one of their equals…. He became an academic and he was going to stay an academic. And also he knew he was going to stay a social psychologist; that was certain.[50]

What had also become certain by the end of this year at Harvard was the personal importance of Henri's relationship with Bruner. Two weeks before his departure, in his tiny spidery hand-writing, Henri wrote a poignant letter to his friend:

3 Phillips Street   13/9/59
Dear Jerry,
    You are welcome to keep this letter, though I would hate the prospect of anyone outside you ever reading it. As a naturalised British citizen I have a duty to keep stiff at least one of my lips. Besides, I have passed the age of 40, and it seems to me that I should have outgrown by at least 25 years (a quarter of a century!) the writing of letters such as this.
    It all started as I was examining in more detail this morning the IBM data of the ambiguity experiment. They are exciting and intriguing (*really* so!) – and we shall talk about them when you get back. At the same time, in this room your presence is strong, obvious and insinuating. All this suddenly somehow

fused together, and I felt the urge of writing to you. First, I brushed it aside – an adolescent sort of thing to do. And then I thought: so what? Maybe at some point of one's life it is possible to become sufficiently mature not to mind lapsing into adolescence from time to time. Just the same, it is very possible that I will destroy this as soon as it's written. Then again, perhaps I will not.

In about a fortnight we shall say goodbye to each other and I at least will do it very awkwardly – I am no good at managing stage exits gracefully. The nonsense I am writing now is probably an effort to compensate. It is being written in the good old tradition – that we presumably share – of not knowing what the next sentence may bring.

Enough of hedging. Probably the main thing I want to say is that I should like you to know that this year you made a friend (two friends, counting Anne). I feel the need of saying this primarily because at the beginning of the year things were not what they could have been – we both know why, and there is no need going into it again. However, I still feel that even later this initial drag was to some extent with us, exercising a sort of progressively remote control. This letter is an effort to wage total war on this drag, and, incidentally (you know me too well not to have understood it already), an offering on the altar of my guilt feelings. I owe you a lot for this year. Specifically, I owe you a lot for having done so well at removing (sometimes forcibly) many of my intellectual inhibitions. I find it hard to discover what I have done in return. I have the feeling that this discrepancy was due to that initial unease which lingered on and on. You are a self-centered bastard. So am I. You are a self-centered bastard who manages to be extremely sensitive to other people. This, I think, is also the case with me.

I care about my relationship with you. I think that you also care about your relationship with me. The resulting mixture of ingredients such as these cannot be an easy one. But there is no reason why it should be. Put it this way: one remains young as long as one grows and changes. You have helped me a great deal (probably more than you know) to do just this. I have failed to do this in return because I have *discovered* you too late in the year – and this again because several smoke-screens were thrown. Therefore, I feel the *need* (in the proper unadulterated sense of the term) of offering something in return. I don't know what to call it: a secure friendship is a clumsy term, but it will do. It includes irritation and the right (given to me by myself) of expressing it when I feel I should. But it is secure and you have it.

I will *not* destroy this letter; though I feel now it is one more clumsy stage exit.

Henri.[51]

A man in a hurry

Harvard, then, provided a hugely stimulating tonic for Henri, both professionally and personally. He had been exposed to some of the most influential psychologists in America, and had been given the time (and the resources) to conduct new research and to write about the relevance of psychophysical experimentation to social phenomena. On his return to Oxford in the autumn of 1959, he threw himself into his work with all his usual vigour: he lost no opportunity to present at conferences (BPS Conferences 1959, 1960 (two papers), 1962, 1965; International Congresses, 1960, 1966; European social psychology conferences, 1963 and 1964 (Italy), 1966 (France)); he published several papers that grew out of the collaborations he had established at Harvard, and also started to write and broadcast for non-specialist audiences; he set about rectifying a gap in his CV (the absence of a PhD); and he had a new grant to direct.

By any standards, Henri's first seven years at Oxford were unusually productive. He published ten articles in scientific journals, more than any contemporary British social psychologists in the same period (Argyle (6), Himmelweit (1), G. Jahoda (9) and H. Beloff (8)). But more telling than the mere number of publications is the impact that his articles have had on succeeding generations of scholars. At a recent count, his papers between 1956 and 1963 had attracted more citations (886) than those of the four aforementioned social psychologists combined (669).[52]

In addition to these academic papers, in May 1960, he broadcast a short talk on the BBC General Overseas Service on the topic, 'The Nation and the Individual', the text of which subsequently appeared in *The Listener*, the BBC house magazine.[53] The article is worth considering in some detail because it is the first time he published a social psychological analysis of a real-world social issue (nationalism). It also contains his first published thoughts on group identification, a concept with which he would later become preoccupied:

> We can say that the psychological basis of nationalism is an individual's identification with a large group of people whom he [*sic*] conceives to be his nation. And, like most other group identifications, nationalism can vary in two ways at least: first, in the intensity of the reactions that it may arouse; and, secondly, in the nature of those reactions.[54]

A little further on he wrote:

> Nationalism can scale the heights of emotion for which a parallel can hardly be found; it also encompasses a tremendously rich range of feelings: love and hatred, joy and anger, pride and humiliation, admiration and contempt.[55]

Although these observations are unexceptionable, it is interesting to see him mentioning emotions so explicitly in connection with social identity; this would not always be the case in his later writings (Chapter 8).

He notes, too, that our (national) group identities are situationally contingent; it is rare that people feel nationalistic all the time and in every context. This flexibility in our experienced identities was also to become a hallmark of his later theorising. Nevertheless, he also speculates that the nation may be one of two elemental and especially potent identities, the other being the family.

The impact of his recent year in America is also clear. He discusses the acquisition of national identification in young children, drawing on some early work by American psychologists on the development of ethnic identification.[56] In a chillingly prescient comment on how deeply entwined American national identity is with gun ownership, he quotes a four-year American boy:

> I was an American when I had my gun, but when they took my gun away I wasn't an American any more.[57]

It is hard to read those words without a shiver of apprehension, especially as it is estimated that there is now approximately one shooting every eight school days in US schools.[58]

The article concludes with an interesting discussion of some potentially positive aspects of group identification:

> a strongly felt identification with one's national group, or with any group, need not be aggressive; it need not be nationalism 'against', it may be nationalism 'for'. It could then become a useful psychological lever for constructive action, and it could help to preserve a diversity of identities which, in our age of rapid mass communication, seems more worth preserving than ever.[59]

Here, Henri was drawing a distinction between patriotism and chauvinism, an issue that was to receive proper theoretical and empirical attention by social psychologists only many years later.[60]

This first venture into broadcasting and popular journalism was soon followed by others. In August 1962, he did another broadcast for the BBC on the topic of 'Similarity and Dissimilarity', probably for the Third Programme. This was an engaging rehearsal of some of the technical arguments and empirical findings about classification and perceptual judgement that he had already published in various academic articles. Then there was an article on prejudice and stereotypes that he wrote in *Race,* the house journal of the Institute of Race Relations.[61] Once again, Henri's gift for writing lucidly – and, at times, wittily – for the non-specialist is apparent. In this article he brilliantly summarises what was then known about the links between prejudice and stereotyping, as ever being careful not to claim too much for his discipline:

> No psychologist who has a sense of proportion about the possibilities and the limitations of his discipline would claim that prejudice can be 'explained' and dealt with on the psychological level alone. This is an infinitely complex problem, and in its handling we need the cooperation of legislators, social workers, economists, historians, sociologists, psychologists and many others.[62]

He then takes the reader on a guided tour of the classical perceptual overestimation studies on which he had cut his teeth a few years before, and gives an early preview of his findings on the effects of categorisation. A recurring idea in this article is the normalcy of stereotyping and its functionality for everyday living:

> Stereotyping can, therefore, be considered an inescapable adjunct to the human activity of categorising. As such, it is neither 'bad' nor 'good', it is there and presumably it serves some purpose in our continuous efforts to simplify the world around us.[63]

He finishes with a careful discussion of the possibilities (and the limitations) of educational programmes to reduce prejudice in young children, underlining the importance of gearing interventions to the child's level of socio-cognitive development and the concrete realities of their daily lives. Many of the ideas he presented in this *Race* article he reiterated in subsequent essays in *New Society*, *Common Factor* and in other broadcasts for the BBC.[64]

Henri also did some consultancy work for an advertising agency (Dorland Ltd) at about this time. In his papers, are two memoranda which are proposals for some market research, presumably to be overseen by Henri, to support two of Dorland's clients, Control Motor Oil and Pirelli car tyres. Although they are undated, one of them refers to some previous market research conducted in June 1959, shortly before he returned from America. Both proposals suggest a conventional mix of qualitative (interviews) and quantitative (questionnaires) methods to gauge potential customers' attitudes toward some new products. It is possible that money was a little tight in the Tajfel household on their return to Oxford. They just had Henri's (tutor) salary to survive on and maybe that was why he agreed to do such commercial work.

Perhaps, too, it was financial motivation, as well as a desire for professional advancement, that led him to make a series of applications for Chairs not long after his return from Harvard. Correspondence in Bruner's papers reveals that he had asked Bruner to write recommendation letters for professorial positions at Leicester and Cardiff (1960), the New School for Social Research in New York (1961), Hull (1962), University of Western Ontario (1963) and, a little later, University of California at Santa Cruz (1966). In 1961 he also applied for a seven-month Fellowship to work with Herman Witkin in New York to pursue some research in clinical psychology.[65] It is indicative of Henri's unbounded self-confidence that the first two of these applications were made when he had but five publications to his name! Truly, he was a 'man in a hurry', as one of his later colleagues described him.[66] Another, a colleague at Barnett House, described him as 'enormously ambitious'.[67]

Since obtaining his bachelors degree in 1954, Henri had needed to work to support himself and his family. This financial imperative had denied him the opportunity to obtain a doctorate. Fortunately, he was able to take advantage of a London University regulation that allowed external candidates to submit a PhD thesis based on previously published work. So this is what he did in January 1961, submitting a 151 page dissertation entitled, 'The role of value in the formation of a scale of judgements'. This was essentially an amalgam of three of his publications,[68] 'bookended' by introductory and concluding chapters. Because Henri prepared his thesis in this way, he did not have a formal supervisor for it. Nevertheless, it is significant that the first person he records in Acknowledgements is Bruner, underlining once again the pivotal role that he played in Henri's early career. Others acknowledged were Bailey (an Oxford biometrist), Audley and Jonckheere (two psychologists from London, the second of whom was often a source of statistical advice for Henri), Howarth (Hull), Brown (a lecturer at Birkbeck), and his former Durham colleagues, Sluckin and Graham.

Without doubt, though, Henri's main professional preoccupation on his return to Oxford was the direction of the grant he had obtained from the DSIR. Alan Wilkes, his research assistant on the project, described Henri like this:

> Henri was deeply impressive as a thinker, in the sense that I found he thought very quickly and could get through to an argument, the essence of it, quite fast. But he would only put a fraction of what he was thinking into what he was saying, so you were forever four or five steps back in the chain.[69]

Working with Henri could also be quite a challenge:

> The other thing about Henri, and working with Henri, particularly as a research assistant, he was always impatient to know the results of an experiment and, if they hadn't turned out as he expected, that was always the fault of something or other, not so much the hypothesis. And he did get <u>very</u> involved in the research and the outcomes. But we tended to design the experiments together … in that sense, he wasn't dictatorial. He would listen, for a bit…. Impatience is the thing which comes through most clearly, either in terms of impatience with the results or with getting the next experiment up and under way.[70]

In all other respects, though, Henri was a most considerate and supportive supervisor. He insisted that the university enrolled Wilkes into the staff pension scheme, even though it wasn't then a normal part of a research assistant's contract. He also was very helpful in assisting him to find another position once the research project was over.

The principal publication to emerge from this project was called 'Classification and quantitative judgement',[71] which currently stands as Henri's seventh most cited journal article (379 citations[72]). Undoubtedly inspired by Bruner's bold claim – 'perception involves an act of categorisation'[73]– the central hypotheses of this paper were taken from his two earlier theoretical articles on accentuation:[74] when an arbitrary classification is imposed on a set of stimuli in a systematic way, one can expect a perceptual *exaggeration* of the differences between members of different categories, and a corresponding *diminution* of the differences among members of the same category.

They tested these ideas by showing participants a series of eight lines drawn diagonally on large sheets of cardboard (one line per sheet). The lines ranged in length from 16.2 cm to 22.9 cm, each differing from its neighbour by around 5%. Sometimes the lines were presented successively in order of length, sometimes they were all visible simultaneously (again ordered by length). The participants' task could not have been simpler: s/he had to estimate the length of each line in centimetres.[75] One week later, they returned for repeat testing. The experimental manipulation involved the presentation of one additional piece of information to each card. This was the letter 'A' or 'B'. In one condition ('Classified'), the four shorter lines were labelled 'A' and the four larger lines 'B'; in another ('Random'), the letters appeared randomly on each card so that there was no correlation between category membership and length; in the Control condition, no letters appeared. A second experiment was a partial replication of the first.

The results only partly supported Henri's predictions. The expected between category accentuation was visible, especially in the estimates of the lengths of the crucial 'boundary' lines (line 4 in class A and line 5 in class B). The true difference between these two lines was 0.9 cm, yet those in the Classified condition saw it as 1.8 cm (combining across the two experiments), an overestimation of 100%. Participants in the Random and Control conditions were fairly accurate – their mean estimated difference was 1.0 cm. But support for Henri's second hypothesis (reduced differences within each category) was much less evident. He chose to examine it by looking at the slopes of each participant's estimates of the four lines within each category – flatter slopes would indicate reduced differentiation or assimilation. Across both experiments and at both testing points there was no sign that the slopes in the Classified condition were any smaller than in the Random or Control conditions; if anything, they were slightly steeper. The only – albeit tenuous – evidence for within category assimilation came from an internal analysis of one of the experiments where he compared participants' first six estimates from the first session of experiment 1 with their final six estimates. Here he did find that the within category slopes in Classified reduced more than did those in the other two conditions.

What should we make of this paper which has achieved something of a 'classic' status in the field, routinely being cited in social psychology textbooks, even if not always accurately?[76] Gordon Allport certainly seemed to appreciate the paper. He wrote to Henri shortly after its appearance, noting its implications for social stereotyping. Henri was obviously flattered to have received his feedback.[77]

At a purely technical level, these experiments suffered from a number of deficiencies: the degree of control in the presentation of the stimuli was quite rudimentary, even making allowances for the technology at the time – in some sessions, the sheets of cardboard were displayed on tables and participants could wander around and inspect them as they wished; the order of presentation of stimuli was not randomised; participants had to make their estimates in (to them) unfamiliar metric units of length.[78] It is also worth noting that this paper was not the first to demonstrate accentuation effects caused by the imposition of a classification. Campbell had already shown both accentuation *and* assimilation effects in an experiment where participants had to learn the spatial position of nonsense syllables, half of which contained the letter 'E' (associated with positions towards the left) and the remainder which contained the letter 'X' (associated with the right).[79] Using more realistic materials (photographs of faces), Secord and his colleagues had observed that participants' personality judgements of Black and White faces manifested both within ethnic category assimilation and between category accentuation (especially at the Black–White boundary),[80] and Razran had also found intergroup accentuation in liking by the simple expedient of adding stereotypical names (for Jewish, Italian, Irish and Euro American communities) to previously unidentified photographs.[81] None of these earlier papers is cited in the Tajfel and Wilkes paper.

All that said, this paper has stood the test of time, still routinely cited in ten or more articles a year (unlike the earlier papers on the same topic which have sunk without trace). Although it has seldom been replicated exactly – a study by Corneille and colleagues[82] is a partial exception – the between category accentuation effect that it uncovered has been observed in several other domains[83] and so, too, though somewhat less reliably, has the within category assimilation phenomenon that it failed to find.[84] One reason for the durability of this article with Wilkes, and why I have dwelt upon it at such length here, is that it is emblematic of Henri's life-long concern with how the human mind is predisposed to create or exaggerate difference where none may actually exist. It also paved the way for his later experiments on intergroup discrimination and formed one of the corner-stones for his theorising on identity, another of his enduring legacies.

Meanwhile, Henri's position at Oxford took a decided turn for the better with the arrival of Chelly Halsey as Director of Barnett House in 1962. Halsey was an up and coming educational sociologist who would subsequently exert considerable influence over successive British governments' educational policies. Unlike Barnes, he was an active researcher and he was keen to create an environment at Barnett House that would be more conducive to his colleagues' research also. He soon became aware of the marginal status of the Barnett House staff, including Henri. As we know, they mostly only held 'tutorships' and were excluded from participation in College Life. As he put it:

> The place (Barnett House) was run down both in itself and in the mouths of mainstream Oxonians. '*Nous allons changer tout cela*' was the motto to be adapted from the French Revolution. There were three urgencies. First, all tutors should become full-time lecturers and be offered fellowships. Second, there should be an immediate and marked expansion of social research. Third, the department teaching should be extended to include undergraduates, a master's degree in social work, BPhil in sociology, and doctoral students attached to all senior members.[85]

With the help of Oldfield, then Professor of Psychology at Oxford, he secured a new position for Henri, 'University Lecturer in Social Psychology'. He was still based in Barnett House (and not in Experimental Psychology that he would surely have preferred), but at least he now had a formal status within the university. Halsey was also instrumental in obtaining 'Senior Member' (later 'Fellow') status for Henri at the newly created Linacre House (subsequently, in 1965, Linacre *College*). It also helped that John Bamborough, the first Principal of Linacre, was a neighbour of the Tajfels in Bainton Road.

Among the other Senior Members invited along with Henri were Gilbert Ryle and Isaiah Berlin, the famous philosophers, and Hugh Blashcko, a physiologist and later Fellow of the Royal Society, and seven others.[86] Membership of Linacre carried no additional stipend (unlike some of the wealthier Oxford colleges) but it did offer free meals and an entertainment allowance of £20 per year (soon increased to £36). Apparently, the latter was drawn on extensively for wine at Linacre dinners,[87] something Henri might well have appreciated – later, he became well known for his enthusiastic consumption of alcohol. Henri seems to have been quite an active member of this new college. In thirty-nine meetings of the Governing Body between October 1963 and June 1966, he gave his apologies only nine times, and he is quite often recorded as having been deputed to form a sub-committee to carry out some delegated business.[88]

His new status as a university lecturer seems to have done little to increase his enthusiasm for his teaching duties at Barnett House, however. Juliet Cheetham, a member of staff at Barnett House in 1965, recalls that Henri was not the easiest of colleagues:

> He was a temperamental and difficult colleague. There would be shouting in the common room upstairs and Olive (Stevenson) would shout at him that he hadn't taught them, and he would say he was much too busy and he was going off elsewhere. And Chelly (Halsey) would come in and say, 'Ah, we have to make allowances for our Eastern European colleague.[89]

So, now Henri was 'Dr Tajfel', a university lecturer, and (almost) a bona fide Oxford college fellow to boot, none of which would have done any harm to his national – and increasingly, international – standing in the world of psychology. Unfortunately, whatever material and psychological benefits that he might have accrued from these titular changes did not seem to have been transferred to his physical health. At about this time, Henri experienced three serious episodes of ill health.

In 1960, during a holiday in Italy, he slipped a disc in his back, which laid him up for the holiday and which was to become a chronic condition for him – '*la maladie d'élite*', as he complained in a letter to Bruner in September of that year. Wilkes, his research assistant, recalled another health issue occurred whilst Henri was visiting Ragnar Rommetveit, a well-known social psychologist of language, in Norway. Apparently, he discovered blood in his urine which, on further investigation back in Oxford, turned out to be due to pre-cancerous growths in his bladder that had to be cauterised. A third health scare was a heart attack which landed him in the Radcliffe Infirmary in the summer of 1963. This experience did nothing to deter him from smoking however (he had a forty–a–day habit for much of his life). Wilkes remembers visiting him in hospital:

> There he was, smoking away and calculating – he'd taken his calculator with him. He'd made a special plea to be allowed to smoke because it would be worse if he didn't. And I remember Anne saying: 'I'm not surprised because Henri would barter food for cigarettes in the concentration camp, and that was his predilection.[90]

Even whilst convalescing at home, with instructions from his doctors to cut down, he showed no inclination to do so. Anne told me how she once hid his trousers in an attempt to prevent him leaving the house to buy cigarettes. Undaunted, Henri nipped out to the nearby corner shop in his pyjamas and dressing gown![91]

A Crisis of Identity

For all this bravado, his heart attack seems to have provoked some earnest self-reflection. Amongst Henri's papers is a four-page typed document entitled, 'A Crisis of Identity'. I have no idea for whom it was intended and, as far as I know, it was never published.[92] I reproduce it here in full, incorporating the handwritten corrections that he made to the typescript. Not only does it reveal his penchant for irony and self-mockery, but it is revealing also about his own doubts (and aspirations) for his newly adopted discipline of social psychology.

> First draft
> A Crisis of Identity
> The readers (if any) will forgive me, I hope, a short biographical note to introduce these meditations. But such a note is necessary, I feel, for those who wish to understand how my crisis became overdetermined.
> A short time ago, Oxford University bestowed on me a new title in which the term <u>Social</u> became rather prominently coupled with <u>Psychology</u>. At about the same time I landed in hospital – where I still am while writing this – with a mild heart condition and a strict doctor's injunction to keep quiet. One dares hope that there is no causal connection between the two events. But I know of no better way of raising around one's bed a host of minor ghosts than doctors' order to leave one's frenzies behind, to behave for once like all the other people who apparently have not a care in the world, and if they have one apparently never pay the slightest attention to it.
> After a few days in hospital during which my peace and quiet were only disturbed by increasing suspicions about the criteria for selection of nurses at Radcliffe Infirmary (or do they all seem more beautiful from a supine position?) a minor ghost appeared. It came in the form of: 'Who am I?' It is, of course, not an unfashionable ghost, but mine had a nasty twist to it. When I asked: 'What do you mean 'Who am I'?', it said: 'I mean professionwise.' I guessed then that it was a ghost of mixed origin.

I tried to argue. I said that the question was unanswerable. Everyone who is With It knows that it's definitely in bad taste nowadays to try and define one's discipline. Everyone knows that they all merge into one another, that the range of uncertainty is wide and fluid, that the same subject-matter can be approached in different ways by asking different questions about it, etc., etc.

It was no use. He said sharply: (it became he by that time as it grew and grew) 'Who do you take me for? Do you think this is a first introductory tutorial? Don't forget where you are.'

I sank into my pillows, thinking and worrying about my heart. But then, in the recesses of it, I had to admit that he was right. This was an answer which might, with luck, just do at an introductory tutorial; it would disintegrate in the hands of an enterprising undergraduate at a second meeting.

Indeed, who am I? Some years ago, I remember, I had a call from the B.B.C. They asked whether I would take part in a series of six talks on nationalism, and talk about it from the psychological point of view. My first reaction was that of panic. Nationalism? What is it? But, showing great courage, I accepted. It's always possible, I thought, to open a few books and crib twenty minutes of wisdom (at a ratio of 1.5 guineas per unit) to feed the masses. The next wave of panic was much stronger, I scanned the indexes of 7 (seven) textbooks of social psychology. The word appeared in one only. When, in that particular one, I read the five-and-a-half lines devoted to the issue I was wishing I had never been born.

Presumably, some aspects of nationalism are of some slight interest to social psychologists. Why so much about social attitudes and so little about nationalism? So much about leadership and so little about totalitarianism? So much about small groups and so little about isolated communities? So much about 'cognitive maps' and so little about teaching geography?

But now came my crushing reply to the bore: I am not a vulgar technician, I said to him, and anyhow the vulgar technicians would not be here had it not been for pure scientists, such as my friends and I, who spend devotedly their lives studying processes, aiming at theoretical understanding, providing foundations from which one can generalize about social behaviour. We do know, my friends and I, that there are a few social problems here and there, some of them not quite solved; however, one must have patience. It is only through the slow and painful accumulation of theoretical knowledge that, one day, social psychology will be able to….etc., etc.

He came back at me with his old ploy about the first tutorial, and threatened that if I did not stop talking nonsense he would start behaving as an intelligent student should at a third tutorial. This was an effective threat, and it sent me on a fool's errand into another vicious circle.

What processes, what theoretical understanding and what generalisation? Then I thought of a good one: in a very respectable symposium someone once wrote that from his quantification of the emotional dimensions of security and insecurity in group life the following prediction could be arrived at: If you leave a small child in a strange room on its own it will be more afraid than if left in a strange room with a friendly adult. This prediction was experimentally confirmed. (Interested readers can obtain the reference from me on receipt of a stamped addressed envelope). Here we had a theory (the dimensions of security and insecurity were miraculously and impressively quantified by the author in the form of a ratio) and we had generalization which was undoubtedly valid.

I was very proud of it. Thinking of this theoretically-based generalization was like opening floodgates. Dozens more came hurtling through, all claiming attention: the keener you are to belong to a group the harder you will work at it; the less you agree with a group the more your friends will try to convince you that you are wrong; the more cohesive a group the greater its likelihood to agree about a number of things; the more the members of a group agree about a number of things the greater the cohesiveness of the group....(Approximate references for all these generalizations can also be sent on request).

But the ghost remained unconvinced. He became quite rude and challenged me to produce something more startling. As I did so with some difficulty and a great number of qualifying conditions, he accused me of living beyond my means, entirely on H.P. – Hedging Parameters, he explained scornfully. He produced a few out of his pocket and as soon as he put them on the table they began to multiply by mitosis. Finally, we had on the table 1,024 generalizations, each applying to one unique case.

At this stage, I clutched at my heart and nearly gave up. To my surprise, as soon as I did this he relented. He said: 'There, there.....Don't worry so much. I know from long experience that there are in the world some real problems and there are in the world some real theories. The very fact that you are so worried makes me think that you and your friends will one day find some way of putting the two together.'

But I am still worried. Did he say that just because he wanted to be kind?

Henri Tajfel

Meanwhile, Henri continued to be a hospitable academic host. Bruner had already visited him at least once since his return from the States. David Winter, the undergraduate he had met at Harvard and employed as a research assistant, obtained a Rhodes Scholarship and visited him at Oxford (Figure 5.4). He recalls:

[he treated me] as a colleague. The opposite of arrogant. Seemed to be interested in whatever I was talking about, whether it was the food in Bulgaria, or McClelland's theory of achievement motivation, or Keynesian economics, or whatever. He was kind of a respectful listener.[93]

Although Henri's appetite for work in this period was prodigious, he loved to play too. Wilkes recalls:

FIGURE 5.4 Anne, Paul, Henri, and Michael, Oxford 1962.
Source: Courtesy of David Winter.

One of the things he loved to do was to say, 'I'm not going to work this afternoon; I'm off to the cinema'. And he would then spend the afternoon at some film. He <u>loved</u> doing that.[94]

It is also at about this time that we have the first intimation of another facet of Henri, his habit of making uninvited and usually unwanted advances to women. Here is how Wilkes recalled one occasion:

Although I never witnessed it directly, he did chase other female students. I remember one party where the babysitter came over and said, 'please could I go home with her when Henri drove her back?' And I said, 'Yes, OK', and then got caught up in the most convoluted argument with Henri as to why I had to come back: 'I want to pick up some cigarettes'; 'No, I'll buy them for you'. I insisted and he was not happy about that.[95]

On another occasion, a former student and his girlfriend went to lunch with Henri. Afterwards, she complained about Henri's 'roving hand' on her leg. This will not be the last time that I shall have occasion to note Henri's proclivity for sexually harassing young women.

Spreading his wings

The next four years at Oxford (1963–1967) were important ones for Henri's career since they were marked by a significant broadening of his research interests and professional activities, both of which involved a notable increase in his international wanderings. He had always loved to travel but now his work took him further afield and more frequently than it had ever done before.

He continued to publish prolifically. His CV records that in those four years he had 18 publications of various kinds to his name. In strictly scientific terms there was little of great originality or import: in academic journals he published a few more articles arising out of his collaboration with Bruner on individual differences in categorisation;[96] there were two more minor papers from his DSIR grant;[97] and one on inter-category similarity and stereotyping.[98]

However, if his writing for academic outlets yielded little of interest, he started to publish more frequently for a wider audience and it is in these more accessible articles that his metamorphosis into a fully fledged social psychologist can be observed. He wrote on prejudice in a chapter in a BBC publication, *Colour in Britain*.[99] He wrote on judgemental biases and children's concepts of and preferences for their own and other countries for *New Society*,[100] and encouraged one of his research assistants to write on children's consumption of war comics for the same publication.[101] Together with a with a young Oxford social anthropologist, John Dawson, he edited a book on overseas students' experiences of racism in Britain, *Disappointed Guests*.[102] He wrote a heartfelt plea in the *Bulletin of the British Psychological Society* for more investment by wealthy Western countries in international cooperation and training in social psychology, an article which he also used as an advertisement for the recently inaugurated *European Association of Experimental Social Psychology*, an organisation into which he would pour much of his energy over the following years.[103] And, finally, he wrote an essay in *The Eugenics Review* (of all places!) on 'Cooperation between human groups', an incisive critique of both 'instinctivist' and 'utilitarian' accounts of intergroup relations.[104]

Apart from the bizarre choice of journal, this article is notable for his first published formal definition of what constitutes a group:

> I shall define a group as a category of people fulfilling two criteria: the first, that an individual identifies himself [*sic*] as belonging to that category; and the second, that this identification is to him of some emotional significance.[105]

This period of Henri's career also saw him achieve considerable success in winning grants, both to support his own research and to promote the research of others. Following the DSIR grant on categorisation that he had obtained soon after moving to Oxford, he managed to persuade the American National Science Foundation (NSF) to fund his research on individual differences in categorising. I suspect that this must have been with the assistance of Bruner since NSF does not normally directly fund the research of scholars not affiliated to an American institution.

More American grant success followed, this time for a large cross-cultural study of children's national and international attitudes, sponsored by the United States Air Force of Scientific Research via its European outpost, the European Office of Aerospace Research (AF-EOAR). This also was a substantial grant. Lasting for four years (1963–1967), it involved data collection in seven countries and employed three research assistants at Oxford. The project tackled several research questions. The most basic of these was to assess when in childhood a preference for one's own country over others emerges, and how this favouritism develops during middle childhood (6–12 years). Henri was also interested to relate these nationality preferences to children's factual knowledge of countries – is increased familiarity with countries related to inter-nation attitudes? And then there were several subsidiary questions relating to cognitive decentering (ability to judge other countries according to the same principles as one judges one's own), balance theory (is the enemy of our enemy our ally?), and how foreigners are depicted in children's comics.

Although these issues were not particularly new – Piaget and Jahoda had already investigated many of them[106] – what was innovative about the research were the techniques that Henri and his colleagues devised to assess children's attitudes. A key one was an indirect measure of nationality preference. Rather than asking children outright what they thought about a country, which would have been susceptible to social desirability biases, Henri and his colleagues came up with an ingenious two step procedure. In the first session the children, tested individually, were given 20 photographs and asked how much they liked each one on a simple four-point scale (see Figure 5.5 for some examples). Then, two to three weeks later, they were given the same pictures and asked to decide which were of people of their own nationality and which were not, putting them into two clearly labelled boxes (e.g., 'Italian', 'Not Italian').[107] A simple measure of nationality preference is to compare the mean liking scores of the pictures (elicited in session 1) placed in the two boxes. A positive difference indicates that those placed in the own-nationality box were liked more than those in the other-nationality box. In most countries, the difference scores were clearly (and significantly) positive, and they were usually a little higher for younger (6–8 years) than older children (9–12 years).[108]

However, two exceptions to this general own-country preference were observed: Scottish children and Israeli children of Arabic origin seemed to favour the 'other' group ('English' and 'European Israelis' respectively).[109] Henri interpreted these 'anomalous' findings with reference to the children's apparent sensitivity to the socially prevalent devaluations of their nationality/ethnicity, drawing a direct parallel with similar ingroup derogation observed amongst ethnic minority children.[110] He would return to these observations in his later writing on identity.

What was it like to work with Henri on this project? Charlan Nemeth, one of his research assistants, remembered the experience fondly:

> Nic (Johnson) and I felt we were Henri's favourites in those days. We were really treated in many ways as colleagues, in the sense that we felt that how

FIGURE 5.5 Some examples of photographic stimuli used in the cross-cultural project on children's national and international attitudes.

we thought about a phenomenon, or how we wanted to analyse it, or what we thought mattered, were all taken seriously.[111]

By any standards, the grant was a considerable success. Henri succeeded in coordinating data collection in cities as far-flung as Glasgow, Haifa, Leiden, Leuven, Naples, Oxford, and Vienna, no mean feat in an era when email and international video conference calls were still the stuff of science fiction. It kept Henri and his colleagues busy on the conference circuit for several years and resulted in no fewer than six publications.[112] And while it is true that few of these papers ever attracted much attention from the scientific community (the highest lifetime citation count from this set is currently only 35), the key findings on the early emergence of own national/ethnic preference have proved replicable.[113] But the real significance of the project and its associated publications was that it established Henri's reputation firmly as a mainstream *social* psychologist in the eyes of his colleagues in Britain and elsewhere.

Henri wrote one other article in this period which is worth considering briefly. Entitled, 'The formation of national attitudes: a social psychological perspective', it was essentially a reprise of the *Listener* article on nationalism he had published nine years before, but this time at much greater length and for a more academic readership.[114] It is a wide-ranging essay on how we should conceptualise and study nationalism, simultaneously a critique of biological and personality perspectives and a plea for a contextual approach in which social psychological processes take proper account of the political and economic structures in which they are embedded. This would be a recurrent theme of much of his writing over the next decade. It also contains an almost throw-away remark that group identifications may develop without the presence of hostile outgroups. This was a clue that he was already thinking about investigating the minimal conditions for group attachment and intergroup discrimination (Chapter 6).

He seems to have been popular with the US Air Force because in 1964 they also funded him to carry out a survey of social psychological research in new and developing countries, with a view to considering how international research might best be fostered. This led to another grant in 1967 for 'training in research on psychological aspects of social change in developing countries', funded by the Social Science Research Council.[115]

Quite how Henri found time to do so much writing (of articles and grant proposals) is a bit of a mystery because, over those four years, he travelled *a lot*: 1963, Sorrento (Italy), Greece, Israel; 1964, Washington DC, Ljubljana (Slovenia), Ontario (Canada, one month visit), Frascati (Italy); 1965, Chicago, Cologne (Germany, visiting professor); 1966, Royaumont (France), Warsaw, Czechoslovakia, and Moscow. To these trips, we should also add his efforts to promote social psychology in developing countries, and frequent committee meetings in Belgium, France, Italy, and the Netherlands in connection with the European Association of Experimental Social Psychology (EAESP), then in its infancy but, like any new-born, requiring the constant care and attention of its 'midwives', of whom Henri was surely one of the most assiduous (Chapter 6). Of these many trips, I want to enlarge here on just two – to Poland and Israel.

The visit to Warsaw in June 1966 is of note mainly for personal reasons. Ostensibly, it was to give a research seminar at the Warsaw branch of the Polish Sociological Society. He spoke about his ongoing research with children and national identity. It seems also to have been something of a reconnaissance visit on behalf of the recently formed organisation of EAESP. However, of greater interest is the fact that this was almost certainly the first time he had returned to Poland since he had left it thirty years before; it may also have been his last. During his stay, he took the opportunity to visit Włocławek. Janusz Reykowski remembers Henri telling him about this a few years later, about twelve years after their first meeting in 1959 (Chapter 2). This time Henri was able, if unwillingly, to speak Polish to Reykowski:

> He told me that he visited Poland … and he visited the place of his birth (Włocławek). And it was for him a traumatic experience. Because, he said, the town, the buildings were exactly as he remembered them. But there are no people that he knew. Everything was completely foreign. It was a recollection of the tragic experience that he had.[116]

This anecdote was confirmed by Charlan Nemeth, then working on the children and nationality project. As she recalled it:

> He'd been on a trip back to Poland, and it frightened him … he was very worried he wouldn't be able to leave, that they might keep him there. It sounded – to use contemporary language – like a mini panic attack.[117]

The details of his visit to Israel in May 1962 are a little less clear. It is possible that it was for professional purposes. Alan Wilkes recalled that he had quite close political links with Israel. Apparently, members of the then Israeli cabinet periodically used to visit him in Oxford. But there was a personal reason for the visit too. A former school-friend from Włocławek days, Alexander Fuks, had emigrated to Israel in the 1930s and Henri stayed at his house in Jerusalem for the duration of his stay. Fuks' son, the historian Gideon Fuks, found the first part of a handwritten letter from Henri to his parents, dated 1 June:

> Dear Bela and Olek,
>
> I must apologise for not having written earlier. On my return home, there was a tremendous amount of accumulated work coinciding with the beginning of term. In addition, I had to go to Paris unexpectedly for some committee meeting. I hope that all this together amounts to a reasonable excuse – plus the fact that I am one of the worst correspondents in the world.
>
> I hardly know how to thank you for your kind and unfussy hospitality in Jerusalem. In one way or another, this whole visit seems to me now – at only about one month distance – like a dream. It was an emotional experience of greater intensity than I ever expected it would be. It left very strong but not easily defined feelings – perhaps one way to describe them would be to say that no other place can be quite 'home' again. I couldn't bear the idea of not returning, and there is a new element to one's life which puts Oxford life in a completely new – and unimportant – perspective. But there is no use boring you with all this. You must have seen many half-immigrants and immigrants manqués. One day perhaps I will be able to spring a surprise on you.[118]

From this fragment, it seems clear that the visit had been a deeply affecting experience for Henri. I was particularly stuck by the sentence which refers to his feeling 'at home' in Israel, in a way that he apparently did not at Oxford.

Earlier, I noted how Henri initially felt himself to be somewhat marginalised at Oxford. Despite acquiring a lectureship and a college fellowship, and despite his growing international reputation as a researcher, this sense of being somewhat on the periphery of Oxford life seems to have remained with him. Here is Charlan Nemeth again:

> He loved Oxford and yet I think he felt he never really belonged. He wasn't at the high end colleges (like Christchurch or Magdalen or Balliol). I think

he also felt that his professional advancement would be hampered by the fact that he was not quintessentially British. Whereas, by contrast, Michael Argyle was......Henri didn't fit the prototype of an Oxford 'don'.[119]

His continued exclusion from the Institute of Experimental Psychology did not help. Although he occasionally attended research seminars there, and even gave one himself,[120] it was clear that he would be unlikely to be able to transfer his lectureship there from Barnett House. As for the prospect of obtaining a Chair in the Institute (or in Barnett House, for that matter), that was even more remote. In those days, Oxford clung fast to the tradition that there was only a single professor in each department; the idea of internal promotion to a Chair was not introduced at Oxford for another thirty years. Meanwhile, he would have been aware that several of his new-found European colleagues did already occupy Chairs: Himmelweit (LSE), Gustav Jahoda (Glasgow), Marie Jahoda (Sussex), Moscovici (Paris), Mulder (Utrecht), Nuttin (Leuven), and Rommetveit (Oslo), to name but a few. Thus it was that at some point in 1966, Henri started to think seriously about a move that would secure him a professorial title as well.

Notes

1 A. Tajfel interview, September 2014.
2 Smith, Peretz, and Smith (2014).
3 Halsey (1996); Smith *et al.* (2014).
4 Smith *et al.* (2014).
5 A. Tajfel interview, September 2014.
6 www.psy.ox.ac.uk/about-us.
7 Harré interview, October 2017.
8 A. Tajfel interview, September 2014.
9 Eiser interview, October 2016.
10 UK National Archives, Kew.
11 www.Brittanica.com/event/Algerian-War.
12 The explanation for my chosen title of this section ('A city of perspiring dreams') should now be apparent. This phrase is a nice pun on Matthew Arnold's famous description of Oxford as 'a sweet city of dreaming spires'. It is uttered by a character in Anthony Quinn's (2017) novel *Freya* (Penguin).
13 Collison (1963).
14 Tajfel (1959a).
15 Tajfel (1959b).
16 Tajfel (1959b), p. 16.
17 Asch (1951); Pettigrew, Allport, and Barnett (1958); Secord, Bevan, and Katz (1956).
18 Tajfel and Cawasjee (1959).
19 Tajfel (1959c).
20 Tajfel (1958).
21 Tajfel (1958), p. 25.
22 Cheetham interview, December 2017.
23 Letter to Bruner, 14 November 1955; HUA box HUG4242.5.
24 Tajfel and Cawasjee (1959).

25 Letter to Bruner, 23 January 1958; HUA box HUG4242.5.
26 Letter to Bruner, 24 May 1958, HUA box HUG4242.5.
27 Letter to Eleanor Horan, Harvard, 19 August 1958, HUA box HUG4242.5.
28 Bruner (1983).
29 Bruner and Allport (1940).
30 Bruner (1957).
31 Bruner (1957), p. 124.
32 Another characteristic he shared with Henri.
33 Bruner (1983), p. 287.
34 Bruner interview, October 2014.
35 Bruner and Tajfel (1961).
36 E.g., Tajfel (1962a, 1977).
37 Tajfel, Richardson, and Everstine (1964ab); Tajfel and Bruner (1966).
38 Winter interview, December 2015.
39 Lambert, Solomon, and Watson (1949).
40 Tajfel and Winter (1963).
41 Winter interview, December 2015. Winter is, indeed rather tall (6'8' or 2.03 m). Apparently, Winter had mentioned to someone that probably all he'd get out of the weeks of work with pre-school research participants would be a footnote, and this remark may have got back to Henri.
42 Winter interview, December 2015.
43 Pettigrew interview, October 2014.
44 Bruner and Tajfel (1961); Tajfel and Winter (1963).
45 Tajfel (1962a).
46 Tajfel (1962a), p. 20; my emphasis.
47 Katz and Braly (1933).
48 Tajfel (1962a), p. 33.
49 Tajfel (1962a), p. 35.
50 A. Tajfel interview, September 2014.
51 HUA box HUG4242.5.
52 WoS, February 2019.
53 Tajfel (1960).
54 Tajfel (1960), p. 846.
55 p. 846.
56 Clark and Clark (1947).
57 Tajfel (1960), p. 846.
58 www.bbc.co.uk/news/business-46507514.
59 p. 847
60 E.g., Kosterman and Feshbach (1989); Mummendey, Klink, and Brown (2001); Staub (1997).
61 Tajfel (1963).
62 Tajfel (1963), p. 5.
63 Tajfel (1963), p. 8.
64 Tajfel (1964ab); Tajfel (1965), p. 66; Tajfel (1966a).
65 Bruner warned him off this fellowship in no uncertain terms: 'you'd get so bored with Witkin in the course of a year that you'd cheerfully go to Patagonia to get away from him'. He was more encouraging about the Cardiff job, writing that he looked forward to addressing him as the '*père de la psychologie galloise*' (letter from Bruner to Henri, 14 February 1961, HUA box 4242.5).

66 Eiser interview, October 2016.
67 Interview with Peter Collison for the centenary history of Barnett House (*Social Enquiry, Social Reform and Social Action,* Oxford 2014), conducted by Dr Katie Field, c. 2012.
68 Tajfel (1957, 1959a, 1959b).
69 Wilkes interview, February 2015.
70 Wilkes interview, February 2015.
71 Tajfel and Wilkes (1963).
72 WoS, February 2019.
73 Bruner (1957), p. 123.
74 Tajfel (1957, 1959b).
75 Thus, the task may not have been so easy. The experiment was conducted in a pre-metric era when measurements in Britain were made in feet and inches. To circumvent this problem – if problem it was – the experimenter showed each participant a ruler marked in both centimetres and inches so they could familiarise themselves with the imperial-metric conversion.
76 For example, Sutton and Douglas (2013) and Myers, Abell, and Sani (2010) state that *both* inter-category accentuation and intra-category assimilation were found. Even Henri himself was not averse to the occasional misrepresentation of the findings, sometimes unqualifiedly claiming that intra-category assimilation effects were observed (e.g., Wilkes and Tajfel, 1966; Tajfel, 1963).
77 Letter from Henri to Allport, 8 July 1963, HUA box 4118.10.
78 Corneille, Kelin, Lambert, and Judd (2002).
79 Campbell (1956).
80 Secord *et al.* (1956).
81 Razran (1950).
82 Corneille *et al.* (2002).
83 E.g., Eiser (1971); Krueger and Clement (1994).
84 E.g., Doise, Deschamps, and Meyer (1978); McGarty and Penny (1988); Tajfel, Sheikh, and Gardner (1964).
85 Halsey (1996), p. 75.
86 Linacre College Governing Body minutes, 12 June 1962.
87 Harré, personal communication, November 2017.
88 Linacre College Governing Body records.
89 Cheetham interview, December 2017.
90 Wilkes interview, February 2015.
91 A. Tajfel interview, September 2014.
92 The only other copy of this paper I have located was in Bruner's papers in the Harvard Library.
93 Winter interview, December 2015.
94 Wilkes interview, February 2015.
95 Wilkes interview, February 2015.
96 Bruner and Tajfel (1965); Tajfel *et al.* (1964ab); Tajfel and Bruner (1966).
97 Tajfel and Wilkes (1964); Wilkes and Tajfel (1966).
98 Tajfel *et al.* (1964).
99 Tajfel (1965).
100 Tajfel, 1964a, 1966a).
101 Johnson (1966).
102 Tajfel and Dawson (1965).
103 Tajfel (1966b).

104 Tajfel (1966c).
105 Tajfel (1966c), p. 78.
106 Piaget and Weil (1951); Jahoda (1963).
107 The order of the two tasks was counterbalanced.
108 Tajfel, Nemeth, Jahoda, Campbell, and Johnson (1970).
109 Tajfel *et al.* (1970); Tajfel, Jahoda, Nemeth, Rim, and Johnson (1972).
110 Clark and Clark (1947); Milner (1975).
111 Nemeth interview, January 2017.
112 Jaspars, Van de Geer, and Tajfel (1972); Johnson, Middleton and Tajfel (1970); Middleton, Tajfel, and Johnson (1970); Simon, Tajfel, and Johnson (1967); Tajfel *et al.* (1970, 1972).
113 Aboud (1988); Barrett (2007).
114 Tajfel (1969a).
115 It is unclear if this was the British or American funding body, since they shared the same name.
116 Reykowski interview, March 2017.
117 Nemeth interview, January 2017.
118 Letter courtesy of Gideon Fuks.
119 Nemeth interview, January 2017.
120 Allegedly described by Stuart Sutherland, rather condescendingly, as 'not as bad as I thought it would be' (A. Tajfel interview, August 2014).

6

PALO ALTO AND EARLY YEARS AT BRISTOL

1966–1972

Go west, young man

As we saw in Chapter 5, Henri had been assiduous in his search for a Chair ever since his return from Harvard in 1959. His next hopes centred on the London School of Economics (LSE). Outside of Oxbridge, LSE was probably the most prestigious British institution for social sciences at the time. An added attraction was that LSE had just founded the first ever department of *social* psychology in Britain.

However, there was a problem. One of the people responsible for setting up that new department was Hilde Himmelweit, one of the most prominent British social psychologists of the 1960s. When LSE advertised a Chair, Henri duly applied for it,[1] but Himmelweit had the inside track – she had been at LSE since 1948 – and it was she who got it, thus dashing Henri's hopes for a return to London.

Still, to paraphrase Jane Austen, it is a truth universally acknowledged that an academic in possession of a good CV must be in need of a Chair, and so, when another vacancy was advertised in 1966, this time for Professor of Psychology and Head of Department at Bristol University, Henri threw his hat in the ring. Though it was outside the golden Oxford–Cambridge–London triangle, by the 1960s Bristol could fairly claim to be one of the leading 'red-brick' universities. The same could not be said about its Psychology Department. Most of the staff there at the time were not very active in research and some of them were also rather delinquent in their teaching duties. Mick Billig, who was an undergraduate student at Bristol at the time, recalls that several of the lecturers were poor teachers, when they bothered to show up at all. Some of their attitudes were pretty antediluvian as well. He remembers one woman student being told by a male lecturer that she had only obtained her place because she was a blonde.[2]

It was this rather moribund department that Henri was contemplating joining. To some, this might have been too daunting a proposition, but Henri was seldom a man lacking in self-confidence. He may have seen this position as an opportunity, not only to establish himself among the elite of British social psychology – there were only three other professors of social psychology at the time: Himmelweit (LSE), Gustav Jahoda (Strathclyde), and Marie Jahoda (Sussex) – but also to realise his growing ambition to build a distinctively European brand of social psychology.

At some point in 1966, Henri was interviewed for the position, and shortly afterwards (in September), departed for the United States to spend a year's sabbatical as a Fellow at the prestigious Center for Advanced Study in the Behavioural Sciences at Palo Alto, California.

Such fellowships were by invitation only and required the nomination of past Fellows. Among his acquaintances, Festinger (Stanford), Mandler (Harvard) and Argyle (Oxford) had all spent sabbaticals at the Center in the 1950s and it seems likely that they would have extolled its virtues to him. In any event, this Fellowship represented another significant milestone of the esteem in which Henri was held by his peers.

The Center was (and is) an exceedingly pleasant place to spend a sabbatical. Here is how Michael Argyle described it:

> On a distant hilltop in California – a land of palm trees, orange groves and perpetual high summer – is a social scientist's dream world, known to its inhabitants as 'the Center'. Here the fifty fellows can be found lunching in shirt sleeves under the blue sky, arguing in seminar rooms, working in their studies or sleeping on their couches. The buildings, which were given an architectural award, are in contemporary redwood and glass and are specially strengthened against earthquakes. They consist of fifty identical and luxuriously equipped studies, together with various meeting rooms, a dining room and library. There are tremendous views in all directions – of the mountains, San Francisco Bay, the red-tiled buildings of Stanford University, and on clear days the white buildings of San Francisco 32 miles away…
>
> …. Fellowships are awarded on a generous scale and cover salary, travel (family included) and research expenses. There is a staff of administrators, research assistants, secretaries, librarians, computers, and a resident statistician, who all combine to make work easy.[3]

Each Fellow is given his or her own study in which to work. A tradition of the Center is that each study has pinned to its door a list of former occupants, 'the ghosts of the study'. Henri's was No. 42. By a nice coincidence, the previous year's occupant of that study was William Bevan who had been the co-author of the experiment on weight estimation that had inspired Henri's first published experiments[4] (Chapter 4).

In the class of 1966–67 there were forty-five Fellows (Figure 6.1). Apart from Henri himself, there were eight other psychologists, including: Justin Aronfreed, a developmental social psychologist; Henri's colleague from LSE, Hilde Himmelweit; Arthur Jensen, author of some later controversial views on race and intelligence;

FIGURE 6.1 The Class of 1966/67 at the Center for Advanced Study in the Behavioral Sciences.

Source: Picture courtesy of the Center for Advanced Study in the Behavioral Sciences. Henri is seventh from left in the third row. Hilde Himmelweit, his LSE colleague, is seated second from left (reproduced with permission).

and Herbert Kelman, an authority on intergroup conflict resolution. And, consistent with the interdisciplinary ethos of the Center, there were also anthropologists, economists, scholars of English literature and linguistics, political scientists, sociologists, historians, lawyers, psychiatrists, a biologist, a philosopher, and an educationalist.

Unfortunately, despite the Center's idyllic surroundings and the stimulating ambience provided by his fellow Fellows, Henri's stay at Palo Alto did not get off to a happy start. In October 1966, just five weeks after his arrival, he suffered his second heart attack.[5] According to Anne, the coronary occurred on their way back from a wine-tasting in one of the famous Californian vineyards. Fortunately, John Beattie (a colleague from Oxford) was with them and was able to drive them to a hospital at Stanford. At first, the hospital was reluctant to admit him because their health insurance documents had not yet arrived from the UK. It was only when Anne threatened to sue the hospital if Henri died that he was admitted. When it came to his discharge two weeks later, there was the opposite problem. This time the hospital were unwilling to let him leave until the medical bill had been paid. In response, Anne told them that if that was their attitude they could keep him! This threat seemed to have its desired effect and soon Henri was back at the Center convalescing.[6]

Because of the heart attack Henri reluctantly had to cancel his plans to attend an international conference on *Social Psychological Research in Developing Countries* in Ibadan, Nigeria, a meeting that had been Henri's brain-child. It arose out of the piece of commissioned research that he had done for the US Airforce (Chapter 5).

He, together with Herbert Kelman and Brewster Smith, had been the organising committee for the conference. True to its title, the conference participants were a properly international group. Although it was rather dominated by Americans – fifteen in all, including the famous cross-culturalists Otto Klineberg and Harry Triandis – twenty-three other nations were represented, mostly developing countries.[7] His friend from Strathclyde, Gustav Jahoda, was there, as was his fellow Birkbeck graduate from 1954, Douglas Price-Williams (Chapter 4). At the conference an international committee was formed, which laid the ground-work for a new organisation, the International Association of Cross-Cultural Psychology (IACCP). Kelman, who was on that committee, offered this tribute to Henri's efforts to promote cross-cultural psychology in the 1960s: 'Henri can rightfully be considered a godfather to IACCP.'[8]

Meanwhile, things were progressing on the Bristol front. He had obviously impressed the selection committee and was made an initial offer. After several months of negotiations, not the least of which concerned the title of the position ('Professor of *Social* Psychology' rather than the originally advertised more generic title[9]), and an agreement from Bristol that someone else would soon be responsible for running the department,[10] he received the final offer in early February 1967, followed by the formal contract letter one month later.[11] The agreed annual salary was £3885 (equivalent to about £69,260 in 2018[12]).

It is clear that Henri felt quite conflicted about accepting the Bristol offer. It meant leaving his beloved Oxford for a town in the West country that he regarded as rather provincial. On the day he received the offer letter from Bristol he wrote to John Bamborough, the Principal of Linacre College:

4th February 1967

Dear Bam,

Well, it's happened. I received this morning official confirmation from Bristol and accepted the appointment to the Chair of Social Psychology. Together with this, I am sending my resignation to Halsey as from the 1st September. Presumably, this means that I must also resign my present fellowship as from that date.

There is nothing much to add really, apart from saying that I feel I have taken the right decision, though it involves the choice of an alternative which is in many ways less attractive. I suppose in situations like this one should say that one will keep an active interest in the College: I do say it and do mean it.

[........]
Yours ever,
Henri[13]

Notice his ambivalence in the first sentence of the second paragraph. Of the remainder of his stay in California, there is little to report. According to Anne, they did quite a bit of travelling, visiting Big Sur and other areas of the Californian coast. Perhaps it was on one of those trips that Nic Johnson took the photograph shown

FIGURE 6.2 Anne, Henri, and Michael on a beach in California.

Source: Photograph courtesy of Nicholas Johnson (reproduced with permission).

in Figure 6.2. Nic had visited them around Christmas 1966, flown out from Oxford on a military plane (paid for by the US Airforce grant).

During ongoing negotiations with Bristol, Henri was also discussing other job possibilities. One such was at the University of Santa Cruz which had just opened its doors the year before. Indeed, Henri had actually received an offer from them in 1965 but had postponed any decision until he had had a chance to visit the university in person.[14] But, according to Anne, this would never have worked for Henri who was essentially an 'urban man' and found Santa Cruz all rather parochial:

> He was (still) a bit fragile … but mainly it (Santa Cruz) was too healthy! (It) simply wasn't his cup of tea.…They had barbecues. Imagine having barbecues! The whole thing simply wasn't his scene.[15]

Besides, Bruner had also been rather discouraging when Henri had told him of the offer:

> I absolutely forbid you to take a professorship at Santa Cruz until you see what a wretched place it is.[16]

For the rest of his sabbatical in California, it is likely that he was doing at least some of the writing of two major publications that appeared in the next two years. One was a review chapter in the Second Edition of the *Handbook of Social Psychology* entitled, 'Social and Cultural Factors in Perception'.[17] The other was an essay, 'Cognitive aspects of prejudice', published in the *Journal of Social Issues*.[18]

The *Handbook of Social Psychology* was then, as it still is, the major reference book for social psychologists. Typically, the chapters – 45 of them in this Second Edition – are detailed overviews of a field. Henri's was no exception. It consisted of 64 printed pages of text plus a further 14 pages of references. It is an extremely thorough review of how people's perceptions can (or may not) be influenced both by proximal social factors – for example, other people in the immediate situation[19] – and by more distal factors such as cultural values, language or exposure to certain physical environments.[20] Unsurprisingly, there is a very knowledgeable coverage of the *New Look* research, since a central argument of that approach is the joint influence of the stimulus *and* the perceiver's background or motives on what is perceived (Chapter 4). Reflecting his long-standing interest in art, there is a brief discussion of the role of culture in the perception and appreciation of pictorial representation, with reference to Dürr, Giotto, and others.

This chapter is notable for several reasons. The first is his appearance at all in the list of contributors who, by and large, were well-established scholars in anyone's A–Z of the discipline: from Gordon Allport to Robert Zajonc. Finally, then, he was rubbing shoulders with the big boys (there was not a single woman first author among the 45 chapters). Second, almost certainly he was the only contributor from outside North America, although not all the authors' affiliations are given. This was another indicator of his international visibility, partly attributable, no doubt, to his frequent appearance at international conferences in the preceding years. Third, the chapter, whilst heavy-going in places (it would have benefited from some editing), is remarkable for the wide range of sources that he drew on, including several German and French publications. Such diversity is almost completely absent from the resolutely Anglophonic reference lists of the other chapters. This reflected his multilingual competence and his familiarity with non-English psychology, but also his nascent desire to have the contributions of European social psychology more widely appreciated. Fourth, there is an interesting and quasi-autobiographical exegesis of the factors involved in the identifiability of Jews from physiognomic cues. This included what must have been for him a personally poignant discussion of Jews who escaped persecution by the Nazis in the Second World War by 'passing' as non-Jews[21] (Chapter 2). This is one of the few occasions in Henri's scholarly output where he explicitly discusses issues relating to anti-Semitism and the Holocaust.

The chapter garners only 84 citations on Web of Science.[22] There is little to suggest, therefore, that it has had much impact on the discipline.

Henri's second publication from that same year (in the *Journal of Social Issues*) has enjoyed greater success. 'Cognitive aspects of prejudice' is at once an uncompromising critique of the then fashionable evolutionary theories of aggression[23] and a plea for theories of prejudice to take more account of people's efforts to understand their social environments. In the opening pages of the article, especially in the slightly longer version,[24] Henri lambasts both ethological and psychoanalytic attempts to explain prejudice and intergroup conflict in terms of biological instincts:

> There is no doubt that under some conditions all men can and do display hostility towards groups other than their own, be they social, national, racial, religious, or any other. There is also no doubt, however, that under other conditions this hostility either does not appear or can be modified. The scientifically minded biologist (as distinct from Lorenz's biologically minded scientist) would have to specify for us in the case of human behaviour, as he does so often and so successfully for animal behaviour, the invariances of the waxing and waning of the aggressive drive. Until he does so, statements such as that of Lorenz are just about as useful as would be statements relating to the development of the rich variety of gastronomic traditions to man's undeniably innate need for food and drink.[25]

In place of these 'blood and guts' models of human behaviour (as he called them), we need:

> A psychological theory of intergroup relations (which) must provide a two-way link between situations and behaviour, and it can do this through an analysis of the motivational and the cognitive structures which intervene between the two.[26]

The remainder of the article is a summary of some of his own work on the cognitive processes involved in stereotyping and prejudice. Pride of place goes to his research on categorisation and inter-category accentuation (Chapter 5). From there, he passes to his work on children and national preferences, also discussed in Chapter 5. There is a brief and approving mention of Pettigrew's classic paper[27] on socio-cultural determinants of prejudice before he spends the five concluding pages introducing some interesting speculations on future directions that people's 'search for meaning' might take. He extends Heider's attribution theory[28] to ask what kinds of causal attributions group members might make of events in their intergroup worlds.[29] Henri concluded his argument by pointing out how such group-based attributions can be found in ideologies used by dominant groups to justify their superior status and power. Then there is this telling passage:

> An intensified affiliation with a group is only possible when the group is capable of supplying some satisfactory aspects of an individual's social identity. This can be defined as the attribution by the individual to the ingroup of certain characteristics from the sharing of which he derives some satisfaction.[30]

In these two sentences he anticipates the kernel of this theorising on social identity that would only properly be articulated five years later.

This article won Henri the 1968 Gordon Allport Prize, awarded annually by the Society for the Psychological Study of Social Issues for the best publication on intergroup relations. It also won him high praise from his Harvard friend Jerry Bruner:

> I have finally read your prize essay on cognitive factors in prejudice. It is very, very fine and I could not help but think how pleased Gordon [Allport] would have been with it. [....] I can't begin to tell you how much the paper delighted me and how much it felt like an extrapolation and growth from where you were when we were close enough by to chat about these things.[31]

It is his fifth most frequently cited journal article, with lifetime citations of 509.[32] These show no signs of diminishing. Over the past twenty years the article has consistently been cited about 16 times a year, a remarkable achievement for one that is nearly fifty years old. The range of papers citing it is quite astonishing. Just in 2017, it was cited in outlets as varied as *Sport Marketing Quarterly, Comparative Literature Studies, Journal of Revenue and Pricing Management, Personnel Review, Meditari Accountancy Research, Journal of Pedagogic Development,* as well as more conventional publications like *Political Psychology* and *PLoSOne.*

It is indicative of the significance of this article that it continued to provoke debate on the nature of prejudice three decades after its publication. Billig wrote a careful appreciation of it, acknowledging the force of its arguments against instinctivist and psychodynamic accounts of conflict whilst, at the same time, pointing out its inadequacies in providing an explanation of horrific phenomena like genocide.[33] Amongst Billig's concerns, two in particular stand out. The first is that part of Tajfel's argument against 'blood and guts' models (that they fail to account for historical variations in conflict) might also be used against his own account. To the extent that he (Henri) was seeking to propose a generally applicable theory of prejudice, there is the risk that its contextual specifics get overlooked. The second limitation concerns the failure of the kind of cognitive approach advanced by Henri to do justice to the kinds of powerful emotions of hatred and disgust that drive genocidal rhetoric and behaviour.

There is a particular irony about the success of this paper of Henri's. It might fairly be argued that 'Cognitive aspects....' laid the foundations for much of the socio-cognitive revolution that took social psychology by storm in the 1970s and 1980s.[34] Indeed, Hamilton paid generous tribute to Henri in the final chapter of his volume on *'Cognitive Processes in Stereotyping and Intergroup Behaviour'*:

> The more specific catalyst for the resurgence of interest in a cognitive approach to this domain (stereotyping) is found, I believe, in the work of Henri Tajfel.[35]

Metaphors of people as 'cognitive misers', 'information processors', or 'naïve scientists' became popular, as researchers sought to account for biases and errors in people's thinking about their social worlds. In some of the narrower social cognition approaches that became fashionable in those years, the goal was to provide explanations of phenomena like stereotyping and prejudice in terms of the operation of people's cognitive processes, abstracted from the group and intergroup contexts in which those people were embedded. All this, of course, would have been a complete anathema to Henri, who was later to rail against such a lop-sided view of a truly *social* cognition.[36]

Building an empire

On their return from California in the summer of 1967, Henri and Anne packed up their Oxford home – this was in Polstead Road, a substantial four-storey house where they had moved to from Bainton Road – and completed the move to Bristol. For the first several months they lived in Westbury-on-Trym, an area on the north side of Bristol, in rented accommodation. In July 1968 they bought a large Victorian semi-detached house in Richmond Park Road, just five minutes' walk from the Department of Psychology in Berkeley Square. The department occupied the corner of an elegant Georgian square which enclosed a pleasant tree-filled garden (Figure 6.3). Although beautiful to look at from the outside, with a rather grand entrance flanked by four pillars, the building which housed Henri's new academic home was rather unsuited for an experimental discipline like psychology.

FIGURE 6.3 The Psychology Department at Berkeley Square, Bristol.

Source: Picture courtesy of Grazebrook Architects, Bristol (reproduced with permission).

Laboratories and lecture theatres had been created from former school-rooms, as had staff offices, of which there were too few to accommodate Henri's ambitions for a greatly expanded department. Henri's own office was on the third floor. It was large, big enough for his desk in one corner by the window, a couch against one wall, and a table and a dozen or so chairs. This meant that it could double as his office and a room for research meetings and visiting speaker colloquia. A small room across from his office accommodated his secretary.

Soon after his arrival in Bristol, Henri got cold feet about the move. The position he had vacated at Oxford was advertised and, reportedly, he rang Chelley Halsey, his former head of department, to enquire whether he might apply to get his old job back.[37] Halsey talked him out of this retrograde step but this would not be the last time that Henri's ambivalence about Bristol manifested itself. As Anne told me:

> He wasn't happy to go (to Bristol). He wasn't ever happy there, ever, ever, ever.....it was a provincial place.... he never felt at home there.[38]

Rom Harré, his former colleague at Linacre College, recalled an incident a year or two later, when Henri returned to Oxford for a college dinner:

> After dinner, we were sitting around in the common-room and Henri got up and he began to weep. And he looked around and he said, 'I should never have left, I should never have gone to Bristol'. And he left, still weeping.[39]

Like it or not, Henri was stuck with (and in) Bristol at least for the time being. He set about rebuilding the department, if not exactly in his own image, certainly with a strong infusion of social psychologists. It is clear that he was pushing at an open door as far as the university was concerned. They had agreed to his title as professor of *social* psychology, so they must have envisaged new strategic investment in that direction (there was just one social psychologist in the department when Henri arrived). They soon gave the green light for several new appointments – Henri appointed no fewer than four lecturers in his first year.

While he probably enjoyed the challenge of building up the Bristol department, I suspect that Henri found other aspects of his head of department role rather irksome. Being head of a university department necessarily involves attending many committees, writing innumerable memoranda, and at least some degree of engagement with institutional practices and regulations. Yet, attention to detail and bureaucratic procedures were never really Henri's forte, not to mention the amount of his time that such activities demanded; time that he would much rather have spent on new research, on his writing and, above all, on his travels in connection with his beloved EAESP, of which he was soon to be elected President.

In December 1968, students at Bristol, like others around the country in that year and the next, became more than usually restive. Over an issue concerning the Students' Union, they occupied the university's Senate House for eleven days, disrupting the running of the university and causing much consternation to the university's management. At least two psychology postgraduates were leading lights in the occupation (David Milner and Bob Bundy). Whether because of this, or whether because of Henri's naturally liberal inclinations, it seems that he spoke out at a university senate meeting where the occupation was discussed, urging a conciliatory approach against some hawkish colleagues who were advocating eviction and prosecution. This, apparently, earned him much opprobrium from his fellow senators, one even branding him 'a traitor'.[40]

These and other factors may have reinforced Henri's conviction that he was not really cut out to run a department and, before long, he held the university to their promise to make another professorial appointment in psychology to take over Henri's administrative duties. The person who got the job (in 1969) was John Brown, whom Henri had known from Birkbeck.[41] Brown and Henri were polar opposites on every dimension: research interests (recondite problems in short-term memory versus 'how was the Holocaust possible?'); academic ambitions (fitting some pieces of the cognitive jigsaw versus revolutionising social psychology); temperament and culture (reserved Englishman versus flamboyant Continental); and management style ('Mr Diplomacy' versus 'suffer no fools'). And yet, they became firm friends. Brown reported that Henri had once told him that he (Brown) was his best friend and they certainly saw a lot of each other over the next few years, both at work and outside.[42]

Although Brown's arrival liberated Henri from most of his managerial responsibilities, he still had his pedagogic duties to attend to. It is fair to say that he was not very conscientious in the fulfilment of these. He was forever asking colleagues to substitute for him at short notice[43] and his frequent absences occasionally created resentment amongst colleagues.[44] When he did end up in front of a class, he was not always easy to understand. Billig, who was taught by Henri in his final year, recalls:

> They weren't easy (his lectures). He would come in and the first thing he would do would be to ask someone for a cigarette – I think he was nervous lecturing. (He was) difficult to follow. His accent was stronger when he lectured, or at least in the early days it was. It was difficult to follow but, really, it was so rewarding. I'd never had any lectures like that before, certainly not in psychology.... I certainly had the feeling that I was in the presence of a great thinker, someone who was unusually perceptive, even if I couldn't understand it.[45]

Brown related an anecdote about how, after Henri had gabbled his way through a first year lecture at record speed, he found himself with time to spare before the end of the class. So he invited questions. After a long pause, one student finally plucked up the courage to ask: 'Excuse me, but who are you?'[46]

His PhD supervisions were not much better. Except at the very beginning of his time at Bristol when he had only one student and managed to see him regularly, his other commitments (principally his trips abroad) meant that he saw his PhD students only sporadically. David Milner, his first PhD student, explained the problem:

I had realised by than that he was immensely busy and that he was basically busying himself building an empire. And increasingly it became clear to me that he hadn't got an …. idea what I was talking about from one session to the next. He would contradict himself on the advice he'd given previously. He would send me off on totally blind alleys by saying, essentially, the first thing that came into his head that might be relevant.[47]

This was not an uncommon experience among his PhD students, as we will see in the next chapter. Among Henri's many competing commitments, time for his students was unfortunately seldom accorded very high priority.

Meanwhile, Henri's appetite for travel proved as insatiable as ever. In addition to frequent committee meetings for EAESP (usually in Leuven or Paris), he attended conferences in Vienna (1967), Spain (1968), Montevideo (1968), Prague (1968), Leuven (1969), Cannes (1969), revisiting California (1968), and trips to Copenhagen, Hungary, Switzerland, and Germany (1970).

When he was not frequenting airport lounges around the world, he was writing letters. Unfortunately, most of his correspondence before the move to Bristol is lost but nearly all of the letters he wrote and received after that are preserved in an archive of the Wellcome Library in London. This archive reveals Henri to have been an indefatigable correspondent, and not only to his academic colleagues around the world; dozens of random enquiries from complete strangers, PhD students, undergraduates or would-be students are responded to politely, often with helpful suggestions as to whom they should more usefully direct their requests for information. Of these hundreds of letters, a few are worth detailing.

In December 1966 (whilst at Palo Alto), he had written to Muzafer Sherif, then one of the leading intergroup researchers in the world. He received this appreciative reply:

> Dear Henri,
>   First, let me express my appreciation for the kind words you expressed in your letter to O. J. (Harvey) concerning the character of our work in social psychology… I certainly share deeply your conviction that especially a social scientist has to be a scientist and, at the same time, he has to be (in no lesser degree) a 'man imbued with the deepest sense of human values'. If they lack in either of these, they either become crass elephants not matter what preconceived and highfalutin model or contrived embroidery they try to tread on, or they become breast beating ineffective do-gooders. We tried to incorporate the scientific hard-headedness and intensely felt human concern in our latest book – 'In common predicament: social psychology of intergroup conflict and cooperation', which we believe is our best synthesis of all our work in this vital problem area…
>   Cordially,
>   Muzafer[48]

In March 1968, he wrote to his friend Gustav Jahoda: 'Bristol is *not* humming. I find it hard enough just to keep my head above water.'[49]

In that same letter he mentions his inaugural lecture which he has just given on 'The psychology of social comparisons', a topic that was to preoccupy him for much of the rest of his life.

Of Henri's many epistolic exchanges in this period, his correspondence with Leon Festinger, then at the height of his fame as a social psychologist, particularly stands out. Between January 1968 and November 1971 they exchanged forty-five letters and one telegram. One particular sequence in the spring of 1968 is a real gem. In April, Festinger wrote to Henri:

> I want you to know that I no longer have any sympathy for you or for your choice in the way you live. I am entitled to feel this way now because one week ago I had a mild cardiac infarction and now that 'you and I' are in a similar situation you get no more sympathy from me. Just in case you are wondering, it was not serious; I smoke a little bit more than I did before because it made me a bit nervous; I counteract the effect of nicotine by drinking a lot more and I will soon be fine.[50]

Henri was so alarmed by this news that he replied by *telegram* (at a cost of £1-5s-10d) five days later:

> PLEASE REPEAT PLEASE TAKE SOME MINIMAL CARE TO PREVENT RECURRENCE THOUGH OUR FULL AFFECTION WILL REMAIN UNABATED WHATEVER COURSE YOU ADOPT STOP WARMEST REGARDS AND LOVE HENRI TAJFEL[51]

Quickly followed by a fuller letter on the same day:

> There is nothing much I can say in a letter which will make sense or express appropriately my concern and sense of shock; so I won't even try but for heavens sake, don't be a fool; smoke as much as you did before, but there is no reason on earth for smoking *more*. [....]
> See you in October, Leon, and we can then trade cigarettes and drinks.
> A sort of united front against the moaners.
>> With all my very best wishes,
>>> Yours ever,[52]

To which Festinger replied:

> Thanks for your cable and your letter. You also please must remember always that I have a very peculiar and perverted sense of humour. I am certainly not smoking *more* and even smoking less although I do not intend to engage in any effort to stop smoking. I am also taking it easy and remaining relatively

quiescent as I am supposed to do. I have tried to reach some optimum between physical quiescence and mental quiescence.

The whole thing was extremely minor and should worry no one. The main reason I wrote to you was that I could not resist being able to use the phrase 'you and I'....[53]

Eliciting this response from Henri:

You need find no reasons or excuses why you wrote to me, not even in your perverted sense of humour. If something like that had happened to me again (or whenever it does), you will also be one of the first people I shall be writing to without any further excuses or apologies. Perhaps 'you and I' is not as much of a joke as I always tried to make out it was. And I do not say that just because you also had a little bit of trouble in the upper-left quarter. ...[54]

This exchange of letters between two heavy smokers, one of whom was the architect of the famous theory of cognitive dissonance,[55] which hypothesised that the simultaneous presence of two contradictory cognitions (e.g., 'I smoke heavily' and 'I have just had a heart attack') should be psychologically discomfiting and should provoke attempts to reduce that discomfort, is simultaneously ironic and endearing. The two men remained close friends for nearly twenty years, despite the fact that Festinger was a prototypic exemplar of the kind of North American social psychology that Henri would soon be arguing vociferously against.

A scientific community on a European scale

Whilst at Oxford Henri had had a very creditable track record of winning research grants. Within his first year at Bristol he had obtained two more.

One of these grants was from the Nuffield Foundation who made him a two-year grant to support a research fellow and six postgraduates to do cross-cultural psychology, of which three were to be overseas students. Mallory Wober, who was appointed to the research fellowship and to select and supervise the students, described this job as an 'amazingly feather-bedded scheme'.[56] He couldn't remember how much the grant had been but estimated it might have been worth as much as £40,000[57] (worth over £630,000 in 2018). Henri gave him almost complete autonomy in running the project.

However, a second, more substantial grant was to prove much more significant, both for Henri's own career and for the development of European social psychology. It was from the Ford Foundation (FF), an American philanthropic organisation founded by the son of Henry Ford, he of 'model T' fame. During his year at Palo Alto, Henri had corresponded regularly with this organisation, initially in an attempt to get them to support a postgraduate training scheme for students from developing countries.[58] That proposal came to nothing with FF, but as we have just seen, he was able to 'recycle' successfully it for the Nuffield Foundation. Henri was soon setting his sights on a much more ambitious project: to establish three centres for social psychological research in the *developed* world (Bristol[59], Leuven and Paris), as well as to support the activities of a recently formed association of European social psychologists. This time he had more success. A year later FF made an offer of a four-year grant of $275,000, which was to be divided equally between Henri, Jozef Nuttin (Leuven), and Serge Moscovici (Paris) ($80,000 each, worth over £560,000 in 2018[60]), with a further $35,000 to the new organisation for 'facilitating travel and planning, and for European conferences'.[61]

In fact, that grant was the culmination of four years of intensive activity by Henri and several other European colleagues to establish a new professional organisation of European social psychologists. It has undergone various name changes over the years, initially the European Association for the Advancement of Experimental Social Psychology, then the slightly less cumbersome European Association of Experimental Social Psychology, to its current still simpler guise European Association of Social Psychology.

There is no need here to recapitulate the history of the Association; others have already done that job admirably.[62] To begin with, though, we should note the irony that the new organisation owed its existence in no small measure to a few individual North American psychologists and a good deal of North American money.

The story begins with John Lanzetta, an American social psychologist who was financed by the US Office of Naval Research (ONR) to spend a year in London (1962–63). Part of his brief was to assess the state of European Social Psychology. His initial appraisal was not very positive. He identified several active social psychologists, Henri amongst them, but noted that they were scattered across Europe, largely unaware of each other's existence. Moreover, they were usually the only social psychologist in their department. Lanzetta was to write:

> In such a climate, the social psychologist interested in theory and experimental methods finds himself an isolated deviant. Marginal to the applied group and yet not wholly accepted by his academic brethren in experimental psychology, he stands alone – unsupported and unheard.[63]

What a perfect description of Henri's own situation in Oxford at the time (Chapter 5)!

Lanzetta set about bringing those 'isolated deviants' into contact with one another. He formed a small committee comprised of Henri, Robert Pagès (France), Mauk Mulder (Netherlands), and himself to organise a first European conference on experimental social psychology in Sorrento (Italy) in December 1963. It was sponsored by the ONR, together with a grant from the American Social Science Research Council (SSRC). Such was the success of this meeting that they immediately set about organising another (held at Frascati (Italy) a year later).

The second North American who played a pivotal role in establishing the Association was Leon Festinger. In 1964 he was asked by SSRC to chair a Committee on Transnational Social Psychology (henceforth, Transnational Committee) 'to promote research development in social psychology on an international scale'.[64] Eight people served on this committee, four Americans (Festinger, Lanzetta, Stanley Schachter, Ithiel de Sola Pool) and four Europeans (Leonardo Ancona, Jaap Koekebakker, Serge Moscovici, Ragnar Rommetveit). Henri joined the committee a year later, taking the position of Ancona.[65] This committee was instrumental in securing (US) funding for the 1964 Frascati meeting, and several European conferences and summer schools thereafter. The Transnational Committee was technically a sub-committee of SSRC: it had no funds of its own to disburse and relied on making applications to other agencies. One of these, as we have seen, was ONR. But, by far the most important source of support was the Ford Foundation (FF) which, as we have just seen, contributed more than $250,000 to the Association and three of its key players (Henri, Moscovici, and Nuttin).

The genesis of the Association can be traced to that second European meeting in Villa Falconieri, Frascati, in December 1964. In addition to the scientific papers that were presented there, the decision was made to elect a 'planning committee' for the new organisation that the organisers hoped to create. That committee consisted of Henri, Gustav Jahoda, Moscovici, Mulder, and Nuttin (Figure 6.4).

Henri's published account of the Frascati committee meeting gave some clues as to what activities the committee had in mind: a conference of social psychologists, a European exchange visit programme and research training seminars.[66] Two years

FIGURE 6.4 Five go to Leuven: the founding members of the European Association of Experimental Social Psychology. Left to right: Josef Nuttin, Gustav Jahoda, Serge Moscovici, Henri Tajfel, and Mauk Mulder; February 1965.

Source: Picture courtesy of Monika Nuttin (reproduced with permission).

later, once the Association had been formally inaugurated, Jahoda and Moscovici spelt out those aims more fully:

> The Association wishes to be neither a 'learned society' nor a purely formal linkage of specialists, but an agency promoting advancements. Behind the general aim of creating a milieu favourable for social psychology, in Europe, there lies a whole policy for injecting new life into the science.... It will therefore be a matter of enlivening a discipline, promoting a climate for research, and creating a 'scientific community' on a European scale. These goals can be achieved by contact and communication between specialists, the laying open of common interests, the encouragement of joint enterprises, the unified training of researchers, and the formulation of a clear conception of social psychology.[67]

These aims were to be achieved by: *improving communication among researchers,* principally via regular conferences; *promoting research* via exchange visits and small group meetings; *training young researchers* in regular summer schools; and *disseminating research* through the publication of a journal and books. Thus, the fledging Association planned a series of practical activities that it hoped would bring together colleagues from across Europe, including countries behind the Iron Curtain, and would train the next generation of social psychologists. And behind all these concrete measures lay a grander ambition – the creation of an independent European social psychology, free from the shackles of North American theoretical and methodological traditions.

There is no doubt that Henri was passionately committed to this goal of developing an 'indigenous' European social psychology. Indeed, he once described himself and those early pioneers in the Association as a band of 'old pirates', metaphorically roaming the high seas and discovering new intellectual territories (and not being averse to 'robbing' a few rich foundations in the process)[68]. Colin Fraser, who knew both Henri and Moscovici well, also described them as 'a worldly and astute set of pirates'.[69]

In the early years of the Association, an important priority was not just to facilitate communication among colleagues in Western Europe but also to try to penetrate the Iron Curtain, behind which many social psychologists worked, completely insulated from any scientific contact with their Western colleagues. With this in mind, the Association instituted a special kind of conference – so-called 'East–West Meetings' – which aimed to have approximately equal participation from Eastern and Western European countries. Because of his own Eastern European background, Henri was a great enthusiast for these meetings and played a leading role in several of them.[70] It will be recalled from Chapter 5 that he made reconnaissance visits to Poland, Hungary, and Czechoslovakia in 1966. Between 1967 and 1980 five such East–West meetings were held and Henri attended them all, except for one in Poland in 1977.[71]

The Prague conference in October 1968 is worth a special mention. It took place less than two months after the Soviet Union had invaded Czechoslovakia to suppress the liberalising reforms introduced by Dubček – the so-called 'Prague Spring'. Henri had helped to organise this meeting and was acting President when the Soviet tanks rolled into Prague. The Association's continued sponsorship and participation in the Prague conference was highly controversial. Many members, including four members of the executive committee, were opposed to the conference going ahead. Henri, after much prevarication, eventually took executive action and authorised the conference's continuation, arguing that it was important to support their Czechoslovakian colleagues.[72] This decision, and the manner of its taking, greatly upset two of Henri's close friends on the committee (Mulder and Nuttin), leading to mutual resignation threats by them and Henri.[73] Fortunately for the future well-being of the Association, all three threats were eventually rescinded.

The Association's second goal was to promote more collaboration through travel visits and small group meetings. Initially, the first of these initiatives was not a great success. Whether due to difficulties in international travel in the 1960s or to the then conventional way of designing and conducting research in isolated laboratories, social psychologists showed little interest in applying for travel grants to visit other research centres.[74] With time, that rather parochial attitude changed and short visits to other universities became very popular. Small group meetings proved much more attractive from the start, however. Their size (typically just 20–30 participants), duration (usually 2–3 days) and focus on a single topic meant that they were (and are) ideal opportunities for intensive discussion of research and the development of new projects.

Without doubt, the Association's most original and successful innovation was the postgraduate summer school, fulfilling the third objective of the Association to train young scientists. This was necessary, the founders believed, because of the highly variable nature of doctoral training in social psychology in Europe in the 1960s and also because PhD students, like their supervisors, were geographically quite isolated with few opportunities to interact with their peers elsewhere in Europe. To remedy this situation, the Association devised a formula for an intensive residential doctoral training programme which, with minor variations, has been used ever since. A small group of senior scholars was recruited to serve as 'teachers', whose role was to act as leaders of small groups of PhD students (typically 6–8 people), working on a research topic in the teacher's area of expertise. The teachers typically also gave some formal lectures during the summer school. The goal of the workgroups was to devise and, if possible, actually conduct a study over the course of the summer school.[75] The students were recruited not solely on grounds of individual excellence; their geographical background and the stage they had reached in their PhD studies were additional criteria. The aim was to create culturally and intellectually diverse groups so that the students and any resulting research could profit from that diversity.

The Association's fourth objective was to promote the dissemination of social psychological research throughout Europe. With this in mind, the *European Journal of Social Psychology* (EJSP) was launched in 1971 with the goal to:

serve the needs of all social psychologists by providing them with a common forum which, hopefully, may lead both to greater co-operation across national boundaries and to a general strengthening of social psychology in Europe.[76]

To this end, authors could submit their articles in English, but also in French and German, and abstracts were published in these three languages, with Russian thrown in for good measure. Nor was its multi-lingual nature the only unusual feature of the journal. It boasted a distinctive abstract cover design that was instantly recognisable, if not so instantly legible. The editors did not insist on a rigid format for submissions, and articles could be reviews or theoretical pieces, as well as more conventional empirical reports. Diversity was the editors' watch-word.

Henri summed up his hopes for the new journal in his 1972 Presidential address to the Association:

> A journal has no purpose unless it fulfils the function of initiation and transmission of new forms of intellectual influence. This is badly needed today in social psychology; and perhaps we should acknowledge the fact by being less afraid of 'speculation' and unconventionality in what we write, submit for publication, and accept for printing.[77]

I noted earlier that the establishment of the Association was due in no small measure to the energies of one or two North American scholars and to the munificence of various US funding agencies. This raises the question as to why American military and philanthropic organisations should have been willing to fund European social psychology in the 1960s. And let us not forget that the US Airforce had also made personal grants to Henri in that same period (Chapter 5).

Some have argued that such apparent 'philanthropy' was, in reality, a demonstration of the United States' willingness to exercise 'soft power' in Europe as a way to counter the possible attraction of the Soviet Union to Western European intellectuals during the Cold War.[78] Certainly, a number of European activities (e.g., radio stations, newspapers, literary magazines, art exhibitions, and cultural and scientific conferences) were regularly supported by FF and other organisations, at least one of which, the Congress for Cultural Freedom, was most probably used as a cover for initiatives of the American Central Intelligence Agency (CIA).[79] Although the FF always jealously guarded its reputation as an independent foundation, there is no doubt that it was populated by people with direct connections to the CIA and other American national security agencies.[80] One of these was McGeorge Bundy, who became president of FF in 1966; another was Shepard Stone, director of the International Affairs division in the FF until 1967. Both of these men would have been in post while Henri was negotiating for funds for his own research and the Association.

Of course, just because ex- or current CIA operatives were working at FF does not mean that American intelligence services were taking a direct interest in European social psychology. However, a Dutch social psychologist turned historian,

Sandra Schruijer, believes that there are additional grounds for suspecting that the motivations of the founding agencies were not entirely altruistic.[81]

One concerns the presence of de Sola Pool, a political scientist at MIT, on the initial Transnational Committee. De Sola Pool had set up the Center for International Studies at MIT in the 1950s, in part with the assistance of a large FF grant.[82] By his own admission, de Sola Pool was an enthusiastic advocate for social scientists doing research for government agencies and, indeed, had conducted research for the CIA.[83] Schruijer claims that he was invited to that first European conference in Sorrento in 1963, although he seems not to have attended since he is not listed among the delegates.[84] But Schruijer finds his involvement in the Transnational Committee suspicious since De Sola Pool did not have any obvious social psychological credentials.

The second ground for Schruijer's contention that American security services were taking an active interest in the Association's affairs is a 1965 US Government Report on Behavioural Sciences and National Security, located by the American sociologist Irving Horowitz, which lists various research contracts related to foreign areas and populations[85]. Amongst the grants listed is one for 'foreign research symposia' made to SSRC to support 'meetings of American and foreign scholars in Europe in social psychology'.[86] Almost certainly, this was the grant applied for by the Transnational Committee to support the 1964 Frascati meeting.

These, then, are the two further 'smoking guns' that Schruijer has located to implicate the CIA's involvement in the early activities of the Association. For these reasons, she describes the Association as a 'Cold War baby',[87] not just because of its emergence during one of the most Arctic periods of East-West relations, but also because of its possible role in serving US foreign policy interests.

Whatever the truth of the matter – and Schruijer's evidence is more suggestive than conclusive – there is no doubt that Henri was well aware of the political sensitivities in accepting funding from American sources, including military agencies. In early 1967, he wrote to Don Campbell shortly after accepting the Bristol chair, seeking his advice about research funding:

> You could help me – if you wish – in one of two ways: (1) my chances of getting financial support are quite good. But my possible sources of support are, unfortunately, in the politically-not-so-quite-untarnished category. This is not to say that there is any real difficulty – it is only the label which may become embarrassing. I was wondering whether the Carnegie Corporation would be a feasible alternative, but I know nobody there nothing about them. Could you possibly let me know whether you think that there would be any chance of obtaining Carnegie support, and if so, give me some idea when I should approach. In addition, would you be prepared to let me use your name and, if necessary, to perform an incantation on my behalf in appropriate quarters?[88]

Not long after, he approached one of his PhD students, David Milner, to enlist his help in running the first of his minimal group experiments (see next section). According to Milner, the conversation went something like this:

HT: I've got the germ of an idea which I think is going to make me. And I think it will be very good for those people who cooperate with me.

DM: where is the money coming from (for the research)?

HT (*somewhat sheepishly*): Well, it's from the US Airforce, but via NATO, and we're part of NATO.[89]

Milner declined the invitation on political grounds, but later learned that other invitees were not informed about the source of the funding before they signed up to the project.

In public, though, Henri was quite unapologetic about accepting money from military sources. In his 1972 Presidential address he noted how NATO had supported the 1971 Summer School (as it also did in 1976), and justified that grant (and others before it) on the grounds that there had never been any 'conditions inhibiting academic freedom attached to the support'.[90] As far as we know, this was the case, though from the beginning, some more left-wing members of the Association (particularly in France) were always uneasy about being beholden to North American sources of financial support.[91]

Experiments in a vacuum

If I had to hazard a guess as to which of Henri's empirical discoveries would be at the top of most social psychologists' list, I would put my money on his experiments employing the minimal group paradigm.[92] Citation data would certainly support such a bet. His 1971 paper is his most highly cited journal article (1950 citations), and the 1970 article in *Scientific American* is his third most popular (879). In fact, the four papers which reported the first results from the minimal group paradigm account for 41% of all of Henri's journal article citations.[93] The story of its development is a nice tale about scientific priority, and a case study of how a single scientific discovery has the potential to stimulate an enormous volume of new research whilst also generating enduring controversy over the methods and measures it employed, and over the interpretation and implications of its findings.

To understand why this research of Henri's had such an impact it is necessary to remind ourselves of the explanations of prejudice that were current in the 1960s. Allport's monumental essay on prejudice[94] had acknowledged the role of personality, as represented by the *Theory of Authoritarian Personality*,[95] but had placed more emphasis on socio-cultural factors and cognitive processes in the acquisition and expression of prejudice. Henri's own early work on categorical accentuation was very much in that tradition (Chapter 5).

Experimental studies of intergroup *behaviour*, as opposed to stereotyping and attitudes, were rare. A notable exception were the famous field experiments of Sherif, conducted in boys' summer camps.[96] Sherif's contention – well borne out by his data – was that intergroup behaviour was mainly determined by the goals that groups were striving for. Where these clashed, one could expect intergroup conflict and hostility; where they coincided, cooperation and amity were more likely. And yet, one of Sherif's experiments had thrown up an anomalous result. In one experiment reported by Sherif and his colleagues, two groups of boys spent a few days in separate locations, unaware of the existence of the other group.[97] At a certain point in the proceedings, the presence of the other group was made known to the boys. Immediately, Sherif and his colleagues reported, the boys expressed a desire to compete with the other group, with the derogatory 'n_ _ _ _r' word being used by some of them to describe it. The significance of this observation is that the intergroup animosity occurred *before* the experimenters had introduced any explicitly conflictual goals. Another study had observed similar ingroup favour-itism in intergroup evaluations in the absence of competition in a more controlled laboratory setting.[98] These findings, then, raised the question as to whether simply belonging to one group and not to another could be sufficient to trigger intergroup discrimination.

Although Henri was eventually to receive the credit for answering this question definitively, he was not actually the first to tackle it. That credit is due to his Dutch friend and colleague, Jaap Rabbie.[99] Theoretically, Rabbie had been strongly in-fluenced by Lewin[100] and this led him to hypothesise that some minimum degree of 'common fate' between people was a necessary condition for a group to exist psychologically and thus for any intergroup discrimination to occur. In December 1964, at the meeting in Frascati, Rabbie presented a paper entitled, 'The effects of common fate and discrimination upon intergroup attitudes', one of whose object-ives was 'to explore the minimal conditions under which this in– and out-group differentiation occurs'.[101] Two years later, at Royaumont, France, he followed this up with another paper entitled, 'Origins of ingroup–outgroup attitudes'. In the fourth paragraph of this paper, Rabbie enumerates the research questions he would address, of which the first two were:

> The first is whether the mere classification by an authoritative external source leads to discriminatory ingroup-outgroup evaluations. Second, given this classification, does the added experience of common fate in the form of a randomly bestowed group reward or deprivation lead to discriminatory evaluations?[102]

From his findings, Rabbie concluded that the answer to the first question was negative, but to the second it was positive. In other words, he believed that mere categorisation into groups was *not* sufficient to trigger discrimination; it needed some additional experience of common fate (of being rewarded or deprived). This paper was subsequently published in 1969.[103]

At this point in the story, it is necessary to dwell a little on the procedure Rabbie had devised. Dutch school children, unknown to each other, were divided into groups of four persons on a random basis. The groups were labelled 'green' and 'blue', supposedly for administrative reasons. Some children were told that one of the groups was to receive a reward (transistor radios) for helping with the research, while the other would not. This common outcome of reward or deprivation was decided *either* by the toss of a coin, *or* by the experimenter, *or* by one of the two groups. In Lewin's terms, all these groups experienced 'common fate'. However, in the crucial Control condition this experience was omitted: the group members here had nothing in common *except* their colour label. Finally, the participants were asked to stand up to be rated (privately) by the others on a number of evaluative scales. The results showed that only in the conditions in which some interdependence existed did there seem to be a group influence on the ratings; those in the child's own group were rated more favourably than those in the other group. In the Control group, though, the ratings of ingroup and outgroup members did not differ, thus leading Rabbie to conclude that mere classification was *not* enough to form a group and influence people's judgements along group lines.

Henri was present at both the Frascati and Royaumont conferences and it is not difficult to imagine that he would have been simultaneously intrigued by and envious of Rabbie's experiment. Indeed, listening to Rabbie at the Frascati meeting may well have prompted him to begin his investigations into the minimal conditions necessary for intergroup discrimination. In the discussion after Rabbie's subsequent paper at Royaumont, the conference proceedings recorded:

> Henri Tajfel described an experiment he had recently conducted and which seemed to favour the social comparison theory which Jaap Rabbie had rejected. When an experimental group received no more information about another group (which was never seen) than that it was either similar or different from themselves, then the amount of generosity shown (in a sharing out situation) varied directly with the imputed similarity. However, Rabbie did not accept this as support for social comparison theory.[104]

That final telling sentence signified the start of an intellectual disagreement between Rabbie and Henri that was to persist until Henri's death, and that was vigorously prosecuted by one of Henri's collaborators thereafter.[105]

Once Henri had got his feet properly under his desk at Bristol, he began planning how to continue this work on the *minimal group paradigm* (as it later became known). The arrival of his FF Grant in 1968 meant that he now had the resources to recruit research assistants to help him design and conduct the necessary experiments. Henri approached Mick Billig, who had just graduated from Bristol, and Bob Bundy, a postgraduate on the Nuffield project. He told them of his idea for an experiment on the behavioural effects of mere categorisation and gave them the job of figuring out how to implement it.

Their first idea for inducing a social categorisation involved showing school children a series of slides which (briefly) showed a cluster of dots. Unlike in Rabbie's experiment, these children all knew each other because they were in the same class at school, apparently taking part in an experiment on visual judgements. Each child was then put into an 'overestimator' or 'underestimator' group, allegedly on the basis of their estimates (but actually at random). However, each child was told of their group membership privately and, crucially, *they did not know who else was also in their group or the other*. This was the first important difference from Rabbie's procedure where, it will be recalled, the children could actually see who was in which group. Next, the children were asked to distribute rewards (small amounts of money) between various anonymous class-mates, identified only by a number and their group membership ('overestimator'or 'underestimator'). They did this on a number of simple decision matrices in which points (which would later be converted into money) had to be allocated in a zero-sum way between two recipients. Importantly, their own code number never appeared on any of the matrices so they were never awarding money to themselves. The children could be relatively fair in their points allocation (e.g., 7 to one recipient and 8 to the other), or they could show varying degrees of discrimination (e.g., up to a maximum of 14 to one recipient and 1 to the other). This was the second difference from Rabbie's paradigm since, instead of making mere evaluations, the participants were engaging in meaningful intergroup *behaviour* by giving money to their class-mates.[106]

The results of this first experiment were quite astonishing. When the two recipients indicated on the matrix were both members of the same group, whether it was the participant's own or the other, the children tended to be egalitarian in their decisions, giving each about the same amount of money. But when the recipients came from different groups, the children's behaviour changed dramatically. Now they consistently gave more money to the person in their group than to the outgroup person, even though they had no idea who these two recipients were. The point of fairness on these early matrices was 7.5. On average, the children opted for 9.2, a choice which was reliably higher than that fair point in a statistical sense. In fact, 84% of the children showed some ingroup favouritism in their reward allocations.[107]

Billig remembers Henri's excitement when the first results came in:

> Henri was *delighted* with the results from this first experiment … he was so excited. He started looking at the matrices. He was so excited that he started saying things that, under normal circumstances, he wouldn't have said. When he saw someone giving *everything* – 14-1 in favour of the ingroup – he said, 'I bet this is a really authoritarian person'![108]

And this from someone who spent much of his professional life decrying personality explanations of intergroup behaviour!

Other experiments soon followed. One necessary modification, or so it seemed to Henri, was to find an even more arbitrary method of putting the children into groups. He felt that being an 'overestimator' or 'underestimator' might convey some element of value. A second change was to devise some new measures of intergroup discrimination that could more precisely indicate what allocation strategies were being adopted by participants. Were they, for instance, simply favouring their own group members in an absolute sense (a strategy that became known as 'maximum ingroup profit' (MIP)), or in a *relative* sense so that ingroup members received *more than* outgroup members (so called 'maximum difference' (MD))? And it would also be useful to be able to assess participants' interest in non-discriminatory allocations – giving as much as possible to all ('maximum joint profit' (MJP)) or 'fairness (F).

Claude Flament, a French colleague who wrote a statistics book with one of the boys that Henri had looked after in the FOPOGO home after the war (Stèphane Erhlich; Chapter 3), takes up the story:

> I believe it was in September 1968, near Ross River, to the north of San Francisco: Henri particularly excited, told us of his idea to study intergroup relations in a <u>social vacuum</u> (I never heard him talk of minimal group); for him this was the root of that intergroup aggression which, in a less empty social environment, could lead to such things as the Nazi hatred towards the Jews – a problem which Henri always recognised as being the underlying motivation of all his scientific work.
>
> Henri's ideas were very clear: experiment 1 had already been conducted, and experiment 2 was all planned (Henri told us of a pleasant half day spent with the Curator of the Museum of Modern Art – no doubt in Bristol – at the end of which he had chosen reproductions of Klee and Kandinsky). The only problem that worried him was the difficulty in constructing matrices (analogous to those in Experiment 1) that permitted the measurement of the three variables (MIP, MJP and MD) that he wanted to observe.[109]

Flament, being a mathematical psychologist, offered to help and, on the flight back to France, devised a series of decision matrices that could solve the problem that had been bothering Henri.

Thus, the second minimal group experiment involved an initial task of picture preferences (for paintings by Klee and Kandinsky) which was used to categorise participants into the Klee or Kandinsky group. Other aspects of the procedure remained the same except for the introduction of Flament's more sophisticated reward allocation matrices. The results from this experiment were broadly similar to the first effort – the children still gave more money to their fellow group members – and showed, in addition, what seemed to be underlying that ingroup favouritism. Using Flament's new measures it was clear that participants were attempting simultaneously to ensure that ingroup members were handsomely rewarded (MIP), but also rewarded *more than* outgroup members (MD). In fact, on some matrices participants even elected to give a little less to an ingroup recipient if, by doing so, they could give him[110] more than the outgroup recipient.[111] It was also apparent that they were also attempting to be somewhat fair to both groups, but just a little fairer to ingroupers than to outgroupers.

After these first experiments, further variations were introduced. The most important of these was to create the most minimal social categories of all, effected simply by the toss of a coin.[112] Even this most primitive form of group classification was sufficient to elicit intergroup discrimination.

It is worth reflecting how remarkable these findings were: the groups in these experiments could not have been more meaningless; they had had no prior history of interaction, let alone conflict, and no prospect of any future either; there was no rational motive for the children to have favoured their ingroup so consistently; in fact, the 'rational' thing to have done would have always to distribute the rewards fairly, or in such a way as to maximise the total amount of money that the experimenter would have to pay out (MJP) because, in all probability, as many of their friends would have been in the outgroup as in the ingroup. And yet, discriminate they did.

His old friend Bruner was in no doubt about the importance of the work:

> I thought your paper in Scientific American was simply stunning, and one of the best pieces of social psychological writing I had seen in a decade. You are one of the social psychologists who keeps the field from being trivialized by little trick experiments and I salute you.[113]

The discrimination that Henri observed in this minimal group paradigm proved to be a robust phenomenon. It was replicated over twenty times with a range of participants of different ages and from a variety of countries.[114] True, there have been some anomalous results: in some cultures discrimination has not been found;[115] when penalties are allocated instead of rewards, discrimination usually disappears;[116] when multiple outgroups are added, little discrimination is seen;[117] and, of course, there was that initial minimal group experiment of Rabbie,[118] which had set Henri off on his voyage of discovery, and whose Control condition had yielded no evidence of ingroup favouritism.

Henri was nearly always scrupulous in citing Rabbie's earlier research, although he usually went to some lengths to explain why Rabbie's Control condition did not really constitute a bona fide intergroup situation. This point has been debated repeatedly over the years, but there is probably a very simple reason why Rabbie failed to find any ingroup bias in that Control condition – a lack of statistical power. In a subsequent study, when the number of participants was increased, some ingroup favouritism was observed.[119] Still, for all Rabbie's legitimate claims of priority in the invention of a minimal group paradigm, there is no doubt who the field has judged the originator: I noted earlier how Henri's first paper on the subject has been cited over 1900 times over the past forty-eight years; the paper by Rabbie and Horwitz, despite a two-year advantage, has received just 184 citations!

Perhaps it was inevitable that such a ground-breaking discovery would spark methodological and theoretical controversy, occasionally with more rancour than is usual in scientific discourse. These debates have variously focused on: the interpretation of the results as showing discrimination or fairness;[120] the possibility of demand characteristics in the minimal group paradigm;[121] statistical issues;[122] measurement alternatives to the payment matrices;[123] and the extent to which economic self-interest can explain the typically observed discrimination.[124]

Henri's first explanation for the minimal group discrimination was that any division into groups triggered some kind of competitive norm, perhaps endemic in western societies.[125] He quickly abandoned the idea, however, since it begged the question of why a competitive norm, rather than an egalitarian or an economic maximisation norm, both also present in western societies, should prevail. As he and Billig wrote:

(normative) statements of this nature can be made to explain almost everything, and therefore they explain little if anything at all.

Instead, they introduced a new idea:

> We assume that the fundamental problem in any intergroup situation is that
> of defining one's social identity, of placing oneself in relation to others.... A
> group can contribute to the positive aspects of an individual's image of him-
> self only if it can be positively differentiated on some value-laden dimensions
> from other groups.[126]

Here, then, we see one of the first appearances in his writing of the concept of social
identity, an idea that he would soon develop into a full-blown theory.

The minimal group paradigm continues to prove attractive to researchers. Put
'minimal group paradigm' into the Abstract field of a PsychInfo search and you
will discover extraordinary array of experiments that use variants of Henri's original procedure. There you will find neuroscientific studies of brain activation,
neurophysiological experiments on eye gaze and arousal, investigations of implicit
prejudice, memory experiments, and even evolutionary experiments of mate choice
and pathogen perception.[127] Quite what Henri, with his aversion to reductionist and
biological accounts of intergroup behaviour, would have made of this cornucopia of
knowledge we shall never know. But I suspect that he might have felt more than a
soupçon of satisfaction that an idea, first sparked by Rabbie's paper in that sixteenth-
century Villa Falconieri in Frascati in 1964, had garnered such a rich scientific harvest.

At this time, Henri also initiated another project, a new series of books by
European social psychologists, *European Monographs in Social Psychology*. He negotiated publication rights with Academic Press, a prestigious international publisher
with offices in London and New York, and appointed himself Editor-in-Chief. The
second volume of the Series was a book that Henri co-edited with Joachim Israel,
a Swedish sociologist. This was a substantial volume of essays that came to define
European social psychology's preoccupations about the state of the discipline and
its aspiration to develop an alternative to the dominant North American zeitgeist.
The clue to these concerns is in the book's title, *The Context of Social Psychology*.[128]
Although the book did not pretend to offer a single vision of what this alternative
should look like, a common theme of the chapters was that traditional (i.e., North
American) social psychology had become theoretically sterile and methodologically constipated in its attempts to gain respectability as a science. According to
Henri and several of his fellow contributors, those twin defects meant that it too
often ignored the contexts – both macro and micro – in which social behaviour was
embedded. As a result, it was failing to offer adequate explanations of and solutions
to many of the world's most pressing social problems.

Henri himself wrote a chapter in this book entitled, 'Experiments in a Vacuum'.[129]
He seems to have been fond of this phrase. He had used it ten years before in his
chapter on social perception in Argyle and Humphrey's primer on experimental
social psychology when discussing Katz and Braly's famous study of national and

ethnic stereotypes[130] (Chapter 5). In this now long and, at times, rather abstruse chapter, Henri sought to address three issues.

The first concerned the age-old tension between basic and applied research. At the time of this book's publication, social psychology was undergoing one of its periodic 'crises'. There was much soul-searching about the practical relevance of much social psychological research and the external validity of its preferred (experimental) methodologies.[131] Indeed, the book by Israel and Henri came to represent a specifically European perspective on that crisis. In the first two sections of his chapter, Henri added his own observations to the ongoing debate. In many ways, he adopted a conventional stance on methodology. He argued that experiments were, on balance, still the most fruitful way for testing hypotheses. The problem with most experiments was not, he suggested, that they attempted to control conditions and measure (or manipulate) variables, but that they were too often divorced from external social reality. Participants were regarded as interchangeable atoms with no involvement in or connections to the world outside the laboratory. He concluded:

> Therefore, a description of the 'conditions' of an experiment must include the analysis or the description of these aspects of the social context that the researcher considers to be relevant to the conclusion he draws; also any conclusion about the confirmation or invalidation of his hypotheses must relate to these conditions.[132]

And, a little further on:

> Experiments cannot be conducted in a social vacuum. This implies … that an analysis of the social context of the experiment and of the social situation which it represents must always be made.[133]

Then, apparently unaware of the irony, he illustrates his argument with his own minimal group experiments. In reading the procedure of those studies, one searches in vain for any description of the wider social context from which their participants came. Moreover, in designing the paradigm, Henri had gone to some lengths to make the situation as devoid of meaning – as 'vacuous', one might say – as possible. Perhaps that is why he had actually described it to his colleague Flament as a way of studying intergroup relations 'in a social vacuum'!

A second issue discussed by Henri in this chapter was his belief that social psychology, as traditionally practised, tended to favour either biological explanations (e.g., genetic or physiological factors), or generic psychological processes operating within an asocial individual (e.g., cognitive dissonance theory), or sociological determinants (e.g., the link between socio-economic disparities and prejudice). Rarely, he felt, did it adopt a truly social psychological approach in which the origins of social behaviour are to be sought in the *relationship between* people. He thought that such a neglect was especially problematic when it came to studying intergroup behaviour. He singled out for particular criticism

Leonard Berkowitz, then probably the most well-known scholar working on aggression, including intergroup aggression. Henri quoted a few lines from Berkowitz's monograph on aggression:

> Granting all this, the present writer (Berkowitz) is still inclined to emphasize the importance of individualistic considerations in the field of group relations. Dealings between groups ultimately become problems of the psychology of the individual. Individuals decide to go to war; battles are fought by individuals; and peace is established by individuals.[134]

For Henri, such an analysis was deeply flawed because it offered no insights into the uniformities among individuals that so frequently characterised intergroup behaviour. Sarcastically, he observed:

> (According to Berkowitz) social conduct consists of inter-individual uniformities made up of an algebra of individual cognitions and motivations. One possible analogy that this brings to mind is that of a ping-pong table on which many balls might be falling simultaneously from all directions and distances. The balls would, of course, bounce off in their individual ways; but in doing so they obey a few relatively simple laws. One of the essential requirements for these laws to have predictive power is that the balls should not modify each other or the table on mutual impact, nor should the table modify the balls.[135]

Instead, he argued, we need theories of intergroup relations which could explain and predict how uniformities of group members' attitudes and behaviour could arise and, just as important, how the latter would vary with changing intergroup contexts. Quoting approvingly his former teacher, R.S. Peters,[136] he suggested that such theories would need to take account of humans as 'rule-following' creatures. The business of social psychology was to ascertain how such rules were learned and followed in given situations. It is an interesting question as to how far Henri followed this advice when constructing his own theory of intergroup behaviour only two years later (Chapter 7).

The third plank of Henri's argument in this chapter was to enter a plea for social psychology to concern itself more than it currently did with social change. By this, he did not only mean social change as macroscopic transformations of society, but also how people acted on their social environments to produce change, and were themselves changed as a result. A person:

> must create change, resist it, adapt to it or prepare for it; most often he will do all these things at the same time in dealing with the diversity of tasks that he faces in his social environment.[137]

This, he felt, was a very different conception of human psychology from that offered by most of the more reductionist accounts on offer. These implied that people were simply impinged upon by external forces, whether these be biological, environmental, or societal. He was offering, in other words, a more agentic and a more dialectical view of the person.

What kind of impact has this chapter had? Web of Science records a modest 200 citations.[138] Nevertheless, it is notable that it was still attracting citations as recently as 2019, forty-seven years after its appearance.

Predictably, the tenor of reviews of *The Context of Social Psychology* depended on which side of the Atlantic they were written. Brewster Smith, writing in *Science*, described it as a 'serious and difficult book',[139] although he also predicted – correctly as it turned out – that the (intellectual) culture gap between the ideas it contained and North American social psychology meant that it was unlikely to gain much traction there. He also noted that European social psychology seemed to be biting the American hand that fed it, presumably a reference to the generous financial support that EAESP had received from American sources in its early days. Still, his review was mostly sympathetic although, probably gallingly for Henri, he singled out Moscovici's chapter in the book for special attention and praise, devoting to Henri's barely more than a sentence. Some of Smith's American colleagues were less enthusiastic. Philip Shaver, for example, was quite scathing in his assessment of the book:

> My comments reveal that I am as disappointed by the Europeans as they have been by us. They raise few questions that haven't already been asked, and offer even fewer constructive alternatives.[140]

Throughout his review, Shaver constantly complained about the absence of new methodological proposals and the lack of innovative research in the book, rather missing the point of a volume whose goal was a theoretical and metatheoretical critique of traditional social psychology. Henri was quick to point this out in two rather acidic rejoinders.[141]

As usual, Bruner was very supportive:

> I have finally read your 'Experiments in a vacuum' and I enjoyed it, was disturbed and set wondering. The issue, of course, is broader than just social psychology. I was in an hours-long quarrel with Skinner at our Department colloquium the other night in which he would repeatedly want to make generalization from an ecological distorted learning situation used in experiment (the typical 'box') to any and all situations – assuming rather than proving he had a paradigm. So in social psychology as well.....Your paper is very general, properly abrasive, and elegantly written.[142].

As so often in his later letters to Henri, this one was signed in an endearingly affectionate fashion: '*Thine, Jerry*'.

In Europe, the book – and Henri's chapter – got a more sympathetic hearing. Gustav Jahoda recommended the book unreservedly, noting that: 'very few books have had such a powerful impact on the reader'.[143] He gave pride of place in his long (seven-page) review to Henri's own chapter. Perhaps because Jahoda adopted fairly conventional methodologies himself in his cross-cultural research, he appreciated that Henri did not advocate the wholesale abandonment of experimentation, unlike some other contributors to the volume. Nevertheless, he was somewhat critical of Henri's attempt to divorce social psychology so strongly from general (i.e., individual psychology). Jahoda regarded this as an impossibility. Instead, he offered a rather appealing analogy to situate social psychology in relation to individual psychology and sociology. Theories of physics, he wrote, could provide reasonably precise predictions about the movement of a perfectly round ball down a smooth inclined plane in the laboratory. But it ran into difficulties in predicting the path of a boulder rolling down a hillside. For the latter, one needed also geology, which could provide relevant information about the make-up of the boulder and the steepness and irregularities of the terrain through which it was moving. Armed with both disciplines, one might hope to arrive at a set of rough-and-ready generalisations confined to particular geographical areas, rather than aspire to iron-clad laws with universal application. For Jahoda, social psychology was a bit like this fictional discipline of 'boulder-ology', drawing on principles from general psychology which were necessarily constrained by cultural factors in the manner and scope of their operation.

Cherchez les femmes

Whilst Henri was busy concerning himself with building up the Bristol department, establishing his new research projects and helping to run the newly formed European Association, he soon had something else to worry about. In May 1969, he found himself being obliged to write a long letter to the Bristol vice-chancellor after being summoned to see him following a complaint that had been made about him (Henri) by a student. Here is the letter in its entirety:

> Private and confidential.
> Professor A.R. Collar
> Vice-Chancellor,
> Senate House
>
>   31st May, 1969
> Dear Vice-Chancellor,
> Professor Brown told me that you asked him to see you next Wednesday. It is, of course, possible that his appointment with you has nothing to do with the matter we discussed last week; but as you may have felt it necessary to raise the issue with him, I thought I would write to you before you saw him, and also for more general reasons. Please forgive me for burdening you with this letter. I know how busy you are, but I could see no other way at present of conveying to you some of the preoccupations which are obviously important to me and to my future in this University.

(i)   For reasons that you will understand, I did not report to Brown our conversation, but told him that you wished to see me about a routine matter. From the time he arrived here and I turned over to him the headship of the Department, we have been working together in mutual respect and trust in full cooperation. It would be distressing if this relationship, which promises so well for the development of the Department as one of the most active and interesting in this country, were to be affected by an incident which need have no further relevance to our present or to our future work.

(ii)   As you must have seen, I was fairly shaken at our interview. I tried to explain – badly – to you and to the Pro-Vice-Chancellor the background of the whole affair, without denying the fact that it was due to nothing but my own stupidity, I formed the impression that I was given the privilege of trust both by yourself and by the Pro-Vice-Chancellor when I stated that nothing genuinely improper has happened and that nothing will happen in the future which could give rise to any form of misinterpretation; I also felt that I had your sympathy and agreement in dismissing as contemptible any allegations or inferences about the relevance of all this to the academic work of, or decisions about, any individual student.[144]

(iii)   When I was appointed in 1967 to the Chair of Social Psychology, I was given to understand that my task was to be twofold: to hold the fort until the arrival of a permanent Head of Department, and to develop the social aspects of psychology which were practically non-existent in Bristol despite the rapidly growing importance of the subject. In my two years here, I have tried to do both to the best of my ability. As you found yourself so unexpectedly in what you called on Wednesday 'the driving seat', it would perhaps not be improper for me to summarize what has been done in two academic years.

There was one postgraduate student in social psychology in 1967; there are now thirteen; next year there will be at least seventeen, well over half of them supported entirely from outside private funds. Undergraduate training in social psychology has been introduced at all stages. Research grants in social psychology to the Department, of which there were none in 1967, now total very nearly £60.000, including a new grant from the United States of which I was informed this week. Bristol has been put 'on the map' in the international academic community of social psychologists: we had in the last years a large number of distinguished visitors from this country, the United States, and Europe. If I may refer to two items more directly personal: in the last two months alone, I was awarded its first annual prize by a major learned society in the United States, and was elected President of the European Association of Social Psychology.[145]

    The purpose of this enumeration is not, as it might so easily appear, to blow my own trumpet. I should like to make three related points. The first is that

I have gone all out to fulfil the tasks that have been entrusted to me by the University; the second, that – undoubtedly, like many other academics of some reputation – I would find it possible to accept one of a number of pending or potential offers of posts elsewhere; and the third – and by far the most important – that I like it in Bristol, I like the University, and would dearly wish to stay here and to continue my work here. Please do not misunderstand this; the conjunction of the last two points is meant to convey exactly what they express, and nothing else: I very much wish to stay in Bristol and in England[146].

Entirely through my own fault, there is now a possibility that embarrassment and awkwardness may persist for a while despite the fact that I shall not give it at any time the slightest possible provocation. I cannot help feeling that someone is 'gunning' for me, though I do not know who and why. The purpose of writing all this is to ask you to help me, if you can, to avoid future effects on my life in Bristol of something in the past which was not – in the last analysis – either serious in fact or in intent, or improper in any real sense.

As this is a personal letter, I would be extremely grateful if you could treat it as such rather than consigning it to the files. In addition to the impending change in your office, there have been some unfortunate incidents in the recent past in various universities in this country and elsewhere that you will undoubtedly remember as well as I do.

I must apologize again for imposing on you this letter which turned out to be much longer than I intended or expected. Let me also thank you once again for the kindness that you showed me last Wednesday and for your tactful and human dealing with a situation that must have been difficult and embarrassing for you.

Yours sincerely   Henri Tajfel

Two observations are worth making about this letter. The first is how little genuine remorse Henri shows over the incident. In paragraph (ii) he attributes the incident to his 'own stupidity'. Towards the end, he admits some fault again and then expresses 'embarrassment and awkwardness', though it is unclear about what he feels this, especially when, in the next breath, he says, with more than a hint of paranoia, that he feels that someone is 'gunning' for him. And, at the end of the paragraph, he denies again that the incident was 'either serious in fact or intent, or improper in any real sense'. The second – and connected – point is how the absence of any apology is overshadowed by the lengths he goes to (in paragraph (iii)) to list his achievements since coming to Bristol and to make a (not so) veiled threat about how much the university would lose if he were to leave.

With good reason, Henri was obviously worried by this summons to the Vice-Chancellor's office. David Milner remembers a conversation he had with Henri at about this time. Apparently, Henri had said:

For the first time in my life, I don't know what to do about something … some silly bitch has made a complaint about me. I don't know what she said

> so I don't know what I'm supposed to plead guilty or innocent to. She might
> have said I raped her for God's sake....You know Dave, it's so unfair because
> I never do anything. It's just the chase. I need to know that they want to. I've
> never done anything.[147]

If he had expressed only minimal remorse in his letter to the VC, now there is no
hint of any apology. Instead, there is only an irritated expression of injustice that the
student had had the temerity to complain at all.

Henri's harassment of this unfortunate student was by no means an isolated incident. In the previous chapter, I noted two previous occasions at Oxford where he
had attempted to importune young women against their wishes; during his time
at Bristol, this harassing behaviour seems to have increased in its frequency and
flagrancy.

I am conscious of the risks in using current normative standards of conduct in
public life to examine events which occurred over 40 years ago. It is certainly the
case that the climate in universities (and elsewhere in public life) in the late 1960s
and early 1970s was much more permissive about high status men abusing their
power to take sexual advantage of women students and colleagues. However, as I
hope to show, Henri was something of an outlier, even by the standards of those
days. As the distinguished biographer Hermione Lee warns, 'Historical condescen-
sion is a very bad thing.' When writing about the morally questionable behaviour
of one's subject – in her case, the anti-semitism of Edith Wharton and Virginia
Woolf – she advised that 'you should contextualise it – but that doesn't mean that
you excuse it'.[148]

In the research for this book, I interviewed over fifty former colleagues and
students of Henri, of whom twelve were women. Over half of these interviewees
mentioned Henri's reputation for womanising, and four of the women spoke
openly of his sexual advances towards them personally. If we add to this testimony
the evidence from three other women which is held in the Wellcome Library, it
becomes clear that Henri was both persistent and profligate in his advances.

Here, for example, is the experience of a student being interviewed (alone) by
Henri for a PhD place at Bristol. After a few preliminary questions, she reported:

> and he sort of sidled over to me and put his hand on my knee – and, I
> remember this intently – so I thought, 'he's obviously trying to put me at
> ease'....During the interview, his hand slid further and further up my skirt.
> But it was done in a *brilliant* way ... it never went very far, so at no point could
> I stop or change my position. But it ended up *right* up my skirt .... and there
> was nothing on his face to indicate that anything untoward was happening....
> Then he asked, 'You don't mind my hand being there do you?'....[149]

Supervision sessions with him were quite stressful. She intentionally wore dun-
garees to all her meetings but, even so, the harassment continued:

First of all, I'd have to spend a week psyching myself up [for a supervision]. And then I came to see him. And, as I say, he would have some absolutely brilliant insights but you would have to go through this whole rigmarole of, 'why didn't I ever wear a skirt?', 'why don't I sit on the bed with him?' [Henri had a divan bed in his office][150]

A postgraduate student, recently arrived at Bristol, recounted a similar episode:

My first impression was that I thought he was a bit odd. He agreed a meeting at 5 p.m, when the place [the department] was closing. I felt a bit scared … .he was just trying to touch me and I said something like, 'You may touch me because you are my supervisor and there's nothing I can do, but I don't like it.'[151]

Another Bristol postgraduate student reported a similar experience:

There was always a problem doing individual supervisions with Henri … we had a number of occasions where there were just the two of us, and he would always sit far too close to you on the couch.… One time, early on, he insisted that he and I go to Geneva for a weekend.… It was quite difficult to say no. But, actually, I found with him – maybe he was getting old – but he didn't persist, which was interesting. So there'd be a move, but … it almost felt ritu- alistic. Certainly, he took no for an answer if it was firmly given.[152]

Parties at Henri's house were a frequent occurrence during the 1970s. But women attending them learned to avoid goodnight kisses from Henri on the door- step 'because a tongue would invariably be involved', according to another woman informant[153] who, nevertheless, wanted to make it clear that she it felt it was just light-hearted fun at a rather boozy party and that she herself did not in any way feel threatened by it.

Tony Manstead, who studied psychology at Bristol as an undergraduate (1968– 1971), recalled that one of his (female) friends, a fellow student, changed course shortly after some unwanted attentions from Henri in the first weeks of her degree.[154]

Colin Fraser, a colleague of Henri at Bristol for several years, also recalled that he had once got very angry when one of his (Colin's) research assistants told him that some time previously she had been chased by Henri around his office. Colin proposed that he would confront Henri about that but she did not want him to intervene and so he did nothing further.[155] One of Henri's first secretaries used the same expression of 'being chased around his office for ages' by Henri.[156]

It was not just people in his own department who were the object of his sexual predations. Another woman, whilst a postgraduate at another university, approached Henri at a conference with a question about her research:

And so I asked this question and, as I was asking the question, his arm came around my shoulders. And I thought, 'OK, what am I going to do?'. I mean, it was broad daylight – I think we were in a sort of corner – but we weren't off in private anywhere. And I was in my mid-20s. So, he was probably in his 50s. So I thought, 'This is the big noise in the field. What am I going to do?'. And then I thought 'I'm damn well going to get the answer'. So I stuck it out, got the answer and then sort of went down and off. And all the rest of the conference he kept appearing and asking me for a Chinese meal or a drink.[157]

Some of his contemporaries tended to downplay the seriousness of this behaviour. Maureen Brown, wife of the head of department, thought it was little more than flirtation:

I used to think it was just a game. That he loved doing it. He was like a schoolboy....this was really fun for him. This was a game he indulged in. But he didn't expect to be taken seriously, but maybe some people did. To me, it seemed it was a ritual.[158]

Maureen Brown had used the word 'ritual' to describe Henri's philandering. That word was also used by E in her testimony quoted earlier and, as we have seen, Henri himself described his antics as 'just the chase'. However, Maureen Brown's husband, put it slightly differently:

I think it would be fair to say that he had an uninhibited response to his own impulses....whether they were sexual or anything else.[159]

Another of Henri's victims, who had been openly 'groped' by Henri when she and her husband paid him a social call, agreed:

I don't believe it was totally under his control, this attitude [towards women] … it was a compulsion.[160]

Another of his victims reported that Henri had once confided in her about his sexual depredations:

He did talk about it from time to time … he put it down to a very traumatic experience he'd had in the concentration camps during the war … so I think what he was saying was really, 'I'm a bit disturbed'. He would never have used that expression but that's, in essence, as what it was about, was his attribution – having had an exceedingly deprived experience in the concentration camp which had disturbed the way he thought about things, and his needs and motives.[161]

Whatever the explanation for Henri's behaviour – whether harmless flirtation, or a reflection of a more general untrammelled impulsiveness, or symptomatic of some earlier trauma, or, perhaps more simply, a habitual abuse of patriarchal power[162] – there is little doubt that most of his victims found his harassment to be, at best, embarrassing and, at worst, traumatic.

Before closing this discussion, I would make one further observation. In all of Henri's writing – over a hundred articles and chapters, possibly close to a million words – I struggle to recall more than a few lines devoted to sexism or gender relations, even if only by way of illustrative example.[163] For someone whose antennae for problematic intergroup relations in the world were usually so finely tuned, is it not remarkable that he managed so completely to overlook this most fundamental of social fault-lines? Could it be, I wonder, that the defects that he so often displayed in his relationships with women also extended to a wider intellectual myopia when it came to theoretical analysis of gender relations?

Notes

1 Eiser, personal communication, January 2018.
2 Billig, personal communication, January 2018.
3 Argyle (1959, pp. 14–15).
4 Dukes and Bevan (1952).
5 Gaetani, personal communication, May 2017.
6 A. Tajfel interview, September 2014.
7 DeLamater, Hefner, and Clignet (1968).
8 Kelman, personal communication, January 2018.
9 Letter to Campbell, 7 February, 1967; WC, box PSY/TAJ/7/4/9.
10 Letter to Bruner, 23 February, 1967; WC, box PSY/TAJ/7/4/7.
11 Letter from the University of Bristol Registrar and Secretary, March 6, 1967.
12 www.measuringworth.com
13 LCA.
14 Letter to Bruner, 8 March 1966; HUA, box HUG 4242.5.
15 A. Tajfel interview, September 2014.
16 Letter from Bruner, 29 March, 1966; HUA, box HUG 4242.5.
17 Tajfel (1969c).
18 Tajfel (1969b). This article also appeared in a slightly different form in the *Journal of Biosocial Science*. Not for the first – or last – time, Henri showed himself adept at recycling the same material in different publications.
19 As in Asch's (1956) and Sherif's (1936) famous experiments.
20 E.g., Allport and Pettigrew (1957); Brown and Lenneberg (1954); Segall, Campbell, and Herskovits (1963).
21 Tajfel (1969c), pp. 328–31.
22 January 2019, WoS.
23 Lorenz (1966).
24 Tajfel (1969d).
25 Tajfel (1969d), pp. 175–6.
26 Tajfel (1969b), p. 80.
27 Pettigrew (1958).
28 Heider (1958).
29 Ideas later taken up by Pettigrew (1979) and Hewstone (1989).
30 Tajfel (1969b), p. 95.

31 Letter from Bruner, 8 May 1970; HUA, box HUG 4242.5.

32 WoS, February 2019.

33 Billig (2002). See also, Brown (2002); Frosh (2002).

34 E.g., Fiske and Taylor (1984); Hamilton (1981).

35 Hamilton (1981), p. 335.

36 Tajfel (1981a).

37 G. Smith interview, December 2017. I can confirm this story. In 1973 I had a conversation with Henri in which I was trying to tell him that I wanted to quit my PhD, just nine months after starting. In a (vain) attempt to dissuade me, Henri recounted how he had nearly 'run back to Oxford with my tail between my legs' soon after coming to Bristol.

38 A. Tajfel interview, September 2014.

39 Harré interview, October 2017.

40 Eiser interview, October 2016.

41 Although he had not actually taught Henri, arriving there just as Henri graduated. They had met several times at Birkbeck alumni events (J. Brown interview; WC, box PSY/TAJ/8/2).

42 J. Brown interview; WC, box PSY/TAJ/8/2.

43 Eiser interview, October 2016.

44 J. Brown interview; WC, box PSY/TAJ/8/2.

45 Billig interview, October 2016.

46 J. Brown interview; WC, box PSY/TAJ/8/2.

47 Milner interview, December 2016.

48 WC, box, PSY/TAJ/7/5/43.

49 Letter to Jahoda, 3 March 1968; WC, box PSY/TAJ/ 7/4/24.

50 Letter from Festinger, 24 April 1968; WC, box PSY/TAJ/7/5/5.

51 Telegram to Festinger, 29 April 1968; WC, box PSY/TAJ/7/5/5.

52 Letter to Festinger, 29 April 1968; WC, box PSY/TAJ/7/5/5.

53 Letter from Festinger, 3 May 1968; WC, box PSY/TAJ/7/5/5.

54 Letter to Festinger, 13 May 1968; WC, box PSY/TAJ/7/5/5.

55 Festinger (1957).

56 Personal communication, January 2018.

57 Personal communication, 4 February 2018.

58 Letter to Melvin Fox (FF), 9 January 1967; WC, box PSY/TAJ/6/31.

59 Initially, Henri had proposed that FF support a research centre just at Bristol, 'The Centre for Research in Social Psychology at Bristol'. This grandiose plan, with an equally grandiose budget of $47,000 per annum, was to support one or two research fellows to work on: '1. Experimental studies of intergroup relations; 2. Comparative studies of race relations; 3. Training for research in the psychological aspects of social change in developing countries'; 4. Experimental studies of conflict resolution' (letter to Marshall Robinson (FF), 8 June 1967; WC, box PSY/TAJ/6/31).

60 www.measuringworth.com

61 Letter from Robert Schmid (FF), 14 June 1968; WC, box PSY/TAJ/6/31.

62 Graumann (1999); Moscovici and Markova (2006); van Avermaet (2017).

63 Lanzetta (1963), Technical report on Sorrento meeting, December, 1963; KUL.

64 Festinger, undated; BL.

65 Moscovici and Markova (2006), p. 266.

66 Tajfel (1965).

67 Jahoda and Moscovici (1967), pp. 298–99; emphasis in original.

68 Speltini interview, June 2016.

69 Personal communication to author, February 2018.

70 Moscovici and Markova (2006), pp. 145–6.

71 East-West meetings continued into the late 1990s, even after the removal of the Iron Curtain. In all, 11 such meetings were organised by the Association.

72 Letter to Nuttin, 12 September 1968; KUL.

73 Letter from Henri to members of the Executive Committee, 30 September 1968; KUL.

74 Tajfel (1972c).

75 As, indeed, has sometimes happened: e.g., Doise *et al.* (1972); Zimbardo (1969).

76 Editorial, EJSP, *1*(1), p. 5.

77 Tajfel (1972c), p. 315.

78 Berghahn (2001); Saunders (1999).

79 Berghahn (2001); Saunders (1999).

80 Saunders (1999).

81 Schruijer (2007).

82 Simpson (1994).

83 De Sola Pool (1966).

84 Schruijer (2007), p. 73; Moscovici and Markova (2006), p. 270.

85 Horowitz (1967).

86 Horowitz (1967), p. 51.

87 Schruijer (2007), p. 85.

88 Letter to Campbell, 7 February, 1967; WC, PSY/TAJ/7/4/9.

89 Milner interview, December 2016.

90 Tajfel (1972c), p. 316.

91 Flament (2010).

92 Tajfel (1970); Tajfel, Billig, Bundy, and Flament (1971) – Flament's ordinal position in this list of authors is correct. However, when citing this paper, Henri always placed Flament as *second* author. This discrepancy arose out of a proof-reading mix-up as the paper was going to press. Henri had always intended Flament to be second author, in recognition of his role in helping to devise the payment matrices. However, when then paper was published, Flament had mysteriously slipped to last position, a change for which Henri felt himself responsible. In a letter to Flament, informing him of the mistake, Henri promised that he would always cite Flament as second author (letter to Flament, 9 September 1971). Flament, himself, never followed this practice, preferring, both for reasons of '*exactitude bibliographique*' and for the modesty of his contribution, to remain in fourth place (Bourhis, Gagnon, and Sachdev (1997)); Billig and Tajfel (1973); Tajfel and Billig (1974).

93 WoS, February 2019.

94 Allport (1954).

95 Adorno, Frenkel-Brunswik, Levinson, and Sanford (1950).

96 Sherif, Harvey, White, Hood, and Sherif (1961).

97 Sherif *et al.* (1961).

98 Ferguson and Kelley (1964).

99 There is also a literary precedent for the idea of minimalistic groupings that nevertheless can come to assume social significance. This is the concept of '*granfalloon*', invented by Kurt Vonnegut in his 1963 novel, *Cat's Cradle*, to denote a group of people who believe themselves to have some common identity but whose association with each other is actually meaningless. I am grateful to my colleague Viv Vignoles for drawing this to my attention.

100 Lewin (1948).

101 EASP archive, KUL.

102 EASP archive, KUL.

103 Rabbie and Horwitz (1969).

104 EASP archive, KUL.

105 Turner and Bourhis (1996).

106 A useful account of the minimal group paradigm can be found at www.bbc.co.uk/programmes/b00yw6km.

107 Tajfel *et al.* (1971).

108 Billig interview, October 2016.

109 Letter from Flament to Bourhis, 19 September 1996, Bourhis *et al.* (1997); author's translation.

110 The first minimal group experiments only involved boys.

111 Tajfel *et al.* (1971).

112 Billig and Tajfel (1973).

113 Letter from Buner, 1 January 1971; WC, box PSY/TAJ/7/4/7.

114 Brewer (1979); Diehl (1988); Tajfel (1982b).

115 Wetherell (1982).

116 Gardham and Brown (2001); Mummendey and Otten (1998).

117 Hartstone and Augoustinos (1995).

118 Rabbie and Horwitz (1969).

119 Horwitz and Rabbie (1982).

120 Branthwaite, Doyle, and Lightbown (1979); Turner (1980).

121 Gerard and Hoyt (1974); Tajfel (1978a).

122 Aschenbrenner and Schaefer (1980); Brown, Tajfel, and Turner (1980).

123 Bornstein *et al.* (1983a, 1983b); Turner (1983ab).

124 Rabbie, Schot, and Visser (1989); Turner and Bourhis (1996).

125 Tajfel (1970); Tajfel *et al.* (1971).

126 Billig and Tajfel (1973), p. 49.

127 Otten (2016).

128 Israel and Tajfel (1972).

129 Tajfel (1972a).

130 Tajfel (1962a), p. 33.

131 E.g., Elms (1975); Gergen (1973); McGuire (1967; Ring (1967); Silverman (1971).

132 Tajfel (1972a), p. 75.

133 Tajfel (1972a), p. 84.

134 Berkowitz (1962), p. 167.

135 Tajfel (1972a), pp. 95–6.

136 Peters (1960).

137 Tajfel (1972a), p. 108.

138 As of January 2019.

139 Smith (1973), p. 610.

140 Shaver (1974), p. 357.

141 Tajfel (1975ab).

142 Letter from Bruner, 19 March 1971; WC, box PSY/TAJ/7/4/7.

143 Jahoda (1974), p. 111.

144 Although Henri is discreet about the precise topic of the previous conversation, the fact that he denies that anything improper occurred and his strenuous dismissal of any adverse implications for a student's work, makes it clear that some complaint from a student had found its way onto the Vice-Chancellor's desk.

145 Although obviously self-serving in intent, this paragraph is also quite an accurate summary of what he had achieved in his first two years at Bristol. The prize he refers to is the
   Gordon Allport Prize that he was awarded for his 'Cognitive aspects of prejudice' paper.
146 This protestation of his affection for Bristol is rather at variance with how often he
   complained about living and working there.
147 Milner interview, December 2016.
148 *Guardian* Review, 10 February 2018.
149 Testimony of C, WC, box PSY/TAJ/8/1. In this section I have anonymised most of my
   informants due to the sometimes sensitive nature of what they told me, and to the fact
   that they are still alive.
150 Testimony of C; WC, box PSY/TAJ/8/1.
151 Interview with D, March 2017.
152 Testimony of E, WC, box PSY/TAJ/8/1.
153 Personal communication to the author from K, March 2019.
154 Manstead interview, March 2018.
155 Fraser interview, October 2016.
156 Milner interview, December 2016.
157 Interview with H, January 2017.
158 M. Brown interview; WC, box PSY/TAJ/8/1.
159 J. Brown interview, WC, box PSY/TAJ/8/1.
160 Interview with A, June 2016.
161 Testimony of F, WC, box PSY/TAJ/8/1.
162 I am grateful to Jacy Young and Peter Hegarty for illuminating discussions of these
   same issues in relation to Henri's behaviour; see also Young & Hegarty (2019). Whilst
   this book was going to press, the Young & Hegarty article was published. Its revelations
   about Henri's sexual harassment, consistent with those that I have detailed here, led the
   executive committee of EASP to take the unusual step of removing Henri's name from
   the prize it awards triennially for lifetime achievement in social psychology. Its rationale
   for doing so was that the committee felt that he could no longer be regarded as a role
   model as a scientist (communication to members, 1 August 2019).
163 E.g., Tajfel (1974a, p. 78, 1978b, pp. 3, 18, 1978d).

7

BRISTOL

1972–1982

The grass is always greener

By 1972, Henri's star was very much in the ascendant. His 1969 essay on prejudice and his articles on the minimal group experiments had brought him to the attention of colleagues in North America. The *Context of Social Psychology* book, and his own chapter within it, was setting a new agenda for European social psychologists. And for the past three years he had been president of the newly formed European Association of Experimental Social Psychology (EAESP), as well as founding editor of what was proving an influential book series, *European Monographs in Social Psychology*. Despite – or perhaps because of – this new international visibility, Henri was no less ambivalent about Bristol than he had been from the start. The next years saw him making several serious attempts to move, and when those moves did not materialise he stepped up his efforts to obtain visiting positions in continental Europe and beyond. His feet, chronically itchy at the best of times, seemed even more impatient for pastures new.

One of his first relocation attempts was provoked by a long letter from John van de Geer, a Dutch colleague at Leiden University in the Netherlands[1]. Van de Geer told Henri that a mutual friend, Jos Jaspers, would shortly be leaving Leiden, thus creating a vacancy for a full professor. He described the post in some detail (administrative and teaching duties, likely salary) so there could be no doubt that the invitation was serious. Henri was immediately tempted. He saw the position as an opportunity for:

> moulding things in one's own way. I have now a number of ideas, developed in the last two or three years, as to how social psychology <u>should</u> continue in the future in order to survive as an intellectual discipline of some relevance.[2]

The prospective salary must also have been an attraction. It was over four times what he had been appointed on at Bristol three years before.

Several months of negotiations ensued before they were concluded with an offer to Henri as 'Professor Extraordinarius', to run from September 1971 to August 1973. The 'extraordinary' nature of the position indicates that it was not paid from government funds, as would have been usual, but from sources within Leiden University.[3] According to a member of the Leiden department at the time, Frans van der Meer, the post was probably half time,[4] or perhaps even as much as 60%.[5] The managerial duties were to be mostly performed by van der Meer, although it seems that, formally speaking, the university intended Henri to be departmental chair too. In various letters to and from Leiden over those two years, Henri is clearly involved in departmental debates and decisions (e.g., over appointments and appraisals) even, in one letter, referring to himself as 'Head of Department'.[6]

The appointment to Leiden seems to have been a rather secretive affair. According to Leiden colleagues at the time, it was 'to a high degree backstage business':

> the discussion did not result in a visible recruitment and selection procedure. To the contrary, decision-making in a small circle of prominent faculty members, including John van de Geer led to (his appointment).[7]

Neither of Henri's two closest colleagues at Bristol, Colin Fraser and Dick Eiser, knew anything about the Leiden chair. Whether the Bristol head of department or other more senior members of the university knew of or sanctioned the Leiden appointment is not publicly recorded.

Henri seems to have had some difficulty in fulfilling his Leiden responsibilities. Although in a later letter he claimed to make 10–11 visits to Leiden per year,[8] other informants recalled him visiting much less frequently. Ben Emans, then a Masters student at Leiden under Henri's supervision, recalled that he taught an introductory session of a course on intergroup relations in September 1971 and thereafter they met just four times between January 1972 and August 1973.[9] Ad van Knippenberg, Henri's only PhD student at Leiden, seems to have assumed much of the responsibility for teaching that course. He remembers that Henri came to Leiden 'once or twice a year' with reciprocal visits (by Ad) to Bristol about as often.[10]

Henri's appointment to Leiden was initially only for two years. This temporary arrangement probably suited both parties. It gave Henri the time to consider whether he would want something more permanent, and it allowed Leiden to assess whether such an unusual arrangement was really benefitting them. In the end, Henri decided not to extend the appointment. Apart from any professional misgivings that Henri may have had, one further factor was Anne's unwillingness to move to a country where neither she nor Paul spoke the language. Besides, it would have meant Paul moving school yet again.[11]

Leiden was not the only place on Henri's mind. In 1970, he had invited the famous developmental psychologist, Jean Piaget, to Bristol to give a talk. The visit seems to have gone well and, on his return to Geneva, Piaget wrote to

Henri, thanking him for his hospitality. After these niceties, he then enquired whether Henri would be interested in a new (full-time) Chair in social psychology that had just been created in Geneva. This was no idle enquiry. Piaget took two long paragraphs to sketch out the teaching that the post would entail and the generous research facilities he could expect (a '*chef de recherche*' and two assistants).[12]

Obviously flattered, Henri wrote back immediately. Noting how he and some other European colleagues – he mentioned Moscovici and Flament – had become increasingly frustrated by the limitations of social psychology on the other side of the Atlantic, he explained how they were trying to create alternative perspectives. From that point of view:

> the possibility to work in the ambience that you have created ... is a huge temptation.[13]

Nevertheless, because it was such a big decision, he would appreciate the opportunity to visit Piaget at his earliest convenience. Piaget replied immediately with arrangements for a four day visit in November.

Despite these encouraging overtures, nothing came of the Geneva idea. A short while later, he wrote to his friend Claude Flament at Aix-en-Provence, telling him that he decided against accepting Piaget's offer:

> It seems to me that it will be a rocky road ('chemin rocailleux') to build social psychology there.[14]

That 'rocky road' might have been Henri's worry that it would have been too difficult to escape from under Piaget's shadow at Geneva and develop social psychology there as he might have wished.[15]

Leiden and Geneva were not the end of Henri's attempts to escape from Bristol. In the autumn of 1972, he received a letter from Marie Jahoda, then professor of social psychology at the University of Sussex. There was a chair vacancy and Jahoda wondered whether Henri might be interested in it. She held out the promise of putting 'British social psychology on the map' by combining Henri's small group of social psychologists at Bristol with those already at Sussex (apart from LSE, Sussex was then the only other department of social psychology in Britain).[16]

Her letter bore immediate fruit. Henri must have responded enthusiastically because, before long, he was meeting with a pro-Vice Chancellor (a senior manager in the administration) at Sussex, Barry Supple, to discuss the practicalities of such a move.[17] His Bristol colleague, Colin Fraser, remembers the episode well. Henri summoned him to his office once day and asked him outright:

> How would you feel about moving to Sussex? I've been talking to Marie Jahoda and we think we could move social psychology from Bristol lock, stock and barrel, and set up a social psychology research centre.... Marie is very positive about this and I think it might be a very good idea.[18]

Meanwhile, at Sussex members of the social psychology group were also discussing the situation. Wolfgang Stroebe, then on the Sussex faculty, remembers
Henri's name being discussed as a potential professorial appointment, a prospect
which he and other colleagues welcomed enthusiastically.[19] Still, not everyone at
Sussex was entirely convinced by the idea of Henri's arrival and some protracted
negotiations ensued.[20]

In the end, the move to Sussex never happened. Perhaps Henri became uneasy
about swapping one provincial university for another – neither was Oxford, after
all – or maybe Sussex backed out because of the potential financial ramifications of
the move. In any event, he told Fraser a few months later 'that Sussex wasn't going to
work' and that, for the time being, was that.

'Juif errant'

If Henri's hopes for a permanent relocation seemed thwarted, his wanderlust was
unabated. In 1974 he wrote to Festinger explaining:

> the way to deal with the Bristol backwater has become simple: try to spend a
> few months away every year.[21]

And spending a few months away is exactly what he did in the 1970s: Paris
(March–May 1970, January–June 1973, March–May 1975); Michigan (April
1974); Jerusalem (July–September 1976); Bologna (February–June 1978); Helsinki
(September 1978).[22] By my calculation, in the decade 1970–1980 he spent a total of
nearly two years abroad in those visiting positions, to which should be added (albeit
infrequent) trips to Leiden in connection with his Chair there, and many other
shorter journeys for his committee work for EAESP (he was President until 1972),
the Transnational Committee, the European Science Foundation, and innumerable
conferences, at which he was an assiduous attender. Not for nothing was he known
at Bristol as 'the Heathrow Professor of Social Psychology'[23] or 'the Thomas Cook
Professor of Social Psychology'.[24]

There is no doubt that Henri was a restless man. As his widow said:

> That was the thing about Henri, that's why he had to be a social psycholo-
> gist. He spread his wings. He couldn't stay in one place, neither physically nor
> intellectually. He simply had to go out.[25]

Monika Nuttin, widow of his friend Jozef Nuttin, agreed:

> He was like a person who was always going forward but who was never
> happy to be in the same place where we were … Jeff (her husband) said, 'He
> was like a Wandering Jew,[26] always looking forward, never relaxed.'[27]

Henri himself might not have been too unhappy with the label 'Juif errant'.
Annie Beckers, a long-time assistant to Nuttin, saw a lot of Henri during the early

years of EAESP since meetings were often held at Leuven (where Nuttin worked), and she was often given the responsibility for looking after Henri. On one occasion, a song was playing on a record player by the swimming pool at Beckers' house. The song was '*Le Métèque*', sung by Georges Moustaki, an enchanting ballad of a Greek vagabond looking for love. The song's opening lines (and chorus) go like this:

> *Avec ma gueule de métèque*
> *De Juif errant, de pâtre grec....*

Which, roughly translated reads:

> *With my foreigner's face*
> *Of a wandering Jew, of a Greek shepherd....*[28]

Actually, 'foreigner' does not really do justice to '*métèque*'. In today's parlance, '*métèque*' is a rather offensive term for a foreigner, approximately equivalent to 'wog' or 'Paki' in Britain.[29] Beckers told me how, on hearing this song, Henri insisted on replaying it over and over, no fewer than *six* times.[30] Clearly it struck a chord with him.

Henri had a chronic sense of being 'an outsider' (Chapters 4 and 5): he had lived in five countries by the time he was 35; in his two adopted languages (French and English) he spoke with a pronounced accent which, especially in Britain, marked him out as a foreigner with an ambiguous location in the class structure; and, above all, his strongly felt Jewish identity made him acutely sensitive to anti-semitism, a form of prejudice that was hardly uncommon in his three principal countries of residence (Poland, France, and Britain). As he explained to the journalist David Cohen:

> There is no doubt a re-awakening of anti-Semitism. It happens I am a Jew although I have never been an active Zionist or religious. I am strongly a Jew. Here is a phenomenon that seems to exist through history, irrespective of social conditions ... today we have left-wing anti-Semitism as well as right-wing anti-Semitism. There is anti-Semitism in some Eastern countries although it is difficult to see what interest it serves.[31]

His Jewish identity often found expression in a strong attachment to Israel. In the 1970s, he wrote many letters to newspapers, usually to complain about journalists' (or other correspondents') treatment of the fractious situation in the Middle East. In these letters, not all of which were published, he invariably took Israel's side, although not always in a completely partisan way. Here is a particularly heartfelt example, discussing the Law of Return:

> Mr Ruthven (letters, November 20) wrote about the 'infamous' Law of Return which entitles any Jew to immigrate to Israel. ... I was born and

brought up Poland and went to France to study in 1936, at the age of seventeen – a decision of my parents which most probably saved my life. There were three possibilities open at the time to a young Jew from central or eastern Europe: to emigrate to one of the countries where anti-semitism was less virulent than in his home country; to join those who believed that a change of regime in the semi-fascist countries of eastern Europe would automatically solve the 'Jewish problem'; or to become a dedicated Zionist.

In 1939 there were over three million Jews in Poland; shortly after the end of the war there were fewer than one hundred thousand left. Hundreds of thousands of Jews who were 'displaced persons' lived in camps all over Europe; most of them had lost their entire families. Of the three alternatives I mentioned above, the first two did not have much life left in them. For 'displaced persons' from Poland and other ex-fascist countries return 'home' was either meaningless or repulsive. Emancipation to new countries (including Britain and America) was possible but difficult – no country wished to be flooded with 'indiscriminate' immigration. Very large numbers of orphaned Jewish children, many of whom were ex-inmates of concentration camps, were received in France and looked after in various centres by voluntary organizations. I had the honour of working in several of those centres after having come back to France at the end of five years spent in Germany as a prisoner-of-war and discovering on my return that all members of my family were killed in Poland. In the centres one met children who had seen their parents hanged; who could not read or write; who were at the brink of delinquency or psychopathy; who had nowhere to go; who could not speak any language which might have been any use to them. I know nothing of Mr Ruthven's background or experiences, but I can assure him that the Israeli Law of Return, as applied to those children, did not appear 'infamous' at the time. Many of the children did go to Israel, a country which was fully dedicated to their rehabilitation despite the continuing threat to its survival....[32]

On another occasion, he wrote to the publisher of a pamphlet to be used in British schools for the teaching of modern history, complaining about the one-sided treatment it presented of the Middle East situation.[33] He also wrote to several of his former Oxford colleagues (e.g., Alan Bullock, Isaiah Berlin) to enlist their support to get the pamphlet changed. For the most part, whilst sympathetic, they seem not to have done much to support his campaign. Berlin, though, wrote to thank him for his efforts, saying:

> you have done nobly in striking this blow for impartiality; while it is true that no one can be wholly impartial either about the Soviet Union or, it seems, Israel, one can but try. May I congratulate you on your stout-heartedness in seeking to correct this inexcusable bias.[34]

Henri was also an active member of the London based Institute of Jewish Affairs, the Academic Study Group for Israel and the Middle East, and gave at least one talk to the Bristol Zionist Society.[35]

It was not just in the public sphere that Henri argued for Israel. He was prone to having fierce arguments with his son Paul, an ardent pro-Palestinian. And he once remonstrated with Mike Hogg, then a postgraduate at Bristol, for arriving at a research seminar wearing what looked like a Palestinian scarf.[36]

Thus, there is no doubt that he was emotionally very attracted to Israel, like many European Jews of his generation. He had wanted to emigrate there after the war and relented only because Anne had not wanted to (Chapter 4). Much later (in 1976), he was invited to the Van Leer Institute in Jerusalem for three months, a visit which he often wrote about with considerable nostalgia in letters to colleagues.

Work–life (im)balance

When Henri was not occupying himself trying to arrange an exit from Bristol or disappearing on various jaunts to the Continent and elsewhere, he still had his departmental duties to attend to, however reluctantly. Although he had long since ceded the running of the Bristol department to John Brown, he continued to take an interest in its long-term development. According to colleagues who knew him at the time, he proved himself to be quite astute in various decisions over new appointments and departmental strategy. For instance, he recognised the need in the 1970s to broaden the research base of the department, resulting in a new appointment in developmental psychology in 1972.

That appointment was probably occasioned by the departure of one of Henri's initial appointments (Nic Johnson). Not long after, his other two colleagues, Fraser and Eiser, left for positions elsewhere. Although all three were social psychologists, they were not really researchers in Henri's mould, at least not in terms of their research interests. With their departure, he saw an opportunity to build a research group with a clearer focus on intergroup relations. First, he recruited Howard Giles,[37] a specialist in intergroup language and communication. Soon after, he engineered the appointment of John Turner, his personal protégé who had recently completed his PhD with him. So, by 1975, all three of the social psychologists in the department were working on intergroup relations, 'definitely a BLOCK within the department (and) perhaps a little intimidating in our collective productivity, profile, theoretical acumen, and impact', as Giles later described it.[38]

Staff meetings were usually held in Henri's (smoke filled) office, the largest in the department, with his telephone constantly interrupting proceedings. The meetings could be lively affairs and voices would frequently be raised. But, noted a colleague of the time, the rows were without malice:

> They were people feeling safe enough to get cross with one another openly. It was healthy. It was partly *despite* Henri and partly *because* of Henri and John

(Brown's) way of running things….That set a great stamp on the departmental atmosphere. It was a friendly department, very collegiate indeed.[39]

It was not only with permanent academic appointments that Henri was
establishing Bristol as a major European centre for social psychology. Using his
share of the Ford Foundation grant to *EAESP*, he paid for his first two PhD students, David Milner and Mick Billig, to stay on as postdocs. Both used the opportunity to excellent effect, publishing well regarded and influential books as a result.[40]
He also invited Wolfgang Stroebe to spend a year as a post-doc (1971–1972), and
throughout the 1970s there was a steady stream of overseas visitors, eager to spend
sabbaticals at this obviously burgeoning research centre: Marilynn Brewer, Lloyd
Strickland, Donald Taylor, and Graham Vaughan were just four of many visitors.

Henri could be a playful man with his friends and colleagues but sometimes
he completely failed to get the joke. Every year, the department would stage a
Christmas revue for staff and students. Howard Giles, then a lecturer in the department, performed a sketch at one of these in which he mimicked Henri and which
also involved a gangster scenario involving a violin case with '*HT's henchperson*'
chalked on it in true Al Capone style (Figure 7.1). Henri was not at the revue
and when the violin case turned up in his office the next day, he took it seriously
enough to call the police![41]

An important contributor to the intellectual climate of the department was the
research colloquium held on Wednesday afternoons in Henri's office. These seminars were intimidating affairs for the visiting speakers. Henri was an argumentative
man and he encouraged and inculcated a similar disputatious attitude in his colleagues and students. Interrogation of the speaker was never other than robust and
sometimes could be downright hostile. The prerogative of the first question always
went to Henri. He was seldom equivocal – either he loved what the speaker had

FIGURE 7.1 The violin case used in a Christmas revue in the Psychology
Department.

Source: Courtesy of Howard Giles (reproduced with permission).

said, or it left him cold – and his question made it clear which. After Henri's question (or questions – there were often more than one), others would join in the fun. There was a strong sense of a 'Bristol school of thought' being developed and woe betide the speaker whose research seemed to fall outside its ambit.

The sharp questions to the speaker were not the only discomfiting feature of those colloquia however. Just as important was Henri's behaviour during the talks which was, at times, frankly appalling. He would think nothing of taking or making telephone calls whilst the speaker was in full flow, or of tip-toeing in and out of the room to confer with his secretary next door. Wolfgang Stroebe, a young postdoc he had invited to Bristol for a year, captured the whole experience perfectly:

> He asked me to give a seminar and I had just published a JPSP paper on interpersonal attraction dating and marriage.... I was 10 minutes into my talk when Henri phoned up Paris and started talking in French at great length. And, after a while, he left his desk and kept on his phone call outside and only came back at the end of my talk. And then he said, 'Wolfgang, I really have only one question: for an intelligent guy, why do you study such trivial issues?'[42]

It is not clear whether word of the likely reception awaiting one's talk got around the academic community. If it did, it did not seem to deter potential speakers. The list of colloquium invitees in the 1970s reads like the 'who's who' of international social psychologists: Erika Apfelbaum, Carl Backman, Jerry Bruner, Don Campbell, Thomas Cook, Willem Doise, Martin Fishbein, Liam Hudson, John Lanzetta, Josef Nuttin, Jean Piaget, Harold Proshansky, John Schopler, Geoffrey Stephenson, John van de Geer, and Robert Zajonc.

After the gladiatorial atmosphere of the seminar, it was a relief for speaker and audience alike to repair to the Tajfels' house for drinks and sometimes a meal. Henri and Anne were excellent hosts, though Henri's contribution to the hospitality was confined to pouring the drinks ('He couldn't even peel an orange', according to Anne). Anne, on the other hand, was an accomplished cook. Dinners were held in their large kitchen with everyone seated around an enormous wooden table. Conversation was spirited, especially if Henri saw an opportunity to pick an argument, which he frequently did.

Away from work, Henri's life in the 1970s was not always easy. Never the world's healthiest man, he was beset with various ailments. In 1971 he suffered a relapse of his back problems – a slipped disc that he had had eleven years previously[43] – this time requiring surgery.[44] He contracted pleurisy in 1975 and the next year suffered a kidney infection. Soon after, he wrote to his friends, the Elkanas, in Jerusalem:

> This is by no means an easy letter to write. It is now well over a month and a half since I've been away from Jerusalem, and I don't dare to think what you and everybody else must be thinking about my complete severing of contacts for such a long time. There have been several reasons for this, the

least important of which was my health. A few days after arrival here, I had a minor operation which unblocked my kidney, and since then all kinds of tests showed that everything is clear. But other problems and worries accumulated at the same time, all to do with various members of the family. It's all over now, and everyone is well. The result was, however, that as a reaction of it all, I had a prolonged spell of real depression – and for the first time in my life (I think) this affected my public figure, in the sense that for several weeks I was entirely incapable of doing any work, writing any letters, meeting people, etc. I sat at home, read thrillers and listened for hours to music. One conclusion is that, in this kind of state of mind, nothing written after Brahms is of any help at all. Almost anything written up to and including him is an antidote against feeling sorry for oneself.[45]

Professionally, Henri was as busy as ever, heavily occupied with his editorial work, his writing and, of course, his correspondence. In addition to the dozens of letters a month in connection with his European activities, he still found time to write long missives to his friends, chief amongst whom were Jerry Bruner, Morton Deutsch (the famous scholar of conflict resolution), Leon Festinger, Serge Moscovici, and John van de Geer (his Leiden colleague).

In all this work he was hugely dependent on his secretaries. The last one to work for him was Alma Foster (now Dorndorf). According to her, his typical working day involved dealing with his voluminous correspondence in the morning, usually fortified by black coffee and endless (unfiltered) cigarettes (Alma always kept a spare packet in her desk). He dictated everything, sometimes in French, which she typed up later. Afternoons were usually spent at home writing. He wrote in long-hand in tiny spidery writing which Alma typed for him. He would edit that first draft, but not much. Typically, he would need no more than two drafts before he was satisfied. When not attending to her secretarial duties, Alma acted as his personal assistant, helping with his banking, buying presents for Anne and so on. On Friday mornings, she would have to make his coffee early to prepare him for his nine o'clock lecture.[46]

Henri's teaching did not improve. A student from the late 1970s found his teaching somewhat shambolic, a shambles occasionally redeemed by his obvious passion for his subject:

> Henri had two lecture modes: more or less incoherent ramblings about something he'd read in the Guardian that morning.... or a totally spell-binding account of his latest thoughts about identity, conflict and social stratification.[47]

Another student from that same era added:

> I had a strong sense that he wouldn't suffer fools gladly, and that stupid comments and questions could receive quite a cutting response. He seemed something of a contradiction: quite an intimidating individual, but also very human

and intermittently very engaging, but also distant and dismissive. There were certainly some favoured students.[48]

Miles Hewstone, a student in the late 1970s, remembers Henri's lectures fondly though. Even if the lectures themselves weren't always pedagogically perfect, there was something inspiring about being taught by someone so obviously brilliant:

> It was a 9 o'clock lecture. He was the only guy we'd get up for at 9 o'clock.... I remember he used to arrive and he'd hand round these roneo copied sheets – they were the chapter summaries of the book he was working on [Tajfel, 1978)]. He wasn't an inspiring lecturer but, if you really loved that stuff, when you were reading it there was something truly inspiring about being taught by him.... One of my happiest memories: he'd be in the middle of a lecture and there'd be a tap on the door and his secretary, Alma, would come in and say, 'Professor Tajfel, I've got Geneva on the phone.'[49]

Even that final episode was related positively. For Hewstone (and some of his peers) it revealed Henri as an academic of international standing and someone they felt privileged to be taught by.

Henri was also becoming increasingly in demand as a PhD supervisor. During his ten years at Oxford he had not supervised a single PhD; in his first four years at Bristol he supervised just two (Milner, Billig); from 1971–1978 he successfully supervised eight, myself included (Chapter 8). Henri's supervision style gave new meaning to the term '*laissez-faire*'. His frequent absences, sometimes for months at a time, meant that supervisions happened only intermittently. Brian Caddick, who began his PhD in 1974, could count the number of supervisions 'on the fingers of one hand'.[50] My own experience was no different. Henri disappeared to Paris three months after my arrival at Bristol (in 1972) and I did not see him again for half a year.[51] Ad van Knippenberg, Henri's PhD student at Leiden, was obliged to visit him at Bristol a couple of times a year because Henri was in Leiden so rarely (Figure 7.2).[52]

When you did manage to get an appointment, you did not expect much in the way of technical advice on research design or statistical analysis. What interested him were your ideas or your interpretation of the data you had collected. And he could be extraordinarily inspirational. Colin Fraser, though a colleague and not a student, perfectly captured the effect that a meeting with Henri could have:

> If I think of Henri....the word that immediately has been coming into my mind is 'energising'. Obviously, he was himself very energetic, but the really distinctive thing about him ... was his capacity to transmit his energy to other people, to gee you up, to create opportunities and to create possibilities, to send you off feeling more optimistic, a bit more determined than you had been when you went in to see him....he was always creating things and exciting you....The word 'charismatic' is not a word I tend to use a great deal ... but it's a word that does fit Henri nicely.[53]

FIGURE 7.2 Henri at the PhD defence of Ad van Knippenberg, Leiden 1978.
Source: Courtesy of Ad van Knippenberg (reproduced with permission).

He was also a great facilitator, always ready to use his considerable research funds or personal connections to support his students' endeavours. Sik Hung Ng, one of Henri's PhD students, describes a meeting with him where he had been rather nervously explaining how he wanted to change direction (to investigate power change by combining some aspects of Mulder's theory of power with social categorisation and comparison processes):

> He probably had a *sparkle* in his eyes, thinking that this young man, learning the lesson now, turning away from gaming theory, not to be concerned with decision-making, but more concerned with the broad issues in social psychology. And look, he's also interested in the work of a friend of mine, Mulder! And lo and behold, you know what he did? He picked up his phone and he called Mauk Mulder! And he said: 'Hi Mauk, I have got a young man here from Hong Kong; he wants to talk to you. Do you have time?' Of course he had time! And he (Henri) gave me money to go from Dover to the Netherlands.... I spent a full afternoon talking with Mauk Mulder. I think in terms of time ... the three or four hours I spent with Mulder was more than all the time alone I spent with Henri as his student during my two and half years at Bristol![54]

Feedback from Henri on one's written work was also usually rather scant. Ng recalls sending him a draft of his PhD thesis from New Zealand (where he was then lecturing) and, after a delay of several months, received the following telegram from Henri:

THESIS FINE IMPROVE WORDING STOP.

However, Henri could be selective with his favours. It was readily apparent which of us he preferred and who he was less interested in. He once confided to Glynis Breakwell how he arrived at his judgements of people:

> He said to me that his approach to people was that he decided really quickly when he first met you that you were either on the side of the angels or not; that you were either really good or you weren't; and he never changed his mind.[55]

If you were one of his 'favourite sons', as both Eiser and Reicher described it,[56] he could not do enough for you; if you weren't, you were on your own. Perhaps it was no accident that, in my time at Bristol, the three students who experienced significant problems with their PhDs were those who seemed to me to fall into the latter group. This tendency to have favourites seems to have started early in his career. Recall that one of the boys he looked after in the Brussels children's home after the war made a similar observation.[57] This same tendency was visible in his relationships with his two actual sons (Chapter 5).

An idea is born

Despite all his comings and goings in the 1970s, there was no let-up in Henri's productivity. Between 1973 and 1982 he published over forty separate pieces. However, the nature of these publications underwent a marked change. The demands of establishing himself as an experimental psychology dictated that he publish mainly in scientific journals rather than in books early on in his career. Now, though, the balance shifted sharply; most of his publications in the 1970s were theoretical chapters and edited books.

Nevertheless, of his ten most cited journal articles, five appeared in this period. One of these is of particular interest. Appearing in 1974 in an obscure French journal, *Social Science Information*, it was the first published version in English[58] of the theory for which he is most well-known today, Social Identity Theory (SIT[59]). He would go on to elaborate this theory in several other publications in the years to follow, culminating most famously in a chapter co-authored by John Turner, his third PhD student and then colleague at Bristol.[60] SIT is a theory of intergroup behaviour which is at once deceptively simple but also, in places, frustratingly ambiguous. Its formulation also depends somewhat on which of the several versions one chooses to consult;[61] it is possible to discern subtle variations in emphasis in the different versions. Here, I will draw mainly on his 1974 article, the first statement of the theory, and his 1979 chapter with Turner, the most frequently cited version.

The 1974 version starts with some 'ground clearing'. Henri was at pains to establish that he wanted to move away from previous individualistic and decontextualised accounts of intergroup relations, reiterating points he had so forcibly made two years before[62] (Chapter 6). His second preliminary remark was to note, again as he had done in several previous publications, that he had no wish to claim any causal primacy for social psychological variables over other social, political and economic factors. Nevertheless, he proposed that those social psychological variables could, on occasion, operate autonomously. Then came his first assumption:

> In order for the members of an ingroup to be able to hate or dislike an outgroup, or to discriminate against it, they must first have acquired a sense of belonging to a group which is distinct from the one they hate, dislike or discriminate against.[63]

This paved the way for his second assumption: that it is important to distinguish between situations when that sense of group belonging is uppermost in people's minds, because the group is engaged in some meaningful way with other groups, and situations where the sense of belonging is virtually absent (i.e. they are interacting as *individuals* and not as *group members*). In the first case, one can expect people's perceptions, attitudes and behaviour to show a considerable degree of uniformity because they are mainly determined by category-based processes; the second case one should expect the normal range of variability because behaviour is mostly controlled by individual difference factors. He later labelled this distinction the 'interpersonal-intergroup continuum'[64]. His theory was concerned with behaviour towards or at the intergroup pole (people acting as group members).

Four key concepts comprise the theory. The first is the familiar one of *categorisation*, the focus of Henri's early scientific work. Now he argued that categorisation does not only simplify and bring order to our social world, it also provides the basis for our social identity – who we think we are and, just as importantly, who we are not. The second concept, therefore, is *social identity*, which he famously defined as:

> That *part* of an individual's self-concept which derives from his [*sic*] knowledge of his membership of a social group (or groups) together with the value and emotional significance attached to that membership.[65]

Thus, social identity is clearly described as having cognitive ('knowledge'), evaluative ('value') and affective ('emotional') components. In the 1979 version of the theory, this tripartite definition is curiously absent.[66]

The third element provides a motivational component to the theory. Henri assumed that people generally wish to maintain or enhance their self-esteem and hence they will strive for a *positive self concept*. This implies that they will constantly seek ways to make their group(s) be seen in a positive light (since their self concept is often bound up with their group memberships, especially in 'intergroup' contexts).

How can people assess their group's worth to gauge their own positivity? Here Henri introduced the fourth idea, borrowed from his friend Festinger, that we evaluate our group(s) primarily by means of comparisons with other groups in society.[67] Thus, things being equal (which they seldom are, as we shall see), people will look for ways in which they can positively differentiate the ingroup from relevant outgroups. This 'search for positive distinctiveness' might take the form of biased intergroup evaluations ('we are better than them at X'), or behavioural discrimination (giving more points or money to the ingroup will make it seem superior to the outgroup). Such ingroup favouritism was thought to be especially likely when the ingroup's social status was ambiguous, ill-defined or threatened in some way.

Armed with these four ideas, Henri felt able to provide a better explanation for the gratuitous discrimination he had observed in his minimal group experiments. Initially, as we saw in Chapter 6, he had offered a normative explanation but then had realised its deficiencies. His new explanation went like this: participants are allocated to one of two arbitrary groups; nothing differentiates them except for the category labels (Klee or Kandinsky) and hence their – albeit temporary – social identities (as Klee or Kandinsky people) lack positive distinctiveness. How can they achieve some positivity for their group (and themselves)? By allocating more money to fellow ingroup members than to outgroup members. And the frequent observation of maximising difference strategies in those allocations seemed to be particularly pertinent evidence in favour of this new social identity account.

Henri had bigger ambitions than explaining discrimination in artificially contrived groups, however. He was after a general social psychological theory that could also make sense of people's behaviour in real-life groups in society. Of course, in most societies, groups differ in status and access to scarce resources and power. What are the implications for people's social identities of belonging to a higher or lower status group? This is where SIT starts to get complicated.

Let us start with privileged groups, society's 'winners'. At first blush, members of such groups would seem to have few identity concerns. If Henri's reasoning was correct, members of such groups should be in the comfortable position of knowing that, on many important dimensions, they come out on top, or at least better than most. So, their need for positive distinctiveness should be low. In theoretical terms, they are said to enjoy a 'secure social identity'.[68] However, such 'security' can seldom be taken for granted. There may be other similarly high status groups who might threaten the privileged group's 'superiority'; intergroup similarity is one factor that might reactivate distinctiveness needs and so cause groups to jockey with each other for position.[69] Or, more seriously from an identity point of view, economic circumstances or the actions of other groups might destabilise or threaten to undermine the legitimacy of the privileged group's position. Such conditions, Henri thought, would instigate attempts by dominant groups to re-assert their superiority.

What about groups on the bottom rungs of society's ladder? If, as Henri supposed, members of such subordinate groups evaluate themselves via intergroup comparisons, then their lot is not a happy one: they will discover that they earn less than privileged groups (if they have a job at all); their houses, schools, and neighbourhoods will be less desirable; and, in the media, they will encounter frequent reminders of their 'inferiority'. What will they then do, given that they, too, are presumed to prefer a positive to a negative self-concept?

Henri believed that the answer to this question depended initially on how 'permeable' the group boundaries are. If it is physically or psychologically possible to move between groups, then he thought that the members of subordinate groups will first seek to abandon their ingroup for pastures (groups) new, which would offer them the prospect of higher status and hence a more positive social identity. But such individual mobility is not open to everyone. If your skin is of a certain hue, or your accent of a certain timbre, or your faith is this rather than that, members of the group you aspire to join may simply not accept you. In such cases, Henri suggested, other tactics will be employed to 'rescue' that negative social identity. People may become 'creative' in their social comparisons, either by finding new dimensions on which to compare the ingroup to the privileged group, or by reinterpreting conventional criteria so that what was once devalued becomes more positive, or by searching for other subordinate groups with which to compare so that the outcome of the comparisons is less damaging to their self-esteem. There may sometimes be occasions where the status quo – the existing social hierarchy – is sufficiently undermined by political or economic instability or by a breakdown in the consensual legitimacy of groups' positions in society that subordinate group members may directly confront their 'superior' groups in an attempt to bring about social change. Quite which of these tactics will be adopted, and when, is not well spelled out in the theory, however.

These, then, are the bare bones of the theory (SIT) that Henri spent ten years promulgating (sometimes rather repetitively) in over a dozen articles and chapters between 1972 and 1982. In several of these publications, the influence of John Turner is clear. Turner had been his PhD student (1971–1974), then postdoctoral assistant (1974–1975) and, finally, departmental colleague (1975–1982). In the 1974 article, he quotes Turner at length, both from his PhD thesis and an article that grew out of it.[70] Subsequently, he gave explicit recognition of Turner's contribution to his thinking by inviting him to co-author what would prove to be the principal reference for SIT for later generations of scholars.

The story of that invitation and, indeed, of how the chapter came to be written is an interesting one. Steve Worchel, one of the editors of the volume in which it appeared, had met Henri at a European conference in the mid 1970s. On his return to USA, he asked a colleague, John Thibaut, about Henri. He 'is brilliant and doing some of the best work in social psychology', was Thibaut's reply. With such a ringing endorsement, Worchel and his co-editor, Bill Austin, invited Henri to write a chapter in a book on intergroup relations that they were planning.[71] This was in July 1975. After several letters over the (non-arrival) of a contract from the publishers and changes to submission deadlines, a contract finally arrived (in April 1976) with a firm deadline for delivery of the chapter by July 1976. The contract was in Henri's name only. The imminence of the deadline threw Henri into a panic – he was preparing for a trip to Jerusalem and had several other pressing commitments – so he wrote to the editors asking that Turner be added as a co-author. They readily agreed.

What transpired was that Turner wrote almost the *whole chapter* from start to finish. His handwritten version can be found in the Wellcome Library and it

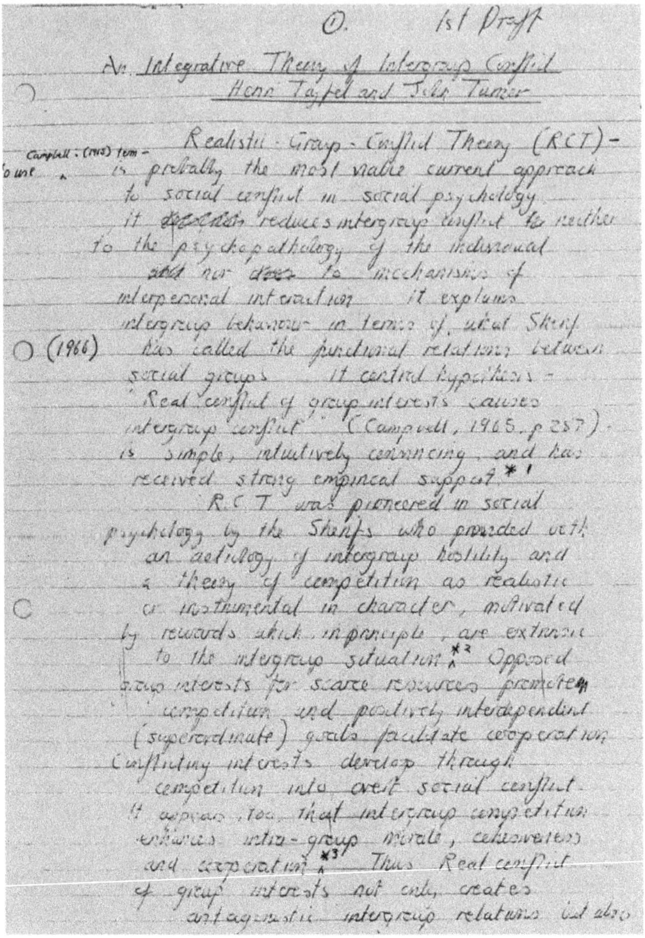

①. 1st Draft

An Integrative Theory of Intergroup Conflict

Henri Tajfel and John Turner

Realistic Group Conflict Theory (RCT) - is probably the most viable current approach to social conflict in social psychology. it reduces intergroup conflict to neither to the psychopathology of the individual nor does to mechanisms of interpersonal interaction it explains intergroup behaviour in terms of what Sherif (1966) has called the functional relations between social groups. Its central hypothesis - "Real conflict of group interests causes intergroup conflict" (Campbell, 1965, p 287) - is simple, intuitively convincing, and has received strong empirical support.*1

R.C.T was pioneered in social psychology by the Sherifs who provided both an aetiology of intergroup hostility and a theory of competition as realistic and instrumental in character, motivated by rewards which, in principle, are extrinsic to the intergroup situation.*2 Opposed group interests for scarce resources promote competition and positively interdependent (superordinate) goals facilitate cooperation. Conflicting interests develop through competition into overt social conflict. It appears, too, that intergroup competition enhances intra-group morale, cohesiveness and cooperation.*3 Thus Real conflict of group interests not only creates antagonistic intergroup relations but also

FIGURE 7.3 The first handwritten page of the famous Tajfel and Turner (1979) chapter.

Source: Wellcome Collection, PSY/TAJ/1/4/14.

closely resembles the published version, with a few subsequent edits from Henri (Figure 7.3).

Worchel describes what happened next:

> When we received the chapter I again understood about 50% of it, but it was clear it was one of the few chapters we had that offered a broad global theory. When we sent it out for review, one of the reviewers argued that we should not include it because it did not really focus on intergroup relations. Then the (publisher's) editor suggested that the book was getting too long and we should drop the two chapters from European authors. Bill (Austin) and I talked again with Thibaut who again sang the praises of Tajfel.... So,

against the reviewer's and editor's advice, we insisted on including the two European chapters.[72]

Austin and Worchel's book, one of the first major volumes to focus entirely on intergroup relations since Sherif's book in 1966,[73] was targeted primarily at the North American market and probably did as much as anything to bring Henri's ideas on social identity to the attention of an audience beyond the continent of Europe.

The partnership of Henri and Turner was a most unlikely one. They could not have been more different in background, political outlook, and intellectual style.[74] Henri was the elder son (of two) of middle-class Jewish parents in Poland; Turner, oldest (of eight), was from a South London working class family. Henri was a left-leaning social democrat; Turner was an active member of a small very left-wing political sect, the Communist Party of Britain (Marxist-Leninist), a group with a fervent adherence, shared by Turner, to the ideologies of Stalin and Mao. Henri was a multilingual and passionate European; Turner was resolutely monolingual and actively campaigned for Britain to leave the European Common Market in 1975. Henri was a strong supporter of Israel; Turner, like most on the British left, was vehemently anti-Zionist. Henri was very open-minded in his receptivity to new ideas, epistemologies and methods, albeit argumentative with it; Turner was much narrower in his academic outlook and was implacably experimental in his methodological preference. What they shared – apart from an addiction to nicotine and a taste for alcohol – was a desire to promote a new way of thinking about groups and intergroup relations and a refusal to compromise with what they saw as impoverished individualistic perspectives.

A close reading of Henri's 1974 exposition of SIT and their 'joint' 1979 chapter reveals some interesting differences, beginning with their titles: 'Social identity and intergroup behaviour' (1974) was not an obvious statement of theoretical intent; 'An integrative theory of intergroup conflict' (1979) was more explicit in its purpose but also narrower in its focus (intergroup conflict). Henri's original definition of social identity included the phrase 'value and emotional significance' (1974); by 1979 the definition had been reduced to, 'those aspects of an individual's self image that derive from the social categories to which he perceives himself as belonging' (p. 40). In 1974, Henri had devoted approximately equal space to how superior and inferior groups expressed and responded to identity concerns. In the later chapter there is much more emphasis on inferior groups' reactions to negative or insecure identity. Indeed, one of those possible reactions, direct 'social competition' with the dominant outgroup,[75] merits only a brief mention in the earlier version. In that sense, the later chapter is more obviously a theory of social change than the 1974 article. Finally, in the preamble to the 1974 exposition, there is an explicit mention of intergroup outcomes with emotional connotations ('hate, dislike or discriminate against', p. 66). Such intergroup emotions are almost entirely absent from the 1979 chapter, where the focus is much more on various strategies of evaluative intergroup differentiation.

Well before these papers were published, Henri was trying out his ideas in research colloquia and conferences. One early public airing of the theory (in December 1971) was at a research seminar to graduate students at Leuven. Norbert Vanbeselaere was in the audience:

> He came in with such a bunch of papers and he started reading ... page after page, after page, after page ... for me, at that time, I couldn't follow him ... I was just lost. And he wanted reactions. But we just got lost in his rea-soning, being totally unfamiliar, and also when you are reading at a very high speed....And then he got angry: 'when I go to other universities, people react and ask questions – they understand what I say'.[76]

Three years later, Henri was invited to give the prestigious Katz–Newcomb lectures at the University of Michigan, the second person to be asked since they were inaugurated (the first was Ivan Steiner). These lectures did not go down any better than his paper in Leuven. His colleague, Dick Eiser, listened to one of them:

> They went down like a lead balloon. They were just not what people ex-pected. The problem was they were thin on data, heavy on theory, a lot of crammed in social history and observations....The sentences were too long, the words too long, the syntax too involved.[77]

Also in the audience for those lectures was Yaacov Trope, then a graduate stu-dent at Michigan. He was not much impressed by Henri's lectures either. In part, this was because they were rather outside his own area of interest at the time (he was working on polarisation of opinions in groups), but also because of the way Henri delivered them. Echoing Vanbeselaere's observations of two years previously, he noted:

> I hate to say it, but no, it was not very charismatic ... he was reading from the paper. He read his talks, one after the other, page after page, after page, after page ... it didn't leave a big mark on me, to tell you the truth.[78]

Henri was no armchair theorist. He used his 1974 article and the Katz–Newcomb lectures, almost verbatim, as the theoretical basis for a grant application he made to the British Social Science Research Council (SSRC) in July 1973. This was for a substantial programme of work – three postdoctoral researchers and two assistants for three years. By today's standards, the proposal was very long (54 pages) and the planned studies were mostly only vaguely described. In current parlance it was a 'multi-methods' project, with an eclectic mix of experimental, quasi-experimental and field studies, including some with an ethnographic element.[79] Its stated objective was to clarify, extend and test some of the hypotheses outlined in the 1974 paper. One of the proposed studies (never actually conducted) drew poignantly on Henri's time at Oxford. In a section entitled 'Marginal Identity', it proposed studying the attitudes of 'Dons' and 'non-Dons' at Oxford, the latter occupying a marginal or ill-defined position within the institution (Chapter 5). The proposal may have been rather sketchily described but it was apparently sufficiently convincing to persuade site visitors Donald Broadbent, Hilde Himmelweit, and Geoffrey Stephenson to recommend to the SSRC to part with nearly £60,000 (around £900,000 at 2018 prices[80]).

The grant was a significant new fillip to Henri's standing within the university as well as enhancing his already considerable reputation in Europe. It also provided full-time employment for no fewer than nine young researchers, myself included. As with his PhD students, Henri took a 'light touch' approach to being principal investigator. Tony Agathangelou, one of the postdoctoral researchers on the grant, described the modus operandi of the research team:

> I was never required to follow any particular directives in terms of the way I did it, but the hypotheses were relatively fixed … my role was to make that (the research) happen and I was given almost complete freedom to do that, to design the experiments. He wasn't that interested (in the particular studies) but more in the long-term view.[81]

Occasionally, there would be team meetings in his office where one of us would present an idea for the next study or the results from the last one (Figure 7.4). There would then be an intense discussion, always led by Henri or Turner, as to how this new study or set of findings could be reconciled with the evolving hypotheses of SIT. The arguments could be heated but there was none of the withering criticism

FIGURE 7.4 The SSRC research team. From left to right: Henri, John Turner, Fred Ross, Richard Bourhis, and the author.

so often on display in the Wednesday afternoon research colloquia. We were the ingroup after all.

The budget of this grant had a generous travel element, sufficiently large to support taking the whole research team to Paris on at least two occasions to confer with Moscovici and his colleagues. I was never quite sure of the purpose of these meetings, apart from giving us all an opportunity to visit various Parisian restaurants, invariably chosen by Henri or Moscovici (they seemed to compete to find establishments with the most interesting menus).[82] Academically, they consisted of two or three members of each group presenting their 'work in progress', often followed by a choleric discussion between Henri and Moscovici, sometimes lapsing into French when they got carried away. As a callow young researcher at the time, I was somewhat awed by these two European 'giants' (as they seemed to me at the time) who cared enough about their work to raise their voices with each other as they disputed the interpretation of a study.

At the same time, it seemed to be more than a battle of ideas. There was something almost ritualistic in their intellectual posturing which reminded me as much as anything of two rutting stags competing for dominance over a herd of deer. Others, too, have noted the rivalry between the two men.[83] From the earliest days of EAESP, there had been constant jockeying for position between them, with Gustav Jahoda often having to play the peace-maker.[84] One colleague, who knew both men well, described them as 'two crocodiles that granted each other little space for peeing'.[85] Moscovici had been *EAESP*'s first president (1966–1969), Henri its second (1969–1972). Moscovici had been one of the founding editors of the *European Journal of Social Psychology* (1971–1972), Henri was in the second editorial team (1973–1977). Although their common Jewish heritage and shared aspiration to create an alternative European social psychology bound them together, their overweening ambition drove them apart.

Henri's successes at Bristol once more brought him to the attention of the media (he had done three radio programmes at Oxford; Chapter 5). In 1975, the producers of the BBC Horizon programme approached him to contribute to a documentary entitled *The Human Conspiracy*. They wanted us to recreate one of the minimal group experiments. Never averse to a bit of publicity, Henri agreed and before long we were filming the experiment live in a secondary school in Bristol. In an amusing reversal of our actual roles on the research project, the director chose me to be the experimenter, with Turner (operating the slide projector showing Klee and Kandinsky pictures) and Henri (apparently coding the boys' picture preferences) as my assistants.[86] Despite the sub-optimal conditions under which the experiment was run, it is a tribute to the robustness of the paradigm that we did, in fact, replicate the usual finding of intergroup discrimination.[87]

Amour propre

As Henri's fame grew in the 1970s so, apparently, did his vanity, sometimes revealing itself as a laughable concern about his standing in the world of social psychology.

David Winter, whom Henri had taught at Harvard, remembers Henri once telling him:

> I know when I have made it, when I have been successful in a professional recognition sense, when, at a conference, when I walk into the large ball-room, reception room, and it takes me the whole evening to work my way across the room.[88]

Occasionally, Henri could be unconscionably rude to people he did not like or respect. Wolfgang Stroebe, a close friend of Henri's, recalled an incident at a conference where he was greeted effusively by his former Oxford colleague, Michael Argyle. Apparently, the encounter went like this:

> Argyle shook Henri's hand five times and said, 'Henri, Henri, it's so nice to see you'. And Henri looked at him and said, 'Michael, do you always have to behave like a fool?' Argyle didn't realise why Henri hated him. He hated him because he had the one job he would have loved.[89]

Then there was the incident after my PhD viva. My external examiner was Jaap Rabbie, Henri's friend but intellectual rival (over the minimal group paradigm; Chapter 6). Rabbie had interrogated me – the choice of verb is apt – for over six hours about my exposition of various intellectual perspectives, including SIT on which the thesis was based. The questioning was courteous and friendly but nevertheless extremely probing (he had brought 30 pages of notes to the examination). Afterwards, during the usual post-viva celebrations, I noticed that Henri and Rabbie were in a corner, locked in a furious argument, which, I learned later, had been instigated by Henri, apparently outraged that Rabbie had had the temerity to challenge the validity of his ideas through the examination of one of his students.

But the real rival was always Moscovici. Three years after the above incident, Henri was the examiner of Miles Hewstone's PhD. During the viva, apropos of nothing, Henri commented:

> I notice you cited Serge Moscovici 16 times. But it's OK, you cited *me* 17 times![90]

Henri's relationship with Moscovici, always a bit fraught, came to a head in 1979. In November of that year, Henri received a letter from Cambridge University Press, asking him to review a proposal for a *Handbook of European Social Psychology*, to be edited by Moscovici and Doise. Doise, then at Geneva (occupying the post Piaget had offered to Henri nine years before), was a colleague of Moscovici's and a friend to both men (Henri used to borrow his flat in Paris). *Quel horreur!* Not only had Henri not been invited to contribute a chapter, but Moscovici had not even told Henri anything about the book. Henri took this as a grievous slight. He surely considered himself as one of the *eminences grises* of European social psychology.

Not to have even been consulted about a major volume 'covering different fields of European social psychology in which original contributions can be found', including a chapter on intergroup relations,[91] was a most stinging slap in the face.

There is no record of how Henri first reacted to Moscovici himself. Probably it was by telephone and I doubt it was the most cordial of conversations. A month later, Moscovici wrote to Henri, referring to a discussion they had had '*L'autre soir*' in which Henri had suggested himself as a third editor. Moscovici rejected this idea for '*trois raisons objectives*': Logistics – it would have multiplied the difficulties and complexity of the project; *finance* – the royalties would have to be split three ways instead of two; and '*paternité*' (authorship or recognition), which I suspect was the real reason for his refusal to accept Henri's self-invitation. He wrote:

> I don't believe anyone can dispute that I had the idea for this handbook and I defended the project against all critics, including yourself. I am the author of this project and its intellectual paternity is mine. If we are three 'editors', we would need to change the alphabetical order (myself, then Willem, and then you) to signify this paternity. Otherwise, I would feel that this paternity has been 'robbed' by you, without you getting anything out of it. A feeling that would be deeply disagreeable for me.[92]

Henri's reply was swift and cutting. He replied in English as he habitually did when corresponding with Moscovici (though not with other French colleagues):

> Thank you very much for your letter which delighted me. As you wrote, you expected from me this kind of proposal. In turn, I fully expected that you would reject it. It is always rewarding to have one's hypotheses confirmed and to know that one's insights are valid.
>
> I respect the reasons for your decision, and I know that you in turn respect me enough not to believe that I could have thought for one moment that they are actually those which you enumerated in your letter. This is why I shall not engage in the exceedingly easy task of presenting the obvious counter arguments....You need not worry either about any further 'pressures' or about my lack of support for the enterprise.[93] It has never been my habit to exercise academic judgement in terms of personal involvements, and this is one of the reasons why my judgement is generally trusted and respected.[94]

As far as I know, the two men, who had known each other for over 15 years, never corresponded again. A year later, Henri wrote to Morton Deutsch, who had invited him to speak at a conference:

> I am sorry not to have replied earlier to your previous letter. To tell you the truth the reason was that I have been (and still am) in a considerable conflict about the whole thing. There has been serious personal trouble between Serge and myself some months ago, and it resulted in our breaking completely our

relationship. As the whole thing hurt me quite a lot (I have no doubt that he was also hurt), I have recently tried not to go to conferences to which Serge comes, and I have the suspicion that the opposite has also been true. Therefore, the reason why I did not quite know what to write was that you informed me that Serge was giving an invited lecture at the Mannheim conference.[95]

Anything Moscovici could do, Henri could do better (and bigger). A matter of weeks later, he set about compiling his own European handbook, a direct competitor to the proposed Doise-Moscovici volume. He wrote to dozens of colleagues around Europe, inviting them:

> to take part in an enterprise which would help us to take stock after these twenty years of development (of European social psychology), and which would provide at the same time a reflection of what has been happening and a useful resource for the future. It is my intention to edit a book the title of which will be: The social dimension. European developments in social psychology.[96]

Needless to say, neither Moscovici nor Doise received an invitation. Most of the invitees accepted and he soon had a convincing table of contents to show to the publishers, Cambridge University Press (who were also handling the Moscovici volume!).

Moscovici was not the only person Henri fell out with in the late 1970s. He and his oldest Belgian friend and co-EAESP founder, Jozef Nuttin, also had a major disagreement. They were both members of the Executive Committee of EAESP (1975–1978), with Nuttin as President, a role Henri had occupied three years before. The committee had to decide on a new editor for the Association's flagship journal. In some preliminary discussions amongst the committee members, one name had emerged as a favoured candidate and they were due to meet in Cambridge to ratify this (apparently) consensual decision. But Henri had another person in mind for the job and, because he was unable to attend the Cambridge meeting, tried to insist that a decision be reached by correspondence amongst the committee prior to the meeting (a most unusual suggestion). Nuttin, as president, felt rather affronted by what he saw as Henri's attempt to subvert the committee's normal decision-making process and promptly resigned.[97] According to Nuttin's widow, Nuttin felt that Henri was engaging in some kind of 'power game' (he felt he hankered to be President again), something he wanted no part of. Out of respect for his long friendship with Henri, and from a wish not to create a public scandal in EAESP, Nuttin pretended that his resignation was for 'health reasons'.[98] The two men hardly spoke again.

Mourir à Bristol

I have already had occasion to note how productive Henri was in this decade. Most of that productivity was crammed into the last few years of that period, especially if we consider the lasting significance (and not just the number) of publications. He edited no fewer than four books,[99] one of which was an introductory text-book,[100] and brought out a volume of his collected writings.[101] There was also an important review article[102] and an essay on minority groups commissioned by a British NGO.[103] And if his publication activities were not enough to keep him busy, he applied for (and won) a personal grant from SSRC, and undertook to lead a large research programme on second generation immigrants in Europe.

His personal letters at that time are full of lamentations about how frantically busy he was. He had always been a man in a hurry; now he seemed to be positively frenetic, almost as if he could sense he did not have long to live. Indeed, intimations of his mortality seemed to have preoccupied him more than once in this decade. In 1974, he wrote rather gloomily to his friend Festinger:

> It's been one of the worst years I can remember (if not *the* worst) since the war, and the prospects for 1975 look no better, to put it mildly. Judging from what you wrote, I don't have to explain any further; me [sic] concerns are par allel, simultaneous and growing at the same pace. Paradoxically, the new and bewildering world we are all entering seems to be inaugurating itself at the same time as one's personal life is, if anything, improving its quality. But this is the rub: general events are becoming an inherent part of personal depressions, and personal satisfactions lose their meaning against the background of the general events. Personally speaking, nothing startling has happened: the children are up and down, as usual. Anne and I grow much closer to one another; my work makes more sense than it has done for many years (but less and less sense in a general perspective); I still dread the idea of 'mourir à Bristol' but am doing something about it (about which more later).[104]

His colleague Norman Freeman told me that he had used that identical phrase, '*mourir à Bristol*', in a conversation with him at about the same time.[105]

Although Henri could scarcely want for international recognition by the late 1970s, like any PhD supervisor he sometimes had qualms about the new directions his favourite 'sons' were taking. Nowhere was this more apparent than with Turner, with whom he had collaborated so successfully over the construction and prom-ulgation of SIT. By the late 1970s, Turner was starting to develop his own ideas for a more general theory of the group, which subsequently found expression as Self Categorisation Theory[106]. This theory was decidedly more cognitive than SIT, and this different emphasis sometimes gave rise to tension between him and Henri[107]. But perhaps more important for Henri was the sense of regret that his baton was being passed to a new generation. Howard Giles, a colleague and friend of Henri's throughout the 1970s, remembers an occasion after a conference on intergroup re-lations that he (Giles) and Turner had organised in 1978. The post-conference party was held at the Tajfels' house. Late on the festivities, Giles found Henri sitting alone in a corner looking rather distraught. When asked what was wrong, Henri replied morosely, 'I've been superseded; JT is taking over.'[108]

Turner would eventually 'take over' Henri's mantle as the standard-bearer for a non-individualistic perspective on group behaviour (Chapter 8), but Henri was by no means a spent force. His two edited books on intergroup relations[109] were significant publications, containing as they did several important theoretical contributions from Henri – three chapters on SIT in 1978, and one in 1982 – and several empirical chapters by his immediate colleagues and students (within the SIT tradition). Both books were substantial (17 and 16 chapters respectively).

The final chapter of his 1982 book was Henri's thoughtful commentary on nearly ten years of empirical testing of SIT. It begins by acknowledging that this theory might be regarded as rather pessimistic in outlook, 'often leaving us stuck in a spiral of conflict between groups from which it is not easy to see an escape'.[110] However, he then goes on to develop an argument, already briefly made in the 1979 chapter with Turner, that the positive distinctiveness sought by groups must be considered together with instrumental factors. Sometimes it will be in groups' materialistic interest not to search for or insist on social superiority.

Much of the chapter is given over to discussing findings which seemed at variance with SIT predictions. Some of these were reported by his Dutch colleague, Jaap Rabbie, who had been a constant critic of the social identity analysis of the minimal group paradigm. Horwitz and Rabbie's chapter in the 1982 book attracted several pages of Henri's attention but this was surprisingly non-defensive in tone. Other chapters by his former PhD student, van Knippenberg and his friend, Jaspars, were also empirically troublesome for SIT since they showed groups apparently failing to maintain or establish distinctiveness in conditions when the theory predicted they should. Henri tried, not always successfully, to rescue his hypotheses.

Henri's own chapter in this book is also notable in two other respects.[111] More than once he diplomatically distances himself from his co-author Turner, suggesting that his new direction was too cognitive[112]. He then linked that veiled criticism to a second concern, the theoretical need to understand the intense emotions that some group affiliations can engender. As I noted earlier, emotion was surprisingly absent in some original formulations of SIT.

The other important publication from this late period of his life was his collected works.[113] The book enjoyed considerable success, not because it contained anything new but because it brought together under a single (paperback) cover his most important theoretical and empirical papers, previously scattered like the four winds in dozens of different outlets. Its organisation also readily permitted the reader the opportunity to discern the common threads that linked his early work on perceptual accentuation (Chapters 4 and 5) to his later work on social identity and intergroup relations (this chapter and Chapter 6).

The book is also noteworthy for two other reasons. One is a touching foreword written by his oldest and dearest friend, Jerry Bruner. In it, he wrote:

> I have known the author well for a quarter of a century and value him as a friend. He is a man of huge hospitality in the broadest sense. He listens, reacts, brings you another drink, argues you down and sets you back up. He sets his guests at each other when he fears pseudo-agreement, thunders at them

when he thinks their differences finical. Add one further element to that. Tajfel is the canonical European, not only linguistically equipped with several languages deployed with breath-taking speed and fluency, but with a deep sense of European culture.[114]

Privately, he wrote to Henri, apologising for the late arrival of the foreword:

> The fact is that it is terribly difficult to write a preface for a book by some-body you love. Just that. I found myself very moved by the essays, often (I suppose) for irrelevant reasons that were more autobiographical than in terms of the contents.....Henri, your book is lovely, rich, spiced with irresolution that you were honest enough not to paper over.....Thine, Jerry.[115]

To which Henri replied, for once rather lost for words:

> I do not quite know how to thank you for the foreword you sent. I suppose it is just as difficult for me to write this letter as it was for you to write the Preface, and for the same reasons plus. I shall therefore leave it at that, just hoping that you know how I feel.[116]

Bruner was not the only person who appreciated the book. It received a glowing review by Tom Pettigrew in *Contemporary Psychology*:

> The volume demonstrates how this remarkable man made critical contribu-tions to virtually every aspect of social psychology's understanding of group prejudice and conflict.[117]

The introductory chapter sets out his vision for social psychology, a discipline which:

> can and must include in its theoretical and research preoccupations a direct concern with the relationship between human psychological functioning and the large-scale social processes and events which shape this functioning and are shaped by it.[118]

The chapter also begins with some brief autobiographical remarks, one of the few times that Henri made public reference to his background as a European Jew.

The only other occasion Henri wrote in such personal terms was in his Preface to the re-issue of a book on anti-semitism written by a German Jew, Peretz Bernstein, in the 1920s.[119] Whilst disagreeing profoundly with Bernstein's main thesis – that prejudice was the result of biologically driven propensities for ingroup love and outgroup hate – he appreciated Bernstein's attempt to describe and explain the *col-lective* nature of anti-semitism (and other bigotries). Henri was also explicit about his shared Jewish heritage with Bernstein and sympathetic to his later struggles to maintain a certain level of scientific dispassion whilst analysing something as horrific as the Holocaust. In that regard, Henri describes his own personal reactions to Chaplin's film *The Great Dictator*, which had satirised Hitler's rise to power in Germany but failed to anticipate the full horror that it gave rise to (apparently, Henri walked out of the film before its end). He also warned of what he saw as a resurgence of anti-semitism in many countries, using as illustration another film, Wajda's *Promised Land*, which he had described to a colleague as:

> one of the most contemptible outbreaks of anti-semitism in very many years. In some ways, it was no better than the old nazi 'Der Jud Süs'.[120]

Henri published four other pieces of note in his last years, three of them in conventional academic outlets and one for a wider readership. The latter was a seventeen-page pamphlet called *The Social Psychology of Minorities*, commissioned by the Minority Rights Group, a UK-based charity.[121] It was a non-technical essay about the psychological effects of minority group membership, drawing heavily on his earlier (1974) theorising about the identity consequences of belonging to subordinate status groups. However, as was often the case when he was not shackled by the conventions of academic publishing, the article is replete with historical and literary references. The infamous Dreyfus trial in nineteenth-century France, the anti-colonial social theorist Frantz Fanon, the American playwright Arthur Miller and the French philosopher Jean-Paul Sartre all make an appearance. Perhaps the most interesting part of this article is the final section entitled, 'Patterns of rejection', where he discusses the social psychological problems associated with various forms of assimilation. One of these – when a few minority members have succeeded in transitioning to the majority group but still do not enjoy complete acceptance – is of particular interest. He notes that this kind of assimilation is:

> an uneasy compromise … between the acceptance and the rejection of their inferior status as members of the minority. Rejection, because they have attempted to leave behind them some at least of the distinguishing marks of their 'inferiority'; acceptance, because they must often do this by achieving and emphasizing a psychological distance between themselves and other members of their previous group.[122]

Is there a hint of autobiography here? By most people's standards he had successfully 'made it' in British academia, and yet perhaps he still felt himself excluded from its highest echelons (a Chair at Oxford) by virtue of his 'foreignness' and his Jewishness.

Henri also warned that, even in the best case, 'assimilation of the few does not solve the problems of the many',[123] and went on to advocate that minorities develop group-based (rather than individual) strategies to deal with their negative social identity. One of these, taken directly from SIT, was for them to develop alternative ideologies which directly challenged (and sought to reverse) society's traditional negative evaluation of the minority group's special attributes (e.g., skin colour; accent, dialect or language).

Henri was obviously pleased with this paper and was soon thinking of expanding it into a paperback book, which would have wide circulation.[124] Bruner, as ever Henri's standard bearer-in-chief, was wildly enthusiastic about the article:

> that MRG booklet, The SP of M, is a brilliant piece of analysis and writing. The only reaction that fits my set of feelings is to congratulate you and throw my hat in the air. When I think back to the naïve state of the field of the social psychology of race relations as represented by Gordon Allport's rather applonian [sic] writing I realize how far we have got – and how crucial you have been to our getting where we are.
>
> It is a delight to find all this so, a total joy. You have brought psychology into the broader community of sociology, history and humane concern and what else can we do but thank you![125]

Henri's second publication from this period was more academic in tone.[126] It was a chapter based on a presentation he had made to the Bristol conference on intergroup relations in 1978 and returned to the topic of stereotypes, the subject of some of his earliest research (Chapter 5). The first part of the chapter rehearsed the usual arguments for the individual cognitive functions of stereotypes – simplification and ordering of people's complex worlds. But then he broadened the argument, taking aim at the emerging 'social cognition' movement in the process, by pointing to two features of stereotypes that are often overlooked by social psychologists: the fact that they are socially constructed – and hence socially shared – entities that have their origins in particular intergroup contexts; and that, in addition to any individual functions they serve, they also frequently provide an ideological justification for some past or intended future treatment of an outgroup.

The third publication, Henri's last in an academic journal, was his review of intergroup relations for the prestigious *Annual Review of Psychology*.[127] It is one of his most well-known publications, still attracting (in the five years prior to 2019) more than 100 citations a year (total citations = 1840[128]). It provided a comprehensive overview of the previous years' research in the field and still provides a useful resource today. The treatment is even-handed – he does not bang the drum too loudly for his own kind of intergroup research – and the coverage is mostly exemplary. In just one respect could it be faulted. His discussion of the reduction of intergroup discrimination is rather cursory – just over two pages in a 31-page article – and is overly pessimistic in tone. It is not as though there was no literature on conflict reduction to review. A later meta-analysis located over 500 studies on prejudice reduction, of which nearly 200 were published before 1980.[129] Henri's coverage of that large literature is confined to a mere twelve sources. But, then, Henri had shown little interest in the positive aspects of intergroup relations throughout his career – publishing just a single article on the topic.[130]

His final book, *The Social Dimension* handbook, his riposte to the Moscovici and Doise volume over which he had fallen out so catastrophically with Moscovici, was published posthumously.[131] It contained thirty-two chapters, including one written by Henri himself on 'Intergroup relations, social myths and social justice in social psychology'.[132] Its central argument was that societal intergroup relations create various social myths about one's own and other groups and that these myths are crucial in determining people's views about what is just (or unjust) treatment of people, especially people who belong to groups other than our own. He used this as a starting point to launch a critique of theories of equity and justice.[133] The burden of his critique was, as usual, that such theories only ever considered relationships (of equity or justice) between *individuals*, and were not relevant to considerations of what people believed was moral, equitable or fair at an intergroup level. The chapter displays all Henri's usual erudition – it contains references to or quotations from such diverse authors as Bourdieu, Hampshire, Homans, Machiavelli, Nagel, S. Runciman, and Tolstoy – and concludes with this interesting admission that his 'social identity perspective' may be inadequate (as currently formulated) to capture the origins and operation of social myths:

> social identity is not enough. The subtle and complex interactions between group strategies striving to achieve positive distinctiveness, and the strategies instrumental in attempts to change or preserve the intergroup status quo must be taken into account as a fundamental issue in theories and research. None of this can be properly understood without considering another set of complex interactions: the interplay between the creation or diffusion of social myths and the processes of social influence *as they operate in the setting of intergroup relations and group affiliations.*[134]

Henri was not just writing and editing books, he was also laying the foundations for future research. Some time in the early 1980s, he received a letter from the Bristol vice-chancellor, inviting him to consider early retirement. Bristol, like other universities in Britain at that time, was feeling the effects of the new Conservative Government's public-sector cuts. To reduce their wage bill, many universities were offering attractive early retirement packages to their senior (or older) staff. Initially, Henri did not take the VC's letter seriously and took no action. However, a little while later he was invited to a meeting with the VC, who indicated that he had taken Henri's non-response as agreement and was expecting Henri to retire. Unsurprisingly, Henri was rather offended by this presumption.[135] Nevertheless, on reflection, he may have viewed early retirement as an opportunity to dedicate himself full-time to his writing, freed from his, albeit minimal, university obligations. Such a prospect would be even more attractive if he could secure some additional income from a new research grant (or two).

Thus it was that in September 1980 he applied to SSRC for a personal research fellowship. If awarded – and it was (in February 1981) – it would free him up for a whole year (October 1981–September 1982) to focus on three publication projects:

the completion of the *Social Dimension* book; the expansion of his pamphlet on minority groups into a book; and a new book, intriguingly called, *Groups and Countergroups*. He described this book thus:

> a synthesis of the perspective on the problems of intergroup relations adopted by my colleagues and myself, the research deriving from this perspective, and a good deal of other research closely related to it.[136]

No sooner had this fellowship started than Henri was in discussion with the European Science Foundation (ESF) about directing a large cross-national project on migration, with particular reference to the 'patterns and choices of belonging of adolescents and young adults of the second generation immigrants in Western Europe'.[137] Henri had been on the original ESF Committee which had approved the project and, indeed, seems to have written the original proposal for it in September 1980.[138] He was asked to step in as Director when the original project director had proved incapable of coordinating such a large and complex research programme.

The primary objective of the project was to obtain data on the acculturation orientations (to use current parlance) of second generation immigrants to Western Europe. Its focus was to be on adolescents (17–21 year olds) and their inclinations towards 'assimilation' or 'separatism' in relation to the majority culture (these terms were used in the original proposal). Originally, four countries were targeted – West Germany and Sweden (as 'receiving' countries), and Turkey and Yugoslavia (as 'sending' countries). Henri quickly set about expanding that number to seven (adding Netherlands, Austria, and Finland). The project was to be comparative, contrasting the aspirations and experiences of adolescent migrants with 'control groups' of adolescents remaining in the countries of origin and from the majority cultures.

This project has an extraordinarily contemporary feel to it. The 1960s and 1970s had seen much westward and northerly migration in Europe, and then, as now, there was considerable public debate about how (well) those migrants were 'integrating', by which was (and is) usually meant 'assimilating' – that is, completely adopting the norms and customs of the majority culture. The 1970s was a period of economic recession in Europe, just as has been the current second decade of the twenty-first century. This, together with the history of the relationships between receiving and sending countries, would undoubtedly be crucial contextual factors to be considered when designing the study and interpreting the data, so the proposal noted. As ever with Henri, 'the context' (of social psychology) was paramount.

It was not just the inclusion of economic and demographic information in the research design that was noteworthy, the way the proposal itself was written would make a more than convincing case for a successful ESF grant today. It proposed an inter-disciplinary (history, sociology, anthropology and linguistics) and mixed-methods (media analysis, semi-structured interviews, observation, and surveys) approach to the study of the immigrant experience.

This was to be a major piece of research. It was logistically complicated – seven national research teams to be coordinated, with data collection not only in those countries but also in the countries of origin of the migrants. The budget was large – for 1981 alone it was more than 850,000 French francs (over £78,000) – and it was projected to last two years. The whole project would probably be the equivalent to around £400,000 at today's prices.[139]

Henri seems to have relished the challenge and he formally accepted ESF's invitation to be the project's coordinator in late 1981.[140] I suspect he saw the grant as another opportunity for him to exercise his not inconsiderable organisational talents, just as he had done fifteen years previously in helping to set up *EAESP*. It would also have given him ample opportunities to satisfy his wanderlust – research sites in seven different countries to be visited, planning meetings to be convened, research seminars to be organised – free from any university commitments in his (to be brought forward) retirement. His readiness to take on such a daunting task was also fuelled by a deeply personal motivation. As he wrote to the leader of the Swedish team:

> One of the major reasons why, after having worried a great deal about it, I have decided to accept the invitation … has to do with my past, both intellectual and 'biographical'. I myself have been an immigrant about three times. Both my children are 'second generation'. Before I was an academic I have worked for several years after the war (after having been a prisoner-of-war in Germany for five years) with refugees and other victims of war (mainly children and young people) in France, Belgium, Germany and elsewhere. The major preoccupation underlying all or nearly all of my academic work has been based on a simple question: how could people have done that to other people? This does *not* mean that my work had become 'subjective' and devoid of the necessary scientific distance from one's problems: but there is no doubt that the underlying passion was there. In very many ways, having now an opportunity to be useful through research to disadvantaged minorities all over Europe would present to me a sort of culmination of many years of intellectual and personal preoccupation. This is the real reason why I decided to accept.[141]

By January 1982, whilst still in the middle of his SSRC Fellowship, Henri started work on the ESF grant. Three weeks into the New Year he sent in his first interim report.[142] Six weeks later, he wrote to a Dr Wilpert, one of the German members of the project who he had co-opted as his assistant, with more plans for further meetings. Rather ominously (with the benefit of hindsight), his letter alluded to him having 'not been well (and (am) still not completely recovered)'.[143] Indeed, he had not been feeling well for some time. The month before, he had written to John Bamborough, Principal of Linacre College, in connection with arrangements for a supernumerary fellowship at the college (he was planning to move back to Oxford in the Spring), complaining of being stuck at home with 'a tummy bug'.[144]

Alma Dorndorf, his secretary at the time, recalled that he had been taken ill abroad with some stomach complaint, causing him severe constipation.[145] Diverticulitis, an inflammation and blockage of the colon, was diagnosed and he was given antibiotics. However, his condition failed to improve and he was then referred for surgery to remove the infected part of his colon. The operation was performed in Bristol on 22 March 1982.[146]

It was then that the surgeon discovered that the diverticulitis was the least of Henri's problems. On gaining access to Henri's abdomen, the surgeon found that Henri had 'terminal cancer somewhere in the region of the pancreas and the liver', and that he had 'a year to go or less', as Henri wrote to his friends the Festingers a short while later.[147]

Naturally, this shocking news put paid to all of Henri's plans, the books he had hoped to write and the ESF project that he had just taken over and which was so dear to his heart. It also meant that he and Anne had to bring forward their planned return to Oxford at the end of April, asking the tenants of their Polstead Road house (the Jaspars) to vacate sooner than expected.

The cancer was terminal and treatment options were limited and would have bought him little time. In any case, Henri did not want them, asking only for pain relief (morphine). According to his colleague Peter Robinson, who visited him several times in hospital, Henri was remarkably pragmatic about the ill luck that had befallen him. Whilst clearly 'diminished' by his illness, he showed few signs of self-pity and retained enough of his old combativeness to engage in a spirited discussion of the Falklands War which had just begun.[148] However, Howard Giles, another Bristol colleague who was much closer to Henri, recalled that he had 'a hard time dealing with this sudden demise' and was loathe to talk about it.[149]

Soon the arrangements had been made and John Brown, his friend and departmental head, took him to Oxford and all his hundreds of books were brought over too. The last weeks were spent with Henri receiving visitors from far and wide and with him rebuilding bridges with those he had fallen out with. He asked to see some of his 'boys' from the FOPOGO home he had run in France and at least one (Maurice Michower) came. Henri gave him a copy of his 1981 book with a touching dedication on the flyleaf (Figure 7.5). He asked Wolfgang Stroebe to tell Moscovici he was dying; Jozef Nuttin was also informed and was much affected by the news.[150]

Ever the organiser, Henri insisted on making the arrangements for his funeral. He wanted a traditional Jewish religious ceremony, at first glance an odd decision for someone who had been an atheist most of his life. Indeed, he seemed to Mick Billig to be a bit defensive about this decision when they discussed it. Billig told him: 'You didn't live like a Goy, why should you be buried like a Goy?'
For Billig, this dying wish of Henri's made perfect sense:

> He always thought of himself as Jewish; he could never be not Jewish. He didn't think of himself as Polish, or particularly French. He liked living in England. He respected the culture of England but he wasn't English. He was Jewish. That was the one constant identity.[151]

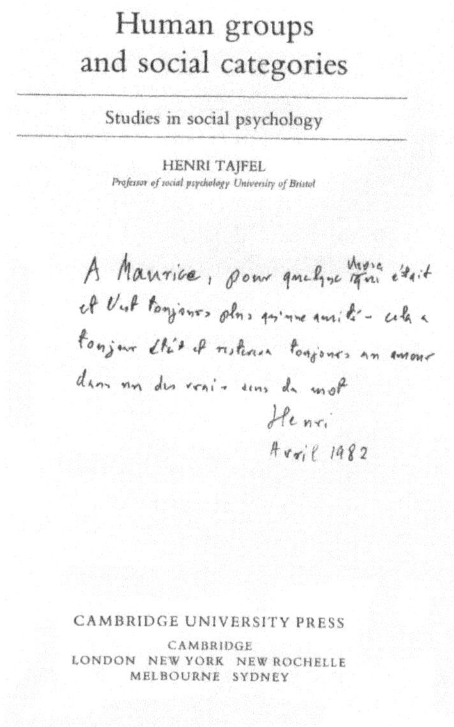

Human groups
and social categories

Studies in social psychology

HENRI TAJFEL
Professor of social psychology University of Bristol

A Maurice, pour quelque chose qui était
et l'est toujours plus qu'une amitié – cela a
toujours été et restera toujours an amour
dans un des vrais sens du mot
Henri
Avril 1982

CAMBRIDGE UNIVERSITY PRESS
CAMBRIDGE
LONDON   NEW YORK   NEW ROCHELLE
MELBOURNE   SYDNEY

FIGURE 7.5 Henri's dedication of his book to Maurice Michower: *'To Maurice, for something that is and has always been more than friendship. It has been and will always be love in one of the true meanings of the word. Henri, April 1982'.*

Henri and Anne talked a lot in those last days. Only half in jest he suggested they take one last holiday together:

> HT: I don't fancy dying here. Why don't we take the car and go somewhere?
> AT: We'd need to find someone to drive us.
> HT (*angrily*): You're taking my masculinity from me. No! No!
> AT: Then you'll have to go on your own!

And, towards the end, he told her: 'We've had a very happy life together'[152]

The end, when it came, was mercifully quick. He started to feel considerable pain and they asked the GP to increase his morphine dose. And so he died, not in Bristol as he had dreaded, but in his beloved Oxford, the city he had been loathe to leave and to which he had always longed to return. The date, appropriately enough for this illustrious son of Poland, was 3 May, Polish National Day.

Post mortem

A few days later, we all gathered in the Jewish section of Wolvercote Cemetery in Oxford to say our farewells. It was a blustery day and those of us without our own kippahs had to improvise with handkerchiefs, and these were constantly in danger of blowing away. Most of the significant people in Henri's life were there: Anne, Michael and Paul, of course; a cousin from Israel; Roger Wachsman, one of the FOPOGO boys; many of his current and former colleagues and students; and several family friends. As he had planned, it was a formal Jewish Burial, officiated by a rabbi. Although he could not have foreseen it, he would have been pleased to have known that just a few metres to the right of his grave (Figure 7.6) his former Oxford colleague, Isaiah Berlin is buried. Also unforeseen, and what would have been devastating for Henri, is the gravestone of his son Paul, just to the left of him. Paul died tragically young at the age of thirty in 1985.

One month later on 9 June 1982, his memorial service was held in St Anne's College, Oxford. If his funeral had been a Jewish affair, this was a more eclectic ceremony with music from Bach, Brahms, and Parry and readings from the bible (Psalms and Ecclestiases) and Yeats. John Bamborough, Principal of Linacre College, gave the address, a detailed account of Henri's life and an eloquent paean to his many achievements.[153]

FIGURE 7.6 Henri's grave in Wolvercote Cemetery, Oxford.

Source: Picture by the author.

Let the last words go to one of his school-friends from Włocławek, the famous French biochemist, Bernard Pullman. Writing to Anne, a few days after Henri's death:

> With Heniek it is part of our youth which definitely disappears and I am sure that it will be a great sorrow to all his friends from Włocławek who are still alive and are dispersed in many places. I am happy that I have at least seen him again in Bristol. I shall communicate this upsetting news to those whose addresses I know, in particular in France and in Israel. He will be remembered by all of us as long as we live'.[154]

Notes

1 Letter from van de Geer, 22 May 1970; WC, PSY/TAJ/7/5/13.
2 Letter to van de Geer, 3 June 1970; WC, PSY/TAJ/ 7/5/13.
3 Van Knippenberg, personal communication, 24 April 2018.
4 As reported by Ben Emans, personal communication, 22 August 2017.
5 Letter from W. van der Kloot, 16 January 1971; WC, PSY/TAJ/ 7/2/9.
6 Letter to Board of the subfaculty of Psychology, 23 December 1973; WC, PSY/TAJ/7/2/9.
7 F. van de Meer, reported by Emans, personal communications 15 and 22 August, 2017.
8 Letter to H. Knegtmans, 19 February 1973; WC, PSY/TAJ/7/2/9.
9 Emans personal communication, 22 August 2017.
10 Van Knippenberg, personal communication, 12 July 2017.
11 A. Tajfel interview, September 2014.
12 Letter from Piaget, 1 October 1970; WC, PSY/TAJ/7/5/39.
13 Letter to Piaget, 6 October 1970; WC, PSY/TAJ/7/5/39.
14 Letter to Flament, 10 December 1970; WC, PSY/TAJ/7/5/7; translation by G. Herman.
15 I am grateful to Ginette Herman for this plausible hypothesis, confirmed by Flament in an interview he gave towards the end of his life (Flament, 2010). The person who got that Geneva chair (Willem Doise) did initially work on some Piagetian hypotheses about social factors in cognitive development.
16 Letter from M. Jahoda, 1 October 1971; WC, PSY/TAJ/7/6/10.
17 Letters from B. Supple, 17 and 19 January 1972; WC, PSY/TAJ/7/3/40.
18 Fraser interview, November 2016.
19 Stroebe interview, February 2016.
20 Letter from Supple, 17 January 1972; WC, PSY/TAJ/7/3/40.
21 Letter to Festinger, 20 December 1974; WC, PSY/TAJ/7/5/5.
22 CV 1980; WC, PSY/TAJ/6/53.
23 Stroebe interview, February 2016.
24 Caddick personal communication, 24 October 2016.
25 A. Tajfel interview, September 2014.
26 'Wandering Jew' is a common English translation of '*Juif errant*', a familiar mythical character in Jewish literature (e.g., Sue, 1845). It is meant to describe the fate of the Jewish diaspora, never (being allowed to be) settled in one place, always in search of the 'promised land'.
27 M. Nuttin interview, November 2016.
28 A version of that song can be found here: www.youtube.com/watch?v=MV8fGf-N06A.
29 I am grateful to Jean-Claude Croizet for assistance with this translation.

30 Beckers interview, November 2016.

31 Cohen (1977) p. 310.

32 Letter to *The Times* (unpublished), 22 November 1975; WC, PSY/TAJ/1/5/18.

33 WC, PSY/TAJ/6/50.

34 Letter from Berlin, 28 March 1980; WC, PSY/TAJ/6/50.

35 In October 1978; WC, PSY/TAJ/ 6/8.

36 Hogg interview, August 2018.

37 Apparently bypassing some of the usual university appointment procedures, according to John Brown (WC, PSY/TAJ/8/1).

38 Personal communication, 27 February 2017.

39 Freeman interview, October 2016.

40 Billig (1976); Milner (1975).

41 Giles, personal communication, 27 February 2017.

42 Stroebe interview, February 2016.

43 Letter to Bruner, 19 September 1960; HUA, HUG 4242.5.

44 Letter to Deutsch, 5 February 1971; WC, PSY/TAJ/7/4/15.

45 Letter to Yehuda and Judith Elkana, 10 November 1976; WC, PSY/TAJ/6/37.

46 Dorndorf interview, October 2014.

47 Oakes, personal communication, 31 May 2018.

48 Culverwell, personal communication, 7 March 2018.

49 Hewstone interview, March 2018.

50 Caddick personal communication, 24 October 2016.

51 With predictable consequences. My initial research plans were so ill-formed that I quickly lost my way and actually dropped out of my PhD for 18 months.

52 Van Knippenberg interview, July 2017

53 Fraser interview, November 2016.

54 Ng interview, August 2017.

55 Breakwell interview, January 2017.

56 Interviews October 2016 and June 2018 respectively.

57 Frydman (2002), p. 110, ch. 3.

58 Some of the ideas in this article were anticipated in an earlier chapter, written in French, for a book edited by Moscovici (Tajfel, 1972b).

59 Tajfel (1974a).

60 Tajfel and Turner (1979).

61 Tajfel (1974a, 1976, 1978, chs 2–4); Tajfel and Turner (1979, 1986). The 1986 chapter is a very slightly amended version of the 1979 piece. Most of the changes involve an updated bibliography; there are few substantive changes to the text, except for the title, which changed from 'An integrative theory of intergroup conflict' (1979) to 'The social identity theory of intergroup behaviour' (1986).

62 Tajfel (1972a).

63 Tajfel (1974a), p. 66.

64 Tajfel (1978a), p. 38.

65 Tajfel (1978b), p. 63.

66 Tajfel and Turner (1979), p. 40.

67 Festinger, in contrast, was concerned only with comparisons among individuals *within* the group (Festinger, 1954).

68 Tajfel (1974a), p. 77.

69 Tajfel and Turner (1979), p. 41.

70 Turner (1975).

71 Worchel personal communication, 24 March 2015.

72 Worchel personal communication, 24 March 2015.

73 Sherif (1966).

74 A colleague once described the Tajfel–Turner partnership as resembling that between Charles Rolls, an aristocratic business man, and Henry Royce, a self-made mechanical engineer from humble origins, who together formed the famous elite motor-car company Rolls Royce in 1906 (Haslam interview, August 2018).

75 Tajfel and Turner (1979), p. 44.

76 Vanbeselare interview, November 2016.

77 Eiser interview, October 2016.

78 Trope interview, April 2019. Michigan at that time was home to the Research Center for Group Dynamics, an institute made famous by Cartwright, Festinger, Lippit, and others in the late 1940s (taking its name from Kurt Lewin's original centre at MIT). Thus, it was no accident that Henri was invited to give a lecture on intergroup relations. The previous year, Ivan Steiner had given a lecture entitled, 'Whatever happened to the group in social psychology?'. Henri's lectures a year later were thus a perfect complement to Steiner's topic. Perhaps he should have called them, 'Whatever happened to the INTERgroup in social psychology?'.

79 Readers interested in the outputs from this project should consult Tajfel (1978, chs 9, 15, and 16, 1982b, chs 6, 14); Turner, Brown, and Tajfel (1979); Brown and Turner (1979); Giles (1977); Giles and Saint-Jacques (1979); and Skevington (1980, 1981).

80 www.measuringworth.com/

81 Agathangelou interview, January 2017.

82 They were also occasions when Henri would give full rein to his sexual importuning (Chapter 6). I recall one occasion when the research team (all men) were enjoying a ribald discussion, led by Henri, as to who would be the first to go to bed with a particular French woman researcher. To my shame, I didn't have the courage to object, although some disapproval must have registered on my face because Henri then singled me out for some sexist banter over my seemingly puritanical attitude.

83 Agathangelou interview, January 2017; Apfelbaum interview, April 2017; Leyens, personal communication, 6 October 2016; Strickland interview, March 2017; Stroebe interview, February 2016.

84 Jahoda interview, February 2015.

85 Schruijer (2007), p. 79.

86 Unfortunately, this documentary is no longer publicly available. Members of EASP can view the portion showing our minimal group experiment at www.easp.eu/.

87 WC, PSY/TAJ/ 6/9.

88 Winter interview, December 2015.

89 Stroebe interview, February 2016.

90 Hewstone interview, June 2018.

91 Proposal to CUP by Moscovici and Doise, October 1979; WC, PSY/TAJ/ 7/5/37.

92 Letter from Moscovici, 3 December 1979, WC, PSY/TAJ/7/5/37; translation by Richard Bourhis and Ginette Herman.

93 However, in the event, he did *not* support it! Sometime later, he wrote a scathing four-page review of the Doise and Moscovici proposal for Cambridge University Press (letter to Jeremy Mynott, 18 December 1980; WC, PSY/TAJ/1/3/5).

94 Letter to Moscovici, 12 December 1979; WC, PSY/TAJ/7/5/37.

95 Letter to Deutsch, 20 January 1981; WC, PSY/TAJ/7/4/15.

96 Letter to the author, 24 January 1980.

97 Letter from Nuttin to EAESP committee, 25 January 1977.

98 M. Nuttin interview, November 2016.

99 Tajfel (1978, 1982a, 1984b).

100 Tajfel and Fraser (1978).

101 Tajfel (1981b).

102 Tajfel (1982b).

103 Tajfel (1978d).

104 Letter to Festinger, 20 December, 1974; WC, PSY/TAJ/7/5/5.

105 Freeman interview, October 2015.

106 Turner (1982); Turner, Hogg, Oakes, Reicher, and Wetherell (1987).

107 Oakes personal communication, 31 May 2018.

108 Giles personal communication, 27 February 2017.

109 Tajfel (1978, 1982a).

110 Tajfel (1982a), p. 483.

111 Tajfel (1982c).

112 Tajfel (1982c), p. 503.

113 Tajfel (1981b).

114 Bruner (1981), pp. xii–xiii.

115 Letter to Henri, 1 June 1980; WC, PSY/TAJ/7/4/7.

116 Letter to Bruner, 10 June 1980; WC, PSY/TAJ/7/4/7.

117 Pettigrew (1982), p. 929.

118 Tajfel (1981b), p. 7.

119 Bernstein (1926/1980); Tajfel (1980). Billig (2014) has provided an incisive analysis of this Preface, linking it to Henri's broader concerns with the Holocaust. I am grateful to Billig for drawing this Preface to my attention.

120 Letter to Lubek, 3 October 1977; WC, PSY/TAJ/7/6/12.

121 Tajfel (1978d).

122 Tajfel (1978d), p. 15.

123 Tajfel (1978d), p. 15.

124 Letter to Bruner, 16 May 1979; WC, PSY/TAJ/7/4/7.

125 Letter to Henri, 6 May 1979; WC, PSY/TAJ/7/4/7.

126 Tajfel (1981a).

127 Tajfel (1982b).

128 WoS, February 2019.

129 Pettigrew and Tropp (2006).

130 Tajfel (1966c).

131 Tajfel (1984b).

132 Tajfel (1984a).

133 E.g., Deutsch (1975); Walster, Berscheid, and Walster (1976).

134 Tajfel (1984a), p. 713; emphasis in original.

135 Stroebe interview, February 2016.

136 Proposal to SSRC, p. 6; WC, PSY/TAJ/6/53.

137 ESF proposal; WC, PSY/TAJ/5/28.

138 Letter to C. Wilpert, 9 March 1982; WC, PSY/TAJ/5/28.

139 www.measuringworth.com/.

140 Letter to J. Goormaghtigh, Secretary General ESF, 24 December 1981; WC, PSY/TAJ/5/28.

141 Letter to T. Hammer, 26 October 1981; WC, PSY/TAJ/5/28.

142 Letter to M. Posner, 22 January 1982; WC, PSY/TAJ/5/28.

143 Letter to C. Wilpert, 9 March 1982; WC, PSY/TAJ/5/28.
144 Letter to Bamborough, 5 February 1982; Linacre College archives.
145 Dorndorf interview, October 2014.
146 Letter from Dorndorf to Nic Johnson, 5 April 1982.
147 Letter to L. and T. Festinger, 6 April 1982; BL, TN63.4.96.
148 Robinson interview, November 2016.
149 Personal communication, 27 February 2017.
150 M. Nuttin interview, November 2016.
151 Billig interview, October 2016.
152 A. Tajfel interview, September 2014.
153 Order of Memorial Service; Linacre College Archive.
154 Letter from Bernard Pullman to Anne Tajfel, 6 May 1982.

8

THE TAJFELLIAN LEGACY

Even in the last months of his life, Henri was brimming with new plans: a large European research programme to direct, new books to edit and write. His tragically premature death at the age of sixty-two meant that he was unable to see those projects through to fruition. It also meant that, unlike several of his contemporaries – Bruner, Moscovici, and (Gustav) Jahoda, all of whom lived into their nineties (or beyond) – he was denied the opportunity to observe how his ideas would be taken up, appraised, and transformed by succeeding generations of scholars. For an intellectual like Henri, for whom ideas and arguments were his life-blood, the hand of fate was cruel indeed to have prevented him from witnessing at least the first few decades of his professional legacy. What, we may ask, would he have made of how the European Association, a project to which he was committed from its outset, has evolved in the years since his death? What would he have thought of the subsequent work of his ten PhD students, the work of their students in turn, and all the succeeding generations of his academic family tree? And, most crucially, what about Social Identity Theory, to which he devoted the last ten years of his life and which he rightly regarded as the culmination of his academic endeavours? To his great frustration, it achieved little purchase in the world of social psychology during his lifetime. That has all completely changed now, but even he might have been surprised (and perhaps occasionally disconcerted) by how the theory has been adopted and adapted, both within social psychology and beyond.

The European project

Throughout his career, a good deal of Henri's considerable energy was devoted to the development of social psychology in Europe. This took its most concrete expression in his dedication to the establishment and running of the European Association of Social Psychology. This organisation has been an astonishing success.

In the fifty years of its existence, it has grown from that small committee of five people elected at that historic meeting in Frascati in 1964 to a membership of over 1000 members based in thirty European countries.[1] In its early years, the Association was forever teetering on a state of insolvency, almost entirely dependent on financial support from North America. Now it is in rude financial health, with an annual budget of over €270,000.[2] But if we go beyond these numbers, impressive though they are, how far has the Association fulfilled the aspirations of Henri and his four co-founders?

The extent to which the *practical* goals of that first committee have been achieved is a straightforward matter to assess. The Association's triennial conferences have been held without a break since the inaugural meeting at Royaumont Abbey (France) in 1966. Then around thirty people attended, with all but two being based in Europe. In 1972, the conference which Henri chaired as President, also had just thirty-three participants, all Europeans (Figure 8.1). Meetings in more recent times regularly attract over 1000 participants, with people coming from all over the world. Today's generation of academics may take such regular conferences for granted, but in the 1960s, such opportunities were virtually unheard of and colleagues from Eastern European countries especially could have almost no contact with those in the West.

EUROPEAN ASSOCIATION OF EXPERIMENTAL SOCIAL PSYCHOLOGY
LEUVEN 1972

Voorste rij (v.l.n.r.): W. DOISE, H. HIMMELWEIT, J.M. NUTTIN, C. FLAMENT, H. TAJFEL, J. RABBIE, M. IRLE, A. BECKERS, J.P. LEYENS
Groep: E. TIMAEUS, G. SEMIN, H. LOCK, S. MIKA, R. GHIGLIONE, L. GARAI, S. TROMMSDORFF, J.P. CODOL, H. WILKE, E. APFELBAUM,
C. FRASER, M. ZAVALLONI, M. ARGYLE, W. STROEBE, T. SLAMA-CAZACU, J. JASPARS, H. HIEBSCH, P. ROBINSON, H. LAMM, M. ANGER,
D. VAN KREVELD, H. MALEWSKA, J. INNES, J.C. ABRIC, P. SCHÖNBACH

FIGURE 8.1 The Leuven General Meeting, 1972; Henri's last as President.
Source: Courtesy of Monika Nuttin.

The other means for facilitating international communication and collaboration dreamt up by the Association's founders have also been a success. Travel grants to support short visits to other universities have become very popular; between 2014 and 2017, the Association provided fifty-eight such bursaries. Small group meetings proved attractive from the start and continue to be well used by Association members (22 financed, 2014–2017). Likewise, those innovative postgraduate summer schools have continued uninterrupted since the first one in The Hague in 1965. Twenty summer schools have been organised (up to 2018) and, by any yardstick, they have been an outstanding success. Talk to anyone who has attended one and they will tell you what a formative experience it was for them and how many of the professional relationships established at them have endured.

As far as the Association's two principal publication ventures are concerned – the *European Journal of Social Psychology* and the *European Monographs in Social Psychology* – they, too, have flourished. However, perhaps inevitably, given the subsequent domination of international psychology by the English language and the increasingly competitive climate of journal publishing, few of the original distinctive features of the *European Journal* have survived. The Russian abstracts only lasted a year; by 1989 the French and German abstracts had disappeared; the possibility to submit articles in a language other than English lasted until 1998; in 1983, a year after Henri's death, the exotic multi-coloured cover had given way to a more prosaic design; and by the mid-1980s articles became increasingly conventional in their format and content. Today (2018) the journal is among the top five social psychology journals in the world with an impact factor of 2.0. It also contributes over 60% of the Association's annual income.

The other publication initiative launched early on in the life of the Association was *The European Monographs in Social Psychology*. This was very much Henri's brainchild and throughout the 1970s he worked tirelessly to recruit authors for it. Over twenty titles were commissioned by him between 1970 and 1980. His vision was to provide a platform for the most interesting theoretical and empirical work in European social psychology. Landmark volumes from that decade included the famous agenda-setting book by Israel and Tajfel (*The Context of Social Psychology;* Chapter 6), Eiser and Stroebe (*Categorisation and Social Judgement*), Giles and Powesland (*Speech Style and Social Evaluation*), Billig (*Social Psychology and Intergroup Relations*), Moscovici (*Social Influence and Social Change*), and Henri himself (*Differentiation between Social Groups: Studies in the Social Psychology of Intergroup Relations*).[3] The book series continues to this day although, with changes in publishing practices and career incentives in psychology, its output has slowed somewhat (from around two books per annum in the 1970s to a book every other year over the past twenty years).

In practical terms, then, the ambitions of Henri and his fellow 'pirates' have been amply fulfilled. They founded an organisation which is still thriving, which holds conferences large and small, which has contributed in no small way to the training of hundreds of young social psychologists, and which sponsors successful journals and books. This is surely a legacy of which Henri would have rightly been proud.

But what of his aspiration to create an autonomous European social psychology, an alternative intellectual tradition that could challenge the supremacy of the North Americans? Has the manifesto for a better, more contextualised social psychology, laid out in various forms in that Israel and Tajfel volume, been realised in the kind of work promulgated by European social psychologists over the succeeding four decades? About this, I suspect he might have felt a little differently.

Let me begin with the 'famous five' founding members of the Association: Gustav Jahoda, Serge Moscovici, Mauk Mulder, Josef Nuttin, and Henri himself. By the 1970s, all had become prominent and productive social psychologists with enviable international reputations. But in what sense was their work distinctively European, independent of the dominant North American research traditions they aimed to challenge?

Jahoda was a leading cross-cultural psychologist, perhaps one of the most pre-eminent of his generation, and, of all the founders, was probably the person who had the least professional contact with the USA. Throughout his career, he was interested in the reciprocal influence of culture and psychological processes and so, in that sense, he was a good exemplar of the kind of 'contextual social psychology' advocated by the contributors to the Israel and Tajfel volume (of whom he was not one, incidentally). Although much of his work can be situated in the earlier cross-cultural tradition initiated by members of the Harvard Department of Social Relations,[4] it is fair to say that a properly contextualised cross-cultural psychology lay rather dormant in North America until the late 1980s and subsequently.

Moscovici's two major contributions to the discipline were his work on minority influence[5] and his theory of social representations.[6] The former was certainly new – prior to his pioneering work, social influence was regarded as being synonymous with majority influence.[7] Moscovici's argument was that such a one-sided view of social influence was inherently conservative and could not account for social change, either on a micro (within groups) or macro (within societies) level. However, in its formulation (presentation of testable hypotheses) and in its methods (mostly experimental) it was conventional enough,[8] so much so that it quickly became absorbed into the North American mainstream.[9] Moscovici's theory of social representations, drawing as it did on Durkheim,[10] is more obviously 'European' in content, epistemology, and methodology and has largely been ignored in North (but not South) America.

Mulder and Nuttin were probably the most conventionally 'mainstream' in their approaches. Mulder's early work was on communication networks, a classic topic in small group research,[11] but became better known later for his power-distance theory of power dynamics within groups.[12] Nuttin worked on dissonance theory[13] and experimental games,[14] and is famous for his discovery of the name letter effect, the phenomenon in which people show an unconscious preference for letters belonging to their first or family name[15]. This may be a variant of his friend Zajonc's mere exposure effect.[16] Both Mulder and Nuttin used traditional experimental methods in their research.

Henri's work has already been discussed extensively elsewhere in this book and I will return to it again shortly. Suffice it to say here that his early work was situated squarely within a traditional psychophysical paradigm (Chapter 5); his work on children's nationality preference, whilst certainly innovative, was otherwise conventional in its chosen methodology and theoretical rationale (Chapter 6); and his most famous empirical discovery (minimal intergroup discrimination – Chapter 6) also emanated from a tightly controlled laboratory paradigm, of which any of his North American colleagues would have been proud and, indeed, which many of whom went on to use.[17] The strongest claim for a uniquely European contribution from Henri can be made for SIT (Chapter 7). This is clearest in its central assumption that, once people's social identities are engaged because of some contextual factor (e.g., presence of clear-cut category boundaries or intergroup competition), people start acting as *group members* rather than in terms of their particular individual attributes. It was also innovative in highlighting the interplay between societal structures (of status and power) and the social psychological processes to be observed among groups in those societies. However, whilst certainly a radical departure from most North American theories of intergroup relations at the time, these ideas were not completely unheard of west of the Atlantic Ocean,[18] even if they were very much in a minority there. As for the rest of SIT, an argument can be made, as for Moscovici's social influence theory, that at least in its *form* it is not radically different from other social psychological theories.[19] Certainly, the vast majority of the empirical research it inspired has been resolutely quantitative, consistent with Henri's consistent advocacy of the experimental approach.[20]

It might reasonably be objected that what demarcated Henri's (and those other pioneers') vision of a distinctively new European social psychology was not so much their preferred methods which, as I have just noted, were often just as conventionally experimental (or at least quantitative) as those practised by North Americans, but in their choice of research problems and in their anti-individualist stance.[21] This was certainly the case for Henri. He remained faithful to the experimental method throughout his career and never embraced other (qualitative) methodologies. The important thing for him, as he laid out in his 'Experiments in a Vacuum' chapter (see Chapter 6), was to tackle important social problems in a non-reductionist way. The same was true of Moscovici, although he was less convinced by the experimental method and positivistic social psychology more generally.[22] Nevertheless, for some other contributors to the *Context of Social Psychology* book, a break with conventional (i.e., North American) methodologies did form a central plank of their critique.[23] It is arguable how much purchase such alternative methods have had on mainstream European social psychology over the past fifty years.

The careers and research profiles of other members of the European 'old guard' – Michael Argyle, Claude Flament, Colin Fraser, Hilde Himmelweit, Martin Irle, Jaap Rabbie, Ragnar Rommetveit, and Peter Schönbach – were not dissimilar from those of the members of the first European planning committee that I have just described. There was little obvious to demarcate their work, in epistemology, content areas or methodology, from that of North American contemporaries, however important it was in its own right (and much of it certainly was).

The same might also be said of those we might call the 'second generation' of European social psychologists – that is, the students or protégés of that 'old guard'. Taking a small and somewhat arbitrary sample of prominent European social psychologists who trained in the 1960s or 1970s – Jean-Paul Codol (France), Jacques-Philippe Leyens (Belgium), Wolfgang Stroebe (Germany), and Ad van Knippenberg (Netherlands) – while all have made a decisive impact in their respective fields, it is not obvious how they can be differentiated from other international scholars of their generation, either in terms of the way they theorised or in the manner in which they conducted their research. Manifest exceptions would be Willem Doise (Switzerland), who was preoccupied with how different levels of analysis in the study of groups could be articulated and with how to analyse social representations quantitatively,[24] and John Turner (Britain) who, extending the ideas of his mentor (Henri), developed a thoroughgoing and non-reductionist theory of the self in group settings.[25]

Earlier, I noted the rising fifty-year trajectory of the *European Journal of Social Psychology* from its launch in 1971 to its current status as one of the world's leading journals for social psychology. Although it was never planned to be an exclusive publication, there is no doubt that it was originally intended to be an outlet run by Europeans for Europeans, a counterweight to what was then seen as the rather rigid orthodoxy of the mainstream North American journals. For twenty-seven years, its editors and associate editors were always affiliated to European universities. Then, in 1998, the first North American associate editor was appointed. Today (in 2019) the editorial team includes two people affiliated to North American universities, one from Australia and one from Israel. And the affiliations of its contributors have undergone a similar transformation. In the first five years of its existence, over 80% of EJSP's authors were European and just 18% were from North America; by 2009, those figures had changed to just over 61%, and 29% respectively.[26] Like much of European social psychology, *EJSP* has become quite globalised and less distinctive in its character.

'Flesh perishes, I live on'[27]: the Tajfel academic family tree

Only ten students completed their PhDs under Henri's supervision, if we don't count the two who transferred to another supervisor and the one who never finished. Of these ten, two pursued careers outside of academia and one supervised no PhDs. Thus, in tracking Henri's academic 'lineage', one begins with a first generation of just seven scholars: Mick Billig, Glynis Breakwell, Rupert Brown, Brian Caddick, Sik-Hung Ng, John Turner, and Ad van Knippenberg. Those, in turn, have supervised a pleasingly symmetrical total of 100 students (second generation, or Tajfellian 'grandchildren'; Figure 8.2), many of whom have gone on to supervise several students of their own ('great grandchildren'; see Appendix 2). In fact, we have now arrived at the fifth generation of Tajfel's descendants. In total, there are over 700 (and counting) social scientists who can claim some kind of

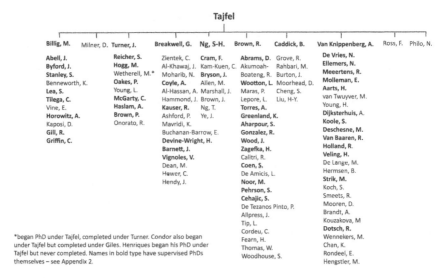

FIGURE 8.2 Henri's academic family tree (first two generations): his ten PhDs and their PhDs.

academic lineage to Henri. Of these, 66 are full professors and three have headed up universities.

In biological genealogy, genetic traces of forebears are irradicably present in succeeding generations, even if in ever-diminishing proportions. Thankfully, academic family trees are not subject to such Mendelian regulation. Not surprisingly, Henri's influence can be most clearly discerned in all ten of the PhDs he supervised: Billig (discrimination in minimal groups), Milner (ethnic preference in young children), and all the remainder on aspects of SIT. Nevertheless, it is striking how divergent the subsequent careers of those first-generation Tajfel scholars proved to be. Billig abandoned experimental social psychology by the late 1970s, and went on to become a world authority on ideology, rhetoric, everyday language, and much else besides[28]. Breakwell developed her own identity process theory before branching out into youth unemployment, social representations, and the analysis of risk, whilst simultaneously pursuing a successful career in university administration.[29] Ng maintained an interest in intergroup relations throughout his career but also became a prominent scholar of language, ageing, and cross-cultural psychology.[30] After his PhD, Caddick worked in a social work department and made contributions to family therapy and the rehabilitation of offenders.[31] Van Knippenberg investigated social identity ideas for a while, principally with his student Ellemers,[32] but eventually abandoned that line of work for mainstream social cognition, studying categorisation processes in memory, associative priming, mimicry, and a host of other core topics in that field.[33] Of all Henri's PhDs, probably Turner and Brown stayed closest to the fold. Turner, Henri's co-author of SIT, famously went on to make a major contribution to our understanding of group behaviour through his

self-categorisation theory, a perspective which he and his colleagues have successfully applied to a wide range of topics – social influence, stereotyping, personality, power, amongst others.[34] It was he who did the most to extend the Tajfellian
legacy theoretically and to encourage its application into new domains. Brown
(the author) investigated ways of measuring group identification before moving to
intergroup contact, prejudice, and acculturation.[35]

Naturally, as one moves to subsequent generations of the Tajfellian lineage, the
diversity of intellectual concerns expands exponentially. Of the 100 'grandchildren'
shown in Figure 8.2, it is doubtful if more than a handful would claim much direct
Tajfellian influence in their work; most of these lie on the 'Turner branch' of the
family tree, most obviously in the work of Reicher, Hogg, Oakes, McGarty, and
Haslam. And by the time one arrives at the third and later generations, the influence has all but completely dissipated, except again among the Turner 'descendants'
(Appendix 2).

I suspect Henri would have been entirely comfortable – proud even – with this
wonderful pot-pourri of scholarship produced by his students and their several
hundred academic descendants. He was rarely a man to impose his ideas on his
protégés and colleagues, however vociferously he might argue his corner.

In the next section, we will go beyond this exercise in academic genealogy to
assess the impact of Henri's ideas more generally. But before doing so, one last
observation is in order. It comes from one of Henri's students, Sik-Hung Ng, who
has worked for much of his career in New Zealand, Hong Kong, and Beijing. He
told me that a significant source of Western influence on contemporary Chinese
social psychology is a series of ten books translated by Wen Fang and his colleagues at Peking University. Six of these are by Europeans, of which no fewer than
three were by direct Tajfellian descendants: Billig's *Arguing and Thinking*,[36] Hogg and
Abrams's *Social Identifications*,[37] and Turner and his colleagues' *Rediscovering the Social
Group*.[38,39]

Given that it is likely that the Chinese psychology student population is one of
the largest in the world, it seems safe to assume that Henri's 'genealogical' legacy has
extended way beyond conventional Western frontiers. Indeed, Fang himself is quite
clear about the impact of Henri's ideas:

> Tajfel is a huge presence in Chinese social psychology, especially in studying
> intergroup relationships. His influence extends also to sociology and other
> social scientific disciplines as long as group processes is concerned. His con-
> ception of social identity has become one of the most important analytical
> tool(s) to understand relationship(s) between different social classes, ethnicity
> groups and religious, as well as social movements in China.[40]

Social Identity Theory: a critical appreciation

In the research for this book, I have interviewed over fifty academic psychologists.
At some point in these interviews, I always asked what they consider to be Henri's

most important and enduring legacy. The overwhelming majority of the replies to this question was that it is his SIT, or some aspect of it, which has been his most significant contribution.

Of course, my sample of interviewees is hardly representative of contemporary social psychologists. Nevertheless, their judgement is borne out by bibliometric data. Following the helpful lead of Postmes and Branscombe,[41] who conducted a 'cited reference' search in Web of Science (WoS) for Tajfel and Turner citations combined, I repeated the exercise *just* for the two Tajfel and Turner chapters and Henri's 1974 article (these are the most common citations for SIT). This yielded over 13,000 records.[42] By way of comparison, this is several hundred more citations than Festinger's famous theory of cognitive dissonance[43] has attracted (12,700), and that had a twenty-year head start.

In passing, it is also worth noting that Henri's influence has been almost entirely through his scientific publications. His one foray into pedagogic publishing was an introductory textbook co-edited with Colin Fraser.[44] Although published by Penguin, a trade publisher with a considerable readership, the book did not make much impact. In part, this was a result of a lack of sufficiently ruthless editing – there is considerable unevenness in level and style (one or two chapters are frankly unreadable). The choice of chapter topics was also somewhat eccentric, especially as compared to contemporary textbooks. Whatever the reason, whilst Henri's name is now probably known to most psychology undergraduates around the world, I doubt that this came about from reading that book. In that respect, his fame has been achieved rather differently than, for example, Solomon Asch, Gordon Allport, or Roger Brown, all of whom published textbooks that exerted considerable influence on the field in their time.[45]

As will be recalled from Chapter 7, SIT purported to be a general theory of intergroup behaviour that rested on a few basic assumptions: that people sometimes see themselves (and act as) *individuals*, at other times as *group members* (the so-called *interpersonal–intergroup* continuum); in the latter case, their *social identities* as members of various groups become engaged, and these identities have cognitive, evaluative, and affective consequences for their self-concepts; people prefer to see themselves in a positive light which implies that there will be a general *search for positive distinctiveness* in their perceptions of and dealings with other groups; this search for distinctiveness may take different forms in socially 'superior' and 'inferior' groups, contingent on various social-structural factors, such as the permeability of group boundaries, the stability of the social system, and the perceived legitimacy of the status relations.

What is interesting about that earlier bibliometric analysis which shows SIT's evergreen popularity is that the vast majority of the recorded citations are not using SIT in order to derive and test specific hypotheses from the theory itself. With some exceptions, to be noted shortly, most of those 13,000 publications have drawn on SIT in a rather general way, *either* to refer to the foundational idea that people may drive their social identity from the groups they belong to, *or* to the fact that, if and when they do so, they will then act in terms of that group membership rather than as an individual, *or* to make the meta-theoretical point that intergroup behaviour must be simultaneously analysed in terms of both social structural variables and subjective group affiliations. From such basic points of departure, researchers have shown remarkable ingenuity in then extending their analyses to an enormous range of fields and applications.

Such creative extrapolations were less in evidence in the first decade or so after SIT's publication. In that period, there was a sustained effort to test hypotheses which were either explicitly stated in SIT or which could be derived from its core propositions. The most salient examples of such work would be: tests of the theory's predictions regarding people's responses to status inequity[46] and similarity;[47] examinations of the motivational status of self-esteem in intergroup behaviour;[48] and attempts to unravel the link between strength of group identification and ingroup bias.[49] I will not attempt a detailed assessment here of how successful this work was in validating key elements of SIT; suffice it to say that not all its hypotheses were unambiguously supported, though several were.[50]

I want now to try to examine the extraordinary popularity of Henri's writings on social identity and intergroup relations especially since the mid-1990s when they started to become more widely diffused.[51] There are, in my view, three main reasons for this growth in popularity: its promise to offer a general theory of intergroup conflict; its account of social identity processes at work in intergroup contexts; and its attempt to provide a new theory of prejudice and discrimination.

Social Identity Theory as a general theory of intergroup conflict

The first reason for the widespread awareness and recognition of SIT within social psychology and beyond lies in its promise to offer a rather general explanation of social conflict that, potentially at least, could be applied to a wide variety of intergroup situations involving organisational, ethnic, or national groups. The idea that threats to people's identities might underlie many kinds of conflicts was a valuable supplement to the other intergroup theories available at the time, such as realistic conflict theory[52] and relative deprivation theory.[53] Like SIT, these theories sought the explanation for intergroup tensions in the nature of the relationships that exist within institutions or societies, but they were somewhat hamstrung when confronted with conflicts which seemed to have a symbolic rather than a realistic (or material) basis.

SIT's primary focus on subordinate or stigmatised groups and its attempts to predict when they might (or might not) be motivated to seek social change was also an attraction, appearing as it did at a period (the 1970s) when many minority or underprivileged groups in the West were agitating for change. And because it set itself so firmly against 'individualistic' or 'reductionist' explanations of intergroup conflict – instinct, drive and personality theories – that still enjoyed some currency in both academic and popular discourse at that time (and since), it was a popular alternative for social scientists of a more 'progressive' persuasion.

But the very generality of SIT's formulation, whilst an obvious strength for many purposes, is also something of a weakness. In crucial respects, SIT lacks the kind of specificity to make it a properly testable theory. Indeed, for some commentators, it is so elastic that it may not deserve the label 'theory' at all.

One example will be sufficient to illustrate this lack of precision. As I noted in Chapter 7, the theory describes several possible reactions by members of low status groups to cope with the negative or insecure identity that their group's inferior status confers on them: they may opt to 'jump ship' (especially if group boundaries are sufficiently permeable to permit this); or they may adopt various 'creative' strategies – find new comparison dimensions, revalue existing comparative dimensions, choose a different outgroup with whom to compare, or even engage in temporal comparisons with how the ingroup fared in the past. Evidence can be found for all of these strategies,[54] although findings have occasionally been somewhat inconsistent with predictions.[55]

But critical questions remain. Do members of subordinate or oppressed groups always opt to leave the groups if they can (if boundaries are permeable)? Henri himself is a case in point. He was a Jew, which, in all the countries he lived, was a consistently stigmatised identity. According to SIT, he might have chosen to hide this identity and tried to 'pass' as a Gentile, especially in France and Britain where he was not geographically embedded in a Jewish community. Yet, as we know, apart from a five-year period during the war when he kept his Jewish identity hidden (Chapter 2), he was always open about (and proud of) his Jewishness throughout his life. Or, to take a less idiographic example, there appear to be developmental trends in the propensity for social mobility among low status group members. Together with a colleague, Mia Yee, I once arranged for young children (3–9 years) to end up in a 'winning' or 'losing' group, based allegedly on their performance in a sporting contest.[56] When offered the option to leave their group, consistent with SIT, most (but not all) the members of the losing groups opted to leave. The exceptions were the five-year-old children who, almost to a boy or girl, elected to remain in their group. Such behaviours, whether of Henri or those five-year-old children, are not easily reconcilable with the proposition in SIT that 'social mobility' will be the default choice of low status group members in permeable group contexts. Evidently, some additional theoretical specification is required.

A similar vagueness can be observed in the preconditions necessary for the 'social creativity' strategies laid out in SIT; it nowhere specifies which strategy will be chosen when. Such an omission is important, given that the various strategies can have very different implications for the subsequent course of intergroup relations in any given context.

Several scholars, from both outside and within the social identity tradition, concur that SIT's generality is, indeed, one of its major strengths but, at the same time, also its Achilles' heel. Anne Maass, for example, one of the most prominent European social psychologists of her generation and not someone who has worked much with SIT ideas, noted:

Although SIT's ability to offer a unifying explanation for multiple phe-nomena and to accommodate seemingly unrelated findings is very appealing, this also constitutes one of its potential limits if one assumes that breadth and predictive power are inversely related (an example is its difficulty in predicting which of many possible identity strategies is likely to emerge in a given situation and how self-esteem is linked to social identity). Although SIT may lack precision, it induced, due to its breadth and flexibility, a pro-found 'paradigm shift' that permeated the entire field and that redirected our attention to social identity as a pervasive motivator of human behaviour.[57]

Marilynn Brewer, who was in the vanguard of North American scholars working on intergroup relations, thinks of SIT as more of a concept than a fully-fledged theory:

> In all honesty, I don't think it's a theory. In contrast, say, with self-categorisation theory which has all the structural elements of a theoretical structure – axioms and so forth. (....) (SIT) is based on a couple of prem-ises but when people think about social identity theory, they're not usually thinking about the disadvantaged social status aspects of it. And so that's one reason why I call it more of a projective test, a stimulus rather than a theory. The idea of a link between the sense of self and a group and the potential implications of that is a really, really important core concept but where it's taken? People just use it as they will.[58]

Constantine Sedikides, an eminent self and identity researcher, is unstinting in his praise for SIT:

> Tajfel's legacy is rich, and I wouldn't know where to begin.... When Tajfel came on the scene the field was still behaviouristically-oriented, and influen-tial theories of intergroup processes emphasised objective reality or behaviour (e.g., realistic conflict theory). Tajfel did not deny the relevance of these ap-proaches, but went beyond them. He made us realise that the subjective is also important. Social identity has implications above and beyond those of real-istic conflict. In doing so, he linked the individual with society in a masterful manner. When groups are incorporated into the self (identity), this matters and has consequences – positive and negative.

But, he continued:

> I am not sure it stands up any more as a coherent set of propositions from which it is possible to derive testable hypotheses. (This is not necessarily a problem with the theory, but it is a problem with the theorists: I've seen SIT being used to support anything under the sun). As such, I am not sure the theory is falsifiable ... it has evolved into a framework.[59]

Michael Hogg is also worried about the theory's falsifiability. He has worked for his entire career broadly under the social identity umbrella and now concludes that it is more of a 'lens' through which one can view many phenomena in a completely different way rather than a tightly bounded theory:

> It's a good and a bad thing about social identity theory.... It's quite a grand theory in many ways, so it can be used to understand a whole array of different phenomena – health behaviour, crowds, the internet, leadership. You name it, it can be used to explain all these things. It's a huge enterprise for a theory to explain all these things ... it helps you understand half of it. My worry it that it's almost like it's been hoist on its own petard, to be honest. It becomes a grand theory that's almost untestable and unfalsifiable.[60]

Perhaps the best depiction of SIT was provided by Dominic Abrams, another prominent European scholar who has worked extensively within the social identity tradition and done much to extend its applicability to understanding the link between intragroup and intergroup dynamics. He regards SIT as 'very robust and strong' for explaining many interesting questions, but likens it to an impressionist painting:

> It's more like impressionism really. You can get some fantastic impressionist art and you know what it's saying, you know what it's telling you. You see the picture and it conveys the emotions as well as the image. And that can be much more powerful than the most precise rendition that looks like a photograph.[61]

Or, to pursue that impressionism metaphor a little further, is it somewhat like Seurat's painting of the River Seine that conveys a wonderful image from a distance but which, on closer inspection, dissolves into a series of meaningless pointillist dots?

Social Identity Theory as a theory of identity

A second reason for the upsurge in interest in SIT over the past thirty years stems from the word 'identity' in the theory's (1986) title. As Postmes and Branscombe noted, 'identity' began to feature prominently in popular and social scientific discourse from the early 1990s onwards.[62]

During the past thirty years, much popular debate and political activism have had identity issues at their core. These debates have focussed on the adoption of new identities or the use of new labels for old identities, and on a growth in the popularity of hyphenated identities. In the realm of gender, an example is the discussion about the wisdom of a continued reliance on a binary gender categorisation ('women' and 'men') which excludes those who choose to transition from one to the other ('Transgender'), or who identify with neither ('agender'). In ethnic relations, indigenous peoples in Australia, Canada, and the United States have agitated for the right to claim 'first nation' status for their communities in recognition of their first occupation of those continents. And, the late twentieth-century saw increases in global migration and a consequent adoption of many bi-cultural or mixed identity labels (e.g., 'British-Asian', 'Turkish-German').

Such cultural trends drew the attention of social scientists. I recently entered the phrase 'identity in social science' into Google Scholar. Henri's (1982) edited book was the third item to appear, neatly sandwiched between a book on fashion and an article on the history of English working-class formation. Calhoun's famous (1994) book, *Social Theory and the Politics of Identity*,[63] headed the list. Further investigation reveals that several other prominent social scientists (e.g., Zygmunt Bauman, Anthony Giddens, Stuart Hall) started to become preoccupied with the concept of identity in the 1990s,[64] an interest that shows no signs of waning.[65]

So, 'social identity' was an idea whose time had come. And yet, for all that SIT fitted perfectly into the emerging cultural and scientific zeitgeist in the final decades of the twentieth century, as a theory of identity it is remarkably simple, perhaps too simple. The core idea, as we know, is that in many intergroup contexts people take on aspects of their group memberships as guides for their thinking and behaviour; they start acting as group members rather than as individuals. Once a relevant social identity is thus engaged, the famous 'search for positive distinctiveness' is instigated. This is the only motivational principle proposed, at least in the original Tajfel and Turner version of the theory.

Thus, as a theory of identity (rather than as a theory of intergroup relations), SIT fails to do justice to the complexities of group-based identities in today's world. There are, I think, three reasons for saying this.

First, to posit the search for positivity as the only motive underlying identity maintenance, enhancement, or restoration is something of an oversimplification. People also belong to, identify with and act in terms of groups in order to reduce uncertainty about their social world.[66] Or they may do so to be able to achieve outcomes that they could not do alone, to be more efficacious.[67] Or they may do so to maintain or re-establish continuity with their past.[68] Or they may do so to gain self-insight and understanding.[69] Vignoles has integrated these different ideas into a motivated identity construction theory which proposes that any or all of the motives of self-esteem, continuity, distinctiveness, meaning, efficacy, and belonging are implicated in group identification.[70] Or, to employ a metaphor that I have used before:

> To say that that any group member always identifies with an ingroup in order to gain or maintain a positive self-esteem is akin to saying that people wear clothes only to look good. Of course, clothes, like social identities, are typically changed according to situational constraints or exigencies. Nevertheless, it would be impossible to hold that enhancement of appearance is the only function served by people's choice of clothing and that other motives (e.g., physical protection, cultural symbolism) are unimportant.[71]

A second reason for doubting the adequacy of SIT as an *identity theory* is that it seems to assume that in any particular context a *single* ingroup identity will become salient and the evaluative positivity of that ingroup versus one outgroup is what drives intergroup behaviour. Yet, as I noted above, the reality of identity construction and expression in many contemporary societies is that identities are often multi-faceted, especially (but not only) for minority groups. Berry[72] is but one of many acculturation scholars to note that many members of immigrant groups choose to be bi-cultural, identifying simultaneously with their heritage culture and the culture to which they have migrated.[73] Add religion and gender into the mix and the intersectional possibilities quickly become quite numerous and complex.[74]

A traditional SIT response to such complexity would be to assume that, in any specific situation, either one identity (of the several available) assumes greater salience, or that some specific combination (e.g., German-Turk) effectively becomes the relevant ingroup. Yet, it is not clear that these two options exhaust the full range of possibilities and, at the very least, a fully fledged theory of social identity would need to specify how particular combined identities come to the fore, or how people reconcile identities which, on the face of it, might be in conflict (e.g., Gay Muslim[75]).

A third doubt about SIT's account of identification has been Henri's (and Turner's) resolute refusal to countenance the possibility that there could be differences among group members in the centrality of the ingroup to their social identity. It is as if a social identity is switched 'on' (or 'off') for all group members in any particular situation. It is easy to understand why the theory's authors adopted this position, given that one of their central objectives in formulating SIT was to account for the uniformity of much intergroup behaviour, in contrast to some previous more individualistic accounts. Probably for that reason, there was no hint in the original versions of SIT that it might be important or even possible to measure people's strength of group identification.

Nevertheless, from the 1980s onward, this has been an issue which has attracted a good deal of research attention.[76] The main reason for this upsurge in interest in identity measurement was researchers' understandable desire to test a basic hypothesis within SIT (that there should be an association between strength of identification and ingroup bias[77]), or to examine if key intergroup processes might be moderated by strength of identification,[78] or to investigate if it might serve an explanatory function as a mediator between the experience of stigmatisation and well-being.[79] For all these reasons, it was odd that the task to develop a reliable and valid indicator of strength of group identification was never initially on Henri's agenda.

Thus, as a theory of social identity, SIT has some weaknesses. Other commentators concur, noting that it is actually more a theory about social conflict and social change than a theory about identity. Sik-Hung Ng, for instance, one of Henri's PhD students, made a telling observation. Noting that the title of Henri's Katz-Newcomb lectures ('Intergroup behaviour, social comparison and social change'; Chapter 7) did not contain the words social identity,[80] he pointed out that Henri himself was at pains to emphasise in his first lecture that 'the crucial pair of terms in the title are intergroup behaviour and social change'.[81] In other words: (social identity theory) is first and last about social change',[82] a view shared by Steve Reicher, one of the most significant contemporary social identity scholars.[83] Glynis Breakwell, another of Henri's students, agrees:

> I don't think Henri was interested in identity; he was interested in intergroup conflict. The extent to which he was interested in identity (identity processes) was in order to explain intergroup conflict.[84]

Indeed, it is quite telling that the original 1979 version of the theory did not actually contain the words 'social identity' in its title; these were added only later by John Turner, when he revised the theory after Henri's death (in 1986). Turner himself once remarked that Henri never liked the term 'social identity theory' because 'he thought it did not do justice to the positive distinctiveness analysis. Tajfel thought it would mislead and in this he has been proven right' (p. 16).[85]

Social Identity Theory as a theory of prejudice and discrimination

A third cause of SIT's growing popularity in recent years was its promise to offer a new explanation of prejudice and discrimination or, indeed, even more catastrophic instances of intergroup hostility like crimes against humanity and genocide. The last three decade of the twentieth century saw little let up in the chronic sectarian conflicts in India, Lebanon, and Northern Ireland. 'Traditional' kinds of ethnic prejudice in the USA and the UK – that is, prejudice based on skin colour – may have subsided somewhat in that same period, even though they were replaced by less obvious forms and were also soon supplanted by anti-immigrant sentiment and Islamaphobia.[86] And, of course, there was unfortunately no shortage of examples of extreme collective violence – for example, in Rwanda, the Balkans, and Sierra Leone, among others.

Social psychologists interested in understanding and reducing such intergroup antipathy not surprisingly looked to a theory variously entitled 'An integrative theory of intergroup conflict' (1979) or 'A social identity theory of intergroup relations' (1986) for answers. And the fact that SIT had started life trying to explain seemingly gratuitous intergroup discrimination instigated solely by the imposition of two arbitrary categories was an added attraction. Certainly, even the most cursory bibliographic survey confirms this growth of interest in SIT as an explanation for prejudice. Putting 'prejudice' or 'discrimination' together with 'social identity' into the Abstracts field of your favourite online database will almost certainly yield several hundred 'hits' between 1974 (the year of the first appearance of a version of SIT) and the present day. Whatever form of prejudice – Islamaphobia, Turkish-Kurdish prejudice, work-place discrimination, ageism, anti-vegetarian prejudice, religious intolerance, prejudice towards transgender people, you name it – you will be able to find research that has tried to employ SIT in its analysis.

Yet, there are reasons to question the utility of SIT as an explanation of prejudice. To be sure, the meta-theoretical point to be drawn from SIT that prejudice involves people acting in terms of their group memberships is a fundamental insight and usefully steers researchers away from searching for personological or individual differences explanations of prejudice. Also, the readiness of people to display ingroup bias on the basis of the most trivial category membership is an important empirical finding, although it is not, strictly, an indispensable element of SIT itself. Beyond these two valuable claims, there is little explicitly stated in the theory which permits specific predictions about when, where, and how prejudice will be shown.

As I noted earlier, and as others have remarked, SIT is at its most detailed when discussing the plight of lower status groups and the conditions when they may agitate for social change; it is much less specific about members of privileged or majority groups who, after all, are the main perpetrators of prejudice and discrimination. To the extent that SIT did discuss possible reactions to threatened or 'insecure' identities, whether of the subordinate or the dominant group, most of its predictions were couched in terms of gaining, maintaining or restoring positive distinctiveness. Such responses were conventionally operationalised in terms of showing increased ingroup favouritism, most often measured as differential evaluations of or reward allocations to the ingroup and the outgroup. In the initial empirical work devoted to testing SIT hypotheses – for instance, in the two Tajfel (1978, 1982) edited volumes – studies that explicitly included measures of negative feelings towards or of outright derogation of the outgroup are notable by their absence.

Indeed, once investigators began to study the differential *negative* treatment of groups – for example, in the allocation of penalties of aversive experiences to ingroup and outgroup, or ingroup favouritism along negatively valenced dimensions – much of the 'usual' ingroup bias seemed to disappear.[87] Now although it proved possible to 'rescue' SIT from these apparently contrary findings – in terms of new contextual norms, or recategorisation of the situation, or normative fit[88] – the fact remains that SIT has always been more capable of explaining when the ingroup is regarded (or treated) more favourably than the outgroup, rather than when the outgroup is treated more negatively than the ingroup.[89] This is important because, as Brewer famously remarked, 'ingroup love is not a necessary precursor of outgroup hate'.[90]

It was not just at an empirical level that early social identity researchers neglected emotion; it was almost completely absent from all the formal statement of SIT. It gets a brief mention in some definitions of social identity,[91] but not all,[92] but that is about the extent of it. The major emphasis was always on predicting differentiation and the search for positive distinctiveness and one can search in vain for hypotheses about when groups might actually dislike or hate each other, or worse. This is both an ironic and a lamentable omission. Ironic because Henri's life mission was to understand how human barbarity, as manifested in the Holocaust and other genocides, could come about. Moreover, Henri himself was a deeply passionate man, quickly moved to laughter, anger or tears. And lamentable because then, as now, many of the most serious manifestations of prejudice in everyday life self-evidently involve strongly felt emotions. When people deface Jewish graves with swastikas, or rip a hijab from a Muslim woman's head, or brutally assault a Gay couple for holding hands in the street, surely the perpetrators are doing something more than seeking to establish some positive distinctiveness for their ingroups? Not for nothing are such behaviours called *hate* crimes.

Others have noted this neglect of emotion in SIT. Tony Manstead, a social emotions researcher, remarked:

> The classic version of social identity theory said nothing about emotion, not explicitly anyway. It's implicit in the ideas of identity threat and the whole idea of the search for positive distinctiveness – presumably there are emotions associated with those and how they manifest themselves in behaviour. But there's no direct treatment of emotion … emotions are an epiphenomenon almost, a side issue.[93]

Jim Sidanius, a leading prejudice researcher, was even blunter:

> It [SIT] is a plausible explanation for ingroup favouritism, but it is an implausible explanation for outgroup aggression, for the Holocaust, for the massacre of the Tutsis etc… .because it doesn't deal with hatred, it doesn't deal with blood. It deals with giving more coins to the ingroup than to the outgroup and then constructing stories around why you did that.[94]

Roger Brown, author of one of the few North American social psychology texts that provided an extensive (and sympathetic) treatment of SIT early in its life-span, also noted the shortcomings of the theory in predicting outright hostility between groups.[95]

And, finally, Mick Billig, a long-term admirer of Henri since his PhD days with him, admitted:

> I think that, technically, it's a theory about how groups which have been discriminated can boost themselves and can campaign against discrimination…. It's not a theory to explain the issue he wanted explained. To say that the Germans persecuted the Jews because they needed to improve their own sense of identity, their self-worth, is not one that should be entertained.[96]

In summary, then, as a formal theory, with clearly stated propositions and hypotheses and well specified boundary conditions, SIT is lacking in several respects. Nevertheless, that lack of precision does not detract from its remarkable generative power in stimulating many diverging and highly productive lines of enquiry. Alex Haslam, one of those who has done most to promote those new developments, suggested that it was only ever 'a blueprint, a hazy blueprint' rather than the finished article, a view echoed by his colleague Steve Reicher, who added the telling observation that it was a theory 'which opens doors' to explain many other phenomena.[97] This is where the true value of SIT's legacy lies: as a valuable general framework – a meta-theory if you will – which provides the foundations, but not the detailed building plan, for understanding the manifold ways in which social behaviour in intergroup settings can be transformed, once people's identities as group members become psychologically salient.

'Let a hundred flowers bloom'[98]: the social identity perspective in contemporary social science and elsewhere

As noted earlier, SIT has attracted over 13,000 citations. WoS conveniently (if only approximately) classifies those citations by discipline and the top ten disciplines (by citation count) are shown in Figure 8.3. Not surprisingly, social psychology is the best represented field (32%). But it is instructive to see the impact of SIT *outside* psychology: apparently scholars in business and management (27% when combined), sociology (6%) and political science (6%) are all finding social identity ideas useful. Not shown in Figure 8.3 are multiple (all >100) citations in fields as diverse as hospitality, leisure, sport and tourism, education, economics, linguistics, women's studies, and environmental studies. Indisputably, then, SIT has spread its tentacles far and wide.

One of the notable omissions in SIT discussed in the previous section was its failure to discuss affective aspects of intergroup relations. Much of the credit for rectifying that omission should go to Eliot Smith who, together with his colleague Diane Mackie, have done the most to put emotion squarely back onto intergroup research agenda.[99] They have developed and extensively tested Intergroup Emotions Theory (IET) which seeks to predict which emotions will be felt by group members in

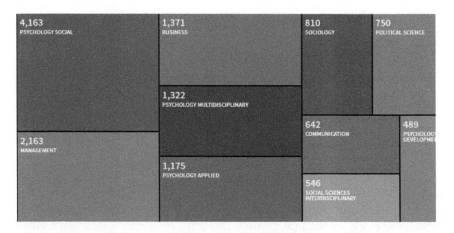

FIGURE 8.3 The bibliometric impact of Social Identity Theory.

Source: Web of Science 'cited reference' search for Tajfel (1974) and Tajfel and Turner (1979, 1986), December 2018 (13,217 records identified; in the above chart there is some double classification so the total exceeds that figure).

particular intergroup contexts, and thence to specify which behavioural responses those emotions will give rise to. The theory begins with the fundamental insight of SIT that, in certain social situations, people's identities as group members are engaged. Once this happens, again drawing directly from SIT, the ingroup's fortunes become its members' fortunes, its misfortunes their misfortunes. Then IET provides the key proposition that those group-based emotions depend on group members' appraisals of the current intergroup context in which they find themselves: if they are confronted with a powerful outgroup that looks set to threaten their existence, they will probably feel fear; if they perceive a weaker outgroup that seems to be challenging their superiority, they will feel anger; if they perceive a subordinate group which appears to endorse moral values at variance with those of the ingroup, they may well feel disgust. From such emotions, specific behaviours follow: fear usually instigates avoidance or withdrawal; anger often gives rise to the opposite – confrontation and aggression; while disgust is thought to stimulate attempts to place the outgroup at a distance or, in extremis, to eliminate it altogether.

Other theories of group-based emotions exist and they all owe a similar debt to SIT of being premised on an initial identification of the self with the ingroup and contextually contingent emotions that are experienced on behalf of the group.[100] As the study of intergroup emotions burgeoned in the 1990s, so did the range of emotions that came under scrutiny. Two particularly interesting emotions are collective guilt and shame, sometimes experienced when group members perceive that their ingroup has behaved immorally or enjoys illegitimate privilege.[101] Again, the hypothesis is that each of these emotions has its own specific behavioural sequelae.[102]

Running in parallel with these developments in intergroup emotions were others which sought to remedy another obvious gap in SIT, namely its neglect of *intra*group processes that might contribute to identity construction, maintenance, and expression. In its original formulation, once an intergroup context had rendered a particular identity salient, various identity serving processes were thought to come into play. But scarcely a line of any of the original formulations of SIT was devoted to the social dynamics among ingroup members that might accelerate or impede those processes.

Fortunately, several lines of research from the early 1990s onwards have largely rectified this situation.[103] Most of these emanated from Turner's Self Categorisation Theory, which grew out of but considerably extended SIT to offer a general theory of group processes. Michael Hogg initiated a programme of work to understand group cohesion from a social identity perspective.[104] Traditionally, cohesion had been understood as the sum total of interpersonal attractions among group members.[105] Hogg showed that very often group cohesion results not from liking one's fellow group members as individuals but from liking the *idea of the group*, as represented by its most prototypical members.

Members of real groups also interact with and influence one another. Such intragroup interaction obviously serves many purposes but sometimes it may be directed at clarifying the ingroup's perception of itself and potential behaviours towards outgroups.[106] In other words, it is by talking to our fellow group members about matters of concern to us – our country's immigration policy, or our political party's manifesto, or our football club's playing style – that we construct images (stereotypes) of our group and others and plan how to give expression to those identities in behaviour.

Our behaviour, whether towards other ingroup members or outgroupers, is usually constrained by norms, and these too are bound up with our social identities. How we *should* behave is part and parcel of what we believe it prototypical for that group. Where there are group norms there are always mechanisms in place to keep deviants in line, as Festinger proposed many years ago.[107] Yet, from a social identity perspective, not all norm deviation is equivalent. Departures from group norms which help sharpen the differences between ingroup and outgroup, and hence contribute to a more distinctive group identity, will be tolerated more readily than those which threaten to blur intergroup boundaries.[108]

Of course, not all group members are equal. Everyday observation, as well as scientific research, confirms that most groups possess a leadership structure which results in some in the group being able to exert more influence over the group's activities than others. The study of how leaders emerge and when they are more (or less) effective has long been of interest to social psychologists.[109] Yet, most theories of leadership treat it as a purely intragroup affair or even, in some cases, as a matter of individual disposition. In recent years, however, there has been a growing recognition that successful leaders are also those who are perceived by their followers as embodying the prototypical attributes of the ingroup.[110] Not only that, but they often play an active role in shaping group members' social identities, in helping to construct what it means to belong to their group (and not to some other). In Haslam, Reicher, and Platow's memorable phrase (borrowed from Yves Besson[111]) they are frequently 'entrepreneurs of identity'.[112]

SIT's influence has also extended in what may seem to some to be quite surprising directions, outside mainstream social psychology. The first of these is in the area of business and management which, as is apparent from Figure 8.3, accounts for over a quarter of the citations of SIT, by far the best represented field outside social psychology. This in itself is quite surprising. Although it is true that four of the early papers testing SIT were conducted in occupational settings,[113] as were a handful after that,[114] it is fair to say that intergroup relations in organisational contexts were never at the forefront of Henri's concerns. For him, interethnic prejudice and conflict and large-scale societal change were always the phenomena of interest.

The application of social identity ideas to business settings was given a significant boost by a 1989 paper by Ashforth and Mael in a leading management journal.[115] They took one of the central ideas in SIT – that groups can become incorporated into people's social identities with a consequent need for positive intergroup differentiation – and sketched out its implications for organisational and sub-organisational loyalty and commitment, institutional socialisation, and intra-organisational conflict. This paper obviously struck a chord amongst business and management scholars: at the last count, it had been cited over 3400 times.[116]

One of the issues dwelt on by these authors was the need for reliable and valid measures of organisational identification. Subsequent researchers obviously resonated to that call and a sizeable number of the 2500 citations of SIT in the business and management fields are concerned with just that. Other popular topics are: workgroup diversity and group performance, customer/client brand identification, work-family balance, mergers and acquisitions, and, of course, leadership.[117] To my knowledge, at least one consultancy company in the UK recognises the potential commercial value of SIT and explicitly employs social identity constructs in plying its trade.[118]

A second innovative development in social identity research has been to explore the implications of group memberships and their associated identities for health and well-being. The credit for this initiative lies with a group of social psychologists at the University of Queensland in Australia.[119] The message of this research can be summarised in a simple five-word phrase, 'groups are good for you'. They can be good for you in providing additional resilience to deal with the challenges presented by natural disasters.[120] They can be beneficial for well-being when imbued with symbolic significance, as studies of participants in mass religious gatherings have shown.[121] They can promote better cognitive functioning and mental health, as research with the elderly, stroke patients, and people suffering from depression has found.[122] Even in surveys of 'normal' populations, those with multiple group memberships have higher well-being than those with few, even controlling for the number of interpersonal relationships.[123] In short, group memberships and the social identities they confer can provide an effective 'Social Cure' for many ailments.[124] Although Henri never wrote about such issues, surely he would have resonated favourably to this conclusion. In his work in the homes for Jewish children in the 1940s, the re-creation of a positive social identity for the children, based on a supportive group environment provided by the homes, was central to his therapeutic philosophy (Chapter 3).

Quite why group memberships can have curative properties is not yet well understood, although it seems likely that they provide people with a sense of belonging, feelings of efficacy, and social support.[125] What is interesting, though, is that, notwithstanding the intellectual debt that social cure research owes to SIT, there is nothing in SIT itself that ever remotely predicted the health and well-being benefits of groups. Once again, it is another brilliant example of how one idea in SIT – that group memberships can become incorporated into the self-concept – has given rise to the flowering of a whole new research literature.

A third offshoot of SIT – and perhaps the most surprising development of all – has been in neuroscience. Since the turn of this century, neuroscientists started to take a concerted interest in the neural substrates of prejudice and intergroup relations, using the full paraphernalia of techniques at their disposal (e.g., fMRI[126]). Much of this research has sought simply to identify the neurophysiological correlates of perceiving various ethnic groups or making perceptual judgements in interethnic contexts, but did not explicitly draw on social identity ideas.[127] However, some of it has been directly inspired by SIT, most notably the work of Jay van

Bavel and Will Cunningham.[128] The general objective of their research has been to examine how mere social categorisation (being classified as a member of group) or social identification (making a meaningful social category temporarily salient) can have neural consequences which are then linked to intergroup attitudes, judgements, or behaviour. This approach is best exemplified by Xiao, Coppin, and van Bavel's 'perceptual model of intergroup relations'.[129] In it, they propose that self-categorisation, collective identification, and features of the intergroup context can all have perceptual effects, whether in the visual, auditory, or olfactory domain, and that these perceptions mediate the relationship between social identification and intergroup relations.

In many ways, this approach is a neuroscientific reprise of the Bruner's *New Look* perspective that was so influential for Henri early in his career (Chapter 4). Indeed, Xiao and her colleagues acknowledge this debt to Bruner explicitly:

> Rather than perceiving the world as it is, people's motives, experiences and expectations can modify how they experience external stimuli.... To the extent that perceptual imprints are afforded social value by way of group affiliations and identities, people should perceive these stimuli differently. These biased representations of the world are more than mere perceptual errors; rather they are evolved adapted biases that are beneficial to survival.[130]

It may be recalled that Henri himself, in his own contribution to the *New Look* literature, concluded his article on the accentuation effects of value on physical judgements with a modest speculation about their potential applicability to the intergroup domain (Chapter 4).[131] In that sense, he might have permitted himself a wry smile at twenty-first-century neuroscientists revisiting some of the phenomena he studied all those years ago. But might that smile not as quickly have given way to a frown of disapproval over this new attempt to reduce social psychological phenomena to neural processes, an argument he railed against so vociferously in that same year?[132] van Bavel thinks not. In answer to the charge of reductionism, he told me:

> I follow the logic of consilience laid out by E.O. Wilson, which is that a theory that operates successfully at multiple levels of analysis is more likely to be true and stand the test of time. On those grounds, I think there is a lot to be gained by not only looking at social psychological aspects of identity, but seeing how these unfold at higher levels of analysis (social systems) and lower levels of analysis (the brain and cognition).... Moving up and down levels of analysis can generate new predictions and insights that might be hard to see if we always stick at the same level of analysis.[133]

Turning to Henri's influence on other disciplines, after business and management the field that has cited SIT most frequently is sociology. However, this impact may be more apparent than real, revealing more about the vagaries of the WoS classificatory system than how seriously sociologists have engaged with Henri's social identity ideas. A review of the several hundred citations attributed by WoS to sociology indicates that many of them should more appropriately be regarded as mainstream social psychology. They deal with such topics as interethnic relations, attitudes towards immigrants and immigration, acculturation, effects of school and organisational diversity, national identity, and nationalism; and many of them are published in psychological journals.

Another approach is to examine how frequently SIT has been cited and discussed in the prestigious *Annual Review of Sociology*. At first glance, here sociologists seem to have taken some interest. Fifteen Annual Review of Sociology articles refer to an original SIT source. All were published after 1996 and cover a wide range of topics, including 'Culture and cognition',[134] 'Ethnic and nationalist violence',[135] 'Ethnic diversity and its effects on social cohesion',[136] and 'Network sampling: from snowball and multiplicity to respondent-driven sampling'.[137] However, closer inspection of these reviews reveals that most offer only the most cursory discussion of SIT, usually restricting themselves to a single sentence, footnote or, at best, a paragraph.[138]

This analysis is consistent with the view of one prominent sociologist, Richard Jenkins, who certainly has engaged with Henri's ideas.[139] He told me:

> I don't think Tajfel's social identity theory has had much impact on sociology at all.[140]

He attributes this lack of impact to two factors: a 'cultural turn' in sociology with a resultant neglect of empirical work; and the isolation of SIT from relevant scholarship outside social psychology – for example, the work of Barth and George Herbert Mead,[141] two authors that Henri never cited. Indeed, such is the general indifference of sociology towards SIT that two influential theorists of the concept of identity could write a thirty-six-page article entitled 'Beyond identity' without mentioning Tajfel once![142]

Henri's ideas have gained more traction in political science, however. Although a search of the *Annual Review of Political Science* revealed only six articles mentioning SIT, four of these provided a detailed treatment of the theory and explored its implications for such topics as minority group formation, voting behaviour and political partisanship, measures of political identity and group consciousness, and American identity.[143] Note, again, that all these reviews appeared after 2000. Henri's ideas have taken some time to gain a foothold outside social psychology.

The only other social science discipline in which SIT has had some, albeit slight, impact is economics. George Akerlof, the Nobel Prize winning economist, has sought to broaden traditional economic models by incorporating and quantifying the concept of group identification into the calculation of an individual's utility function in any particular situation.[144] Adding identity – what he calls the 'missing motivation' – to conventional economic theorising, one is able to make sense of various apparently 'surprising' phenomena: for instance, that people sometimes make choices which are not economically rational but which reflect their loyalty to a group; or how one person's actions can have meaning for and elicit responses from others if they are (in)consistent with group norms; or how people's perceived utilities can change with changing situations when different group identities come into play, instead of remaining invariant as presumed by classical economic models. Akerlof and Kranton make explicit references to SIT in support of their general argument that economic actors incorporate aspects of group memberships into their self-concept. However, the finer details of SIT – the search for positive distinctiveness, strategies for dealing with unsatisfactory identities – are not discussed at all.[145]

SIT has had little impact outside the social sciences. One finds the occasional reference to it in historical treatments of nationalism[146] and, most curiously, in theological studies, where there is a growing interest in using social identity concepts to analyse and interpret biblical texts.[147] Mostly, it seems, this research has focused on the New Testament, although some scholars have also used SIT for interpretations of the Hebrew bible (e.g., analysing intergroup relations between various Judean subgroups). In New Testament studies, a variety of topics have been examined. For example, ingroup–outgroup distinctions in Galatians, subgroup and superordinate group identity formation in Romans and leadership prototypicality among early Christians.[148] Philip Esler, whose work did much to instigate this line of biblical research, estimates that there have been at least twenty monographs published over the last two decades that have explicitly used SIT in their analyses, including a 657-page edited collection entitled, *Social Identity in the New Testament*.[149] I don't know if Henri, a secular Jew but, above all, a committed *social scientist*, would have been more flattered or flabbergasted by his adoption by Christian theologians as a key theorist for their biblical scholarship!

In the late 1970s, Henri was interviewed by the journalist David Cohen. Cohen asked him to predict how well his approach might fare in the future. Henri replied:

> I think it's winning ground. I don't know where it's going to go. If, twenty years from now, someone is interested enough to write that Tajfel was writing nonsense, that's fine. I think it's necessary to stir these issues up because I think they are important.[150]

How right he was! But I suspect that not even Henri, never a man short on self-belief and ambition, could have foreseen the multifarious flowering of his ideas that has happened since his death. This surely is a worthy legacy of this extraordinary social scientist.

Coda

At the end of this story, then, how can we sum up the narrative threads that ran through the complex fabric of Henri's life?

There was, first and foremost, his Jewishness, an identity born out of the horrors of the Holocaust, some of which he evaded himself by enormous good fortune but which nevertheless left him with indelible psychological scars and which propelled all his intellectual work.

From the beginning, that work was marked by a passionate engagement with the social and political issues of the day even though, as an academic, he did no applied work himself (that mantle was taken up later by his descendants).

He was pre-eminently a social *scientist* who, throughout his career, remained faithful to the experimental method, but never dogmatically and seldom to the exclusion of other modes of enquiry.

As that scientist, he evolved from a psychophysicist with a keen eye for experimental detail to a 'big picture' theoretician, often impatient with formal precision and methodological niceties.

He was an intellectual always, who loved to challenge traditional thinking and to stimulate new ideas and research. He did not live long enough to see how those ideas were to bear fruit.

He was a brilliant organiser who managed to persuade colleagues with big egos to work together in the cause of European social psychology, and yet who was prone to occasional bouts of petty rivalry with those same colleagues.

As a man, he was selfless and unfailingly generous in his encouragement of the colleagues and students he liked, but arrogant and dismissive towards those he didn't, and often unconscionable in his mistreatment of women.

Someone, in other words, who could inspire and infuriate in equal measure. Thankfully, in the work of the many hundreds of scholars who have since discovered, adapted, and used his ideas so successfully, the inspiration has proved more durable than the infuriation. Or, to borrow the words of those commemorating the deaths of the two courageous Italian anti-Mafia magistrates, Giovanni Falcone and Paolo Borsellino, he may be dead but *'le sue idee camminano sulle nostre gambe'* ('his ideas walk forward on our legs'[151]).

Notes

1 EASP (2017); van Avermaet (2017).
2 EASP (2017).
3 Israel and Tajfel (1972); Eiser and Stroebe (1972); Giles and Powesland (1975); Billig (1976); Moscovici (1976); Tajfel (1978d).
4 E.g., Kluckhohn and Strodtbeck (1961); Sears, Whiting, Nowlis, and Sears (1953); and others (e.g., Segall, Campbell and Herskovits, 1963).
5 E.g., Moscovici (1976).
6 E.g., Moscovici (1988).
7 Brown and Pehrson (2019).
8 Taylor and Brown (1979).
9 E.g., Nemeth (1986); Wood, Lundgren, Ouellette, Buscerne, and Blackstone (1994).
10 Durkheim (1898).

11 E.g., Mulder (1960).
12 E.g., Mulder, Veen, Hijzen, and Jansen (1973).
13 Nuttin (1966).
14 McClintock and Nuttin (1969).
15 Nuttin (1985).
16 Zajonc (1968).
17 Otten (2016).
18 E.g., Campbell (1965); Sherif (1966).
19 Taylor and Brown (1979).
20 Tajfel (1972a).
21 I am grateful to Steve Reicher and Kay Deaux for this observation.
22 E.g., Moscovici (1972).
23 E.g., Rommetveit (1972); Harré (1972).
24 Doise (1978); Doise, Clemence, and Lorenzi-Cioldi (1993).
25 Turner (1982); Turner, Hogg, Oakes, Reicher, and Wetherell (1987).
26 Schruijer (2012).
27 From Thomas Hardy's poem 'Heredity'.
28 E.g., Billig (1982, 1987, 1992, 2013).
29 E.g., Breakwell (1983, 1986, 1993, 2007).
30 E.g., Ng (1998, 2007); Ng and Lai (2009).
31 Caddick (1988, 1994).
32 E.g., Ellemers, Wilke, and van Knippenberg (1993).
33 E.g., Dijksterhuis and van Knippenberg (1999); van Baaren, Holland, Kawakami, and van Knippenberg (2004); Vonk and van Knippenberg (1995); van Knippenberg, van Twuyver, and Pepels (1994).
34 E.g., Oakes, Haslam, and Turner (1994); Reynolds and Turner (2006); Turner (1991, 2005).
35 E.g., Brown (2010); Brown, Condor, Matthews, Wade, and Williams (1986); Brown and Hewstone (2005); Brown and Zagefka (2011).
36 Billig (1987).
37 Hogg and Abrams (1988).
38 Turner and colleagues (1987).
39 Ng interview, August 2017.
40 Personal communication, 5 January 2019.
41 Postmes and Branscombe (2010).
42 In December 2018.
43 Festinger (1957).
44 Tajfel and Fraser (1978).
45 Asch (1952); Allport (1954); Brown (1965, 1986).
46 E.g., Brown and Ross (1982); Ellemers et al. (1993); Mummendey, Kessler, Klink, and Mielke (1999); van Knippenberg (1984); van Knippenberg and van Oers (1984); Wright, Taylor, and Moghaddam (1990).
47 E.g., Brown (1984); Brown and Abrams (1986); Jetten, Spears, and Manstead (1998).
48 E.g., Abrams and Hogg (1988); Lemyre and Smith (1985); Oakes and Turner (1980).
49 E.g., Hinkle and Brown (1990); Jetten, Spears, and Manstead (1997).
50 Brown (2000).
51 Dumont and Louw (2009).
52 Campbell (1965); Coser (1956); Sherif (1966).
53 E.g, Runciman (1966).
54 Brown and Zagefka (2006); Ellemers et al. (1993); Wright et al. (1990).

55 E.g., Jaspars and Warnaen (1982); Van Knippenberg (1984).
56 Yee and Brown (1992).
57 Personal communication, May 2018.
58 Brewer interview, November 2016.
59 Sedikides personal communication, December 2018.
60 Hogg interview, August 2018.
61 Abrams interview, November 2018.
62 Postmes and Branscombe (2010).
63 Calhoun (1994).
64 E.g., Bauman (1992); Giddens (1991); Hall and Du Gay (1996).
65 E.g., Akerlof and Kranton (2000); Appiah (2018); Brubaker and Cooper (2000); Fukuyama (2018); Mandler (2006).
66 Hogg (2007).
67 Breakwell (1986).
68 Breakwell (1986); Sani, Herrera, and Bowe (2009); Smeekes, Verkuyten, and Martinovic (2015).
69 Aharpour and Brown (2002); Deaux, Reid, Mizrahi, and Cotting (1999).
70 Vignoles (2011).
71 Aharpour and Brown (2002), p. 163.
72 Berry (1997).
73 Nguyen and Benet-Martínez (2013); Schwartz, Vignoles, Brown, and Zagefka (2014).
74 Crenshaw (1994); Deaux and Verkuyten (2014).
75 Roccas and Brewer (2002); Settles and Buchanan (2014); Wiley and Deaux (2010).
76 E.g., Brown, Condor, Matthews, Wade, and Williams (1986); Ellemers, Kortekaas, and Ouwerkerk (1999); Leach, van Zomeren, Zebel, Vliek, Pennekamp, Doosje, Ouwerkerk, and Spears (2008).
77 Hinkle and Brown (1990).
78 E.g., Doosje, Branscombe, Spears, and Manstead (1998); Jetten, Spears, and Manstead (1997).
79 Branscombe, Schmitt, and Harvey (1999).
80 Indeed, the actual phrase 'Social Identity Theory' did not appear until Turner's minor revision of the original 1979 chapter (Tajfel and Turner, 1986).
81 Tajfel (1974b, p. 3; 1974b).
82 Ng interview, August 2017.
83 Reicher interview, June 2018.
84 Breakwell interview, January 2017. Breakwell may be right about this. In 1978 Henri wrote: 'social identity is understood here as an intervening causal mechanism in situations of 'objective' social change, observed, anticipated, feared, desired or prepared by the individuals involved' (Tajfel (1978c), p. 86).
85 Turner and Reynolds (2010); in this same chapter, Turner and Reynolds claim (p. 16) that the first use of the term 'social identity theory' was actually in a chapter Turner co-wrote with the author (Turner and Brown, 1978), p. 203.
86 Brown (2010).
87 E.g., Mummendey and Otten (1998).
88 Gardham and Brown (2001); Mummendey and Otten (1998); Reynolds, Turner, and Haslam (2000).
89 Brewer (1979).
90 Brewer (1999), p. 442.
91 Tajfel (1974a), p. 69.

92 Tajfel and Turner (1979, p. 40, 1986, p. 16).

93 Manstead interview, March 2018.

94 Sidanius interview, May 2018.

95 Brown (1986), p. 574.

96 Billig interview, October 2016.

97 Haslam and Reicher interviews, August and May 2018 respectively.

98 Mao Zedong (1957).

99 Smith (1993); Mackie and Smith (2015, 2018).

100 E.g., Cottrell and Neuberg (2005); Iyer and Leach (2008); Yzerbyt, Dumont, Wigboldus, and Gordijn (2003); Yzerbyt (2006).

101 E.g., Wohl, Branscombe, and Klar (2006).

102 E.g., Allpress, Brown, Giner-Sorolla, Deonna, and Teroni (2014); Gausel, Leach, Vignoles, and Brown (2012).

103 See Brown and Pehrson (2019).

104 Hogg (1992).

105 E.g., Lott and Lott (1965).

106 Postmes, Haslam, and Swaab (2005).

107 Festinger (1950).

108 Abrams, Marques, Bown, and Henson (2000); Marques, Yzerbyt, and Leyens (1988).

109 Brown and Pehrson (2019), ch. 4.

110 Hogg (2001).

111 Besson (1991).

112 Haslam, Reicher, and Platow (2011).

113 Bourhis and Hill (1982); Brown (1978); Skevington (1980, 1981).

114 Brown *et al.* (1986); Brown and Williams (1984).

115 Ashforth and Mael (1989).

116 WoS. February 2019.

117 See Haslam (2001).

118 www.cfte.co.uk.

119 Haslam, Jetten, Cruwys, Dingle, and Haslam (2018); Jetten, Haslam. and Haslam (2012).

120 Drury, Brown, Gonzalez, and Miranda (2016).

121 Alnabulsi and Drury (2014); Tewari, Khan, Hopkins, Srinivasan, and Reicher (2012).

122 Cruwys, Dingle, Haslam, Haslam, Jetten, and Morton (2013); Haslam, Cruwys, and Haslam (2014); Haslam, Holme, Haslam, Iyer, Jetten, and Williams (2008).

123 Helliwell and Barrington-Levy (2012); Jetten, Branscombe, *et al.* (2015).

124 Jetten *et al.* (2012).

125 Greenaway, Cruwys, Haslam, and Jetten (2016); Kyprianides, Easterbrook, and Brown (2019).

126 E.g., Amodio (2008).

127 E.g., Amodio and colleagues (2004); Harris and Fiske (2006).

128 E.g., Cikara and van Bavel (2014); van Bavel and Cunningham (2010).

129 Xiao, Coppin, and van Bavel (2016).

130 Xiao *et al.* (2016), p. 258.

131 Tajfel (1957), pp. 202–3.

132 Peters and Tajfel (1957).

133 Personal communication, 27 May 2018.

134 DiMaggio (1997).

135 Brubaker and Laitin (1998).

136 Van der Meer and Tolsma (2014).

137 Heckathorn and Cameron (2017).

138 Exceptions are DiTomaso, Post, and Parks-Yancy (2007) and Owens, Robinson, and Smith-Lovin (2010), both of which include extended treatments of SIT.

139 E.g., Jenkins (2014).

140 Personal communication, 11 December 2018.

141 Barth (1969); Mead (1934).

142 Brubaker and Cooper (2000).

143 Hechter and Okamoto (2001); Kalin and Sambanis (2018); McClain *et al.* (2009); Schildkraut (2014). See also a lengthy, if critical, appraisal of SIT by Huddy (2001) (cf. Oakes' (2002) rejoinder).

144 E.g., Akerlof (2007); Akerlof and Kranton (2000).

145 See also Shayo (2009).

146 E.g., Mandler (2006).

147 E.g., Baker (2012); Esler (1998, 2000, 2003b); Tucker and Baker (2014).

148 Esler (1998, 2003a); Piper and Esler (2006).

149 Tucker and Baker (2014).

150 Cohen (1977), p. 306.

151 https://scuola.repubblica.it/campania-salerno-itivalitutti/2017/03/21/non-li-avete-uccisile-loro-idee-camminano-sulle-nostre-gambe/.

APPENDIX 1

TAJFEL BIBLIOGRAPHY

During his life, Tajfel published seven books and over 95 articles and book chapters. There are two main strands in Tajfel's intellectual corpus – social perception and intergroup relations – and so the bibliography below is organised along those lines, with a third section of miscellaneous publications and a fourth of radio broadcasts.

Published work 1956–1986

Intergroup relations

Tajfel, H. (1959). A note on Lambert's Evaluation reactions to spoken languages. *Canadian Journal of Psychology, 13,* 86–92.

Tajfel, H. (1960). Nationalism in the modern world: The nation and the individual. *The Listener, 63,* No. 1624, 846–7.

Tajfel, H. (1963). Stereotypes. *Race, V,* 3–14. Reprinted in J.O. Whittaker (ed.), (1972). *Recent Discoveries in Psychology.* Philadelphia: W. B. Saunders.

Tajfel, H. (1964). Cognitive aspects of the development of nationalism. *Proceedings of the XVth International Congress of Applied Psychology,* Ljubljana.

Tajfel, H., Sheikh, A.A., and Gardner, R.C. (1964). Content of stereotypes and the inference of similarity between members of stereotyped groups. *Acta Psychologica. 22,* 191–201.

Jaspars, J.M.F., Van de Geer, J.P., Tajfel, H., and Johnson, N.B. (1965). On the development of national attitudes. University of Leiden, Institute of Psychology, *Report 01-65.* Reprinted in *European Journal of Social Psychology* (1972), *2,* 347–69.

Tajfel, H. (1965). Some psychological aspects of the colour problem. Chapter 10 in *Colour in Britain,* pp. 127–37. London: BBC Publications.

Tajfel, H. (1966). Children and foreigners. *New Society,* June, 30. Reprinted in A. Etzioni and M. Wenglinsky (eds), (1970). *War and Its Prevention.* New York: Harper and Row.

Tajfel, H. (1966). I pregiudizi di colore in Gran Bretagna: l'esperienza degli studenti d'Africa, d'Asia et delle Indie occidentali. *Rivista di Sociologia, 3*, 53–82.

Tajfel, H. (1966). Co-operation between human groups. *The Eugenics Review, 58*, 77–84. Reprinted in *Magyar Filozofiai Szemle* (1967), *3*.

Tajfel, H. and Jahoda, G. (1966). Development in children of concepts and attitudes about their own and other nations: A cross-national study. *Proceedings of the XVIIIth International Congress of Psychology*, Moscow, Symposium 36, pp. 17–33. In translation in *Ceskoslovenska Psychologie* (1966), *11*, 437–44.

Simon, M.D., Tajfel, H., and Johnson, N.B. (1967). Wie erkennt man einen Österreicher? *Kölner Zeitschrift für Soziologie und Sozialpsychologie, 19*, 511–37.

Tajfel, H. (1969). The formation of national attitudes: A social psychological perspective. In M. Sherif (ed.), *Interdisciplinary Relationships in the Social Sciences*. Chicago: Aldine, pp. 137–76.

Tajfel, H. (1969). Cognitive aspects of prejudice. *Journal of Biosocial Sciences, 1,* Suppl. Mon. No. 1, *Biosocial Aspects of Race,* pp. 173–91. Reprinted in *Journal of Social Issues* (1969), *XXV* (No. 4), 79–97; and in P. Watson (e.), (1973). *Psychology and Race.* Harmondsworth: Penguin Books.

Johnson, N.B., Middleton, M., and Tajfel, H. (1970). The relationship between children's preferences for and knowledge about other nations. *British Journal of Social and Clinical Psychology, 9*, 232–40.

Middleton, M., Tajfel, H., and Johnson, N. B. (1970). Cognitive and affective aspects of children's national attitudes. *British Journal of Social and Clinical Psychology, 9,* 122–34.

Tajfel, H. (1970). Aspects of national and ethnic loyalty. *Social Science Information, IX* (3), 119–44.

Tajfel, H. (1970). Experiments in intergroup discrimination. *Scientific American, 233* (5), 96–102. Reprinted in R.C. Atkinson (ed.), (1971). *Contemporary Psychology.* San Francisco: W.H. Freeman.

Tajfel, H., Nemeth, C., Jahoda, G., Campbell, J.D., and Johnson, N.B. (1970). The development of children's preferences for their own country: A cross-national study. *International Journal of Psychology, 5*, 245–53.

Tajfel, H., Flament. C., Billig, M.G., and Bundy, R.P. (1971). Social categorization and intergroup behaviour. *European Journal of Social Psychology, 1*, 149–78.

Tajfel, H. (1972). Vorurteil. In *Lexikon der psychologie, Vol. 111.* Freiburg: Verlag Herde.

Tajfel, H., Jahoda, G., Nemeth, C., Rim, Y., and Johnson, N.B. (1972). Devaluation by children of their own national or ethnic group: Two case studies. *British Journal of Social and Clinical Psychology, 11*, 235–43.

Jaspars, J.M.F., Van de Geer, J.P., and Tajfel, H. (1972). On the development of national attitudes in children. *European Journal of Social Psychology, 2*(4), 347–69.

Billig, M. and Tajfel, H. (1973). Social categorization and similarity in intergroup behaviour. *European Journal of Social Psychology, 3*, 27–52.

Bourhis, R.Y., Giles, H., and Tajfel, H. (1973). Language as a determinant of Welsh identity. *European Journal of Social Psychology, 3* (4), 447–60.

Tajfel, H. (1974). Social Identity and intergroup behaviour. *Social Science Information / Information sur les Sciences Sociales, 13* (2), Apr., 65–93.

Tajfel, H. and Billig, M. (1974). Familiarity and categorization in intergroup behaviour. *Journal of Experimental Social Psychology*, *10*, 159–70.

Tajfel, H. (1975).The exit of social mobility and the voice of social change: Notes on the social psychology of intergroup relations. *Social Science Information/Information sur les Sciences Sociales, 14* (2), 101–18: Reprinted in *Przeglad Psychologiczny* (1979), *22*(1), 17–38.

Tajfel, H. (1976). Exit, voice and intergroup relations. In L. Strickland, F.Aboud, and K. Gergen (eds), *Social Psychology in Transition*. NewYork: Plenum Press.

Tajfel, H. (1976). Against biologism. *New Society, 37* (No. 721), 240–2.

Tajfel, H. (1977). Human intergroup conflict: Useful and less useful forms of analysis. In M. von Cranach, K. Foppa, W. Lepenies, and D. Ploog (eds), (1979). *Human Ethology: The Claims and Limits of a New Discipline*. Proceedings of a Symposium held at theWerner-Reimers-Stiftung, Bad Homburg, October 1977. Cambridge: Cambridge University Press.

Bourhis. R.Y., Gadfield, N.J., Giles, H., and Tajfel. H. (1977). Context and ethnic humour in intergroup relations. In A.J. Chapman and H.C. Foot (eds), *It's a Funny Thing, Humour.* Oxford: Pergamon.

Tajfel, H. (1978) *The Social Psychology of Minorities*. London: Minority Rights Group, report no. 38.

Tajfel, H. (ed.) (1978). *Differentiation between Social Groups: Studies in the Social Psychology of Intergroup Relations.* London: Academic Press. Chapter 1 (H. Tajfel): Introduction; Chapter 2 (H. Tajfel): Interindividual behaviour and intergroup behaviour; Chapter 3 (H.Tajfel): Social categorization, social identity and social comparison; Chapter 4 (H. Tajfel): The achievement of group differentiation.

Bourhis, R.Y., Giles, H., Leyens, J.-P., and Tajfel, H. (1979). Psycholinguistic distinctiveness: Language divergence in Belgium. In H. Giles and R. St. Clair (eds), *Language and Social Psychology.* Oxford: Blackwell.

Gadfield, N.J., Giles, H., Bourhis, R.Y., and Tajfel, H. (1979). Dynamics of humor in ethnic group relations. *Ethnicity, 6*, 373–82.

Tajfel, H. and Turner, J.C. (1979). An integrative theory of intergroup conflict. In W.G. Austin and S.Worchel (eds), *The Social Psychology of Intergroup Relations.* (pp. 33–47). Monterey, CA: Brooks Cole. Also revised as,The social identity theory of intergroup behaviour. In S.Worchel and W.G. Austin (eds), (1986). *Psychology of Intergroup Relations.* (pp. 7–24). Chicago: Nelson Hall.

Turner, J.C., Brown, R.J., and Tajfel, H. (1979). Social comparison and group interest in ingroup favouritism. *European Journal of Social Psychology*, *9*, 187–204.

Brown, R.J., Tajfel, H., and Turner, J.C. (1980). Minimal group situations and intergroup discrimination: Comments on the paper by Aschenbrenner and Schaefer. *European Journal of Social Psychology, 10*, 399–414.

Tajfel, H. (1980). Experimental studies of intergroup behaviour. In M. Jeeves (ed), *Survey of psychology*, No. III. London: George Allen and Unwin.

Tajfel, H. (1981). *Human Groups and Social Categories: Studies in Social Psychology.* Cambridge: Cambridge University Press. German, Portuguese, Spanish and

Italian translations: Stuttgart: Klett-Cotta; Lisbon: Livros Horizontos; Barcelona: Herder; and Bologna: Il Mulino.

Tajfel, H. (1981), Social stereotypes and social groups. In J. Turner and H. Giles (eds), (1981). *Intergroup Behaviour*. (pp. 144–67). Blackwell: Oxford. Translated and reprinted in Tajfel, H. (1982). Stereotype spoleczne I grupy spoleczne. *Social Stereotypes and Social Groups. Studia Psychologisczne, 20* (2), 5–25.

Vaughan, G.M., Tajfel, H., and Williams, J. (1981). Bias in reward allocation in an intergroup and an interpersonal context. *Social Psychology Quarterly, 44,* 37–42.

Tajfel, H. (1982), Social psychology of intergroup relations. *Annual Review of Psychology, 33,* 1–39.

Tajfel, H. (ed.) (1982). *Social Identity and Intergroup Relations.* London/New York: Cambridge University Press. Preface and Introduction: H. Tajfel; Chapter 16 H. Tajfel: Instrumentality, identity and social comparisons.

Tajfel, H. (1983), Prejudice. In R. Harré and R. Lamb (eds), *The Encyclopaedic Dictionary of Psychology.* Oxford: Blackwell.

Social perception and related topics

Tajfel, H. (1957). Value and the perceptual judgement of magnitude. *Psychological Review, 64,* 192–204. Reprinted in M.D.Vernon (ed.), (1966). *Experiments in Visual Perception.* Harmondsworth: Penguin Books; C.W. Backman and P.F. Secord (eds), (1966). *Problems in Social Psychology.* New York: McGraw-Hill; G. Hunyady (ed.), (1972). *Szocialpszichologia.* Budapest: Gondolat; J. R. Torregrosa (ed.), (1973) *Teoria e investigacion en la psicologia social actual.* Madrid: Instituto de la Opinion Publica.

Tajfel, H. (1959). Quantitative judgement in social perception. *British Journal of Psychology, 50,* 16–29. Abbreviated and translated in D. Jodelet, J. Viet, and P. Besnard (1970). *La psychologie sociale.* Paris: Mouton.

Tajfel, H. (1959). The anchoring effects of value in a scale of judgements. *British Journal of Psychology, 50,* 294–304.

Tajfel, H. and Cawasjee, S.D. (1959). Value and the accentuation of judged differences. *Journal of Abnormal and Social Psychology, 59,* 436–9.

Tajfel, H. (1962). Social perception. Chapter 1 in G. Humphrey and M. Argyle (eds), *Social Psychology through Experiment.* (pp. 20–54). London: Methuen.

Tajfel, H. and Wilkes, A.L. (1963). Classification and quantitative judgment. *British Journal of Psychology, 54,* 101–14.

Tajfel, H. and Winter, D.G. (1963). The interdependence of size, number and value in young children's estimates of magnitude. *Journal of Genetic Psychology, 102,* 115–24. Reprinted in F. Dambrot, A. Friedman, and J.A. Popplestone (1965). *Readings for General Psychology.* Wm. C. Brown Book Co.

Tajfel, H. (1964). Human 'judgment' in the laboratory. Categories and Stereotypes. *Common Factor, 1,* 1.

Tajfel, H. (1964). Bias in judgment. *New Society, 4,* 11–12.

Tajfel, H., Everstine, L., and Richardson, A, (1964) Individual judgment consistencies in conditions of risk taking, *Journal of Personality, 32,* 550–65.

Tajfel, H., Richardson, A., and Everstine, L. (1964). Individual consistencies in categorizing: A study of judgmental behaviour. *Journal of Personality, 32*, 90–108. Reprinted in P.B. Warr (ed.), (1970). *Thought and Personality*. Harmondsworth: Penguin Books.

Tajfel, H. and Wilkes, A.L. (1964). Salience of attributes and commitment to extreme judgments in the perception of people. *British Journal of Social and Clinical Psychology, 2*, 40–9.

Bruner, J.S. and Tajfel, H. (1965). Width of category and concept differentiation. *Journal of Personality and Social Psychology, 2*, 261–4, 266–7.

Tajfel, H. (1966). *Study of Cognitive and Affective Attitudes, Final Report*. Grant ΑΓ-EOAR 64–59.

Tajfel, H. (1966). The nature of information in social influence: An unexplored methodological problem. *Proceedings of the XVIIIth International Congress of Psychology*, Moscow, Symposium 34, 50–7.

Tajfel, H. and Bruner, J.S. (1966). The relation between breadth of category and decision time. *British Journal of Psychology, 57*, 71–5.

Wilkes, A.L. and Tajfel, H. (1966). Types de classification et importance du contraste relatif. *Bulletin de C.E.R.P., 15*, 71–81.

Tajfel, H. (1968). Social perception. In *International Encyclopaedia of the social sciences. Vol. XI*, 567–575.

Tajfel, H. (1969). Social and cultural factors in perception. In G. Lindzey and E. Aronson (eds), *Handbook of Social Psychology, Vol. III*, 2nd edn. Cambridge, MA: Addison-Wesley, (pp. 315–94).

Tajfel, H. (1972). La catégorisation sociale. In S. Moscovici (ed.), *Introduction à la psychologie sociale*. Paris: Larousse (Translation).

Tajfel, H. (1976). Social psychology and social processes/La Psicologia sociale e i processi sociali. *Giornale Italiano di Psicologia, 3*(2), 189–221. Reprinted in A. Palmonari (ed.), (1976). *Problemi attuali della psicologia sociale*. Bologna: Il Mulino.

Tajfel, H. and Forgas, J.P. (1981). Social categorization: Cognition, values and groups. In J.P. Forgas (ed.), *Social Cognition: Perspectives on Everyday Understanding*. European Monographs in Social Psychology, No. 26. London: Academic Press.

Other publications

Tajfel, H. (1956) Guide for the psychologist – French. Fontaine, C.G. *British Journal of Psychology, 47*, 237 (book review).

Tajfel, H. (1956) Perception. Symposium of the Association de Psychologie Scientifique de Langue Française. *British Journal of Psychology, 47*, 232–3 (book review).

Peters, R.S. and Tajfel, H. (1957). Hobbes and Hull-metaphysicians of behaviour. *British Journal for the Philosophy of Science, VIII*, 30–44. Reprinted in L.I. Krunerman (ed.), (1969). *The Nature and Scope of Social Science*. New York: Appleton-Century-Crofts; and M. Cranston and R.S. Peters (eds), (1972). *Hobbes and Rousseau: A Collection of Critical Essays*. New York: Doubleday.

Tajfel, H. (1958) The teaching of psychology in social science courses. *Bulletin of the British Psychological Society, 24,* 23–8.

Bruner, J.S. and Tajfel, H. (1961). Cognitive risk and environmental change. *Journal of Abnormal and Social Psychology, 61,* 231–41. Reprinted in R.J.C. Harper, C.C. Anderson, and S.M. Hunka (eds) (1964). *The Cognitive Processes,* NJ: Prentice-Hall and J.C. Mancuso (ed.), 1970. *Readings for a Cognitive Theory of Personality.* New York: Holt, Rinehart and Winston.

Tajfel, H. (1964). *Problems of International Co-operation in Social Psychological Research Concerned with New and Developing Countries.* Mimeo Report, US Airforce, 1–91.

Tajfel, H. (1964). Dei Entstehung der kognitiven und affektiven Einstellungen. In *Vorurteile: Ihre Eforschung und ihre Bekaempfung.* Politische Psychologie, Band 3. Europaeische Veranstaltung, Frankfurt a.M., 1964, Reprinted in Tajfel. H. (1987). The Formation of Cognitive and Affective Attitudes. In Werner Bergmann (ed.), *Error without Trial: Psychological Research on Antisemitism,* Vol. 2. Berlin, Federal Republic of Germany: Walter de Gruyter, pp. 542–6.

Tajfel, H. (1965) European Association for the Advancement of Experimental Social Psychology. *Social Science Information, 4,* 190–2.

Tajfel, H. and Dawson, J.K. (eds) (1965). *Disappointed Guests: Essays by African, Asian and West Indian Students.* Oxford University Press. Preface and Epilogue by H. Tajfel and J.L. Dawson.

Tajfel, H. (1966). International co-operation in social psychology: Some problems and possibilities. *Bulletin of the British Psychological Society, 19,* 29–36.

Tajfel, H. (1968). G.W. Allport: obituary. *British Journal of Psychology, 59,* 103–4.

Tajfel, H. (1968). Second thoughts about cross-cultural research and international relations. *International Journal of Psychology,* 213–19.

Tajfel, H. (1971) Research collaboration in Europe. *Social Science Research Council Newsletter, 12,* 13.

Eiser, J.R. and Tajfel, H. '(1972). Acquisition of information in dyadic interaction. *Journal of Personality and Social Psychology, 23*(2), 340–5.

Israel, J. and Tajfel, H. (1972). *The Context of Social Psychology: A Critical Assessment.* Introduction (pp. 1-13); Chapter 3, Experiments in a vacuum (pp. 69-119). London/New York: Academic Press.

Tajfel, H. (1972). Some developments in European social psychology. *European Journal of Social Psychology, 2*(3), 307–21.

Hoffman, S., Leontief, W., and Tajfel, H. (1975). Book II in *Social Sciences Policy, France.* Paris: OECD (published simultaneously in French).

Tajfel, H. (1975) Tajfel takes a turn. *Contemporary Psychology, 20,* 78–9.

Tajfel, H. (1975) Shaver's view....not a serious analysis. *Contemporary Psychology, 20,* 264–5.

Tajfel, H. and Moscovici, S. (1976). The renaissance of old myths in social psychology. *Zeitschrift für Sozialpsychologie* (in German translation), 7, 292–7.

Tajfel, H. (1977). Social psychology and social reality. *New Society, 39,* 757, 31 March, 653–4.

Strickland, L.H., Aboud, F., Gergen, K., Jahoda, G., and Tajfel, H. (1977) General theory in social psychology. *Personality and Social Psychology Bulletin, 2,* 148–53.

Tajfel, H (1977). Social psychology. In A. Bullock and O Stalleybrass (eds), *The Fontana Dictionary of Modern Thought.* London: Fontana and New York: Harper.

Tajfel, H. and Fraser, C. (eds) (1978). *Introducing Social Psychology: An Analysis of Individual Reaction and Response.* Harmondsworth: Penguin. Reprinted in 1987. Chapter 1 (H. Tajfel and C. Fraser): Social psychology as social science; Chapter 12 (H. Tajfel): The structure of our views about society; Chapter 16 (H. Tajfel): Intergroup behaviour: I. Individualistic perspectives; Chapter 17 (H. Tajfel): Intergroup behaviour: II. Group perspectives.

Tajfel, H. (1979). Individuals and groups in social psychology. *British Journal of Social and Clinical Psychology, 18,* 183–90.

Tajfel, H. (1980). Nachwort zur Neuauflage. (Foreword; German translation.) In Fritz Bernstein (ed.), *Der Antisemitismus als Gruppenerscheinung: Versuch einer Sociologie des Judenhasses,* Königstein/Taunus: Jüdischer Verlag im Athenäum Verlag. (First edition, 1926).

Tajfel, H. (1980). The 'New Look' and social differentiations: A semi-Brunerian perspective. In D. Olson (ed.), *The Social Foundations of Language and Thought: Essays in Honor of J. S. Bruner.* New York: Norton.

Tajfel, H. (1982). Social justice in social psychology. In Paul Fraisse (ed.), *La psychologie du futur.* Paris: Presses Universitaires de France.

Tajfel, H. (ed.) (1984). *The Social Dimension: European Developments in Social Psychology,* 2 Vols. Cambridge: Cambridge University Press. Chapter 1 (H. Tajfel, J. Jaspars, and C. Fraser): The social dimension in European social psychology; Chapter 33 (H. Tajfel): Intergroup relations, social myths and social justice in social psychology.

Radio broadcasts

Tajfel, H. (1960) *The Nation and the Individual.* BBC General Overseas Service, May 1960.

Tajfel, H. (1962) *As Like as Not.* BBC Third Programme, November 7, 1962.

Tajfel, H. (1962) *Similarity and Dissimilarity.* BBC, August 1962.

APPENDIX 2

THE TAJFEL ACADEMIC GENEALOGY

Here may be found the names of Tajfel's PhD students and those of succeeding generations of scholars. This list (of over 700 names) is incomplete. Despite my best efforts, some people proved untraceable or unresponsive.

*denotes full professor; those in upper case are Tajfel's own PhD students (1st generation); those in **bold type** have had PhDs of their own (number shown in parentheses).

*BILLIG, M. (11)

Griffin, C. (12)
    Weate, P.
    Bailey, L.
    Tekola, B.
    Bengry-Howell, A.
    Holt, M. (3)
        Callander, D.
        Conway, D.
        Thu Vu, N.
    Burns, A.
    Willott, S.
    Corr, K.
    Petkova, B.
    Huxley, J.
    *Hepworth, J.
    Al-Talib, N.
Abell, J. (2)
    Collins, M.
    Bryn Coles, A. (3)

Coenraad, J.

Meakin, S.

Waqas, T.

Byford, J. (3)

Smart, C.

Scully, M.

McAvoy, J.

Stanley, S. (1)

Parker, S.

Benneworth-Gray, K.

★Lea, S. (8)

Abey, S.

Lynn, M.

McMullan, M.

Clarke, S.

Farbus, L.

Callaghan, L.

Barnes, R.

Liness, S.

Cristian, T. (2)

Demasi, M.

Popoviciu, S.

Vine, E.

Horowitz, A. (1)

  Kirby, L. (1)

   Lennon, H.

Kaposi, D.

★Gill, R. (19)

Toms, K.

Elias, A.

Kohrs, K.

Figiel, J.

Garcia, L.

O'Neill, R.

Dosekun, S.

de Benedictis, S.

Akinerdem, F.

Watts, A.

Kozic, M.

Harvey, L.

  ★Kelan, E. (3)

   Brown, S.

   Baker, D.

   Carr, M.

Scharff, C. (3)
  McClure, B.
  Wreyford, N.
  Elzerbi, C.
Ryan Flood, R. (1)
  Msosa, A.
Simpson, R.
Jensen, T.
MacDonald, N.
Crisci, R.

*TURNER, J. (9)

★**Reicher, S.** (22)
  Ashraf, M.
  Cronin, P.
  ★**Dixon, J.** (3)
    Hunsberger, A.
    Di Masso, A.
    Clack, B.
  ★**Drury, J.** (8)
    Jansen, B.
    Vestrgren, S.
    Alnabulsi, H.
    Novelli, D.
    Carter, H.
    Templeton, A.
    Alfadhi, K.
    Ntonti, E.
  Eaton, L.
  ★**Hopkins, N.** (2)
    Wakefield, J. (1)
      McIntosh, J.
    Dobai, A.
  Jogdand, Y. (2)
    Sharma, S.
    Thangal, R.
  Lauenstein, O.
  ★**Levine, M.** (8)
    Vanessa Trowell, V.
    Manning, R.
    Lowe, R.
    Palasinski, M. (1)
    Starkey, J.

Wilson, N.
Philpot, R.
Keil, T.
Wilkins, D.
Loth, E. (3)
   Cattrell, A.
   Oakley, B.
   Crawley, D.
McLung, J.
*Phil McNaghten, P.
Neville, F.
Rath, R.
Ryan, C.
Robertson, T.
*****Sani, F.** (7)
   Swartzman, S.
   Miller, K.
   Bowe, M.
   Hale, D. (1)
      Bevilacqua, L.
   Svirydzenka, N.
   Hoey, J.
   Smith, R. (1)
      Tamplin-Wilson, J.
Sindic, D.
Sonnenberg, S. (2)
   Rohlfing, S.
   Shingler, J.
*****Stott, C.** (2)
   Hoggett, J.
   Radburn, M.
Kellezi, B. (2)
   Siddall, Y.
   Shala, A.
Ramos, M.
*****Hogg, M.** (26)
  *****White, K.** (8)
    Obst, P. (2)
      Haydon, H.
      Brayley, N.
    Robinson, N.
    O'Connor, E.
    Walsh, S.
    Hyde, M.

Hamilton, K. (6)
  Jenkins, K.
  Phipps, D.
  Smith, S.
  Brown, D.
  Keech, J.
  Arnautovska, U.
 Starfelt, L.
 Zhao, X.
*Zinkiewicz, L.
Mullin, B.
*Hornsey, M. (4)
 Ariyanto, A.
 Jeffries, C. (1)
  Machin, T.
 Abel, L.
 Harris, E.
Masel, C.
*Reid, S.
McKimmie, B. (5)
 Butler, T.
 Baguley, C.
 Antrobus, E.
 Rijnbout, J.
 Strub, T.
Fielding, K. (6)
 Schultz, T.
 Bissing-Olsen, M.
 Hooper, M.
 McDonald, R.
 Ross, V.
 Cheng, G.
Wellen, J.
Smith, J. (1)
 Onu, D.
McAuliffe, B.
Cameira, M.
Lai, S.
Cheng, H.
Blaylock, D.
Healy, D.
Adelman, J.
Mahajan, N.
Turcotte, D.

    Hohman, Z. (1)

      Dahl, E.

    Rast, D.

    Gaffney, A.

    Goldman, L.

    Grant, F.

    Özyeğin, Y.

    Duggan-Herd, T.

★Wetherell, M.

★Haslam, A. (14)

    Eggins, R.

    Veenstra, K.

    Wright, R.

    Adarves-Yorno, I. (1)

      Rook, C.

    Livingstone, A. (1)

      Jasper, C.

    Mols, F.

    Ashby, J.

    Knight, C.

    Saroyan, S.

    Steffens, N.

    Bjerregaardd, K.

    Butler, T.

    Kwok, N.

    Bentley, S.

★McGarty, C. (11)

    ★Douglas, K. (5)

      Elder, T.

      Skipper, Y. (2)

        Garnett, N.

        Bagnall, C.

      Wood, M.

      Jolley, D. (2)

        Cookson, D.

        Schrader, T.

      Chotpitayasunondh, V.

    Taylor, N.

    Bopping, D.

    Bliuc, A-M.

    Thomas, E. (1)

      Stuart, A.

    Lala, G.

    Blink, C.

Musgrove, L.
Hartley, L. (1)
Gill, G.
Gee, A.
Nikolova, E.
⋆**Oakes, P.** (5)
Morrison, B. (7)
Abramson, A.
Arvanitidis, T.
Asadullah, M.
Glowatski, K.
Wadhwa, A.
Brown, M.
Pearl, T.
⋆**Reynolds, K.** (5)
Krins, P.
Lamberts, R.
Lin, H.
Mohammed, S.
Subasic, E.
⋆**Nolan, M.** (7)
Walker, A.
McEwan, A.
Chandrasen, A.
Lawson, C.
Bishop, S.
Spiers Williams, M.
Liddy, J.
Khoo, A.
Verhagen, A.
Brown, P. (1)
Larkings, J.
Onorato, R.
Young, L.

⋆BREAKWELL, G. (16)

⋆Zientek, C.
Al-Khawaj, J.
Moharib, N.
⋆**Coyle, A.** (3)
Rolfe, M.
Slater, R.
Herron, A.

Al-Hassan, A.

Hammond, J.

★Kausar, R. (10)

    Shahnila, T.

    Shazia, I.

    Mehnaz, Y.

    Attiya, I.

    Fauzia, N.

    Shaista, J.

    Tanvir, N.

    Mohsina, N.

    Tahira, R.

    Nashi, K.

Ashford, P.

Mavridi, K.

Buchanan-Barrow, E.

Devine-Wright, H. (1)

    Sherry-Brennan, F.

★Barnett, J (3)

    Vasileiou, K.

    Hamshaw, R.

    Rempel, E.

Vignoles, V. (10)

    Brown, J.

    Costin, V.

    Koc, Y.

    Yang, S.

    Hassan, B.

    Unanue, W.

    Easterbrook, M. (2)

        Kyprianides, A.

        Moldes, O.

    Owe, E.

    ★Gausel, N. (3)

        Løkkeberg, S.

        Zahl-Olsen, R.

        Pardede, S.

    Gheorghiu, M. (3)

        Coymak, A.

        Flack, P.

        Dickey-Sagherian, T.

Dean, M.

Hewer, C.

★Hendy, J. (1)

    Edematie, T.

*BROWN, R. (24)

⋆Abrams, D. (34)
    ⋆Kakimoto, T.
    Battersby, S.
    ⋆Masser, B. (6)
      Lizzio-Wilson, M.
      Nesic, M.
      Dane, S.
      Zande, R.
      Xiang, N
      Moffat, K.
    Morris, L.
    ⋆Eller, A.
    Viki, T. (2)
      Pina, A. (3)
        Page, T.
        Sagrillo-Scarpati, A.
        Denyer, K.
      Thomae, M.
    Hutchison, P.
    ⋆Randsley de Moura, G. (7)
      Steeden, B.
      Tresh, F.
      Marques, A.
      Morais, C.
      Leite, A.
      Player, A.
      Leicht, C.
    Calogero, R.
    Hopthrow, T. (3)
      Meleady, R. (1)
        Alston, L.
      Mahmood, L.
      ⋆Eriksson, K.
    Leader, T.
    Pelletier, J.
    Zimmerman, A.
    Boehling, M.
    Frings, D. (3)
      Bartlett, G.
      Jn-Pierre, K.
      Aihio, N.
    Tasiopoulou, K.
    Norohna, M.

Petritsis–Chaikalis, E.
Shirley Samson, S.
Wardrop, H.
Swift, H. (1)
 Dias, V.
Yetkili, O.
Travaglino, G. (1)
 Heering, M.
Powell, C.
Palmer, S.
Lamont, R.
Van De Vyver, J.
Drury, L.
Tappin, B.
Webster, K.
Ali, S.
Farrahar, C.
Kapantai, I.
Goodbun, K.
★Maras, P.
Akumoah–Boateng, R.
Lepore, L.
Torres, A. (9)
 Souza de Lima, T.
 Dubeux Lopes Barros, C.
 Vilar Greco Ramalho, J.
 Paula Rodrigues Cavalcanti, A.
 Lins de Almeida, J.
 Roniere Morais Batista, J.
 do Amparo Carvalho Patatas, L.
 Esteves Neto, H.
 Morais Oliveira, T.
Greenland, K. (6)
 Vickery, A.
 Dumangane, C.
 Slater, T.
 Taulke-Johnson, R.
 Gee, H.
 Court, H.
Wootton-Millward, L. (5)
 Banks, A. (2)
  Husted, M.
  Gamblin, D.

Cleveland, M.
Brewerton, P.
Russell, E. (4)
 Price, A.
 Oez, G.
 Abrams, R.
 D'Mello, D.
 Cachia, M.
★**Gonzalez, R.** (4)
 Sirlopu, D.
 Gómez, F.
 Amo, C.
 Jiménez, V.
Hulbert, S. (2)
 Cooper, E.
 Durrant, I.
★**Wood, J.** (7)
 Alleyne, E. (1)
  Parfitt, C.
 James, M.
 Mozova, K.
 Dickens, T.
 Ruddle, A.
 Beresford, H.
 Osman, S.
★**Zagefka, H.** (3)
 Martinez, S.
 Kinshuck, S.
 James, T.
Calitri, R.
De Amicis, L.
Coen, S. (3)
 Olawale, O.
 Mesawa, M.
 Szeto, S.
Noor, M. (2)
 Wood, C.
 Carew, M.
Cehajic, S. (1)
 Savic-Bojanic, M.
De Tezanos Pinto, P.
Allpress, J.
Tip, L.

Pehrson, S. (2)
    Urbanska, K.
    McNeill, A.
Fearn, H.
Cordeu, C.
Thomas, W.
Woodhouse, S.

CADDICK, B. (6)

Grove, R.
Rahbari, M.
Burton, J.
Moorhead, D.
Cheng, S.
Liu, H-Y.

*VAN KNIPPENBERG, A. (26)

★De Vries, N. (41)
    Ahlers, J.
    Richard, R.
    ★Zeelenberg, M. (23)
        Louro, M.
        Bougie, R.
        Giorgetta, C.
        Wetzer, I.
        Coelho do Vale, R.
        Shani, Y.
        van Putten, M.
        de Hooge, I.
        van de Ven, N.
        Martinez, L.
        Welten, S.
        van Osch, Y.
        van de Calseyde, P.
        van Wolferen, J.
        van Doorn, J.
        Evers, E.
        Blanken, I.
        Estrada-Mejia, C.
        Meijs, M.
        Seuntjens, T.

Krijnen, J.
Wagemans, F.
Plantinga, A.
★Gordijn, E. (11)
van Mourik Broekman, A.
Sasse, J.
Greijdanus, H.
Vos, B.
Veldhuis, T.
Koudenburg, N.
Kamans, E.
Braun, M.
Lammers, J.
Oldenhuis, H.
Ruys, K.
Mann, M.
Ruijs, K.
Moukhyer, M.
Harting, J.
Nelissen, R.
★de Vet, E.
Hoeijmakers, M.
Dreezens, E.
Verkooijen, E.
Alberts, H.
★Jansen, M.
Reinaerts, E.
★Crutzen, R. (8)
Peetoom, K.
Nalukwago, J.
Okafor, U.
Jonas, K.
Beaujean, D.
Reinwand, D.
Jander, A.
Badri, A.
Smerecnik, C.
Mbonu, N.
Gubbels, J.
Schickenberg, B.
Heinrich, E.
Boot, N.
Rutten, G.
Steenbakkers, M.

Helmink, J.
Vermeer, A.
Sleddens, E.
Grispen, J.
Alayli-Goebbels, A.
Gerards, S.
Mukhayer, A.
Karavetian, M.
Raaijmakers, L.
Pucher, K.
Hendriks, A.
Diep, P.
van Kann, D.
van der Geugten, J.
Roy, A.
Haidar, S.

⋆**Ellemers, N.** (27)

Scholten, W.
Mooijman, M.
Koot, C.
Beudeker, D.
Shafa, S.
de Vries-Engel, G.
van Nunspeet, F. (2)

Rösler, I.
Hoffmann-Harnisch, M.

Rexwinkel, R.
van der Lee, R.
Does, S.
Zaal, M.
Bleeker, D.
ter Mors, E.
Terwel, B.
Stroebe, K. (1)

Armenta, B.

Boezeman, E.
Faddegon, K.
Cihangir, S.
van Steenbergen, E. (2)

Coffeng, T.
Aarntzen, L.

⋆**Derks, B.** (5)

Does, S.
Maloku, E.
Vink, M.

Aarntzen, L.
Domen, I.
Ståhl, T.
★Rink, F. (12)
  Kosenkranius, M.
  Chuk, E.
  de Waal, M.
  Laurijssen, M.
  Prompeler, J.
  Ahrens, F.
  Cantimur, Y.
  van de Brake, J.
  Oedzes, J.
  Bucur, R.
  Zhang, J.
  Pit, M.
Sleebos, E. (1)
    van der Stoep, J.
van Rijswijk, W.
van Leeuwen, E. (2)
  Hopman, P.
  Mashuri, A.
Ouwerkerk, J.
★Barreto, M. (6)
  Ciftci, E.
  Dasci, E.
  Dimitriou, E.
  Janbakhsh, M.
  Richins, M.
  Rego, M.
Meertens, R. (8)
  den Boer, D-J.
  van Kar-Huisman, A.
  Lion, R.
  Mesters, E. (12)
    Alewijnse, D.
    Ausems, M.
    Fransen, G.
    Gijsbers, B.
    Korstjens, I.
    Lotrean, L.
    van Keulen, H.
    Dörenkamp, S.
    Beekman, E.

   Kanera, I.
   Willems, R.
   Rewald, S.
  Mevissen, F. (3)
   Krugu, J.
   Schutte, L.
   van Lieshout, S.
  Visschers, V. (5)
   Tobler, C.
   Wallquist, L.
   Hess, R.
   Shi, J.
   Lazzarini, G.
Völlink, T.
★Van Vugt, M. (16)
  Grabo, A.
  Gerpott, F.
  Knapen, J.
  Blaker, N.
  Horstmeier, C.
  Gundemir, S.
  Deinert, A.
  ★Buengeler, C.
  Redeker, M.
  Spisak, B.
  Iredale, W.
  May, C.
  Hart, C. (1)
   Paas, K.
  Stiff, C. (1)
   Bosworth, G.
  Powell, C.
  ★De Cremer, D.
★Molleman, E. (13)
  van den Beukel, A.
  Hellenthal, A.
  Hong, Y.
  Zoethout, K.
  Turusbekova, N.
  ★de Jong, S. (3)
   Udall, A.
   Schmitte, K.
   Jayaweera, A.
  Stoffels, R.

Oosterhuis, M.
Veltrop, D. (1).
   Mostert, I.
Grutterink, H. (1)
   Stichling, M.
Regts, G.
Ponsioen, S.
Petkova, B.
★**Aarts, H.** (16)
   van den Berg, S. (2)
      van Leeuwen, M.
      Schwabe, I.
   Mensink, W.
   Custers, R. (3)
      Pilditch, T.
      Magis–Weinberg, L.
      Rochal, I.
   Danner, U. (2)
      Elzakkers, I.
      Jansingh, A.
   Papies, E. (2)
      Versluis, I.
      Keesman, M.
   Dik, G.
   Veltkamp, M.
   Bijleveld, E. (1)
      Rusz, D.
   Terburg, D.
   van der Weiden, A.
   Zedelius, C.
   Marien, H.
   Renes, R.
   Stoeckart, P.
   Keesman, M.
   Prikken, M.
van Twuyver, M..
Young, H.
★**Dijksterhuis, A**. (5)
   Bongers, K.
   Albers, L.
   Sjoerdsma, A.
   Spronken, M.
   Zhu, Y.
★**Koole, S**. (8)

Samur, D.

Schlinkert, C.

Ruigendijk, H.

Veenstra, L.

van Dillen, L. (1)

Zech, H.

Fockenberg, D.

Wisman, A. (1)

Perach, R.

Jostmann, N.

Deschesne, M. (1)

van den Berg, C.

★Van Baaren, R. (6)

van Leeuwen, M.

Damen, T.

Kouzakova, M.

Muller, B. (5)

Loman, J.

Nijssen, S.

Li, S.

Beke, T.

de Sá Siqueira, M.

Ritter, S. (3)

Zhu, Y.

Gu, X.

Verpalen, I.

Bos, M.

★Holland, R. (3)

Chen, Z.

Becker, D.

Bijlstra, G.

Harm, V. (2)

Zedelius, C.

Chen, Z.

de Lange, M.

Hermsen, B.

Strik, M. (1)

Stoeckart, P.

Koch, S.

Smeets, R.

Mooren, D.

Brandt, A.

Kouzakova, M.

★Dotsch, R. (5)

        Jansen, L.
        van den Brule, R.
        Oliveira, M.
        Klapper, A.
        Sofer, C.
    Wennekers, A.
    Chan, K.
    Rondeel, E.
    Hengstler, M.

*NG, S-H. (8)

    Cram, F. (6)
        Jackson, S.
        Pocock, T.
        *McCreanor, T.
        Wolfenden, J.
        Hammond, K.
        Eruera, M.
    Chan, K-K
    Bryson, J. (4)
        Blake, S.
        Parkes, L.
        Foley, M.
        Menzies, M.
    Allen, M.
    Marshall, J.
    Brown, J.
    Ng, T.
    Ye, J.

REFERENCES

Aboud, F. (1988). *Children and Prejudice.* Oxford: Basil Blackwell.

Abrams, D. and Hogg, M. (1988). Comments on the motivational status of self-esteem in social identity and intergroup discrimination. *European Journal of Social Psychology*(18), 317–34.

Abrams, D., Marques, J.M., Bown, N., and Henson, M. (2000). Pro-norm and anti-norm deviance within and between groups. *Journal of Personality and Social Psychology, 78,* 906–12.

Adorno, T.W., Frenkel-Brunswik, E., Levinson, D.J., and Sanford, R.M. (1950). *The Authoritarian Personality.* New York: Harper.

Aharpour, S. and Brown, R. (2002). Functions of group identification: An exploratory analysis. *Revue Internationale de Psychologie Sociale, 15,* 157–86.

Akerlof, G.A. (2007). The missing motivation in macroeconomics. *The American Economic Review, 97,* 5–36.

Akerlof, G.A. and Kranton, R.E. (2000). Economics and Identity. *Quarterly Journal of Economics, CXV,* 715–53.

Allport, F.H. (1924). *Social Psychology.* New York: Houghton Mifflin.

Allport, G.W. (1954). *The Nature of Prejudice.* New York: Addison-Wesley.

Allport, G.W. and Pettigrew, T.F. (1957). Cultural influence on the perception of movement: The trapezoidal illusion among Zulus. *Journal of Abnormal and Social Psychology, 55,* 104–13.

Allpress, J.A., Brown, R., Giner-Sorolla, R., Deonna, J.A., and Teroni, F. (2014). Two faces of group-based shame: Moral shame and image shame differentially predict positive and negative orientations to ingroup wrongdoing. *Personality and Social Psychology Bulletin, 40,* 1270–84.

Alnabulsi, H. and Drury, J. (2014). Social identification moderates the effect of crowd density on safety at the Hajj. *Proceedings of the National Academy of the United States of America, 111,* 9091–6.

Amodio, D.M. (2008). The social neuroscience of intergroup relations. *European Review of Social Psychology, 19,* 1–54.

Amodio, D.M., Harmon-Jones, E., Devine, P.G., Curtin, J.J., Hartley, S.L., *et al.* (2004). Neural signals for the detection of unintentional race bias. *Psychological Science, 15,* 88–93.

Apfelbaum, E. (2009). Against the tide: Making waves and breaking silences. In L. P. Mos (ed.), *History of Psychology in Autobiography* (pp. 1–36). Berlin: Springer.

Appiah, K.A. (2018). *The Lies that Bind: Rethinking Identity*. London: W.W. Norton & Co.

Argyle, M. (1959). The Center for Advanced Study in the Behavioral Sciences. *Bulletin of the British Psychological Society, 38*, 14–15.

Asch, S.E. (1951). Effects of group pressure upon the modification and distortion of judgements. In *Groups, Leadership, and Men*. Pittsburgh: Carnegie Press.

Asch, S.E. (1952). *Social Psychology*. New Jersey: Prentice Hall.

Asch, S.E. (1956). Studies of independence and conformity: I. A minority of one against a unanimous majority. *Psychological Monographs 70*(a), 1–70.

Aschenbrenner, K.M. and Schaefer, R.E. (1980). Minimal group situations: comments on a mathematical model and on the research paradigm. *European Journal of Social Psychology 10*, 389–98.

Ashforth, B.E. and Mael, F. (1989). Social identity theory and the organization. *The Academy of Management Review, 14*, 20–39.

Auslander, L. (2005). Coming home? Jews in postwar Paris. *Journal of Contemporary History, 40*(2), 237–59.

Baker, C.A. (2012). Social identity theory and biblical interpretation. *Biblical Theology Bulletin, 42*, 129–38.

Barrett, M. (2007). *Children's Knowledge, Beliefs and Feelings about Nations and National Groups*. Hove: Psychology Press.

Barth, F. (ed.). (1969). *Ethnic Groups and Boundaries: The Social Organization of Culture Difference*. Prospect Heights, IL: Waveland Press.

Bauman, Z. (1992). Soil, blood and identity. *The Sociological Review, 40*, 675–701.

Beevor, A. and Cooper, A. (1994). *Paris after the Liberation, 1944–1949*. London: Penguin Books.

Berghahn, V.R. (2001). *America and the Intellectual Cold Wars in Europe*. Princeton, NJ: Princeton University Press.

Berkowitz, L. (1962). *Aggression: A Social Psychological Analysis*. New York: McGraw Hill.

Bernstein, P.F. (1926/1980). *Der Antisemitismus als eine Gruppenerscheinung: versuch einer Soziologie des Judenhasses*. Berlin: Jüdischer Verlag.

Berry, J.W. (1997). Immigration, acculturation, and adaptation. *Applied Psychology: An International Review, 46*(1), 5–68.

Besson, Y. (1991). *Identités et conflits au Proche-Orient*. Paris: L'Harmattan

Biderman, I. M. (ed.). (1969). *Włocławek and Kujawy: A Memorial Book*. New York: Włocławek Memorial Book Committee of USA.

Billig, M. (1976). *Social Psychology and Intergroup Relations*. London: Academic Press.

Billig, M. (1982). *Ideology and Social Psychology: Extremism, Moderation, and Contradiction*. Oxford: Blackwell.

Billig, M. (1987). *Arguing and Thinking*. Cambridge: Cambridge University Press.

Billig, M. (1992). *Talking of the Royal Family*. Abingdon: Routledge.

Billig, M. (2002). Henri Tajfel's 'cognitive aspects of prejudice' and the psychology of bigotry. *British Journal of Social Psychology, 41*, 171–88.

Billig, M. (2013). *Learn to Write Badly: How to Succeed in the Social Sciences*. Cambridge: Cambridge University Press.

Billig, M. (2014). Henri Tajfel, Peretz Bernstein and the history of Der Antisemitismus. In C. Tileaga and J. Byford (eds), *Psychology and History* (pp. 223–41). Cambridge: Cambridge University Press.

Billig, M. and Tajfel, H. (1973). Social categorization and similarity in intergroup behaviour. *European Journal of Social Psychology, 3*, 27–52.

Bornstein, F., Crum, L., Wittenbraker, J., Harring, K., Insko, C.A., and Thibaut, J. (1983a). On the measurement of social orientations in the Minimal Group Paradigm. *European Journal of Social Psychology*(13), 321–50.

Bornstein, F., Crum, L., Wittenbraker, J., Harring, K., Insko, C.A., and Thibaut, J. (1983b). Reply to Turner's comments. *European Journal of Social Psychology*, 13, 369–81.

Bourhis, R., Gagnon, A., and Sachdev, I. (1997). Les matrices de Tajfel: Un guide méthodologique pour la recherche intergroupe. *Les Cahiers Internationaux de psychologie Sociale, 34*, 11–28.

Bourhis, R. and Hill, P. (1982). Intergroup perceptions in British higher education: A field study. In H. Tajfel (ed.), *Social Identity and Intergroup Relations* (pp. 423–68). Cambridge: Cambridge University Press.

Branscombe, N., Schmitt, M., and Harvey, R.D. (1999). Perceiving pervasive discrimination among African Americans: Implications for group identification and well-being. *Journal of Personality and Social Psychology, 77*, 135–49.

Branthwaite, A., Doyle, S., and Lightbown, N. (1979). The balance between fairness and discrimination. *European Journal of Social Psychology, 9*, 149–63.

Breakwell, G.M. (ed.) (1983). *Threatened Identities*. Chichester: Wiley.

Breakwell, G.M. (1986), *Coping with Threatened Identities*. London: Methuen.

Breakwell, G.M. (1993). Integrating paradigms, methodological implications. In G. M. Breakwell, and D.V. Canter (eds), *Empirical Approaches to Social Representations*. Oxford: Oxford University Press.

Breakwell, G.M. (2007) *The Psychology of Risk*. New York: Cambridge University Press.

Brewer, M.B. (1979). Ingroup Bias in the Minimal Intergroup Situation: A Cognitive-Motivational Analysis. *Psychological Bulletin*, 86, 307–24.

Brewer, M.B. (1999). The psychology of prejudice: ingroup love or outgroup hate? *Journal of Social Issues, 55*, 429–44.

Brown, R. (2000). Social Identity Theory: Past Achievements, Current Problems and Future Challenges. *European Journal of Social Psychology, 30*(6), 745–78.

Brown, R. (2002). 'Henri Tajfel's 'Cognitive aspects of prejudice' and the psychology of bigotry': Comment. *British Journal of Social Psychology, 41*, 195–8.

Brown, R. and Hewstone, M. (2005). An integrative theory of intergroup contact. *Advances in Experimental Social Psychology, 37*, 255–343.

Brown, R. and Pehrson, S. (2019). *Group Processes: Dynamics Within and Between Groups, 3rd edition*. Chichester: Wiley.

Brown, R., and Zagefka, H. (2006). Choice of comparisons in intergroup settings: the role of temporal information and comparison motives. *European Journal of Social Psychology, 36*, 649–671.

Brown, R., and Zagefka, H. (2011). The dynamics of acculturation: an intergroup perspective. *Advances in Experimental Social Psychology, 44*, 129–184.

Brown, R.J. (1978). Divided we fall: An analysis of relations between sections of a factory work-force, in Tajfel, H (ed.), *Differentiation between Social Groups: Studies in the Social Psychology of Intergroup Relations* (pp. 395–429). London: Academic Press.

Brown, R.J. (1984). The effects of intergroup similarity and cooperative vs. competitive orientation on intergroup discrimination. *British Journal of Social Psychology, 23*, 21–33.

Brown, R.J. (2010). *Prejudice: Its Social Psychology, 2nd Edition*. Chichester: Wiley-Blackwell.

Brown, R.J. and Abrams, D. (1986). The effects of intergroup similarity and goal interdependence on intergroup attitudes and task performance. *Journal of Experimental Social Psychology, 22*, 78–92.

Brown, R.J., Condor, S., Matthews, A., Wade, G., and Williams, J.A. (1986). Explaining intergroup differentiation in an industrial organisation. *Journal of Occupational Psychology, 59,* 273–86.

Brown, R.J. and Ross, G.F. (1982). The battle for acceptance: An investigation into the dynamics of intergroup behaviour. In H. Tajfel (ed.), *Social Identity and Intergroup Relations* (pp. 155–78). Cambridge: Cambridge University Press.

Brown, R.J., Tajfel, H., and Turner, J.C. (1980). Minimal group situations and intergroup discrimination: Comments on the paper by Aschenbrenner and Schaefer *European Journal of Social Psychology, 10,* 399–414.

Brown, R.J., and Turner, J. C. (1979). The criss–cross categorization effect in intergroup discrimination. *British Journal of Social and Clinical Psychology, 18,* 371–383.

Brown, R.J., and Williams, J. (1984). Group identification: the same thing to all people? *Human Relations, 37*(7), 547–564.

Brown, R.W. and Lenneberg, E.H. (1954). A study in language and cognition. *Journal of Abnormal and Social Psychology, 49,* 454–62.

Brown, Roger (1965). *Social Psychology.* New York: Macmillan.

Brown, Roger (1986). *Social Psychology, The Second edition.* New York: The Free Press.

Brubaker, R. and Cooper, F. (2000). Beyond 'identity'. *Theory and Society, 29,* 1–47.

Brubaker, R. and Laitin, D.D. (1998). Ethnic and nationalist violence. *Annual Review of Sociology, 24,* 423–52.

Bruner, J.S. (1957). On perceptual readiness. *Psychological Review, 64,* 123–51.

Bruner, J.S. (1973). *Beyond the Information Given.* New York: Norton.

Bruner, J.S. (1981). Foreword. In H. Tajfel (ed.), *Human Groups and Social Categories* (pp. xi–xiii). Cambridge: Cambridge University Press.

Bruner, J.S. (1983). *In Search of Mind: Essays in Autobiography.* New York: Harper & Row.

Bruner, J.S. and Allport, G.W. (1940). Fifty years of change in American psychology *Psychological Bulletin, 37,* 757–76.

Bruner, J.S. and Goodman, C. (1947). Value and need as organizing factors in perception. *Journal of Abnormal and Social Psychology, 42,* 33–44.

Bruner, J.S. and Postman, L. (1948). Symbolic value as an organizing factor in perception. *Journal of Social Psychology, 27,* 203–8.

Bruner, J.S. and Postman, L. (1949). On the perception of incongruity: A paradigm. *Journal of Personality, 18,* 206–23.

Bruner, J.S. and Tajfel, H. (1961). Cognitive risk and environmental change. *Journal of Abnormal and Social Psychology, 61,* 231–41.

Bruner, J.S. and Tajfel, H. (1965). Width of category and concept differentiation. *Journal of Personality and Social Psychology, 2,* 261–4.

Buruma, I. (2013). *Year Zero: A History of 1945.* London: Atlantic Books.

Caddick, B. (1988). Equity in the family: Some social psychological contributions to family therapy. *Journal of Family Therapy, 10,* 255–69.

Caddick, B. (1994). The 'new careers' experiment in rehabilitating offenders: Last messages from a fading star. *British Journal of Social Work, 24,* 449–60.

Cala, A. (1994). The social consciousness of young Jews in Interwar Poland. In A. Polansky, E. Mendelsohn, and J. Tomaszewski (eds), *Jews in Independent Poland, 1918–1939* (pp. 42–65). London: The Littman Library of Jewsih Civilization.

Calhoun, C. (ed.). (1994). *Social Theory and the Politics of Identity.* Oxford: Blackwell.

Campbell, D.T. (1956). Enhancement of contrast as a composite habit. *Journal of Abnormal and Social Psychology, 53,* 350–5.

Campbell, D.T. (1965). Ethnocentric and other altruistic motives. *Nebraska Symposium on Motivation*, 283–311.

Campbell, E. (2006). Le Traitement des insultes sexistes et racistes dans les dictionnaires bilingues *The French Review, 80*, 112–37.

Caron, V. (1999). *Uneasy Asylum: France and the Jewish Refugee Crisis, 1933–1942*. Stanford: Stanford University Press.

Cikara, M. and Van Bavel, J.J. (2014). The neuroscience of intergroup relations: An integrative review. *Perspectives on Psychological Science, 9*, 245–74.

Clark, K.B. and Clark, M.P. (1947). Racial identification and preference in Negro children. In H. Proshansky and B. Seidenberg (eds), *Basic Studies in Social Psychology* (pp. 308–17). New York: Holt Rinehart and Winston.

Cohen, D. (1977). *Psychologists on Psychology*. London: Routledge and Kegan Paul.

Collison, P. (1963). *The Cutteslowe Walls: A Study in Social Class*. London: Faber & Faber.

Corneille, O., Klein, O., Lambert, S., and Judd, C. M. (2002). On the role of familiarity with units of measurement in categorical accentuation: Tajfel and Wilkes (1963) revisited and replicated *Psychological Science, 13*, 380–3.

Coser, L.A. (1956). *The Functions of Social Conflict*. Abingdon: Routledge.

Cottrell, C.A. and Neuberg, S.L. (2005). Different emotional reactions to different groups: A sociofunctional threat-based approach to 'prejudice'. *Journal of Personality and Social Psychology, 88*, 770–89.

Crenshaw, K.W. (1994). Mapping the margins: Intersectionality, identity politics, and violence against women of color. In M. Fineman and R. Mykitiuk (eds), *The Public Nature of Private Violence* (pp. 93–118). Abingdon: Routledge.

Cruwys, T., Dingle, G., Haslam, C., Haslam, S.A., Jetten, J., and Morton, T. (2013). Social group memberships protect against future depression, alleviate depression symptoms and prevent depression relapse. *Social Science and Medicine, 98*, 179–86.

Davies, N. (1972). *White Eagle, Red Star: the Polish-Soviet War, 1919–1920*. London: Macdonald.

Davies, N. (1981). *God's Playground: A History of Poland 1795 – The Present, Volume 2*. Oxford: Oxford University Press.

Davies, N. (2001). *The Heart of Europe: The Past in Poland's Present*. Oxford: Oxford University Press.

Deaux, K., Reid, A., Mizrahi, K., and Cotting, D. (1999). Connecting the person to the social: The functions of social identification. In T.R. Tyler, R.M. Kramer, and O.P. John (eds), *The Psychology of the Social Self*. Mahwah, NJ: Lawrence Erlbaum.

Deaux, K. and Verkuyten, M. (2014). The social psychology of multiculturalism: Identity and intergroup relations. In V. Benet-Martinez and Y.-Y. Hong (eds), *The Oxford Handbook of Multicultural Identity* (pp. 118–38). Oxford: Oxford University Press.

DeLamater, J., Hefner, R., and Clignet, R. (1968). Social psychological research in developing countries. *Journal of Social Issues, 24*, 1–298.

De Sola Pool, I. (1966). The necessity for social scientists doing research for governments. *Background, 10*, 111–22.

Deutsch, M. (1975). Equity, equality and need: What determines which value will be used as a basis of distributive justice. *Journal of Social Issues, 31*, 137–49.

Diehl, M. (1988). Social identity and minimal groups: The effects of interpersonal and intergroup attitudinal similarity on intergroup discrimination. *British Journal of Social Psychology, 27*, 289–300.

Dijksterhuis, A. and van Knippenberg, A. (1999). On the parameters of associative strength: Central tendency and variability as determinants of stereotype accessibility. *Personality and Social Psychology Bulletin, 25*, 527–36.

DiMaggio, P. (1997). Culture and cognition. *Annual Review of Sociology, 23*, 263–87.

DiTomaso, N., Post, C., and Parks-Yancy, R. (2007). Workforce diversity and inequality: Power, status, and numbers. *Annual Review of Sociology, 33*, 473–501.

Doise, W. (1978). *Groups and Individuals: Explanations in Social Psychology*. Cambridge: Cambridge University Press.

Doise, W., Clemence, A., and Lorenzi-Cioldi, F. (1993). *The Quantitative Analysis of Social Representations*. Hove: Harvester.

Doise, W., Csepeli, G., Dann, H.-D., Gouge, C., Larsen, K., and Ostell, A. (1972). An experimental investigation into the formation of intergroup representations. *European Journal of Social Psychology, 2*, 202–4.

Doise, W., Deschamps, J.C., and Meyer, G. (1978). The accentuation of intracategory similarities. In H. Tajfel (ed.), *Differentiation between Social Groups: Studies in the Social Psychology of Intergroup Relations*. London: Academic Press.

Doosje, B., Branscombe, N.R., Spears, R., and Manstead, A.S.R. (1998). Guilty by association: When one's group has a negative history. *Journal of Personality and Social Psychology, 75*, 872–86.

Drury, J., Brown, R., Gonzalez, R., and Miranda, D. (2016). Emergent social identity and observing social support predict social support provided by survivors in a disaster: Solidarity in the 2010 Chile earthquake. *European Journal of Social Psychology, 46*, 209–23.

Dukes, W.F. and Bevan, W. (1952). Accentuation and response variability in the perception of personally relevant objects. *Journal of Personality, 20*, 457–65.

Dumont, K. and Louw, J. (2009). A citation analysis of Henri Tajfel's work on intergroup relations. *International Journal of Psychology, 44*, 46–59.

Durand, Y. (1980). *La Captivité: Histoire des Prisonniers de Guerre français, 1939–1945* Paris: FNCPG-CATM.

Durand, Y. (1987). *La Vie Quotidienne des Prisonniers de Guerre dans les Stalags, les Oflags et les Kommandos 1939–1945* Paris: Hachette.

Durkheim, E. (1898). *Sociologie et Philosophie*. Paris: PUF.

EASP (2017). European Association of Social Psychology: Report to members (2014–2017). Granada.

Eiser, J.R. (1971). Enhancement of contrast in the absolute judgement of attitude statements. *Journal of Personality and Social Psychology, 17*, 1–10.

Eiser, J.R. and Stroebe, W. (1972). *Categorisation and Social Judgement*. London: Academic Press.

Ellemers, N., Kortekaas, P., and Ouwerkerk, J.K. (1999). Self-categorisation, commitment to the group and group self-esteem as related but distinct aspects of social identity. *European Journal of Social Psychology, 29*, 371–89.

Ellemers, N., Wilke, H., and van Knippenberg, A. (1993). Effects of the legitimacy of low group or individual status on individual and collective status-enhancement strategies. *Journal of Personality and Social Psychology, 64*(5), 766–78.

Elms, A.C. (1975). The crisis of confidence in social psychology *American Psychologist, 30*, 967–76.

Esler, P.F. (1998). *Galations*. London: Routledge.

Esler, P.F. (2000). Jesus and the reduction of intergroup conflict: The parable of the Good Samaritan in the light of Social Identity Theory. *Biblical Interpretation, 8*, 325–57.

Esler, P.F. (2003a). *Conflict and Identity in Romans: The Social Setting of Paul's Letter*. Minneapolis, MN: Fortress.

Esler, P.F. (2003b). Social identity, the virtues and the good life: A new approach to Romans 12:1–15:13. *Biblical Theology Bulletin, 33*, 51–63.

Ferguson, C.K. and Kelley, H.H. (1964). Significant factors in overevaluation of own-group's product. *Journal of Abnormal and Social Psychology, 69*, 223–8.

Festinger, L. (1950). Informal social communication. *Psychological Review, 57,* 271–82.

Festinger, L. (1954). A theory of social comparison processes. *Human Relations, 7,* 117–40.

Festinger, L. (1957). *A Theory of Cognitive Dissonance.* Evanston, Ill: Row, Peterson & Co.

Fiddick, T. (1973). The 'Miracle of the Vistula'. *Journal of Modern History, 45,* 626–43.

Fiske, S.T. and Taylor, S.E. (1984). *Social Cognition.* MA: Addison-Wesley.

Flament, C. (2010). Conversation between Xenia Chryssochoou and Claude Flament. *European Bulletin of Social Psychology, 22*(2), 5–17.

Frosh, S. (2002). Enjoyment, bigotry, discourse and cognition. *British Journal of Social Psychology, 41,* 189–94.

Frydman, M. (2002). *Le Traumatisme de l'enfant caché: Repercussions psychologiques à court et à long termes…* Paris: L'Harmattan.

Fukuyama, F. (2018). *Identity: The Demand for Dignity and the Politics of Resentment.* London: Profile Books.

Gardham, K. and Brown, R. (2001). Two forms of intergroup discrimination with positive and negative outcomes: Explaining the positive-negative asymmetry effect. *British Journal of Social Psychology, 40,* 23–34.

Gausel, N., Leach, C.W., Vignoles, V.L., and Brown, R. (2012). Defend or repair? Explaining responses to in-group moral failure by disentangling feelings of shame, rejection, and inferiority. *Journal of Personality and Social Psychology, 102,* 941–60.

Gerard, H.B. and Hoyt, M.F. (1974). Distinctiveness of social categorization and attitude toward ingroup members *Journal of Personality and Social Psychology, 29,* 836–42.

Gerassi, J. (1989). *Jean-Paul Sartre: Hated Conscience of His Century.* Chicago: University of Chciago Press.

Gergen, K.J. (1973). Social psychology as history. *Journal of Personality and Social Psychology, 26,* 309–20.

Gibson, J.J. (1950). *The Perception of the Visual World.* Oxford: Houghton Mifflin.

Giddens, A. (1991). *Modernity and Self-identity: Self and Society in the Late Modern Age.* Stanford, CA: Stanford University Press.

Giles, G.J. (ed.). (1997). *STUNDE NULL: The End and the Beginning Fifty Years Ago.* Washington DC: German Historical Institute.

Giles, H. and Powesland, P.F. (1975). *Speech Style and Social Evaluation.* London: Academic Press.

Giles, H. and Saint-Jacques, B. (eds) (1979). *Language and Ethnic Relations.* Oxford: Pergamon.

Greenaway, K.H., Cruwys, T., Haslam, S.A., and Jetten, J. (2016). Social identities promote well-being because they satisfy global psychological needs. *European Journal of Social Psychology, 46,* 294–307.

Greenaway, K.H., Haslam, S.A., Cruwys, T., Branscombe, N.R., Ysseldyk, R., *et al.* (2015). From 'we' to 'me': Group identification enhances perceived personal control with consequences for health and well-being. *Journal of Personality and Social Psychology, 109,* 53–74.

Guthmann, J.-F. (2012). OSE: 100 years of history. In Oevre de Secours des Enfants (OSE) (ed.). Paris: OSE.

Hall, S. and P. du Gay (eds) (1996). *Questions of Cultural Identity.* London, Sage.

Halsey, A.H. (1996). *No Discouragement: An Autobiography.* Basingstoke: Macmillan.

Hamilton, D.L. (ed.). (1981). *Cognitive Processes in Stereotyping and Intergroup Behavior.* Hillsdale, NJ: Erlbaum.

Harré, R. (1972). The analysis of episodes. In J. Israel and H. Tajfel (eds), *The Context of Social Psychology* (pp. 407–24). London: Academic Press.

Harris, L.T. and Fiske, S.T. (2006). Dehumanizing the lowest of the low: Neuroimaging responses to extreme out-groups. *Psychological Science, 17,* 847–53.

Hartstone, M. and Augoustinos, M. (1995). The minimal group paradigm: categorization into two versus three groups. *European Journal of Social Psychology, 25,* 179–93.

Haslam, C., Cruwys, T., and Haslam, S.A. (2014). 'The we's have it': Evidence for the distinctive benefits of group engagement in enhancing cognitive health in aging. *Social Science and Medicine, 120*, 57–66.

Haslam, C., Holme, A., Haslam, S.A., Iyer, A., Jetten, J., and Williams. (2008). Maintaining group memberships: Social identity continuity predicts well-being after stroke. *Neuropsychological Rehabilitation, 18*, 671–91.

Haslam, C., Jetten, J., Cruwys, T., Dingle, G., and Haslam, S.A. (2018). *The New Psychology of Health: Unlocking the Social Cure.* London: Routledge.

Haslam, S.A. (2001). *Psychology in Organizations: The Social Identity Approach.* London: Sage.

Haslam, S.A., Reicher, S.D., and Platow, M.J. (2011). *The New Social Psychology of Leadership: Identity, Influence and Power.* New York, NY: Psychology Press.

Hazan, K. (2012). *Les enfants de l'apres-guerre dans les maisons de l'OSE.* Paris: OSE and Somogy.

Hechter, M. and Okamoto, D. (2001). Political consequences of minority group formation. *Annual Review of Political Science, 4*, 189–215.

Heckathorn, D.D. and Cameron, C.J. (2017). Network sampling: From snowball and multiplicity to respondent-driven sampling. *Annual Review of Sociology, 43*, 101–19.

Heider, F. (1958). *The Psychology of Interpersonal Relations.* New York: Wiley.

Helliwell, J.F. and Barrington-Levy, C.P. (2012). How much is social capital worth? In J. Jetten, C. Haslam, and S.A. Haslam (eds), *The Social Cure: Identity, Health and Well-being* (pp. 55–71). Hove: Psychology Press.

Hewstone, M. (1989). *Causal Attribution.* Oxford: Blackwell.

Himmelweit, H. (1982). Obituary: Henri Tajfel, FBPsS. *Bulletin of the British Psychogical Society*, 288–9.

Hinkle, S. and Brown, R. (1990). Intergroup comparisons and social identity: Some links and lacunae. In D. Abrams and M.A. Hogg (eds), *Social Identity Theory. Constructive and Critical Advances* (pp. 48–70). London: Harvester-Wheatsheaf.

Hirsch, S. (2004). La reconstruction. In A. Nysenholc (ed.), *Le Livre des Homes: enfants de la Shoah, AIVG 1945–1959* (pp. 33–7). Bruxelles: Didier Devillez.

Hogg, M.A. (1992). *The Social Psychology of Group Cohesiveness.* London: Harvester Wheatsheaf.

Hogg, M.A. (2001). A social identity theory of leadership. *European Review of Social Psychology, 5*, 184–200.

Hogg, M.A. (2007). Uncertainty-Identity Theory. *Advances in Experimental Social Psychology, 39*, 69–126.

Hogg, M.A. and Abrams, D. (1988). *Social Identifications: A Social Psychology of Intergroup Relations and Group Processes.* London: Routledge.

Holborn, L.W. (1956). *The International Refugee Organization: A Specialized Agency of the United Nations, Its History and Work, 1946–1952.* London: Oxford University Press.

Holzer, J. (1977). The Political Right in Poland, 1918–39. *Journal of Contemporary History, 12*, 395–412.

Horowitz, I.L. (1967). Social science and public policy: an examination of the political foundations of modern research. *International Studies Quarterly, 11*, 32–62.

Horwitz, M. and Rabbie, J.M. (1982). Individuality and membership in the intergroup system. In H. Tajfel (ed.), *Social Identity and Intergroup Relations* (pp. 241–74). Cambridge: Cambridge University Press.

Howes, D.H. and Solomon, R.L. (1951). Visual duration thresholds as a function of word probability. *Journal of Experimental Psychology, 41*, 401–9.

Howie, D. (1952). Perceptual defense. *Psychological Review, 59*, 308–15.

Huddy, L. (2001). From social to political identity: A critical examination of social identity theory. *Political Psychology, 22*(1), 127–56.

Hull, C.L. (1952). *A Behavior System: An Introduction to Behavior Theory Concerning the Individual Organism*. New Haven: Yale University Press.

Hyman, P.E. (1998). *The Jews of Modern France*. Berkeley: University of California Press.

Israel, J. and Tajfel, H. (eds). (1972). *The Context of Social Psychology*. London: Academic Press.

Iyer, A. and Leach, C.W. (2008). Emotion in inter-group relations. *European Review of Social Psychology, 19,* 86–125.

Jahoda, G. (1963). The development of children's ideas about country and nationality. *British Journal of Educational Psychology, 33,* 47–60.

Jahoda, G. (1974). Review of Context of Social Psychology. *European Journal of Social Psychology, 4,* 105–12.

Jahoda, G. and Moscovici, S. (1967). EAESP. *Social Science Information, 6,* 297–305.

Jaspars, J.M.F., Van de Geer, J.P., and Tajfel, H. (1972). On the development of national attitudes in children. *European Journal of Social Psychology, 2,* 347–69.

Jaspars, J.M.F. and Warnaen, S. (1982). Intergroup relations, ethnic identity and self-evaluation in Indonesia. In H. Tajfel (ed.), *Social Identity and Intergroup Relations* (pp. 335–66). Cambridge: Cambridge University Press.

Jenkins, R. (2014). *Social Identity*. Abingdon: Routledge.

Jetten, J., Branscombe, N.R., Haslam, S.A., Cruwys, T., Jones, J.M., and Zhang, A. (2015). Having a lot of a good thing: Multiple important group memberships as a source of self-esteem. *PLoS One.* doi: 10.1371/journal.pone.0124609

Jetten, J., Haslam, C., and Haslam, S.A. (eds) (2012). *The Social Cure: Identity, Health and Well-being*. Hove: Psychology Press.

Jetten, J., Spears, R., and Manstead, A.S.R. (1997). Strength of identification and intergroup differentiation: The influence of group norms. *European Journal of Social Psychology, 27,* 603–9.

Jetten, J., Spears, R., and Manstead, A.S.R. (1998). Defining dimensions of distinctiveness: Group variability makes a difference to differentiation. *Journal of Personality and Social Psychology, 74,* 1481–92.

Johnson, N. (1966). What do children learn from war comics? *New Society, 7 July,* 7–12.

Johnson, N.B., Middleton, M., and Tajfel, H. (1970). The relationship between children's preferences for and knowledge about other nations. *British Journal of Social and Clinical Psychology, 9,* 232–40.

Jones, E.E. (1998). Major developments in five decades of social psychology. In D.T. Gilbert, S.T. Fiske, and G. Lindzey (eds), *The Handbook of Social Psychology, 4th Edition* (Vol. 1, pp. 3–57). New York: McGraw-Hill.

Judt, T. (2008). *Reappraisals*. London: Vintage Books.

Kalin, M. and Sambanis, N. (2018). How to think about social identity. *Annual Review of Political Science, 21,* 239–57.

Katz, D. and Braly, K. (1933). Racial stereotypes of one hundred college students. *Journal of Abnormal and Social Psychology, 28,* 280–90.

Kluckholn, F.R. and Strodtbeck, F.L. (1961). *Variations in Value Orientations*. Oxford: Row, Peterson.

Koestler, A. (1941). *Scum of the Earth*. London: Jonathan Cape.

Koffka, K. (1935). *Principles of Gestalt Psychology*. London: Lund Humphries.

Korzen, M. (1969). The Jewish Gimnasium. In I.M. Biderman (ed.), *Włocławek and Kujawy Memorial (Yizkor) Book* (pp. 84–94).

Kosterman, R. and Feshbach, S. (1989). Towards a measure of patriotic and nationalistic attitudes. *Political Psychology, 10,* 257–74.

Krech, D. (1949). Notes toward a psychological theory. *Journal of Personality, 18,* 66–87.

Krueger, J. and Clement, R.W. (1994). Memory-based judgements about multiple categories: A revision and extension of Tajfel's Accentuation Theory. *Journal of Personality and Social Psychology, 67*, 35–47.

Kyprianides, A., Easterbrook, M.J., and Brown, R. (2019). Group identities benefit well-being by satisfying needs. *Journal of Experimental Social Psychology, 84*. doi: 10.1016/j.jesp.2019.103836

Lacy, O.W., Lewinger, N., and Adamson, J.F. (1953). Foreknowledge as a factor affecting perceptual defense and alertness. *Journal of Experimental Psychology, 45*, 169–74.

Lambert, W.W., Solomon, R.L., and Watson, P.D. (1949). Reinforcement and extinction as factors in size estimation *Journal of Experimental Psychology, 39*, 637–41.

Landau-Czajka, A. (1994). The image of the Jew in the Catholic press during the Second Republic. *Polin: A Journal of Polish-Jewish Studies, 8*, 46–175.

Lane, M.D. (1952). 'Who share our concern for these people': The resettlement of unwanted refugees by the International Refugee Organization. *Social Service Review 26*(3), 270–83.

Leach, C.W., van Zomeren, M., Zebel, S., Vliek, M.L.W., Pennekamp, S.F., Doosje, B., Ouwerkerk, J.W., and Spears, R. (2008). Group-level self-definition and self-investment: A hierarchical (multi-component) model of in-group identification. *Journal of Personality and Social Psychology, 95*, 144–65.

Lee, D. (2014). *Petain's Jewish Children*. Oxford: Oxford University Press.

Lemyre, L. and Smith, P.M. (1985). Intergroup discrimination and self esteem in the Minimal Group Paradigm. *Journal of Personality and Social Psychology, 49*, 660–70.

Leroy, S. (2012). L'engagement des Juifs étrangers dans l'armée française et dans la Résistance pendant la Seconde Guerre Mondiale. *Disphoriques, 22*, 57–61.

Lewin, K. (1948). *Resolving Social Conflicts*. New York: Harper and Row.

Lichten, J. (1986). Notes on the assimilation and acculturation of Jews in Poland, 1863–1943. In C. Abramsky, M. Jachimiczyk, and A. Polonsky (eds), *The Jews in Poland*. Oxford: Blackwell.

Lorenz, K. (1966). *On Aggression*. Fakenham: Cox & Wyman.

Lott, A.J. and Lott, B.E. (1965). Group cohesiveness as interpersonal attraction. *Psychological Bulletin, 64*, 259–309.

Lowe, K. (2012). *Savage Continent: Europe in the Aftermath of World War Two*. London: Viking.

Luchins, A.S. (1950). On an approach to social perceptions. *Journal of Personality, 19*, 64–84.

Lukowski, J. and Zawalski, H. (2001). *A Concise History of Poland*. Cambridge: Cambridge University Press.

Mackie, D.M. and Smith, E.R. (2015). Intergroup emotions. In M. Mikulincer and P.R. Shaver (eds), *APA Handbook of Personality and Social Psychology, Vol 2* (pp. 1–31). Washington: American Psychological Association.

Mackie, D.M. and Smith, E.R. (2018). Intergroup emotions theory: Production, regulation, and modification of group-based emotions. In J.M. Olson (ed.), *Advances in Experimental Social Psychology* (pp. 1–69). San Diego, CA: Academic Press.

Mandler, P. (2006). What is 'national identity'? Definitions and applications in modern British historiography. *Modern Intellectual History, 3*, 271–97.

Marques, J.M., Yzerbyt, V.Y., and Leyens, J.-P. (1988). The 'Black Sheep Effect': Extremity of judgments towards ingroup members as a function of group identification. *European Journal of Social Psychology, 18*, 1–16.

Marrus, M. (1985). *The Unwanted. European Refugees from the First World War through the Cold War*. Oxford: Oxford University Press.

Marrus, M.R. and Paxton, R.O. (1981). *Vichy France and the Jews*. New York: Basic Books.

McClain, P.D., JohnsonCarew, J.D., Walton, E., and Watts, C.S. (2009). Group membership, group identity, and group consciousness: Measures of racial identity in American politics? *Annual Review of Political Science, 12*, 471–85.

McClintock, C.G. and Nuttin, J.M. (1969). Development of competitive game behavior in children across two cultures. *Journal of Experimental Social Psychology, 5*, 203–18.

McGarty, C. and Penny, R.E.C. (1988). Categorization, accentuation and social judgement. *British Journal of Social Psychology, 27*, 147–57.

McGinnies, E. (1949). Emotionality and perceptual defense. *Psychological Review, 56*, 244–51.

McGinnies, E. (1950). Discussion of Howes' and Solomon's note on 'Emotionality and perceptual defense'. *Psychological Review, 57*, 235–40.

McGuire, W.J. (1967). Some impending reorientations in social psychology: Some thoughts provoked by Kenneth Ring. *Journal of Experimental Social Psychology, 3*, 124–39.

Mead, G.H. (1934). *Mind, Self and Society*. Chicago: University of Chicago Press.

Mendelsohn, E. (1994). Historiography. In A. Polonsky, E. Mendelsohn, and J. Tomaszewski (eds), *Jews in Independent Poland, 1918–1939*. London: The Littman Library of Jewish Civilization.

Michower, M. (ed.). (2012). *Lendemains: par les jeunes, pour les jeunes*. Paris: OSE et l'Amicale des Anciens et Sympathisants de l'OSE.

Middleton, M., Tajfel, H., and Johnson, N.B. (1970). Cognitive and affective asapects of children's national attitudes. *British Journal of Social and Clinical Psychology, 9*, 122–34.

Militaria1940. (2016). Information about various stalags. http://militaria1940.forumactif. com/

Milner, D. (1975). *Children and Race*. Harmondsworth: Penguin.

Milner, D. (2015). *Fess: An Autobiography*. Peterborough: Compass Publishing.

Mooslechner, M. (2014). The prison of war STALAG XVIII C 'Markt Pongau'. Stand: Samson Druck.

Moray, N. (1959). Attention in dichotic listening: Affective cues and the influence of instructions *The Quarterly Journal of Experimental Psychology, 11*, 56–60.

Moscovici, S. (1972). Society and theory in social psychology. In J. Israel and H. Tajfel (eds), *The Context of Social Psychology* (pp. 17–68). London: Academic Press.

Moscovici, S. (1976). *Social Influence and Social Change*. London: Academic Press.

Moscovici, S. (1988). Notes towards a description of social representations. *European Journal of Social Psychology, 18*, 211–50.

Moscovici, S. and Markova, I. (2006). *The Making of Modern Social Psychology*. Cambridge: Polity Press.

Mulder, M. (1960). Communication structure, decision structure and group performance. *Sociometry, 23*, 1–14.

Mulder, M., Veen, P., Hijzen, T., and Jansen, P. (1973). On power equalization: A behavioral example of power-distance reduction. *Journal of Personality and Social Psychology, 26*, 151–8.

Mummendey, A., Kessler, T., Klink, A., and Mielke, R. (1999). Strategies to cope with negative social identity: Predictions by social identity theory and relative deprivation theory. *Journal of Personality and Social Psychology 76*, 229–45.

Mummendey, A., Klink, A., and Brown, R. (2001). Nationalism and patriotism: National identification and outgroup rejection. *British Journal of Social Psychology, 40*, 159–72.

Mummendey, A., Klink, A., Mielke, R., Wenzel, M., and Blanz, M. (1999). Socio-structural characteristics of intergroup relations and identity management strategies: Results from a field study in East Germany. *European Journal of Social Psychology, 29*, 259–86.

Mummendey, A. and Otten, S. (1998). Positive-negative asymmetry in social discrimination. In W. Stroebe and M. Hewstone (eds), *European Review of Social Psychology* (Vol. 8, pp. 107–43). Chichester: Wiley.

Myers, D., Abell, J., Kolstad, A., and Sani, F. (2010). *Social Psychology*. New York: McGraw Hill.

Nemeth, C.J. (1986). Differential contributions of majority and minority influence. *Psychological Review, 93*, 23–32.

Ng, S.H. (1998). Social psychology in an ageing world: Ageism and intergenerational relations. *Asian Journal of Social Psychology, 1*, 99–116.

Ng, S.H. (2007). Language-based discrimination: Blatant and subtle forms. *Journal of Language and Social Psychology, 26*, 106–22.

Ng, S.H. and Lai, J.C.L. (2009). Effects of culture priming on the social connectedness of the bicultural self: A self-reference effect approach. *Journal of Cross-Cultural Psychology, 40*, 170–86.

Nguyen, A.-M.T.D. and Benet-Martínez, V. (2013). Biculturalism and adjustment: a meta-analysis. *Journal of Cross-Cultural Psychology, 44*, 122–59.

Nuttin, J.M. (1966). Attitude change after rewarded dissonant and consonant 'forced compliance': A critical replication of the Festinger and Carlsmith experiment. *International Journal of Psychology, 1*, 39–57.

Nuttin, J.M. (1985). Narcissism beyond Gestalt and awareness: The name letter effect. *European Journal of Social Psychology, 15*, 353–61.

Nysenholc, A. (ed.). (2004). *Le Livre des homes: enfants de la Shoah, AIVG 1945–1959*. Bruxelles: Didier Devillez.

Oakes, P. (2002). Psychological groups and political psychology: A response to Huddy's 'Critical examination of social identity theory'. *Political Psychology, 23*, 809–24.

Oakes, P.J. and Turner, J.C. (1980). Social categorization and intergroup behaviour: Does minimal intergroup discrimination make social identity more positive? *European Journal of Social Psychology, 10*, 295–302.

Oakes, P.J., Haslam, A., and Turner, J.C. (1994). *Stereotyping and Social Reality*. Oxford: Blackwell.

Ordelheide, K. (1982). *Am Ende war der Anfang*. Osnabruck: Verlag Karl Ordelheide.

Orwell, G. (1933). *Down and Out in Paris and London*. Harmondsworth: Penguin Books.

Otten, S. (2016). The Minimal Group Paradigm and its maximal impact in research on social categorization. *Current Opinion in Psychology, 11*, 85–9.

Owens, T.J., Robinson, D.T., and Smith-Lovin, L. (2010). Three faces of identity. *Annual Review of Sociology, 36*, 477–99.

Peters, R.S. (1960). *The Concept of Motivation, 2nd edition*. London: Routledge and Kegan Paul.

Peters, R.S. and Tajfel, H. (1957). Hobbes and Hull: Metaphysicians of behaviour. *British Journal for the Philosophy of Science 8*, 30–44.

Pettigrew, T.F. (1958). Personality and sociocultural factors in intergroup attitudes: A cross-national comparison. *Journal of Conflict Resolution, 2*, 29–42.

Pettigrew, T.F. (1979). The ultimate attribution error: Extending Allport's cognitive analysis of prejudice. *Personality and Social Psychology Bulletin, 5*, 461–76.

Pettigrew, T.F. (1982). A summing up of major contributions. *Contemporary Psychology, 27*, 927–9.

Pettigrew, T.F., Allport, G.W., and Barnett, E.O. (1958). Biocular resolution and perception of race in South Africa. *British Journal of Psychology, 49*, 265–8.

Pettigrew, T.F. and Tropp, L. (2006). A meta-analytic test of intergroup contact theory. *Journal of Personality and Social Psychology, 90*, 751–83.

Piaget, J. and Weil, A.M. (1951). The development in children of the idea of the homeland and of relations to other countries. *International Social Science Journal, 3,* 361–78.

Pickersgill, M.J. (1998). Brian Foss: Obituary. *The Independent,* 1 January 1998.

Piper, R.A. and Esler, P.F. (2006). *Lazarus, Mary and Martha: A Social Scientific and Theological Reading of John.* London: SCM Press.

Plant, E.A. and Peruche, B.M. (2005). The consequences of race for police officers' responses to criminal suspects. *Psychological Science, 16,* 180–3.

Postman, L., Bruner, J.S., and McGinnies, E. (1948). Personal values as selective factors in perception. *Journal of Abnormal and Social Psychology, 43,* 142–54.

Postmes, T. and Branscombe, N.R. (eds) (2010). *Rediscovering Social Identity.* Hove: Psychology Press.

Postmes, T., Haslam, S.A., and Swaab, R.I. (2005). Social influence in small groups: An interactive model of social identity formation. *European Review of Social Psychology, 16,* 1–42.

Price-Williams, D. (1978). Cognition: Anthropological and psychological nexus. In G. D. Spindler (ed.), *The Making of Psychological Anthropology* (pp. 586–611). Los Angeles: University of California Press.

Proudfoot, M.J. (1956). *European Refugees, 1939–1952: A Study in Forced Population Movement.* London: Faber & Faber.

Quinn, J. (2007). Shared sacrifice and the return of the French deportees in 1945. *Proceedings of the Western Society for French History, 35,* 277–88.

Rabbie, J.M. and Horwitz, M. (1969). Arousal of ingroup bias by a chance win or loss. *Journal of Personality and Social Psychology, 13,* 269–77.

Rabbie, J.M., Schot, J.C. and Visser, L. (1989). Social identity theory: A conceptual and empirical critique from the perspective of a behavioural interaction model *European Journal of Social Psychology, 19,* 171–202.

Razran, G. (1950). Ethnic dislikes and stereotypes: A laboratory study *Journal of Abnormal and Social Psychology, 45,* 7–27.

Reynolds, K.J. and Turner, J.C. (2006). Individuality and the prejudiced personality. *European Review of Social Psychology, 17,* 233–70.

Reynolds, K.J., Turner, J.C., and Haslam, S.A. (2000). When are we better than them and they worse than us? A closer look at social discrimination in positive and negative domains. *Journal of Personality and Social Psychology, 78*(1), 64–80.

Ring, K. (1967). Experimental social psychology: Some sober questions about some frivolous values *Journal of Experimental Social Psychology, 3,* 113–23.

Roccas, S. and Brewer, M.B. (2002). Social identity complexity. *Personality and Social Psychology Review, 6*(2), 88–106.

Rommetveit, R. (1972). Language games, syntactic structures and hermeneutics. In J. Israel and H. Tajfel (eds), *The Context of Social Psychology* (pp. 212–57). London: Academic Press.

Roth, J. (1926/2001). *The Wandering Jews (translation: Michael Hofmann).* London: Granta.

Rudnicki, S. (2011). Jews in Poland between the two World Wars. *Shofar, 29*(3), 4–23.

Runciman, W.G. (1966). *Relative Deprivation and Social Justice. A Study of Attitudes to Social Inequality in Twentieth Century England.* London: Routledge and Kegan Paul.

Sani, F., Herrera, M., and Bowe, M. (2009). Perceived collective continuity and ingroup identification as defence against death awareness. *Journal of Experimental Social Psychology, 45,* 242–5.

Saunders, F.S. (1999). *Who Paid the Piper?: The CIA and the Cultural Cold War.* London: Granta Books.

Schildkraut, D.J. (2014). Boundaries of American identity: Evolving understandings of 'Us'. *Annual Review of Political Science, 17,* 441–60.

Schruijer, S.G.L. (2007). *The Cold War and the Institutionalization of European Social Psychology: 'Having Supper with the Devil?'* Utrecht: University of Utrecht.

Schruijer, S.G.L. (2012). Whatever happened to the 'European' in European social psychology? A study of the ambitions in founding the European Association of Experimental Social Psychology. *History of the Human Sciences, 25,* 88–107.

Schwartz, S.J., Vignoles, V.L., Brown, R., and Zagefka, H. (2014). The identity dynamics of acculturation and multiculturalism: Situating acculturation in context. In V. Benet-Martinez and Y.-Y. Hong (eds), *The Oxford Handbook of Multicultural Identity* (pp. 57–93). Oxford: Oxford University Press.

Sears, R.R., Whiting, J.W.M., Nowlis, V., and Sears, P.S. (1953). Some child-rearing antecedents of aggression and dependency in young children. *Genetic Psychology Monographs, 47,* 135–236.

Secord, P.F., Bevan, W., and Katz, B. (1956). The Negro stereotype and perceptual accentuation. *Journal of Abnormal and Social Psychology, 53,* 78–83.

Segall, M.H., Campbell, D.T., and Herskovits, M. J. (1963). Cultural differences in the perception of geometrical illusions. *Science, 139,* 769–71.

Settles, I.H. and Buchanan, N.T. (2014). Multiple groups, multiple identities, and intersectionality. In V. Benet-Martinez and Y.-Y. Hong (eds), *The Oxford Handbook of Multicultural Identity* (pp. 160–80). Oxford: Oxford University Press.

Shaver, P. (1974). European perspectives on the crisis in social psychology *Contemporary Psychology, 19,* 356–8.

Shayo, M. (2009). A model of social identity with an application to political economy: nation, class, and redistribution. *American Political Science Review, 103,* 147–74.

Shephard, B. (2010). *The Long Road Home: The Aftermath of the Second World War.* London: Vintage Books.

Sherif, M. (1936). *The Psychology of Social Norms.* New York: Harper and Row.

Sherif, M. (1966). *Group Conflict and Cooperation.* London: Routledge.

Sherif, M., Harvey, O.J., White, B.J., Hood, W.R., and Sherif, C.W. (1961). *Intergroup Conflict and Cooperation: The Robbers Cave Experiment.* Norman, Oklahoma: University of Oklahoma Book Exchange.

Silverman, I. (1971). Crisis in social psychology: The relevance of relevance. *American Psychologist, 26,* 583–4.

Simon, M.D., Tajfel, H., and Johnson, N.B. (1967). Wie erkennt man einen Osterreicher? *Kolner Zeitschrift fur Soziologie und Sozialpsychologie, 19,* 511–37.

Simpson, C. (1994). *Science of Coercion: Communication Research and Psychological Warfare, 1945–1960.* New York: Oxford University Press.

Skevington, S.M. (1980). Intergroup relations and social change within a nursing context. *British Journal of Social and Clinical Psychology, 19,* 201–13.

Skevington, S.M. (1981). Intergroup relations and nursing. *European Journal of Social Psychology, 11,* 43–59.

Smeekes, A., Verkuyten, M., and Martinovic, B. (2015). Longing for the country's good old days: National nostalgia, autochthony beliefs, and opposition to Muslim expressive rights. *British Journal of Social Psychology, 54,* 561–80.

Smith, E.R. (1993). Social identity and social emotions: Toward new conceptualizations of prejudice. In D.M. Mackie and D.L. Hamilton (eds), *Affect, Cognition and Stereotyping* (pp. 297–315). San Diego: Academic Press.

Smith, G., Peretz, E., and Smith, T. (2014). *Social Enquiry, Social Reform and Social Action: One Hundred Years of Barnett House.* Oxford: Department of Social Policy and Intervention, Oxford University.

Smith, M.B. (1973). Review of Context of Social Psychology. *Science, 180.*

Stachura, P. (1998). *Poland between the Wars, 1919–1939.* London: Macmillan.

Staub, E. (1997). Blind versus constructive patriotism: Moving from embeddedness in the group to critical loyalty and action In D. Bar-Tal and E. Staub (eds), *Patriotism: In the lives of Individuals and Nations* (pp. 213–28). Chicago: Neslon-Hall.

Stevens, S.S. (1951). *Handbook of Experimental Psychology.* New York: Wiley.

Stroebe, W. (1982). Obituary: Henri Tajfel (1919–1982). *European Journal of Social Psychology, 12*(3), iv–vi.

Sue, E. (1845). *Le Juif Errant.* Paris: Paulin.

Sutton, R., and Douglas, K. (2013). *Social Psychology.* London: Palgrave.

Tajfel, H. (1957). Value and the perceptual judgment of magnitude. *Psychological Review, 64,* 192–204.

Tajfel, H. (1958). The teaching of psychology in social sciences courses. *Bulletin of the British Psychological Society, 24,* 23–8.

Tajfel, H. (1959a). The anchoring effects of value in a scale of judgements. *British Journal of Psychology, 50,* 294–304.

Tajfel, H. (1959b). Quantitative judgement in social perception. *British Journal of Psychology, 50,* 16–29.

Tajfel, H. (1959c). A note on Lambert's 'Evaluation reactions to spoken languages'. *Canadian Journal of Psychology, 13,* 86–92.

Tajfel, H. (1960). The nation and the individual. *The Listener, 63,* 846–7.

Tajfel, H. (1962). Social perception. In G. Humphrey and M. Argyle (eds), *Social Psychology through Experiment.* London: Methuen.

Tajfel, H. (1963). Stereotypes. *Race, 5,* 3–14.

Tajfel, H. (1964a). Bias in judgment. *New Society, 4,* 11–12.

Tajfel, H. (1964b). Human 'judgment' in the laboratory: Categories and stereotypes. *Common Factor, 1,* 1.

Tajfel, H. (1965). Some psychological aspects of the colour problem. In BBC (ed.), *Colour in Britain.* London: British Broadcasting Corporation.

Tajfel, H. (1966a). Children and Foreigners. *New Society.*

Tajfel, H. (1966b). International cooperation in social psychology. *Bulletin of the British Psychological Society, 19,* 29–36.

Tajfel, H. (1966c). Co-operation between human groups. *Eugenics Review, 58,* 77–84.

Tajfel, H. (1969a). The formation of national attitudes: A social psychological perspective. In M. Sherif (ed.), *Interdisciplinary Relationships in the Social Sciences* (pp. 137–76). Chicago: Aldine.

Tajfel, H. (1969b). Cognitive aspects of prejudice. *Journal of Social Issues, 25,* 79–97.

Tajfel, H. (1969c). Social and cultural factors in perception. In G. Lindzey & E. Aronson (Eds.), *Handbook of Social Psychology, 2nd edition* (Vol. III, pp. 315–394). Reading, Mass.: Addison-Wesley.

Tajfel, H. (1969d). Cognitive aspects of prejudice. *Journal of Biosocial Science, 1,* 173–91.

Tajfel, H. (1970). Experiments in intergroup discrimination. *Scientific American, 233,* 96–102.

Tajfel, H. (1972a). Experiments in a vacuum. In J. Israel and H. Tajfel (eds), *The Context of Social Psychology: A Critical Assessment* (pp. 69–119). London: Academic Press.

Tajfel, H. (1972b). La catégorisation sociale. In S. Moscovici (ed.), *Introduction à la psychologie sociale.* Paris: Larousse.

Tajfel, H. (1972c). Some developments in European social psychology. *European Journal of Social Psychology, 2,* 307–22.

Tajfel, H. (1974a). Social identity and intergroup behaviour. *Social Sciences Information, 13,* 65–93.

Tajfel, H. (1974b). Intergroup behaviour, social comparison and social change. Paper presented at the The Katz-Newcomb Lectures, Ann Arbor, Michigan, USA.

Tajfel, H. (1975). The exit of social mobility and the voice of social change: Notes on the social psychology of intergroup relations. *Social Science Information, 14*(2), 101–18.

Tajfel, H. (1975a). Tajfel takes a turn. *Contemporary Psychology, 20*, 78–9.

Tajfel, H. (1975b). Shaver's review ... Not a serious analysis. *Contemporary Psychology, 20*, 264–5.

Tajfel, H. (1976). La psicologia sociale e i processi sociali. *Giorno Italiano di Psicologia, 3*, 189–221.

Tajfel, H. (1977). Social psychology and social reality. *New Society, 39*, 653–4.

Tajfel, H. (ed.). (1978). *Differentiation between Social Groups: Studies in the Social Psychology of Intergroup Relations*. London: Academic Press.

Tajfel, H. (1978a). Interindividual and intergroup behaviour. In H. Tajfel (ed.), *Differentiation between Social Groups: Studies in the Social Psychology of Intergroup Relations* (pp. 27–60). London: Academic Press.

Tajfel, H. (1978b). Social categorization, social identity and social comparison. In H. Tajfel (ed.), *Differentiation between Social Groups: Studies in the Social Psychology of Intergroup Relations* (pp. 61–76). London: Academic Press.

Tajfel, H. (1978c). The achievement of group differentiation. In H. Tajfel (ed.), *Differentiation between Social Groups: Studies in the Social Psychology of Intergroup Relations* (pp. 77–98). London: Academic Press.

Tajfel, H. (1978d). *The Social Psychology of Minorities*. London: The Minority Rights Group.

Tajfel, H. (1980). Nachwort. In P.F. Peretz (ed.), *Der Antisemitismus als eine Gruppenerscheinung: versuch einer Soziologie des Judenhasses* Königstein: Jüdischer Verlag.

Tajfel, H. (1981a). Social stereotypes and social groups. In J. C. Turner and H. Giles (eds), *Intergroup Behaviour* (pp. 144–67). Oxford: Blackwell.

Tajfel, H. (1981b). *Human Groups and Social Categories*. Cambridge: Cambridge University Press.

Tajfel, H. (ed.). (1982a). *Social Identity and Intergroup Relations*. Cambridge: Cambridge University Press.

Tajfel, H. (1982b). Social psychology of intergroup relations. *Annual Review of Psychology, 33*, 1–30.

Tajfel, H. (1982c). Instrumentality, identity and social comparisons. In H. Tajfel (ed.), *Social Identity and Intergroup Relations* (pp. 483–507). Cambridge: Cambridge University Press.

Tajfel, H. (1984a). Intergroup relations, social myths and social justice in social psychology. In H. Tajfel (ed.), *The Social Dimension* (Vol. 2, pp. 695–715). Cambridge: Cambridge University Press.

Tajfel, H. (ed.). (1984b). *The Social Dimension: European Developments in Social Psychology*. Cambridge Cambridge University Press.

Tajfel, H. and Billig, M. (1974). Familiarity and categorization in intergroup behaviour. *Journal of Experimental Social Psychology, 10*, 159–70.

Tajfel, H., Billig, M.G., Bundy, R.P., and Flament, C. (1971). Social categorization and intergroup behaviour. *European Journal of Social Psychology, 1*, 149–78.

Tajfel, H., and Bruner, J.S. (1966). The relation between breadth of category and decision time. *British Journal of Psychology, 57*, 71–5.

Tajfel, H. and Cawasjee, S.D. (1959). Value and the accentuation of judged differences. *Journal of Abnormal and Social Psychology, 59*, 436–9.

Tajfel, H. and Dawson, J.K. (1965). *Disappointed Guests: Essays by African, Asian and West Indian Students*. Oxford: Oxford University Press.

Tajfel, H. and Fraser, C. (eds) (1978). *Introducing Social Psychology: An Analysis of Individual Reaction and Response*. Harmondsworth: Penguin.

Tajfel, H., Jahoda, G., Nemeth, C., Rim, Y., and Johnson, N.B. (1972). Devaluation by children of their own national or ethnic gorup: Two case studies. *British Journal of Social and Clinical Psychology, 11*, 235–43.

Tajfel, H., Nemeth, C., Jahoda, G., Campbell, J.D., and Johnson, N.B. (1970). The development of children's preferences for their own country: A cross-national study. *International Journal of Psychology, 5*, 245–53.

Tajfel, H., Richardson, A., and Everstine, L. (1964a). Individual consistencies in categorizing: A study of judgmental behavior. *Journal of Personality, 32*, 90–108.

Tajfel, H., Richardson, A., and Everstine, L. (1964b). Individual judgment consistencies in conditions of risk taking. *Journal of Personality, 32*, 550–65.

Tajfel, H., Sheikh, A.A., and Gardner, R. C. (1964). Content of stereotypes and the inference of similarity between members of stereotyped groups. *Acta Psychologica, 22*, 191–201.

Tajfel, H. and Turner, J. (1979). An integrative theory of intergroup conflict. In W. G. Austin and S. Worchel (eds), *The Social Psychology of Intergroup Relations* (pp. 33–47). California: Brooks & Cole.

Tajfel, H. and Turner, J.C. (1986). The social identity theory of intergroup behavior. In S. Worchel and W.G. Austin (eds), *Psychology of Intergroup Relations* (pp. 7–24). Chicago: Nelson Hall.

Tajfel, H. and Wilkes, A.L. (1963). Classification and quantitative judgement. *British Journal of Psychology, 54*, 101–14.

Tajfel, H. and Wilkes, A.L. (1964). Salience of attributes and commitment to extreme judgments in the perception of people. *British Journal of Social and Clinical Psychology, 2*, 40–9.

Tajfel, H. and Winter, D.G. (1963). The interdependence of size, number and value in young children's estimates of magnitude. *Journal of Genetic Psychology, 102*, 115–24.

Taylor, D.M. and Brown, R.J. (1979). Towards a more social social psychology? *British Journal of Social and Clinical Psychology, 18*, 173–80.

Tewari, S., Khan, S., Hopkins, N., Srinivasan, N., and Reicher, S. (2012). Participation in mass gatherings can benefit well-being: Longitudinal and control data from a North Indian Hindu pilgrimage event. *PLoS One, 7.* doi: 10.1371/journal.pone.0047291

Tucker, J.B. and Baker, A.C. (eds) (2014). *T & T Clark Handbook to Social Identity in the New Testament.* London: Bloomsbury/T&T Clark.

Turner, J.C. (1975). Social comparison and social identity: Some prospects for intergroup behaviour. *European Journal of Social Psychology, 5*, 5–34.

Turner, J.C. (1980). Fairness or discrimination in intergroup behaviour? A reply to Branthwaite, Doyle and Lightbown. *European Journal of Social Psychology, 10*, 131–47.

Turner, J.C. (1982). Towards a cognitive redefinition of the social group. In H. Tajfel (ed.), *Social Identity and Intergroup Relations* (pp. 15–40). Cambridge: Cambridge University Press.

Turner, J.C. (1983a). Some comments on… 'the measurement of social orientations in the minimal group paradigm.' *European Journal of Social Psychology, 13*, 351–67.

Turner, J.C. (1983b). A second reply to Bornstein, Crum, Wittenbraker, Harring, Insko and Thibaut on the measurement of social orientations *European Journal of Social Psychology, 13*, 383–7.

Turner, J.C. (1991). *Social Influence.* Milton Keynes: Open University Press.

Turner, J.C. (1996). Henri Tajfel: an introduction. In W.P. Robinson (ed.), *Social Groups and Identities: Developing the Legacy of Henri Tajfel* (pp. 1–23). Oxford: Butterworth-Heinemann.

Turner, J.C. (2005). Explaining the nature of power: A three-process theory. *European Journal of Social Psychology, 35*, 1–22.

Turner, J.C. and Bourhis, R.Y. (1996). Social identity, interdependence and the social group: A reply to Rabbie *et al.* In W.P. Robinson (ed.), *Social Groups and Identities: Developing the Legacy of Henri Tajfel* (pp. 25–63). Oxford: Butterworth-Heinemann.

Turner, J.C. and Brown, R. (1978). Social status, cognitive alternatives, and intergroup relations. In H. Tajfel (ed.), *Differentiation between Social Groups: Studies in the Social Psychology of Intergroup Relations* (pp. 201–34). London: Academic Press.

Turner, J.C., Brown, R.J., and Tajfel, H. (1979). Social comparison and group interest in ingroup favouritism. *European Journal of Social Psychology, 9,* 187–204.

Turner, J.C., Hogg, M.A., Oakes, P.J., Reicher, S.D., and Wetherell, M.S. (1987). *Rediscovering the Social Group: A Self-Categorization Theory.* Oxford: Blackwell.

Turner, J.C. and Reynolds, K.J. (2010). The story of social identity. In T. Postmes and N.R. Branscombe (eds), *Rediscovering Social Identity* (pp. 13–32). NY: Psychology Press.

UNHCR. (2010). 1951 Refugee Convention. www.unhcr.org/uk/3b66c2aa10

van Avermaet, E. (2017). 50 years of the EASP: The history of the European Association of Social Psychology (1967–2017). In European Association of Social Psychology (ed.). Granada: European Association of Social Psychology

van Baaren, R.B., Holland, R.W., Kawakami, K., and Van Knippenberg, A. (2004). Mimicry and prosocial behavior. *Psychological Science, 15,* 71–4.

van Bavel, J.J. and Cunningham, W.A. (2010). A social neuroscience approach to self and social categorisation: A new look at an old issue. *European Review of Social Psychology, 21,* 237–84.

Van der Meer, T. and Tolsma, J. (2014). Ethnic diversity and its effects on social cohesion. *Annual Review of Sociology, 40,* 459–78.

van Knippenberg, A. (1984). Intergroup differences in group perceptions. In H. Tajfel (ed.), *The Social Dimension* (Vol. 2, pp. 560–78). Cambridge: Cambridge University Press.

van Knippenberg, A. and van Oers, H. (1984). Social identity and equity concerns in intergroup perceptions. *British Journal of Social Psychology, 23,* 351–61.

van Knippenberg, A., van Twuyver, M., and Pepels, J. (1994). Factors affecting social categorization processes in memory. *British Journal of Social Psychology, 33,* 419–31.

Veil, S. (2012). Preface. In M. Michower (ed.), *Lendemains: par les jeunes, pour les jeunes* (pp. 7–9). Paris: OSE et Amicale des Anciens et Sympathisants de l'OSE.

Vignoles, V.L. (2011). Identity motives. In S. Schwartz, K. Luyckx, and V.L. Vignoles (eds), *Handbook of Identity Theory and Research* (pp. 403–32). New York: Springer.

Vinen, R. (2006). *The Unfree French: life under the Occupation.* London: Penguin.

Vonk, R. and van Knippenberg, A. (1995). Processing attitude statements from in-group and out-group members: Effects of within-group and within-person inconsistencies on reading times. *Journal of Personality and Social Psychology, 68,* 215–27.

Walster, E., Berscheid, E., and Walster, G.W. (1976). New directions in equity research. In L. Berkowitz and E. Walster (eds), *Equity Theory: Toward a General Theory of Social Interaction.* New York: Academic Press.

Wegner, D.M. and Bargh, J.A. (1998). Control and automaticity in social life. In D.T. Gilbert, S.T. Fiske, and G. Lindzey (eds), *Handbook of Social Psychology, 4th Edition* (pp. 446–96). New York: McGraw Hill.

Weinberg, D.H. (1977). *A Community on Trial: The Jews of Paris in the 1930s.* Chicago: University of Chicago Press.

Wetherell, M. (1982). Cross-cultural studies of minimal groups: Implications for the social identity theory of intergroup relations. In H. Tajfel (ed.), *Social Identity and Intergroup Relations* (pp. 207–40). Cambridge: Cambridge University Press.

Wiley, S. and Deaux, K. (2010). The bicultural identity performance of immigrants. In A.E. Azzi, X. Chryssochoou, B. Klandermans, and B. Simon (eds), *Identity and Participation in Culturally Diverse Societies: A Multidisciplinary Perspective* (pp. 49–68). Oxford: Blackwell.

Wilkes, A.L. and Tajfel, H. (1966). Types de classification et importance du contraste relatif. *Bulletin de CERP, 15,* 71–81.

Winkelman, M. (2015). *Keeping the Promise: To Tell My Story of Survival in Warsaw during WWII.* Sarasota, FL: Bardolf & Co.

Wohl, M.J A., Branscombe, N.R., and Klar, Y. (2006). Collective guilt: Emotional reactions when one's group has done wrong or been wronged. *European Review of Social Psychology, 17,* 1–37.

Wood, W., Lundgren, S., Ouellette, J.A., Buscerne, S., and Blackstone, T. (1994). Minority influence: A meta-analytic review of social influence processes. *Psychological Bulletin, 115,* 323–45.

Wright, S.C., Taylor, D.M., and Moghaddam, F.M. (1990). Responding to membership in a disadvantaged group: From acceptance to collective protest. *Journal of Personality and Social Psychology, 58,* 994–1003.

Xiao, Y.J., Coppin, G., and van Bavel, J.J. (2016). Perceiving the world through group-colored glasses: A perceptual model of intergroup relations. *Psychological Inquiry, 27,* 255–74.

Yee, M., and Brown, R. (1992). Self-evaluations and intergroup attitudes in children aged three to nine. *Child Development, 63,* 619–29.

Young, J.L. and Hegarty, P. (2019). Reasonable men: Sexual harassment and norms of conduct in social psychology. *Feminism and Psychology.*

Yzerbyt, V. (2006). From subtle cues to profound influences: The impact of changing identities on emotions and behaviors. In P.A. Van Lange (ed.), *Bridging Social Psychology: Benefits of Transdisicpinary Approaches* (pp. 391–6). Mahwah, NJ: Lawrence Erlbaum.

Yzerbyt, V., Dumont, M., Wigboldus, D., and Gordijn, E. (2003). I feel for us: The impact of categorization and identification on emotions and action tendencies. *British Journal of Social Psychology, 42,* 533–49.

Zajonc, R.B. (1968). Attitudinal effects of mere exposure. *Journal of Personality and Social Psychology, 9,* 1–27.

Zedong, M. (1957). On the correct handling of contradictions among the people. Paper presented at the Supreme State Conference of the Chinese Communist Party, Peking.

Zimbardo, P.G. (1969). The human choice: Individuation, reason, and order versus deindividuation, impulse, and chaos. *Nebraska Symposium on Motivation, 17,* 237–307.

Zuccotti, S. (1993). *The Holocaust, the French and the Jews.* New York: Basic Books.

INDEX

Note: Entries for Heniek/Henri Tajfel are not included since they were ubiquitous. Page references in **bold** refer to figures.